Proverbs

OPENING THE SCRIPTURES

Opening the Scriptures is neither a new series of technical commentaries nor is it a collection of sermons. Instead it offers devout church members a series of popularly accessible primers so that the average churchgoer can easily grasp them.

The organization of this series follows the four main sectional divisions of Holy Scripture: the Torah, the many prophetic books, the Psalms and wisdom books, and the New Testament. The authors of Opening the Scriptures show throughout that Holy Scripture is from A to Z the book of God's covenant with his people.

Proverbs

GOD'S LIFE-PROTECTING WISDOM

FRANS VAN DEURSEN

Nelson D. Kloosterman, Translator

WIPF & STOCK · Eugene, Oregon

PROVERBS
God's Life-Protecting Wisdom

Copyright © 2025 Paideia Press. All rights reserved. Except for brief quotations in critical publications or reviews, no part of this book may be reproduced in any manner without prior written permission from the publisher. Write: Permissions, Wipf and Stock Publishers, 199 W. 8th Ave., Suite 3, Eugene, OR 97401.

Wipf & Stock
An Imprint of Wipf and Stock Publishers
199 W. 8th Ave., Suite 3
Eugene, OR 97401

www.wipfandstock.com

PAPERBACK ISBN: 979-8-3852-3252-9
HARDCOVER ISBN: 979-8-3852-3253-6
EBOOK ISBN: 979-8-3852-3254-3

VERSION NUMBER 07/11/25

Unless otherwise indicated, Scripture quotations are from the ESV® Bible (The Holy Bible, English Standard Version®), copyright © 2001 by Crossway, a publishing ministry of Good News Publishers. Used by permission. All rights reserved.

Scripture quotations marked ASV are taken from the American Standard Version®. This translation of the Bible is in the public domain.

Scripture quotations marked KJV are from the King James Version. Public domain.

Scripture quotations marked NASB are taken from the (NASB®) New American Standard Bible®, Copyright © 1960, 1971, 1977, 1995, 2020 by The Lockman Foundation. Used by permission. All rights reserved. lockman.org.

Scripture quotations marked (NIV) are taken from the Holy Bible, New International Version®, NIV®. Copyright © 1973, 1978, 1984, 2011 by Biblica, Inc.™ Used by permission of Zondervan. All rights reserved worldwide. www.zondervan.com. The "NIV" and "New International Version" are trademarks registered in the United States Patent and Trademark Office by Biblica, Inc.™

Scripture quotations marked NKJV are taken from the New King James Version®. Copyright © 1982 by Thomas Nelson. Used by permission. All rights reserved.

Scripture quotations marked (NRSV) are from the New Revised Standard Version Bible, copyright © 1989 National Council of the Churches of Christ in the United States of America. Used by permission. All rights reserved worldwide.

Contents

Translator's Introduction   vii
Foreword   ix

1	Proverbs or *Mashals*?	1
2	The Origin of the Book of Proverbs	19

PART 1 | PROVERBS 1–9: A PRIMER FOR USING THE BOOK OF PROVERBS

3	Proverbs 1:1–6: Proverbs Offers Life-Wisdom, Especially for Young People	33
4	Proverbs 1:7: The Fear of the Lord Is the Beginning of Knowledge	44
5	Proverbs 1:8–33: Listening Makes One Wise, and Wisdom Brings Life, but Then Listen Early	64
6	Proverbs 2: The Treasure Hunter Looking for Wisdom Discovers Life-Insight and Life-Preservation	78
7	Proverbs 3: In Keeping God's Commandments Lies Rich Reward for Our Entire Life	84
8	Proverbs 4: What Solomon Himself Learned as a Child from His Father David	131
9	Proverbs 5–7: Adultery and Prostitution: Folly Is Crowned	137
10	Proverbs 8: A Canticle Celebrating Wisdom	161
11	Proverbs 9: Which Invitation Will You Accept?	185

PART 2 | PROVERBS 10–31: THE "REAL" BOOK OF PROVERBS

12	Some Proverbs of Solomon and of Other Sages: A Selection from Proverbs 10–31	199

| 13 | Proverbs 31:10–31: Hymn to a Proficient Wife | 323 |

Bibliography   333
Subject Index   335
Scripture Index   367

Translator's Introduction

THIS VOLUME IS PART of the original multivolume Dutch commentary series entitled De Voorzeide Leer, which means "the aforesaid doctrine," a phrase found in the Reformed liturgical form used in connection with the baptism of infants. In their responsive vows, the child's parents promise to teach their child "in the aforesaid doctrine," referring to the teachings of the Bible, the ecumenical creeds, and the Reformed confessions. We have chosen to entitle the series Opening the Scriptures as an encouragement to readers to take in hand these commentaries as handbooks for working through portions of Scripture that may be unfamiliar.

Opening the Scriptures is not a new series of technical commentaries that explain the Bible word for word, although this series of volumes does rest upon careful exegesis. Nor is it a collection of sermons, although now and then the authors shine the light of Scripture on our modern world. Actually, there is no familiar category of Bible studies that serves as a suitable classification for Opening the Scriptures. This series has a unique character. It offers devout church members a series of popularly accessible primers, with no display of scholarly expertise, so that the average churchgoer can easily grasp them.

As far as their approach is concerned, these volumes begin by telling you about the structure of the biblical book that you want to study. This is because an overview of the whole enhances insight into the parts. After all, Scripture is neither a loose-leaf assortment of essays nor a collection of isolated texts. The ABC guidelines of the authors of this series are these: pay attention to the text, the context, and the canonical place of the biblical book (or the other way around). What is the scope of a particular book, and how is it organized? What is its place in the totality of Scripture? For example, what ties Joshua, Judges, Samuel, and Kings together? In short, Opening the Scriptures resembles a museum guidebook that opens your eyes to the beauty and meaning for today of the treasures, large and small, being exhibited.

The organization of this series follows the four main sectional divisions of Holy Scripture (Luke 24:44). For the Holy Spirit has joined together all the books of the Bible into an imposing edifice. The Torah, or the five books of Moses, is the foundation upon which the entire Scripture rests. Therefore this section of the Bible is discussed most extensively in Opening the Scriptures. The many prophetic books form the walls. The Psalms and wisdom books are the windows. Over all of this the Holy Spirit has laid the golden dome roof of the New Testament. The authors of Opening the Scriptures would like to guide you through this immense building. They will ask, "Have you seen this, and did you notice that?" And when you respond, "Surely the Bible is a wonderful book, and I would like to know more about it!" then they will have achieved their purpose.

Finally, two concluding translator comments may be helpful.

In the original Dutch volume, each chapter concludes with "Notes"—endnotes referring the reader to commentaries and other relevant studies, most of them in Dutch or German. The usefulness of these endnotes to the English-language reader is dubious. Where substantive explanations of the main text appear in these notes, they have been incorporated into the main text in English.

The English Bible translation usually cited is the ESV. But where the Tetragrammaton is rendered "the Lord" in English, the author has substituted "Yahweh."

Foreword

THIS BOOK WAS PUBLISHED in the Netherlands in 1979, fifty years after Reverend C. Vonk, the founder and principal author of this commentary series, began his work in the ministry and service of the Word. By God's grace, during that half-century he became a teacher of Holy Scripture for many, including myself. Therefore, now as his collaborator, I gratefully dedicate this volume of our series to his memory.

Throughout the years, I received heartfelt support and encouragement in my work from my wife. According to Solomon, he who finds such a "fellow worker" has found happiness and received favor from the LORD (Prov 18:22). She fell asleep in Christ in 2021.

May the Holy Spirit use our books to show readers that his own book is a lamp on our life's path. And may he bless this new volume to open many eyes, especially those of young people, to the wisdom that is from above (Jas 3:17), so that they may learn to hate the death- and destruction-sowing foolishness of Satan and increasingly love the healing wisdom of the book of Proverbs.

> November 24, 2024
> Barneveld
> Frans van Deursen

1

Proverbs or *Mashals*?

"FOR THIS YOU NEED the wisdom of Solomon!" Perhaps you've uttered that sigh as you wondered: How do I raise my children as believers? May discipline play a role in that context? How do I protect my marital happiness? What is a responsible use of money? I read newspapers and books, I listen to religious speakers on radio and TV; how do I learn to distinguish truth and falsehood in that material? What should I think about the use of alcohol? How do I achieve a biblical, rather than a humanistic, knowledge of people? To find answers to these and many more questions like them, you don't get very far with a school diploma. For these answers, you need *wisdom*.

To obtain that, must God's children first attend the harsh school of injury and embarrassment? Providentially not. God has preserved for us an entire arsenal of Solomon's wisdom. In the book of Proverbs, he offers it to us on a platter. Here the wise prince shines his light upon our marital life and business life, our strengths and desires, our eyes and ears, our love and hatred, our work and rest. There is no better oracle for life's questions than the Proverbs of Solomon.

But is that book, then, a maverick among the books of the Bible? A somewhat humanistically tinted guidebook for successful living? Not at all. Proverbs also belong to the books of the old and new *covenants*. Living in that covenant is not exhausted by religious matters, but includes really all kinds of activities. Therefore, in this book, God gave us wisdom for our entire lives. Because Proverbs is a genuine *covenant book*, its teaching is squarely opposed to "the counsel of the wicked" (Ps 1:1), which presses upon you perhaps every day. But whereas those counsels of the wicked set us on a dead-end path (Ps 1:6), in Proverbs you read words that heal, words that can make our life healthy.

An incidental delight in that connection is the attractive *form* in which Proverbs offers its life lessons. For that, Israel's sages chose the stimulating style of the *mashal*. Did you know that our Savior also frequently used this pedagogical form in his instruction?

Let's first study that teaching style a bit further.

1. PROVERBS: A TITLE THAT DOES NOT ENTIRELY FIT THE CONTENTS

In the Hebrew Bible our book is entitled *mišlê*, which is the plural form of the word *māšāl*. (From now on, we will use the transliteration *mashal*.) Our English Bibles provide the title *Proverbs*, but that word only partially fits the meaning of *mashal*. For we think of a proverb as a pithy saying of one or two lines, summarizing a piece of life wisdom. Now, in our book of Proverbs there are hundreds of such short sayings, but the word *mashal* covers more than simply brief proverbs.

The term *mashal* is, in fact, a collective term.

You can detect that already from the book of Proverbs itself, for there we encounter, in addition to the two- or three-line proverbs, also entire discourses—of a father to his son, and, at the end, even a complete poem in praise of the ideal wife. All of this falls under the term *mashal*. Precisely because this is clearly a collective term for various kinds of prose and poetry, we would know of no better equivalent English word than what we have as the title of this Bible book. But why don't we incorporate into our vocabulary as a Christian term the word *mashal*?

Mashal: collective term for saying, proverb, taunt, prophecy, parable, psalm, and speech

During their captivity the Jews were sulking in Babylon: "The fathers have eaten sour grapes, and the children's teeth are set on edge" (Ezek 18:2). A short *saying* like this, taken from popular speech, is also called a *mashal* (Ezek 18:2–3; cf. 12:22–23; 1 Sam 24:14; Jer 31:29). "Therefore it became a proverb, 'Is Saul also among the prophets?'" (1 Sam 10:12).

Taunts also belong to this genre. In Isa 14:4–21 we read the welcome song with which the ghosts of dead rulers welcomed the king of Babylon into the realm of the dead: Is this the man before whom the earth trembled? Such mockery is there called "this taunt [*mashal*] against the king of Babylon" (v. 4). Unfaithful Israel would suffer the same fate: "I will make them . . . a reproach, a byword [*mashal*], a taunt," Yahweh threatened through Jeremiah (Jer 24:9; see Deut 28:37; 1 Kgs 9:7).

Often a *parable* is also called a *mashal*. When David had taken Bathsheba as his wife and had her husband Uriah killed, Yahweh sent the prophet Nathan to David with the story about a rich man who had stolen the only ewe lamb of a poor man. Although the word does not appear here, this parable was a genuine *mashal*. This is like Isaiah's well-known "love song [of Yahweh] concerning his vineyard Israel" in Isa 5:1–7. That this could also be a *mashal* we see in Ezek 17:2, where Ezekiel receives the commission, "Son of man, propound a riddle, and speak a parable [Heb., *mashal*] to the house of Israel"—which is followed with a parable like those of Nathan and Isaiah.

Thus, with his parables, our Lord Jesus Christ was using an ancient and trusted teaching style in Israel. In a Hebrew translation of the Greek New Testament, Jesus' parables are properly called *mashals*. Thus the disciples ask, "Why do you speak to them in *mashals*?" (Matt 13:10), and the Lord continues then by saying, "Hear the *mashal* of the sower" (Matt 13:18). A bit later we read, "He spoke another *mashal* to them" (Matt 13:24, 31, 33–34). The Proverbs of Solomon, with respect to its style, belong to the family or the category of the parables of our Savior.

To this large *mashal* family belong several *psalms* as well. "I will incline my ear to a proverb [*mashal*]; I will solve my riddle to the music of the lyre," says Ps 49:4. "I will open my mouth in a parable [*mashal*]," we read in Ps 78:2. And Job says of the speeches of his friends, "Your maxims are proverbs [*mashals*] of ashes" (Job 13:12; 27:1; 29:1).

These examples show us what an extensive area is covered by the word *mashal*. We encounter it as a reference to short sayings, maxims, and proverbs; entire poems, like the taunt of the king of Babylon; the future predictions of Balaam; the parables of Isaiah and Ezekiel; the speeches of Job and his friends; and even a few psalms. Not only sages but also prophets and psalmists used the *mashal* form in connection with their teaching.

This very inclusive word is the title of our Bible book: *Mashals of Solomon*. The translation *Proverbs of Solomon* has become coin of the realm, so to speak, but is in fact too narrow to cover the content—especially because this book, as we stated, contains not only short proverbs but also longer explanations, especially in Prov 1–9 (cf. 5:1–23; 6:20—7:27; 8:1–36; 23:29–35; 31:10–31).

We will better understand Proverbs when we pause a moment to consider a few eye-catching features of the *mashal*.

2. A *MASHAL* OFTEN DISPLAYS HEBREW PARALLELISM

Although Proverbs does contain longer *mashals*, it consists largely of proverbs stated in two lines. What is remarkable in that connection is that a certain balance exists between the content of these lines. With this feature we have encountered one of the prominent characteristics of Hebrew, indeed, all Semitic, poetry.

We enjoy it when two lines of a poem rhyme, but the Israelites and their neighbors had a different taste in this regard. Whether you study a Babylonian, a Canaanite, or an Israelite poem, these lines would perhaps not rhyme, but by the same token they did display an artistic choral dance of ideas. Often the poets composed their piece with sections of two or three lines, whose content displayed a certain balance. This so-called parallelism comes out more clearly in modern Bible translations, because they do not print the lines of a psalm or proverb after each other in prose style, but beneath one another.

Those who wrote proverbs were godly artists who possessed gifts of wisdom, prophecy, and poetry.

At first glance, this art of writing seems perhaps less artistic and easier to practice than ours, but don't be mistaken. Try it for yourself once, and you will quickly notice that appearances deceive. God the Holy Spirit must have granted to the sages, through whose ministry he gave us the book of Proverbs, rich gifts of knowledge and skill.

They must have been able to observe more acutely than the superficial masses, for their proverbs ought to contain no random claims, but had to rest on facts that every believer could investigate. They had to view these facts, however, exclusively out of a deep respect for Yahweh, for all wisdom begins with fear of him (Prov 1:7; 9:10). Therefore they had to possess an especially rich faith-knowledge of the Word and deeds of Yahweh. In addition, they needed deep insight into the regularities to which God had subjected human society. How else would they be able to point their students to the connection between our actions and their consequences? In fact, they also had to know how former generations had experienced these things. Moreover, they were expected to know the values central to human living and be able to prioritize them. As God-fearing nurturers they could not lose from view the limits of human ability, and had to take God's sovereignty into account with just as much respect.

Once they had drawn a life lesson from Scripture and experience, however, they still had to be able to summarize it in an artistic manner. Not in a long-winded argument filled with talking but in a pithy, proverbial style of only two or three lines. One line must clarify the other, whether by an image, an expansion, or a contrast (in a moment we will show examples of each of these). And then that proverb also had to stimulate reflection and be easily stored in the memory.

Those who wrote biblical proverbs had to have the Scripture knowledge of the prophet, the life insight of the elderly, the imaginative capacity of the painter, the pedagogy of the teacher, and the experience of their ancestors. Remember, finally, that our *mashal*-composing Savior said, concerning all these gifts and skills, which Solomon had displayed above all other sages, "One greater than Solomon is here" (Matt 12:42)—referring, of course, to himself.

A book full of synonyms

This technique of composition naturally requires a singular adeptness in the use of synonymous expressions and refined shades of verbal meaning. Those who wrote psalms and proverbs demonstrate genuine mastery of these skills. A book like Proverbs teems with synonyms. The main characters in this book are the wise person and the fool, but what a rich supply of expressions is provided in the book to describe these two types of people. Let's arrange them in columns.

The wise person	*The fool*
Understanding	Stupid
Humble in spirit	Proud
Avoids evil	Commits unrighteousness
Righteous	Wicked
A man of knowledge	Without understanding
Godly	Faithless
Good	Wicked
One who does good	Wrong
Upright in walk	Evil
Upright	Forgets God
Faithful	Overconfident
One who is just	Audacious
Pays attention to his way	Sinner
Walks above reproach	Blameworthy
Pious	Mocker
Honorable	Sloth

Naturally these expressions overlap somewhat, but they nevertheless do contain refined nuances. When a writer had summarized his lesson in the first line of a proverb, he could still refine or deepen it in the second line by means of such synonymous expressions. For formulating such balanced lines, the *mashal* writers had richly varied techniques at their disposal. We will not strive to provide a complete overview of this art of verbal variety, but will identify four main classes and give examples of them, since these kinds of proverbs appear very often in the book of Proverbs.

Both lines say the same thing in different words.

> Whoever loves transgression loves strife;
> > he who makes his door high seeks destruction. (Prov 17:19)
>
> Whoever restrains his words has knowledge,
> > and he who has a cool spirit is a man of understanding. (Prov 17:27)

Both lines clarify each other by means of a contrast.

> A joyful heart is good medicine,
> > but a crushed spirit dries up the bones. (Prov 17:22)
>
> A slack hand causes poverty,
> > but the hand of the diligent makes rich. (Prov 10:4)

The second line supplements the first line.

> Leave the presence of a fool,
> > for there you do not meet words of knowledge. (Prov 14:7)
>
> A man of great wrath will pay the penalty,
> > for if you deliver him, you will only have to do it again. (Prov 19:19)

One or both lines contain(s) a comparison.

> Like a gold ring in a pig's snout
>   is a beautiful woman without discretion. (Prov 11:22)

> Like vinegar to the teeth and smoke to the eyes,
>   so is the sluggard to those who send him. (Prov 10:26)

If you take this linguistic phenomenon into consideration, you will understand many a line from the Psalms or Proverbs more easily. You need only compare it with the accompanying line and you have the key in hand. The lines explain each other, supplement each other, illustrate each other with an image, or clarify each other by means of a contrast.

This technique of composing with balanced lines also makes it easier for someone to learn a psalm or proverb by memory. People have occasionally stated their assumption that the ancient wisdom teachers imprinted their *mashals* by reciting the first line themselves and having their class or student finish with the accompanying line.

Parallelism in the preaching of our Lord Jesus

Our Savior also used such balanced sentences. He often employed a brief *mashal*, whereby he explained one line by means of another. We encounter this linguistic usage especially in the Sermon on the Mount, especially in the Beatitudes (Matt 5:1–12).

> Blessed are the poor in spirit,
>   For theirs is the kingdom of heaven. (Matt 5:3)

> Blessed are those who mourn,
>   For they shall be comforted. (Matt 5:4)

> Give to the one who begs from you,
>   and do not refuse the one who would borrow from you. (Matt 5:42)

> Not everyone who says to me, "Lord, Lord,"
>   will enter the kingdom of heaven,
>   but the one who does the will of my Father
>   who is in heaven. (Matt 7:21)

3. A *MASHAL* PREFERS TO SPEAK GRAPHICALLY AND OFTEN CONTAINS A COMPARISON

A second characteristic of many *mashals* is their graphic language and manifold use of images and comparisons. The Israelites loved such lively forms of speaking, as did all Semites. When Nathan came to rebuke King David, he did that by way of a detour using his well-known *mashal* (2 Sam 12). Isaiah compared Israel to a vineyard, and the men of Judah to the vines (Isa 5). Holy Scripture knows nothing of the scholarly, abstract language of our theologians. (That arises from the Greek system of thinking, which has so strongly overtaken the scriptural manner of speaking that we have difficulty understanding the Scriptures.) God's Word comes to us with *things* (and not with perspectives), and sets these before our eyes with liveliness and concreteness.

Those who wrote the *mashals* did the same. They tired themselves out thinking up new images and comparisons. Just look through their book. They did not approach their readers with dry theories—they had none, after all—but had them walk through an image gallery. Reading proverbs means looking at pictures: lazy farmers and quarrelsome women, depressed and happy people, the tight-lipped and the loquacious, judges and witnesses. It is as if the sages tap us on the shoulder time and again, and say, "Look!"

One comparison is more attractive than another:

> The beginning of strife is like letting out water,
> so quit before the quarrel breaks out. (Prov 17:14)

> A stone is heavy, and sand is weighty,
> but a fool's provocation is heavier than both. (Prov 27:3)

The incarnate Word employed the same method.

The *mashals* are characteristic of the speaking style of the Lord God in his Word. So it could not go any other way than that the incarnate Word of Yahweh, our Lord Jesus Christ, employed this same method. It was the method of his Father, of Yahweh. Therefore, our Chief Prophet and Teacher did not come with foreign and strange perspectives, but with the great *thing* known as the kingdom. That is what he *painted* for the eyes of his hearers. In his *mashals* he compared this kingdom to a mustard seed, a hidden treasure, a fishnet, seed that someone sowed in a field, and yeast that a woman kneaded into a few measures of dough (Matt 13).

Nevertheless, we need not look to his parables to hear him speak graphically. Take the Sermon on the Mount once again (Matt 5–7), where he points his anxious believers to the birds that had perhaps just flown overhead, and to the flowers among which he was sitting to teach. He compared the life of the church to walking down a narrow path or entering through a small gate, something that many of his hearers probably did every day.

4. A *MASHAL* CAN MOCK SOMEONE EITHER COVERTLY OR OPENLY

Earlier we referred to the *mashal* in which Isaiah gave the taunting welcome with which the ghosts in the realm of the dead would one day welcome the fearsome king of Babylon (Isa 14). But those who wrote the proverbs could also poke fun at somebody, as in these proverbs:

> The sluggard buries his hand in the dish
> and will not even bring it back to his mouth. (Prov 19:24)

> Like a gold ring in a pig's snout
> is a beautiful woman without discretion. (Prov 11:22)

We do not find any such taunting *mashals* in the teaching of our Lord, although he could speak with deep irony (see, e.g., Matt 7:15; 23:16, 24).

5. A *MASHAL* CAN OCCASIONALLY SPEAK ENIGMATICALLY

When Nathan told David the *mashal* about the rich miser who stole the only ewe lamb that a poor man owned, the king cried out in indignation, "As the LORD lives, the man who has done this deserves to die, and he shall restore the lamb fourfold, because he did this thing, and because he had no pity" (2 Sam 12:5–6). From this you can see how someone can hear an apparently simple *mashal without grasping its meaning*. Only when the prophet explained it ("You are that man") did the light go on for David, and he figured out the *mashal*.

As genuine Easterners, the Israelites were fond of such riddles; recall the wedding of Samson (Judg 14). This kind of apparently clear but simultaneously enigmatic manner of expression could provoke reflection very powerfully. This is why the sages intentionally formulated their life lessons with less transparency, in order to stimulate the reflection and acuity of their listeners. *Mashals* were designed to grab and hold the hearer. Thus, the design of the book of Proverbs was that the reader "understand a proverb [*mashal*] and a saying, the words of the wise and their *riddles*"[1] (Prov 1:6). Some proverbs need to be read more than once before one understands them.

The Preacher in Ecclesiastes is also fond of presenting readers now and then with a riddle. The occasionally enigmatic writing style provokes the reader a bit, and that was exactly the intention. This we can see from the conclusion of his book: "The words of the wise are like goads, and like nails firmly fixed are the collected sayings" (Eccl 12:11). They are designed to stimulate reflection.

The concealing mashals of an offended King Jesus

On a particular day in his ministry, our Lord Jesus Christ also taught with *mashals* that did not *clarify* his teaching but *obscured* it. He did not come with these at the beginning of his instruction. For a period of time he first gave all Israel a friendly invitation to accept him as the promised Messiah-King. In that connection he had told them a number of *mashals*—see the Sermon on the Mount—but those were still, at that point, parables that explained his preaching. Only when the majority of Jews had rejected him did the Lord turn to telling *mashals* that *concealed* his teaching. These were provocative *mashal* riddles.

On first hearing, these parables also looked so simple that a child could grasp them. "A sower went out to sow . . . . The kingdom of heaven is like leaven that a woman took and hid in three measures of flour, till it was all leavened" (Matt 13:3, 33). They seemed as clear as day, but don't be misled. David also thought that he had understood Nathan's parable, but he hadn't. That's how it went with those apparently simple *mashals* like those of the sower and the leaven. Most of the Jews did not understand what Jesus was actually intending to teach there, and a large number of Christians do not understand them today either.

His disciples were amazed about this change in the style of Jesus' instruction. "Why do you speak to them in parables?" they asked (Matt 13:10). Of course, what they meant was "in such obscure parables," for they themselves did not understand either. So now you can see how irritated and angry Jesus was when he turned to giving instruction in puzzling *mashals*, for he directed his disciples, for their requested explanation, to the prophecy of Isaiah: "Go, and say to this people: 'Keep on hearing, but do not understand; keep on seeing, but do not perceive.' Make the heart of this people dull, and their ears heavy, and blind their eyes; lest they see with their eyes,

---

1. Unless otherwise noted, italics in Scripture quotations are added for emphasis.

and hear with their ears, and understand with their hearts, and turn and be healed" (Isa 6:9–10; Matt 13:14–15).

That is how matters stood between Jesus and Israel when he turned to teaching by means of concealing *mashals*. Most of the Jews had, while listening to him, stopped their ears to what he was teaching. "That is why I speak to them in parables, because seeing they do not see, and hearing they do not hear, nor do they understand" (Matt 13:13). He did not want to make it easier with his parables for those malicious and ill-disposed Jews to believe in him, but exactly the opposite!

They had become "outsiders" (Mark 4:11), who got to hear the kingdom of God proclaimed to them only in parables "*so that* [!] 'they may indeed see but not perceive, and may indeed hear but not understand, lest they should turn and be forgiven'" (Mark 4:12). When we place this Scripture passage alongside the one cited above from Matt 13, we discover the following historical sequence of events: The Jews rejected Jesus—that was the action that started everything else. Next came Jesus' angry response: Therefore (Matt 13:13) I will turn to telling them obscure parables. *So that* (Mark 4:12) from now on they will have an even more difficult time understanding my preaching!

And that is what they did, given the impact that those parables had on the listeners. Most of them perhaps found the stories to contain "smooth things" (Isa 30:10), but the quintessential meaning escaped them: that the kingdom of God does not come through carnal violence but only through God's Word and Spirit, both of which work like seed in a field and yeast in dough. Though seeing they *wanted* to remain blind (Matt 13:15), so they did not see that Jesus was thereby smashing their political image of a messiah. Nor did they ask for further explanation. When he finished speaking, they went back to the order of the day, no wiser than before.

Jesus' disciples, by contrast, responded differently. They, too, had not understood what the Lord was intending with these *mashals*, but these stories had at least provoked them to ask him for further explanation (Matt 13:10–17; Mark 4:10; Luke 8:9). And, when everyone had gone home, he gave *them* the requested clarification (Matt 13:18–23, 36–52; 21:31; Luke 7:42–43; 10:36). In this way, by means of these *mashals*, Jesus separated his listeners, bringing to light those who were superficial chasers and who were teachable disciples.

In so doing, he was not bringing peace but division (Matt 10:34–35). For then he could say, "Learn from me, for I am gentle and lowly in heart" (Matt 11:29), but that is not to deny that he was at the same time the great King of prophecy. Israel's unbelief was nothing less than desecration of the Majesty, rejection of their King. And that, after all his beneficent words and miracles! Therefore he was putting off this unwilling audience with these particular *mashals. Obscuring* lessons. Were they unwilling to listen to him? If so, they would not be allowed any longer to listen to him! He would *hide* from them the kingdom of God. Therefore he chose the most veiled teaching style of the *mashal* riddles, with which Israel was familiar from its wisdom books.

Read the parables, then, especially not as saccharine or short, idyllic stories of a Jesus who implores endlessly for people to believe. Rather, view them as proofs of the fearsome reality that God's people, too, can hear a *judgment* from God's Word. Of course, Jesus' priestly heart continued to be moved with regard to this people, for he continued to speak to them, and even, on the way to Golgotha, wept over Jerusalem. But that is not to deny that such apparently nice *mashals* were the *disciplinary preaching* of a scorned Ruler, whereby he said, You refuse to listen? Then you may not listen any longer. Now I will not clarify my message for you, but obscure it. You might just decide to believe in me, and that would be too bad!

This kind of Jesus came to Israel with *mashals*. A scorned king, who effected the result that things went this way with respect to the faith-knowledge pertaining to God's kingdom: "For to the one who has, more will be given, and he will have an abundance, but from the one who has not, even what he has will be taken away" (Matt 13:12). From then on, those ill-disposed toward Jesus understood him even less, while those desiring to be saved stepped over the threshold with these *mashals*.

Those concealing *mashals* are still contained in the Bible today. In that particular form, Holy Scripture offers us a portion of Jesus' teaching about the coming of the kingdom. Thereby, in our age as well, Christ makes manifest "thoughts from many hearts," as Simeon prophesied about him (Luke 2:34–35). Even now the *mashals* sift and separate the fleshly from the spiritual disciples, just as they did among ancient Israel.

The kingdom of heaven does not come through fleshly activism, but through the sowing of God's Word and the leaven of God's Spirit. This is what Jesus taught in his *mashals*. It was the ancient lesson, "Not by might, nor by power, but by my Spirit, says the Lord of hosts" (Zech 4:6). Thereby Jesus was condemning not only Jewish revolutionary and military messianic expectations, but also various Christian variations of that. Who continues to sense, however, that antithetical "stinger" (Eccl 12:11) in Jesus' parables?

When one sees or hears or reads about particular Christians engaged in activism, one fears that they scarcely realize how much Jesus' parables apply to them. They perhaps view them as nice illustrations accompanying Jesus' preaching, but in hearing them they are simultaneously deaf to the fact that here the judgment of Christ is being given about various contemporary fussing over the kingdom of God. For that kingdom comes, after all, just as quietly as a seed in a field and yeast in dough. You can continue to hear and read these *mashals* without *understanding* them.

But in this era, these words are fulfilled among a remnant: "But blessed are your eyes, for they see, and your ears, for they hear" (Matt 13:16).

6. A *MASHAL* OCCASIONALLY CONTAINS A BLUNT FORMULATION

A *mashal* can provoke not only by means of its veiled manner of speaking, however, but also by means of its *pithy* manner of speech. Some of them are so strongly formulated that people wonder: Didn't the writer know that the matter has other dimensions? Especially in Proverbs and Ecclesiastes you can find many of those blunt formulations. We might weaken them somewhat by adding "so to speak" and "in a manner of speaking," but the writers themselves did not soften their proverbs.

You can see many examples of this brought together in Prov 3. The thematic lesson of this chapter is: "In keeping God's commandment lies rich reward." For that can extend your life, advance your health, benefit your night's sleep, smooth out your path, and supply you with wealth and honor. Perhaps you've wondered at one time or another: But this doesn't always work out this way, does it? These are not rules without any exceptions, are they? These questions can arise on every page of Proverbs.

To mention a few examples: "Yahweh does not let the righteous *go hungry*" (Prov 10:3). But Israel knew famine, during which the righteous suffered along with everyone else, didn't they? During a severe famine, the prophet Elisha stayed in besieged Samaria (2 Kgs 6:24–33). In fact, we know of believers in the Netherlands who died of hunger, or ate cats and sugar beets, during the so-called hunger winter of 1944–1945. So sometimes God permits the righteous to go hungry, but is it the case that the proverb cited above is not *always* valid?

Here are two more examples. "*No ill* befalls the righteous, but the wicked are filled with trouble" (Prov 12:21). But David said, "*Many* are the afflictions of the righteous, but the Lord delivers him out of them all" (Ps 34:19). "Gray hair is a crown of glory; it is gained in a righteous life" (Prov 16:31). But was this true of Simeon, to whom David entrusted his son Solomon, saying, You know what you must do to "bring his gray head down with blood to Sheol" (1 Kgs 2:9). So gray hair is not always an adorning crown.

How must we understand such strong proverbs?

1. *In Proverbs the emphasis is placed on the general rule.*

To begin with, we must read such *mashals* as poetry, which is licensed to use language in a way that could lead a curmudgeon to criticize this or that. Moreover, the sages wanted definitely to reach their readers, so they expressed their ideas not only graphically and enigmatically but also pithily and strongly. Intense colors make a stronger impression, and exaggeration makes a point more clearly.

Don't forget as well that the sages wanted to nurture young people, and young people simply have no patience for long-windedness. A pithy formulation is also easier to memorize (for the believer must have a certain number of proverbs at the ready). As good teachers, the sages place more emphasis on the rules than on the exceptions. In fact, we ourselves do the same thing, don't we? "If you do your best, you will get ahead in the world," we tell our children. *At that moment*, we remain silent about industrious workers who nonetheless face poverty.

As far as that goes, the sages themselves realized that they were exaggerating one dimension of the truth. Therefore we should not read these proverbs apart from the larger context of the book in which they appear. The one proverb supplements the other. "Answer not a fool according to his folly, lest you be like him yourself" (Prov 26:4). The author did not mean that as an absolute rule, for in the next verse we read, "Answer a fool according to his folly, lest he be wise in his own eyes" (Prov 26:5). We find something similar in the proverbs about the advantages of working industriously. "In all toil there is profit, but mere talk tends only to poverty" (Prov 14:23). Nevertheless, the same book says, "The blessing of the LORD makes rich, and he adds no [!] sorrow with it" (Prov 10:22).

It is clear that the sages are here providing *general rules*, without mentioning the exceptions at the same time. Poetic *mashals*, designed to provoke reflection. Formulations that supplement each other back and forth. Therefore they may never be pried loose from the large unit of this instruction. Then we will have less trouble with "contradictions" and "one-sidedness" in Proverbs.

2. *Don't create a contradiction between Proverbs and Ecclesiastes.*

Perhaps someone will object to the foregoing, however, by asserting, "That's all good and well, but when David was driven into the wilderness with hundreds of righteous people, or when the entire city of Samaria suffers hunger, including the prophet Elisha, or when the pious Daniel is one of the first to go into captivity, then we are not encountering exceptions to the general rules in Proverbs. But then, in such situations, those rules themselves don't apply. What must we do then? When the promises of Proverbs appear not to be valid? Then we cannot suffice with reference to the occasionally pithy, provocative manner of speaking that we find in the *mashal*."

Some expositions of the Bible's wisdom books solve this problem with the help of a particular construction. The expectation of Israel's sages supposedly shifted over the course of time, moving downward from a high point in Proverbs, via the lower level of expectations in Job, to the virtually hopeless depths of Ecclesiastes. Using this construction, one could summarize these three books this way:

Proverbs: Whoever fears Yahweh will have it good.

Job: Whoever fears Yahweh will not always have it good.

Ecclesiastes: Whoever fears Yahweh will have it as good as the one who does not fear him.

This construction, for starters, runs aground on the book of Proverbs itself, which describes *much pain and injustice* in the life of the righteous. According to Proverbs, the godly *do not always have it good* (we will come back to this later). And if the alleged "optimistic" teaching of Proverbs is really under attack in the book of Job, and then altogether vanquished in the book of Ecclesiastes, then why does the later apocryphal wisdom book of Jesus Sirach reach back beyond Ecclesiastes and Job once again to Proverbs?

Moreover, with this construction people are ignoring the characteristics of the *mashal*, which is designed to drive its listeners to reflection. Therefore, it speaks not only metaphorically and concretely but occasionally also pithily and strongly, and several times even intentionally one-sidedly. Anyone who forgets that is taking the Preacher for an arch-pessimist whose biblical life-wisdom is bankrupt.

We view the construction mentioned above as an evolutionistic invention, and certainly not as a suitable aid for understanding Proverbs when here and there it appears not to fit together—for example, when the situation arises that a David has to flee, and an Elisha suffers hunger, and a Daniel is led away into captivity. For, in such cases, the book of Proverbs is not outdated, but people are reading it wrongly.

3. *Read Proverbs not as a disparate collection, a timeless book, but as one of the books of the old and new covenants.*

Because Proverbs contains so many disparate maxims, we could easily come to view it as a loose-leaf notebook, one that has found somewhat of an uneasy home in the Bible. Nothing is less true, however. Proverbs belongs, together with all of the other Bible books, to the canonical books of the old and new *covenants*. Like the Psalms, it rests upon the Torah; it is intimately connected to the Torah (we will come back to this in connection with Prov 1:7). You can be sure that those who wrote the proverbs knew the blessing and the curse that Moses had pronounced upon Israel *as covenant stipulations* (Lev 26; Deut 28). And that they knew how God's blessing and curse were connected with Israel's obedient living according to the requirements of God's covenant (see our comments in connection with Prov 11:11).

So, then, you hear the echo of this instruction in Proverbs. This book is not offering a neutral, universally human wisdom nor a collection of trans-historical religious propositions that are valid in every place and time. Proverbs contains *covenantal* wisdom. It echoes the covenant blessing and covenant curse of the Torah. Therefore you must always take into consideration the *situation* of God's people whenever you wonder whether some of the proverbs are still applicable. Are we reading and applying them in a time of covenant abandonment or a time of return? A time of judgment and breakdown, or a time of peace and refreshing? We may not simply apply Scripture unthinkingly; we discussed this more extensively in connection with Ps 46.[2]

This applies to Proverbs as well.

Indeed, it does promise to the righteous that along the route of fearing the LORD they will not suffer hunger, they will walk smooth paths, will obtain affection and approval in the eyes of God and men, will see their barns filled with abundance, and will walk safely without stumbling. Nevertheless, a person like the prophet Jeremiah—and there were more like him—saw few of these promises fulfilled. But he was living in a time when the flames of God's wrath were burning throughout Israel! When the curse of God's covenant afflicts his people, then we should not expect that the blessings of the book of Proverbs will descend unabridged. This book does indeed promise honor and smooth paths to the godly, but Jeremiah was cast unceremoniously into a pit, and he certainly did not travel smooth paths but ended up in prison. At that point, *in that situation*, surely he could not say, "I demand bread, rest, and a long and secure life, because Proverbs promises these," could he?

This is so even though God the Almighty can feed a godly remnant among his people who are dwelling in caves (1 Kgs 18). For in many respects the righteous must suffer along with the wicked during times of covenant wrath; but many times God does place them in exceptional circumstances

---

2. See van Deursen, *Psalms I*, 368–69.

(1 Kgs 18; Isa 7:14–15, 21–25; Jer 45; Daniel). During such times, dependent, humble, righteous believers will not pressure God with the promises of Proverbs, but rather hide in the inner room until the divine wrath has passed (Isa 26; Amos 5:13; see our comments on Prov 28:28).

In fact, Proverbs itself shows that the wise do not always experience things in the same way. "Whoever works his land will have plenty of bread" (Prov 28:19). But you cannot turn this into an ironclad rule, for Solomon also knew, "The fallow ground of the poor would yield much food, but [*sometimes*] it is swept away *through injustice*" (Prov 13:23). When God punishes his people with the domination of the wicked or by means of a hostile attack, then Prov 28:19 does *not* apply. At that point "the people cast off restraint" (Prov 29:18) and at that point "people hide themselves" (Prov 28:28). When God removes his peace (Jer 16:5), this often involves the peace that is mentioned repeatedly in Proverbs.

So we must not forget, especially, that we are reading the book of Proverbs in the twenty-first century, and we are seeing, and have seen in the previous century, severe judgments coming upon formerly Christian nations. We see our culture and population descending into a post-Christian period, when people everywhere are elevating the *science* of autonomous man above the *wisdom* of Solomon. The godly remnant in our day may pray, of course, that, in his long-suffering, God will permit it to taste the peace of the wisdom of Proverbs. But if they should see some of the proverbs not being fulfilled, they have every reason to ask the humble question: Will the revolution as a scourge of God perhaps break into even more pieces the good life that Proverbs proclaims? And rather than level accusations against God, they will humbly acknowledge, "The Lord is righteous" (by applying his rod of correction to us) (2 Chr 12:6).

We hope that this chapter about the uniquenesses of the *mashal* can prevent misunderstandings as we now proceed to read Proverbs. In any case, we have issued an advance warning. In this Bible book, we do not receive a hermetically sealed system explained to us. The book offers what its title promises: *mashals*. These are proverbs of wise men who discovered rules that certainly have exceptions, but who omitted mentioning them in part for reasons having to do with nurture. These proverbs communicate effectively as long as you don't remove and isolate the wisdom of this book from the context of God's covenant and the general situation of God's people in our own day.

As we saw, in his own teaching, our Lord Jesus Christ followed very closely the didactic style of those who wrote the proverbs. Neither did he avoid strong *mashals*, for example, when he advised us to pluck out our right eye or cut off our right hand if they would tempt us to sin (Matt 5:29–30;

cf. John 6:27a; Matt 19:12). It is remarkable that he often ended his *mashals* with the words, "He who has ears, let him hear!" (Matt 13:9; Luke 14:35).

How he—the one who himself has composed such wonderful *mashals* of various kinds—must have loved the book of Proverbs! Naturally, first of all for its wisdom but also for its beautiful style: the style of visual, concise, and occasionally veiled *mashals*.

2

The Origin of the Book of Proverbs

WHOM MUST WE THANK for the book of Proverbs? Of course, first of all, God the Holy Spirit, the author of the entire Scriptures, including the book of Proverbs (2 Tim 3:16; 2 Pet 1:21). But the Spirit of wisdom made use in that connection of wise men. Especially of King Solomon, but also of sages like Agur and King Lemuel. Solomon, however, provided far and away the largest amount of material, and for that reason the book is named after him: Proverbs of Solomon (Prov 1:1; cf. 10:1; 25:1). In what follows, we will first provide a bit of information about these *authors*.

These writers of proverbs did not work simultaneously or as a group. The *mashals* that have been collected in Proverbs were written over the course of many years and existed separately for a time or belonged to other existing collections. In the time of King Hezekiah people collected various proverbs (or groups of them). We will say something about this *collecting activity* in the second place.

But can we discover any *order* or arrangement in Proverbs? Did the authors or collectors follow any particular arrangement, or does the book from beginning to end resemble a collection of marbles? Indeed, Proverbs does show a particular structure, which provides us much delight as we read this book. We will discuss this in the third place.

1. PROVERBS OF SOLOMON

According to the testimony of the book itself, by far the largest amount of material in Proverbs comes from the hand of Solomon—almost twenty-seven of its thirty-one chapters (Prov 1–9; 10—22:16; 25–29; see the superscriptions above Prov 1:1; 10:1; 22:17; 25:1; 30:1; 31:1).

Since the 1800s, Scripture-critical scholars have argued that this is not true. According to some, not a single proverb in this Bible book comes from Solomon; others make a less bold claim, but people in these circles accept rather generally that Proverbs as a book did not come from Solomon.

What is the basis of this claim? In ancient Egypt people honored a king by making a collection of proverbs in his name. He himself had not written them, but people considered them as his. In this way the book acquired greater authority, for a king must surely have been a wise man! Such a ruler was being honored in this way. Without proof people simply believed that men in Israel had done the same thing: ascribed laws to the famous Moses, psalms to David, and proverbs to Solomon.

In this connection, naturally, the evolutionary paradigm was playing a role. According to this paradigm, short works of poetry must have been older than long ones, because in primitive times people could not yet compose large works. Therefore Prov 1–9 could not have come from the hand of Solomon. His name was above it, but that had been placed above it in order to bestow on these proverbs more prestige. This part of the book contains longer, and thus more recent, compositions, dating from the time after Solomon. This is the argument of especially older Scripture-critical commentaries.

But what does Scripture itself say? It reports to us three clear facts that give us a decisive answer to our question: (1) Solomon indeed possessed unprecedented wisdom; (2) Solomon really did publish wisdom literature; and (3) Solomon's name appears often as a superscription in the book of Proverbs.

Let us examine these three facts in detail.

Solomon possessed unprecedented wisdom.

In his day, King Solomon was a universal genius. When, at a young age, he was permitted to make a wish from God, he did not ask for riches, honor, and long life, but for the *capacity to discern* between good and evil in order to be able to reign over Israel as a righteous ruler. This desire was so pleasing to Yahweh that he replied, "Behold, I give you a wise and discerning mind, so that none like you has been before you and none shall arise after you," incomparable to you also in riches and honor (1 Kgs 3:4–15). Then God gave Solomon not only a deep insight into good and evil but also an extraordinarily wide field of interest (literally, "space of heart"). His insight was not only in matters of justice and injustice but Solomon's wisdom and understanding were "beyond measure, and breadth of mind like the sea on the seashore" (1 Kgs 4:29).

To cite a few examples: "He spoke of trees, from the cedar that is in Lebanon to the hyssop that grows out of the wall. He spoke also of beasts, and of birds, and of reptiles, and of fish" (1 Kgs 4:33; about Agur, cf. Prov 30:15–16, 18–20, 24–31). The king was interested in so many things, and in so many things he excelled above everyone else. So it is understandable that we should speak of a universal genius, is it not? Solomon was the wisest man, after the Lord Jesus.

For that reason, with regard to the matter of authorship, we should keep in mind the difference between biblical and extrabiblical books of proverbs. The ancient Egyptians liked to associate this kind of literature with the name of a renowned king, presumably without considering whether the man was in fact all that wise. Perhaps in so doing they were honoring a fool (Prov 9:11; 10:6). But Solomon was genuinely extraordinarily wise. Other than the Lord Jesus, no one had ever possessed the kind of insight that he did.

When people *ascribe* the book of Proverbs to Solomon alone, by virtue of a particular literary convention, they face difficult problems. For then the book must have come from someone who was no less wise than Solomon. But who would that have been? The content of Proverbs rises like a church steeple above those other ancient Near Eastern collections of proverbs. Would their wisdom really need to be puffed up by putting Solomon's name over it? Or do people apply such an ancient Egyptian literary custom to an essentially incomparable phenomenon? Do not the immeasurable breadth and unmatched wealth of Proverbs constitute an argument for a single author: King Solomon? Who else could account for twenty-five chapters of such a book? Other than this uniquely wise man, who else could have composed so many proverbs of this quality?

Solomon wrote genuine wisdom literature.

Ancient Eastern proverb collections might well have been identified with the name of a king who had never composed one proverb himself. But regarding Solomon, Scripture says explicitly that he wrote various collections of wisdom literature. For those, he chose the form of songs as well as of proverbs (1 Kgs 4:32).

In so doing, Solomon was following a centuries-old international tradition of his time. In the world surrounding Israel, people had practiced the art of composing proverbs for hundreds of years. Prospective officials were taught at school all kinds of good advice in the form of proverbs. Babylon, Edom, and especially Egypt had acquired great fame in the arena of practical wisdom for living (Isa 19:12; Jer 49:7; 50:35; 51:57). The Egyptian proverbs of Ptah-Hotep, (dating from 2450 BC) are some fifteen hundred years older than those of Solomon.

And yet his wisdom rose above that of everyone else! Yes, it attracted interested even beyond Israel's boundaries. It did so even though people in that foreign land had been familiar with wisdom literature for centuries. But the insights of this great mind surpassed those of all other Easterners, indeed, surpassed even the wisdom of Egypt (1 Kgs 4:30; Sir 47:14–12). The knowledge of famous wise men like Ethan, Heman, Calcol, and Darda (1 Kgs 4:31) did not extend to the breadth and depth of Solomon's insight. Many foreigners made excursions to Israel in order to become knowledgeable about Solomon's wisdom (1 Kgs 4:34; cf. 10:1–10).

Would the equally exceptional wisdom of the book of Proverbs then have come from anyone except the man whose name stands at its beginning? Why may Proverbs not have really come from Solomon? Or are we catching here a whiff of the destructive activity of Scripture criticism?

Solomon's name is mentioned three times in Proverbs.

So Solomon's name was known the world over. The book of Proverbs names him as its primary author, not once but three times (Prov 1:1; 10:1; 25:1). Doesn't that tell us something? Why should we doubt these superscriptions, after all, since the book of 1 Kings has told us about Solomon's wisdom and his publications in this area? The excavations done in our century have certainly not added fuel to this skepticism.

At the close of the nineteenth century and the opening of the twentieth century, people considered the superscriptions in Proverbs rather generally to be incorrect. Solomon could never have made such long compositions as we find in Prov 1–9. But the excavations have taught us something different. People discovered poetic works that in terms of language and literary quality resemble Proverbs, but which date from the time *of Abraham* or earlier, as far back as fifteen hundred years before Solomon! This itself has led to increased respect for the credibility of the superscriptions in question.

A genuinely convincing proof against the authorship of Solomon has in fact never been provided by anyone. Even the argument that, according to 1 Kgs 4:32, Solomon composed some three thousand proverbs, whereas the Bible book of Proverbs contains only about eight hundred, is not all that strong. If we render the Hebrew word for three thousand (for three *elaphim*) as *three units*, then this argument doesn't work. For then 1 Kgs 5 would have meant to say that Solomon wrote *three collections*.

For these reasons, we will simply continue to speak of the Proverbs of Solomon. Even though the book itself bears witness that other hands have collaborated on it, the lion's share was undoubtedly contributed by Israel's most wise ruler. Initially, God's good Spirit endowed him as a young man with extraordinary wisdom. Thereafter, the Spirit ensured that a rich wealth of Solomon's insights was preserved for God's people. Thus we can "hear" him three thousand years later. And we need not be embarrassed when citing one of his proverbs simply to say, "Solomon said."

In this way we are at the same time honoring the Lord Jesus Christ, who said, "Behold, something greater than Solomon is here" (Matt 12:42). In saying this, he was referring not to Solomon's wealth and glory, for in those respects our humble Savior was far less than Solomon but he was referring to the latter's royal wisdom. In that respect our Messiah King far surpassed Solomon. For in him the prophecy of Isaiah was fulfilled: "His name shall be called Wonderful Counselor" (Isa 9:6). "And the Spirit of the LORD shall rest upon him, the Spirit of wisdom and understanding, the Spirit of counsel and might, the Spirit of the knowledge and the fear of the LORD" (Isa 11:2; cf. Luke 2:40, 52; Col 2:3).

Other composers of proverbs

In addition to a large quantity of Solomonic proverbs, we possess in this book several smaller collections from other composers of proverbs. Some of these people we know by name like Agur the son of Jakeh (Prov 30:1) and Lemuel the king of Massa (Prov 31:1), but not others. One of the anonymous collections has this superscription: "Incline your ear, and hear the words of the wise" (Prov 22:17). Another begins with, "These also are sayings of the wise" (Prov 24:23). Nor do we know who composed the song praising the ideal woman (Prov 31:10–31).

In connection with such unknown composers of proverbs, one might think of the woman from Tekoa, who at Joab's request went to David to urge him to receive back his son (2 Sam 14). Or of that woman from Abel-Beth-Maacah who rescued the city by means of her wisdom (2 Sam 20:16–22).

Or of that poor man in Eccl 9:15 who also could have rescued his city if only people had listened to him. But above the work of such unknown and lesser known sages stands the name of Solomon as the principal author of this book.

All of them driven by the Spirit of wisdom

We have now adequately discussed the known and unknown composers of proverbs, for in the final analysis they all had obtained their wisdom from God. For all wisdom comes from God (Prov 2:6; 8:22–31). All the collections of proverbs "are given by one Shepherd" (Eccl 12:11). The renowned Solomon also imparted only that wisdom that he in turn had *received*. "Behold, I have given you a wise and discerning mind," Yahweh had said to him (1 Kgs 3:12; 4:29). In that connection, God surely used the means of Solomon's own study and powers of observation. But in the final analysis we owe this Bible book not to people, but to "the Spirit of wisdom and understanding" (Isa 11:2), who also "drove" the composers of biblical proverbs on behalf of God (2 Pet 1:21; cf. 2 Tim 3:16).

Proverbs, too, belongs to God's own Word!

2. HEZEKIAH'S CARE FOR ISRAEL'S PROVERBIAL WISDOM

Presumably other visitors beside the queen of Sheba heard the wisdom of Solomon from his own mouth (1 Kgs 10:1–10). Did he perhaps speak personally with all these foreigners, and give them lessons in wisdom? We would not be surprised if many people had become acquainted with Solomon's insights at that time already on the basis of his writings. What this ruler taught to the sages, and these sages learned from this ruler, would have been written down and copied by scribes. Already in his lifetime, three collections of proverbs of Solomon were published. Foreign visitors who made a trip to Jerusalem, which at that time was the world-renowned center of wisdom, could presumably read many of Solomon's songs and proverbs.

But just as many of our English proverbs are used without ever having consulted a book of proverbs, so, too, the Israelites certainly learned many proverbs by memory and passed them on orally. They would have used them just as freely as we do, in order to add spice to our daily conversations. For generations Israel must have preserved a treasury of proverbial wisdom in the safe deposit box of their memory. It took at least until the time of Hezekiah before our Bible book of Proverbs received its present form.

This godly king was zealous not only for the reformation of the temple ministry but also for preserving Israel's wisdom proverbs. We learn of this in Prov 25:1, where we read, "These also are proverbs of Solomon which the men of Hezekiah king of Judah copied." According to this translation, King Hezekiah appointed a commission whose mandate was to gather together Israel's treasury of proverbs. Perhaps a number of collections of Solomon's proverbs already existed; that seems to be the case when we read, "*These also are proverbs of Solomon*" (Prov 25:1). In that connection, we might think of the collections identified as Prov 1–9 and 10:1—22:16. But we could also translate Prov 25:1 this way: "These also are proverbs of Solomon, which the men of Hezekiah copied *to another scroll*." In that case, they would have gathered together already existing collections of Solomon's proverbs and perhaps of other sages, and written them on a new scroll.

Would Hezekiah have undertaken this work because of the critical urgency of his day? The Assyrian empire had led the ten tribes into captivity and were threatening Judah as well. Was it with an eye to these developments that the king wanted to safeguard the immense treasure of the proverbial wisdom that had been handed down, and do so by gathering it beforehand and putting it down on new scrolls?

In any case, between those loose collections and our modern book of Proverbs lay a path of at least two hundred fifty years, from Solomon to Hezekiah. But over all those proverbs, whether stored in Israel's memory or preserved on scrolls, the watchful eye of God the Holy Spirit was superintending throughout all those years. He not only "drove" the composers to their work of composing proverbs but he also preserved that work. And he saw to it that this work has come down to us in the form of the book we possess in Holy Scripture.

3. DESIGN AND ARRANGEMENT OF THE BOOK

Is there anything to discover with regard to the order and arrangement within this Bible book? Aren't these proverbs more or less randomly arranged? To a certain extent they are, and, if you pay attention simply to the subjects they address, from Prov 10:1 onward they bounce from one topic to another, and seem connected only very loosely. What motivated the collectors to place these proverbs in their current order is hard to determine. They even repeat various proverbs, not only in different parts of the book but even in the same section (see 2:16 and 7:5; 3:15 and 8:11; 10:1 and 15:20;

14:12 and 16:25; 14:20 and 19:4). It would be difficult to find a satisfying explanation of this phenomenon.

Due to this loose interconnection, some commentators have organized the book of Proverbs in various ways. Some have arranged the proverbs according to topics: what the book teaches about the person who serves God in the family, in society, or what it teaches about laziness, industry, nurture, and social relationships Others organized the proverbs according to the Ten Commandments. This is a good approach, in view of the close connection between the Torah and Israel's wisdom proverbs.

Nevertheless, for our commentary, we have not followed such arrangements, despite the attractiveness they afford. We have taken this route, first, because an explanation of all the proverbs lies beyond the purpose of this volume. In addition, we have chosen our method because so many proverbs really break the categories being imposed. Regarding the Ten Commandments, it is striking that the collectors themselves did not arrange Proverbs this way, even though they already possessed an example of that in the book of Deuteronomy. Moreover, numerous *mashals* can be categorized under more than one of the Ten Commandments. Or when one seeks to arrange them topically, one discovers that often they can be categorized under more than one topic.

Our principal objection, however, is that upon further investigation Proverbs does display a certain organization and order, and such rearranging disrupts the structure that God the Holy Spirit was pleased to use in handing down this wisdom to us.

A collection of eight proverb compilations

The book of Proverbs is actually a collection of proverb compilations, compiled by "the men of Hezekiah." The book shows clearly various seams where people sewed the proverb collections together. For we have superscriptions that describe the collections we are reading. We will list these superscriptions, with their references, so you can see that Proverbs constitutes a compilation of at least eight booklets of proverbs.

1. The Proverbs of Solomon (Prov 1:1—9:18)
2. The Proverbs of Solomon (Prov 10:1—22:16)
3. Words of the wise (Prov 22:17—24:22)
4. These too are the words of the wise (Prov 24:23–34)
5. These too are proverbs of Solomon, which the men of Hezekiah, the king of Judah, collected (Prov 25:1—29:27)

6. The words of Agur, the son of Jakeh (Prov 30:1–33)
7. The words of Lemuel, the king of Massa, with which his mother warned him (Prov 31:1–9)
8. The ideal woman (Prov 31:10–31)

When we investigate these booklets of proverbs further, then we observe a remarkable difference between Prov 1–9, on the one hand, and Prov 10–31, on the other hand. The first nine chapters clearly show a different character from the rest of the book. If we were to compare Proverbs to a palace, then, in Prov 1:1–7, we are entering the main hall. Next, in Prov 1:8–9, we enter, as it were, into a beautiful corridor that leads us to Prov 10–31. There we find the throne room and the various side rooms. In a certain sense, Proverbs really begins in Prov 10:1. There we find the superscription from Prov 1:1 repeated once more: "The Proverbs of Solomon."

Now we don't want to exaggerate this difference between Prov 1–9 and Prov 10–31. Proverbs 1–9 indisputably teaches the same kind of life lessons that we hear in the rest of the book. For that reason we said that *in a certain sense* the book of Proverbs begins in Prov 10:1. But this does not deny that Prov 1–9 taken as a whole contains other kinds of material than Prov 10–31. You can see that from merely a superficial glance. From Prov 10:1, the proverbs are arranged in small groups with hardly any connection between the groups By contrast, Prov 1–9 displays a far greater mutual dependence, in part because it is dealing with main themes that are clearly different.

If we review these topics more closely, then Prov 1–9 clearly has the character of a *manual* that teaches us how we must read and appreciate Prov 10–31. Something like the *instruction manual* for using the teaching provided in Prov 10–31. So we would like to entitle Prov 1–9 in our subsequent discussion "Instruction Manual for Proverbs." Or more briefly, "Instruction Manual."

Therefore we arrange Proverbs this way:

1. Proverbs 1–9: Instruction Manual for the book of Proverbs
2. Proverbs 10–31: The book of Proverbs

4. INSTRUCTION MANUAL FOR THE BOOK OF PROVERBS

Before discussing Prov 1–9, we first want to tell you something about the characteristic uniquenesses of these instructions for using and understanding the book of Proverbs. By doing so, we can clarify our overview of these chapters and deepen our insight into the structure of this Bible book. Well then, the characteristic features of Prov 1–9 consist of these two main themes:

- The *value* of wisdom
- The *path* to wisdom

Certainly Proverbs itself discusses these topics differently than we will. For the sake of clarity, we are laying these alongside each other; but in Prov 1–9 they are interwoven, even though these are two distinct matters: "What good is wisdom for me?" and "How do I get wisdom?" With great emphasis, the Instruction Manual for Proverbs never tires of repeating, "Know the priceless *value* of wisdom, and walk in wisdom's *ways*." We will make a few comments about each of these main themes.

The value of wisdom

Those who composed the proverbs were intelligent educators. They were not demanding from their pupils blind obedience. As competent pedagogues they knew that sympathetic listeners obey more easily when they perceive *why* someone is encouraging this and discouraging that, more easily than when people demand rote compliance from them. For that reason, you can observe everywhere in Proverbs that the wise ones clothe their instructions with reasons. Nevertheless, we can see in this respect a bit of difference between the Instruction Manual and the actual book of Proverbs itself.

Naturally, in Prov 31 as well, the sages take great pains to show their pupils why wisdom is far preferable to folly. But Prov 1–9 places still greater emphasis on that. Continuously throughout those chapters this main theme returns: "If you are wise, you are wise for yourself" (Prov 9:12). Proverbs 2 and 3 discuss this topic quite extensively. Proverbs 4 tells us how Solomon himself had learned this at home from his godly father David. And Prov 5–7 shows us in that connection a striking example: wisdom can rescue you from the life-destroying seduction of the wicked woman. Proverbs 1, 8, and 9 present wisdom as a woman speaking to us, someone who, in a couple of powerful speeches, illuminates the noble birth and life-enhancing power of wisdom.

In that connection, one might naturally think of all the wisdom in nature and in Scripture, but given the canonical place of Prov 1–9, our thinking is directed by these songs of praise for wisdom especially to the instruction of Prov 10–31. Before we get to read those chapters, Prov 1–9 specifies for us with strong emphasis the priceless value of that instruction: *it can save your life*. In the fullest sense of the word, not only your length of life but also your quality of life, your possessions, your health, your marital delight.

In this way, the Instruction Manual is teaching us at the same time one of the most fundamental lessons in the school of Proverbs: Always ask yourself what *consequences* your actions will have. Proverbs 1–9 shows us by means of many examples from all areas of life that this is a question of life and death. Once we have read through the Instruction Manual concerning this matter, we will also be able to consider Prov 10–31 more vividly in terms of this aspect.

The path to wisdom

How, then, do I get wisdom? About this as well, the Instruction Manual does not leave us in ignorance. We may well call this the second main theme of Prov 1–9.

The ABCs are at the beginning: "The fear of Yahweh is the beginning of knowledge" (Prov 1:7). Would you like to be wise? Then you must adopt the proper attitude in order to proceed. But after this there is naturally more to be done. Proverbs 1–9 talks about that continually. With a wealth of expressions the Instruction Manual emphasizes incessantly: *Listen* to wisdom, for listening makes one wise.

Those who composed the proverbs did not set aside their pedagogical wisdom in this context, as they made use of the same words and expressions, or used similar formulations. They did this in order to lead their readers to walk upon that path, the path of *listening* to wisdom. And that reference would then have been especially to *that wisdom of Prov 10–31*, which had been set forth in this book and is laid upon our hearts by our God-fearing parents and teachers.

The path to wisdom begins, then, at home (Prov 1:8).

Our plan of presentation

It would go beyond the nature of this commentary series if we were to discuss each Bible book verse by verse. We are not writing a commentary on each proverb. Our desire will be met if we could give you a helping hand for learning to read and understand Proverbs on your own.

Therefore, we will devote lots of space in our volume to Prov 1–9, because it is exactly this that constitutes the Instruction Manual for using and understanding this Bible book. Some material we will have to skip or discuss with only a few comments on account of our approach, but the Instruction Manual of Prov 1–9 we will, in any case, discuss extensively. For if we can grasp this material, then Prov 10–31 will open up for us all the more easily.

Part 1

Proverbs 1–9: A Primer
for Using the Book of Proverbs

3

Proverbs 1:1–6

Proverbs Offers Life-Wisdom, Especially for Young People

ANYONE WHO WANTS TO study a textbook would be smart not to dive in immediately, but first read through the table of contents carefully. Then, by means of this overview, one will gain insight and will read the book all the more profitably. We can apply this wise counsel to the book of Proverbs as well. Just like the book of Psalms, the book of Proverbs begins with a preface that at the same time forms a kind of table of contents. You can find it in Prov 1:1–6, which reads as follows:

1. The proverbs of Solomon, son of David, king of Israel:
2. To know wisdom and instruction,
   to understand words of insight,
3. to receive instruction in wise dealing,
   in righteousness, justice, and equity;
4. to give prudence to the simple,
   knowledge and discretion to the youth—
5. Let the wise hear and increase in learning,
   and the one who understands obtain guidance,
6. to understand a proverb and a saying,
   the words of the wise and their riddles.

We need say nothing more about verse 1, since we discussed the genre of proverb and its associated *mashal* forms in chapter 1, and we considered Solomon and the other authors of Proverbs in chapter 2. In this chapter we will deal with the questions: *What* is Proverbs seeking to teach, and *to whom* is it particularly directed? The answers are supplied in the title of this chapter: Proverbs offers *life-wisdom*, especially for *young people*.

1. PROVERBS CAN TEACH YOU WISDOM

The meaning of the various expressions in Prov 1:2–6 are like the colors of the rainbow: these are different colors, of course, but they blend together to form the rainbow. Similarly, words like *wisdom, discipline, insight, discernment, understanding, knowledge,* and *caution* are distinct words, each with its own color, but the boundaries of their meaning are difficult to identify.

Those who composed the proverbs certainly intended them to function not as sharply defined concepts but as associative sayings that complement each other and together reproduce the intention of the composers. As full-blooded teachers they knew the penetrating power on pupils of repeating something in various formulations. So with their different synonyms they painted the colors that together form the rainbow of wisdom.

For that is what Proverbs seeks to provide: wisdom.

But the question becomes: What does Scripture understand by wisdom?

1. Wisdom in Israel: the craftsman's skill, too

The Hebrew word *chokma* (wisdom) possesses in the Hebrew Bible a much wider meaning than our word *wisdom*. We often think exclusively of life skills, but the Israelites could talk about good seamanship as being a question of wisdom (Ps 107:27). If you check any number of rather literal English Bible translations, you will observe a rather wide-ranging use of the word *wisdom*. In the King James Version of Exod 36:4, for example, we read that the tabernacle was built by *the wise men*, whereas the English Standard Version speaks of craftsmen. This is referring to the goldsmiths and silversmiths, the coppersmiths and seamsters, clothiers and weavers, all of whom had participated in building the tabernacle and its associated items (cf. in the KJV, Exod 28:3; 31:3–11; 35:10, 26, 31, 35; 36:1, 4; 1 Chr 22:15).

Scripture also states that the temple was built by *the wise men*. When Solomon undertook the temple building, he requested from King Hiram of Tyre, "Send me now therefore a man *cunning* to work in gold, and in silver, and in brass, and in iron, and in purple, and crimson, and blue, and that can skill to grave with *the cunning men* that *are* with me in Judah and in Jerusalem, whom David my father did provide" (2 Chr 2:7 KJV; cf. 1 Kgs 7:14 KJV). This is how Scripture speaks also about the *business wisdom* whereby Tyre had acquired its wealth (Ezek 28:4–5, 12). In addition, it speaks this way about the *managerial wisdom* with which Joseph led Egypt through some difficult years (Gen 41:39). We have already mentioned the *seafaring wisdom* that can sometimes be in short supply during a storm (Ps 107:27).

These examples show the broad range of usage in Holy Scripture with respect to the Hebrew word *chokma*. It talks about the wisdom of smiths and architects, contractors and stonecutters, tailors and spinners, mariners and apothecaries, kings and merchants. In short, wisdom as used in Scripture can simply refer to someone's skill as a craftsman, his occupational know-how.

From this we begin to learn the thoroughly practical way in which Scripture understands the word *wisdom*. Wisdom is never simply a matter of rarefied, abstract thoughts and theoretical reflections, but has everything to do with our eyes and ears and our hands and feet. Wisdom, then, is not the same as philosophy.

In addition, from this we can learn what life-wisdom really is. For it is clear as day that Proverbs is not offering wisdom in the sense of technical competence, unlike some Egyptian books of proverbs. Those are textbooks for young officials, and they are limited somewhat to the rules of conduct that a prospective politician or palace official needs to learn. But Proverbs offers life-wisdom, and in reality is dealing with all of life.

Nevertheless, the Hebrew Bible does use the same word, *chokma*, for the *occupational skill* of the goldsmith, coppersmith, seafarer, king, and merchant as it uses for the *life-wisdom* of Solomon. Apparently the Israelite saw some kind of correspondence between these, since both uses involved the know-how pertaining to the one and the other.

For in what did the wisdom of the goldsmith consist? That he knew the way in which one was to produce golden ornaments. And in what did the wisdom of the seaman consist? That he knew how to sail a ship into the harbor. In this same sense, the wisdom of every occupation consisted in this, that a person was an expert in his field of labor. He knew his raw material and its characteristics, and he possessed the skill for reaching his goal with that material. He knew what was and was not possible. Every occupation had its regularities, its order of processes, the limits within which one could perform his labor. This is what is called in English occupational know-how, knowing how you need to take hold of something.

Well then, does this apply to our daily living as well?

2. Life-wisdom: the know-how for living

Daily it occurs to us that we know *how* we must live. For we are constantly moving within the parameters of what can and cannot be done, what may and may not be done. Just like the craftsman in his occupation, we daily encounter various realities. Here is one for you: "If the iron is blunt, and one does not sharpen the edge, he must use more strength" (Eccl 10:10). Naturally, this applies to all kinds of situations in life. Therefore Solomon says, "The wisdom of the prudent is *to understand his way*" (Prov 14:8a, ASV).

Just as the craftsman knows the path that leads to his goal, so, too, the one who is wise in living knows *the correct way* to spend his money, raise his children, use his tongue, in short, to direct his entire life. Just as the craftsman masters the correct technique for producing his product, so, too, the godly one who is wise in living knows the correct "technique" for ordering his life, namely, according to the rule that God has established for that (see further in connection with Prov 1:7, discussed in the next chapter).

No one can transgress this divine order and these rules without injury. All of Proverbs teaches, "If you are wise, you are wise for yourself; if you scoff [at God's order], you alone will bear it" (Prov 9:12). The book shows us numerous examples of that. If someone commits adultery, then he brings indelible shame upon himself (Prov 6:33). If someone starts a quarrel, then he does not know where it will end (Prov 17:14). *These actions* are more or less joined by a kind of law to *these consequences*. Life-wisdom means humbly respecting this connection. Such a person will continually pay attention to the order for human living that God has revealed in Scripture and creation, and to the boundaries of what can and may be done in life (for further discussion of this order, see the next chapter).

Those who authored the annotations to the Dutch States Translation (SV) wrote this fine comment for Prov 1:2: Wisdom is "a sure and grounded knowledge of Divine and Humane things how to order ones self aright, both in matter of faith and life. Compare 1 Kgs 3. on verse 14."[1] Wisdom leads a person to adopt Scripture's humble sense of realism, whereby one learns to discern correct relationships and learns to conform to reality.

Wise persons pay attention to their gifts and callings; they do not strive for what God has placed beyond their reach. They know their work *space*. They do not exceed their *competence*. They know what is both possible and fitting for living, just as the goldsmith knows the same with respect to his work of smithing. They also *want* only what is possible and suitable. Like an unwritten constitutional law of the kingdom of heaven, it is written on their

---

1. Schuringa, *Wisdom Literature*, 627.

body: Never force anything! They accept the world as it is, without resigning themselves to it (for that is something altogether different)!

By contrast, folly is idealistically revolutionary. It discounts reality, and lives with fantasy images. The fool refuses to suffer under the iron fist of reality, and does not want to acquiesce to his place in reality. We will discuss the fundamental principles of folly in the next chapter.

There you see the correspondence between the wisdom of the craftsman and the wisdom of Proverbs. Both involve knowing how you can achieve your goal, knowing the correct method for that. Or as Solomon puts it, "The wisdom of the prudent is to discern his *way*" (Prov 14:8a). Naturally this occurs in the fear of God, but we will discuss this further in connection with Prov 1:7. Just as the wisdom of the craftsman consists in the expertise with which he practices his trade, so too the life-wisdom of the righteous consists in the expertise with which he masters all kinds of situations in life.

In addition to this, Solomon comes to give us a helping hand with his *mashals*. Proverbs wants to teach us the correct way of living. With the help of hundreds of examples it shows us what wisdom would do in so many kinds of cases. Here is an initial, somewhat preliminary summary anticipating the next chapter:

Wisdom is the art of living purposefully in the fear of God, according to the order that he has revealed in Scripture and creation, for our own well-being.

2. PROVERBS CAN TEACH YOU DISCIPLINE

We are not born with wisdom, however. On the contrary, in terms of the old nature we are foolish. The old pagan nature in us possesses a dark and foolish heart (Rom 1:22; Eph 4:22). With its misleading desires it still rages within us and our children. Therefore wisdom must be learned and acquired from youth. Our folly must be replaced by insight. Our disobedience must be restrained and our dissoluteness put in chains. For like prancing horses, we by nature refuse the bridles of God's commandments and ordinances. Here there is only one means that helps: "Hear instruction [lit., discipline; Heb., *musar*] and be wise" (Prov 8:33; cf. 19:20).

It is regrettable that in connection with discipline we immediately and exclusively think of punishment and spankings. According to its etymology, the word *discipline* refers first of all to promoting the good, and only in the second place to punishing the evil. The word *discipline* has had the broad meaning of nurture. Only later was its meaning restricted to punishment.

Proverbs uses the word *discipline* in Prov 1:2 to refer first of all to *nurture, teaching, instruction,* and *guidance.* In that connection we must not think first of a rod of chastisement. For here discipline serves as one of the words in the title of a book that itself exercises discipline only through instruction and admonition. The fact that this book wishes to see discipline practiced first of all verbally appears clearly from Prov 4. There we hear Solomon telling us how formerly at home the words rang out, "*Hear,* O sons!" as the beginning of "a father's *instruction* [lit., *discipline,* Heb., *musar*]." In the same breath he continues with, "and be attentive, that you may gain insight, for I give you *good precepts*; and do not forsake my *teaching*" (Prov 4:1–2; cf. 4:4, 11).

From the italicized words you can see what he understood by discipline. It meant hearing something rather than feeling the pain of something. Apparently for him discipline is not simply punishment and certainly not equivalent to a rod, but it is the guidance that he was giving to young people. Certainly it comes with fatherly authority, but nonetheless it comes first of all through friendly instruction. Behind that heartfelt address in Prov 4 there beats a warm fatherly heart. That is the ABC of all discipline in Scripture, including God's discipline of his people: it comes through teaching those who are straying, bringing them back to the right path.

This is not to deny that Solomon recommends the use of more severe means of discipline if necessary. Some pupils are simply ignorant and foolish, who reject friendly instruction. At that point their teachers take in hand more pointed forms of discipline, such as admonitions, corrections, and even beatings (Prov 18:6; 19:29; 20:30). In extreme cases they would not spare the rod. For this, too, is evidence of wise pedagogical insight, when people realize "the rod and reproof give wisdom" (Prov 29:15; cf. 10:13; 13:24; 22:15; 23:13–14; 26:3; see our discussion of these proverbs).

Where should all discipline begin? It should be administered by father and mother at home! That is the very first lesson that Proverbs will teach us in Prov 1:8. Father and mother have the weighty calling to guide their children with a firm hand from their earliest days in the cradle, the calling to be continually teaching them as the children grow up, occasionally warning and correcting them, and, if necessary, leading them to better insight by means of punishment and corporal discipline.

But what is more difficult than teaching yourself and your children wisdom? Rest easy, for God's Spirit comes to our aid with the book of Proverbs. He supplies us with that especially "to know wisdom and *instruction* [Heb., *musar,* discipline]" (Prov 1:2). That is the indispensable "school of discipline" where we can learn wisdom. As we mentioned earlier, our teachers are not demanding rote obedience. They want to teach their pupils insight as to why one thing is good and another is evil, so that their students voluntarily and intentionally conform to God's ordinances for our human living. This is how the proverb writers exercise discipline: they provide guidance through instruction, enforcing it if necessary through correction and punishment.

Whoever listens to them eventually learns *self-discipline* (the word *instruction* in Prov 1:2 can also mean that). Self-discipline is one of the nicest fruits of education in the "school of discipline" of Proverbs. Although its curriculum is in fact lifelong, so that we never graduate from this school, its results do not remain invisible. Whoever has taken its classes for any length of time can observe within themselves: I have acquired some insight, learned some obedience, come to possess some self-control, learned to conform to the realities of life, in short, I have become wiser.

Discipline: God's guidance, exercised through authoritative instruction, admonition, and, if necessary, punishment and chastisement. It is exercised also through parents and other teachers. This guidance is for the purpose of making us wise and nurturing us in terms of insight and self-discipline.

3. PROVERBS CAN FOSTER YOUR ABILITIES OF DISCERNMENT

How often throughout each day do we face a choice? Repeatedly we are confronted with the question: Is that good for me to do? What is that action demonstrating? What kind of person does that? Every day we stand between good and evil, truth and falsehood, right and wrong, humility and pride. In addition, modern Christianity is in danger of losing its bearings more and more. In Christian circles it seems rather fashionable to have fewer certainties and to pepper our talk with more questions than answers. Many people acknowledge that there is no fixed truth, but only subjective *views* and *opinions*. In this rootless society, how does one discern the right path? To do that, one must be able to distinguish between the truth and the lie. And where can one learn that? With the lamp of the Word, through the wisdom of Proverbs. This book also serves

> to understand words of insight,
> to receive instruction in wise dealing,
> in righteousness, justice, and equity. (Prov 1:2b–3)

When Solomon was still young, he had prayed to Yahweh for this: "Give your servant therefore an understanding mind to govern your people, that I may discern between good and evil" (1 Kgs 3:9). Proverbs proves how abundantly God heard this prayer. Solomon's *mashals* are "words full of discernment" between what is good and evil, what is wholesome and harmful. They place their readers under the *discipline* or instruction and admonition that the needed *insight* can teach them.

In this way, one can gain from them capacities for discernment, whereby one can form a *sound judgment* and make correct decisions (Heb., *mishpat*). For that reason, Proverbs is a book that, in a manner of speaking, we must *eat* and *consume*. Notice how Solomon and the other wise men identify the distinction between doing or avoiding this or that. In this way, your capacities for discernment will grow in "knowledge and all discernment, so that you may approve what is excellent" (Phil 1:9–10; cf. Ps 119:66; Heb 5:14).

For us this comes down to nothing other than keeping God's covenant in our daily living. Here, in verse 3, Scripture calls this *righteousness*. That is what Yahweh asked from Israel: "Justice [Heb., *tsedek*], and only justice, you shall follow" (Deut 16:20). This daily obedience we can learn from the wise, so that we live before God uprightly, fearing God and avoiding evil.

4. PROVERBS IS A SPECIAL BOOK FOR THE YOUTH

Pagan collections of proverbs were usually directed to a select public, at least as the initial audience. Most Egyptian wisdom books and Assyrian-Aramean proverbs of Achiqar also served primarily to educate youngsters from the ruling class for a prominent place in the palace or a leading post in society. So these wisdom books were designed especially for the high-ranking politician, though they do contain general suggestions.

Later Jewish and gnostic wisdom literature also was not directed to the general public, but merely to a select segment of the populace. The Greek philosophers strove never to make their ideas common property, but dismissed certain classes of the populace. Once again, they focused exclusively on upper-class schools.

How different were Solomon and the other Israelite sages. The book of Proverbs was not designed for a select group, but for all Israel. Every ordinary Israelite could share in it. We wish to emphasize this at the outset. The book of Proverbs makes no social separations among its readers.

Nevertheless, Israel's proverb writers did think most often of a particular circle of readers among God's people, namely, the young people. Proverbs is a book specially directed to the youth. For it was written "to give prudence to the *simple*, knowledge and discretion to the *youth*" (Prov 1:4). Once more, it does so without dividing this group into the children of wealthy white-collar parents and children of blue-collar parents, as was done in the non-Israelite books of proverbs.

The question naturally arises as to what Proverbs understands by the terms *youth* and *simple ones*. Should we think exclusively of age groups, say, seventeen to twenty-one years old? And perhaps only of unmarried young people?

1. For young people ages fourteen to forty

The Hebrew word *na'ar* that is rendered as *youth* in Prov 1:4 is used in other passages with a very broad range of meaning. We encounter this word in the Hebrew Bible being used for Moses, when as a baby he lay for almost a month in the reed basket (Exod 2:6); for Samuel when he came to Shiloh as a child (1 Sam 1:24); but also for Ishmael when he was fourteen years old (Gen 21:12); for King Josiah, when he was sixteen (2 Chr 34:3); for Joseph when he was seventeen (Gen 37:2); for David, when he went out against Goliath (2 Sam 17:33; cf. v. 42); and for Jeremiah, when he was called to be a prophet (Jer 1:6).

In the latter instances we could also describe them as young people. But when Absalom rebelled, he was already married and father of four children (2 Sam 14:27). Nevertheless David told Joab, "Deal gently for my sake with the young man Absalom" (2 Sam 18:5, 12, 32). He spoke the same way later about Solomon: "Solomon my son is young" (1 Chr 22:5; 29:1; 1 Kgs 3:7). When Rehoboam became king, he was forty-one years old, but Scripture nonetheless uses the word *na'ar* to describe him (2 Chr 13:7), the same word that we find in Prov 1:4.

So we should not misconstrue the meaning of the word *youth* in Prov 1:4, for Scripture uses the Hebrew word *na'ar* both for *young children* and for *young men* who have reached their forties. Even married men and fathers of four children, like Absalom, could be among those addressed by Prov 1:4.

It was to these age groups that the sages directed their teaching through their *mashals*. In that regard, they had in view not only the children and young people like those we encounter nowadays in youth groups or children's clubs, but also their similarly young fathers and mothers. This included every age group all the way up to forty-one-year-olds like Rehoboam. Perhaps the average forty-year-old in Israel was more mature than the average married couple of similar age in the modern West. After all, most Israelites at that age already had grown children and could have been grandparents by then. In short, Proverbs is reading material directed especially to the first half of the average person's life.

At that point, a person is in school or is still young. One has acquired a massive amount of facts, but does he also see through a seductive woman who is making advances (Prov 7)? One knows how children are conceived, but does one also know the Scripture's principles according to which they must be raised? Proverbs speaks often to the father and teacher of young children (Prov 13:24; 19:18; 22:6, 15; 23:13–14). For a person has a head full of "knowledge," but does he or she really know? Know people? Know God?

That knowledge is what Proverbs offers young people.

2. *For anyone who still needs to gain a little experience*

Now in the nature of the case, young people have had little opportunity to gain very much experience. They need not be ashamed of that, for they have not yet lived long enough. This is not to deny, however, that few *years of life* and few *life experiences* often go hand in hand. Seen in this way, it is obvious that the wise one in Prov 1:4 mentions for whom this Bible book is written, for both the *young person* and the *simple person*.

What kind of person was in view here? The meaning of the word *simple* is really "naive." The Hebrew word translated as "simple" (*peti*) can be translated that way. It seems to be related to the notion of "being open toward" something.

Just imagine for a moment a good boy who has not perpetrated anything evil, but his heart is wide open such that both good and bad influences can find entrance there. He is rather unaware about the ways and words of "people." You could characterize him as a *gullible* fellow who has few suspicions. In Prov 14:15 Solomon sketched this type of person with a couple of lines: "*The simple believes everything*, but the prudent gives thought to his steps" (see our discussion of this proverb below). In our world, this type of person is still naive even after ten years of schooling, and allows himself to be influenced far too easily.

Such ignorant or simple people—whom you encounter not only among the youth—are being offered a helping hand by the book of Proverbs. From it you can gain some shrewdness that will serve to overcome any inexperience and gullibility, so that you no longer believe every word that you hear or read, but are able to *test* what "people" are claiming. Young people can also learn from the wise ones not to walk off with somebody, but to carefully examine whether there is any danger afoot. This means being cautious throughout life, just like the young Joseph, who was in every respect the opposite of a naive person. In short, the goal of this special Bible book devoted to the youth is to adorn young people with the virtues and experience of older people.

3. Never too old to learn

We should read Proverbs especially during the first half of one's life. But that does not mean that the book is written exclusively for young people. We see this in Prov 1:5:

> Let the wise hear and increase in learning,
> and the one who understands obtain guidance.

We never graduate from the school of wisdom. For that reason, parents are also encouraged to reread Proverbs. Throughout the years they may very well have learned much wisdom and discernment—we may speak of already acquired knowledge or a fund of insight—but by rereading this book they can increase this treasury.

Therefore, Proverbs is very suitable reading material also for fifty- and sixty-year-olds, even for the elderly, all of whom can still broaden and deepen their insight. This follows the rule of Prov 9:9.

> Give instruction to a wise man, and he will be still wiser;
> teach a righteous man, and he will increase in learning.

"For to the one who has, more will be given, and he will have an abundance," said our Lord Jesus Christ (Matt 13:12; cf. Prov 18:15). The rabbis also encouraged people to continue receiving lessons from the school of wisdom; they insisted that a person is wise only during the time he seeks wisdom; the moment he imagines that he has attained wisdom he is a fool.

Parents who do not imagine that they have graduated can obtain "guidance" from Proverbs. The Hebrew word used here was a term from seafaring, which could be translated "to navigate, the art of navigation." This is a gift that came in handy for parents living in a society in which their wisdom and experience could still hold sway.

At the same time we find summarized here in this single word what Proverbs seeks to teach us by means of all the related theme words in Prov 1:2–5: *the art of navigation.* That is wisdom: to find the seafaring lane between the banks and cliffs that endanger our ship of life.

4

Proverbs 1:7

The Fear of the Lord Is the Beginning of Knowledge

HOW OFTEN HAVE WE not asked for advice throughout our life? "What should I do?" is a question that is asked daily by numerous people. Only God has never needed to ask anyone for advice. Whom would he ask? "Who has measured the Spirit of the Lord, or what man shows him his counsel? Whom did he consult, and who made him understand? Who taught him the path of justice, and taught him knowledge, and showed him the way of understanding?" (Isa 40:13–14).

"His understanding is unsearchable" (Isa 40:28). He alone possesses wisdom in its full breadth (Job 28). For that reason the apostle Paul praised our heavenly Father as "the only wise God" (Rom 16:27; cf. 11:33–36).

1. WISDOM IS A GIFT OF GOD

Happily, God has not kept his wisdom only for himself, but has entrusted some of it to us. All human wisdom is thus a gift of God. That is what Holy Scripture teaches us very clearly. "For Yahweh *gives* wisdom" (Prov 2:6). "He *grants* wisdom to the wise and knowledge to those who have understanding" (Dan 2:21). Solomon, too, had received his unmatched wisdom from God (1 Kgs 3:12; 5:12; cf. Gen 41:39).

As we will see later, this pertained not only to all life-wisdom but also to everything that Scripture understands by wisdom. Thus Bezaleel and Oholiab owed their construction insight (which was also a form of wisdom) to the Spirit of wisdom with whom Yahweh had filled them (Exod 28:3; 31:2–3; Eccl 2:16). Even the practical wisdom whereby a farmer sows corn differently than wheat is a gift of God: "For he is rightly instructed; his God teaches him" (Isa 28:26).

How does a person become wise?

But if wisdom is a gift of God, how does he bestow it upon us? The wise men supply various answers to that question. You must listen to wisdom. You must seek her as you would seek a hidden treasure. You must listen to your father and mother. You must seek interaction with wise people. You must inquire from your ancestors (Job 8:8).

Each of these is a path leading to wisdom.

You could also think of the observation and reflection that lie at the foundation of wisdom. The wise men composed their proverbs only after much investigation (Job 5:27). Their *mashals* contain much experience and observation.

Nevertheless, having said this, we have not yet identified the first step on the path of wisdom. For listening with our ears and observing with our eyes should proceed from a heart that fears the Lord. Whoever wants to become wise must begin with *fearing God*. Otherwise one becomes a fool.

2. WISDOM BEGINS WITH THE FEAR OF THE Lord

"The fear of Yahweh is the beginning of knowledge" (Prov 1:7a). That is the starting point, the core proverb, the chief thing, and the basis of the wisdom that Holy Scripture wishes to teach us. The Holy Spirit apparently found this information so important that we encounter it with some variations at least six times in Holy Scripture (cf. Prov 1:7; 9:10; 15:35; Ps 111:10; Job 28:28; Eccl 12:13).

According to Holy Scripture, knowledge is a matter not first of all of our intellect but of our heart. "For wisdom will come *into your heart*, and knowledge will be pleasant to your soul" (Prov 2:10). Our heart, and not primarily our brain, is the vault where wisdom is stored. Anyone wanting to become wise must cherish deep respect for God and his revelation. The godly heart is decisive, and that is what Proverbs continually emphasizes.

The only wise God has revealed his wisdom to us in two ways. First, in his holy and divine *word*, which constitutes an inexhaustible fountain of wisdom. Second, in *the rest of his works*, which also contain an ocean of wisdom. (We say intentionally: *the rest* of his works, because God's Word is also a work of God, of course, one of preeminent rank. It is a power of God [Rom 1:16]. As such it is a demonstration of the same eternal power and divinity that can be perceived, ever since the creation of the world, from his works [Rom 1:20]. Having taken note of this, in what follows we will speak more concisely of the wisdom of God's Word and works.)

What does Prov 1:7 mean, in the larger context of the book of Proverbs, by the fear of the Lord? At this point, this question is not difficult to answer.

Anyone who fears Yahweh honors him, first, as the all-wise God, the Speaker of the divine Torah, or instruction, that overflows with wisdom, which he gave to Israel through the ministry of Moses. At the same time, one honors Yahweh as the good Giver of all the continuing instruction that he has given to us through the ministry of his prophets and, finally, through the ministry of his Son and his Son's apostles.

But anyone who fears God honors him, second, as the sovereign Creator of heaven and earth, to whose statutes and ordinances all creatures in heaven and on earth are subject. As we will see more extensively later, he established ordinances not only for the conduct of his people (Deut 4:6) but also for the behavior of the sun, moon, and stars, the sea, rain, seedtime, and harvest.

So fearing Yahweh consists in a humble acknowledgement of his sovereign right of supremacy over the entire creation, especially over the people with whom he established a covenant. God revealed this right of supremacy in his Word and in his works. Therefore, the fear of the Lord consists in a childlike respect and love toward the revelation of God's wisdom in his Word and in his works.

Respect for God and for the sources of wisdom that he gave is the *beginning* of all knowledge. Knowledge does not reason its way back to such respect, but proceeds *from* such respect. One could also say: All wisdom begins with humility, more humility, and complete humility toward God and his "order" that he revealed in his Word and works. That forms the ABC and the XYZ of the alphabet used in the school of Solomon.

For Prov 1:7 teaches that the fear of Yahweh is *the beginning* of knowledge. Proverbs 15:33 says that the fear of Yahweh is *instruction* unto wisdom. But other Bible passages go still further and hold before us "the fear of the Lord, that *is* wisdom" (Job 28:28). Those who practice the fear of the Lord have insight (Ps 111:10b). And knowledge of the Holy One *is* understanding (Prov 9:10b).

This corresponds entirely with the character of wisdom, as we have already become acquainted with it. We have seen that the wise person is characterized by his *grasp of reality* in which God has given him a place. The wise person knows that he must adapt himself within the space and dimensions of reality assigned to him. He does not occupy himself with things too great and too marvelous for him (Ps 131:1). He humbly respects the *boundaries* of his *competence*. And Prov 1:7a adds by way of clarifying and deepening its teaching: this is how the wise person can function, because the fear of Yahweh is his starting point.

God is the sovereign Creator of all creation and Holy Scripture is the infallible textbook for his people. That is the root (Heb., *resit*) from which the art of living and the grasp of reality that belong to the wise person will flourish. Therefore, we earlier described wisdom as the art of living purposefully according to the order that God has revealed in his Scripture and creation.

3. WISDOM DRAWS FROM GOD'S WORD

The richest source of wisdom that Israel possessed was the Torah, or instruction, that God had given to them in the wilderness. Moses had foreseen that the pagan nations surrounding Israel would take notice: How wise a people is Israel, how wise are their laws (Deut 4:6)! And in Israel people sang about the Torah, "The law of the Lord is perfect, . . . making wise the simple" (Ps 19:7; cf. Ps 119).

This was not surprising, since Israel had received that instruction directly from the only wise God. And in that instruction he dealt not only with "religious matters" (we would say: praying, reading the Bible, and going to church), but also such everyday things such as labor contracts, poverty relief, protection of animals, building codes (a fence on the rooftop), marriage regulations, rate of interest, laws governing military warfare, treatment of sojourners, military service (not for newlywed husbands), morality regulations, and just weights and measures. These are but a sample drawn from the Torah, which was the Bible of those who wrote these proverbs.

Yahweh caused his light to shine upon all these things at Horeb, and he gave Israel statutes and ordinances that bore pervasive testimony to his divine wisdom. For Yahweh favored his people in every respect with a good life. Moses, Yahweh's fully authorized liaison officer, added, "Keep them and do them, for that will be your wisdom and your understanding in the sight of the peoples" (Deut 4:6).

Solomon and the other proverb writers drew eagerly from this source of wisdom. After all, they wanted to give advice to Israel for the same wide-ranging human living in God's covenant as that for which Yahweh had given his commandments in the Torah. What better thing could they do, therefore, than to reproduce in their beloved *mashal* style what Yahweh had taught in the Bible of their time about marital life, business, education, masters, servants, sojourners, jurisprudence, poverty relief, and all the rest that belongs to human living? Doing what God says is always the wisest, is it not? Who loves human life more than Yahweh, who later did not spare even his own Son to redeem that life (John 3:16)?

It was not as if the wise men had the Torah scrolls lying open before them as they composed their proverbs. They had been instructed in the Torah, and would have known some of it by heart. We see that from their choice of words. Often they use characteristically Deuteronomic expressions, like "written on the tablet of your heart" (Deut 6:6–8; 11:18; Prov 3:3; 6:20–35; 7:3).

Here are several examples of the close connection between the Torah of Moses and the Proverbs of Solomon.

1. Learning wisdom from the Torah of Moses

Business

In a time when there was no minted money yet, the pieces of gold and silver that people used as monetary currency were weighed. Abraham weighed out four hundred shekels of silver for Ephron, the Hittite, as the cost of the cave of Machpelah, where he wanted to bury Sarah (Gen 23:16). But, for reasons that are valid today as well, such dealings depended on the accuracy of the scale and the honesty of the weights.

Yahweh got involved with these nonreligious matters, and the wise men echoed Yahweh's Torah concerning these things almost word for word. How the traveling merchants would have praised Israel and Israel's God when they encountered no false weights in this country! Let's place God's instruction through Moses and what he taught through the wise men alongside each other.

You shall not have in your bag two kinds of weights, a large and a small. You shall not have in your house two kinds of measures, a large and a small. A full and fair weight you shall have, a full and fair measure you shall have, that your days may be long in the land that the LORD your God is giving you. For all who do such things, all who act dishonestly, are an abomination to the LORD your God (Deut 25:13–16; cf. Lev 19:35–36).	Unequal weights and unequal measures are both alike an abomination to the LORD (Prov 20:10). A just balance and scales are the LORD's; all the weights in the bag are his work (Prov 16:11). A false balance is an abomination to the LORD, but a just weight is his delight (Prov 11:1).

The poor and sojourners

By means of all kinds of statutes in the Torah, Yahweh lifted up a shield of protection around the poor and sojourners. Does someone want to borrow from you? Then don't fleece him and don't demand interest from your poor brother (Exod 22:25). Never forget that you yourselves were slaves in Egypt. "You know the heart of a sojourner, for you were sojourners in the land of Egypt" (Exod 23:9). Show it. They too have the right to relax on the seventh day (Exod 23:12). In the Sabbath year you must let them eat freely from what grows in your field (Exod 23:11). You must pay your day laborer in a timely manner. He is poor and is looking forward to his wage (Lev 19:13; cf. 25:39–40).

The echo of this gospel according to Moses is heard in Proverbs as well. It lies beyond the design of this chapter to cite all the *mashals* that encourage people to show compassion toward the poor, sojourners, and others in distress. We will mention only a few examples that show you how the wise men have drawn their wisdom from the Torah. At the same time, you can see clearly how fundamental *social* knowledge also begins with the fear of the LORD.

When you reap the harvest of your land, you shall not reap your field right up to its edge, neither shall you gather the gleanings after your harvest. And you shall not strip your vineyard bare, neither shall you gather the fallen grapes of your vineyard. You shall leave them for the poor and for the sojourner: I am the LORD your God (Lev 19:9–10).

Whoever despises his neighbor is a sinner, but blessed is he who is generous to the poor (Prov 14:21).

Whoever has a bountiful eye will be blessed, for he shares his bread with the poor (Prov 22:9).

Whoever oppresses a poor man insults his Maker, but he who is generous to the needy honors him (Prov 14:31).

Whoever gives to the poor will not want, but he who hides his eyes will get many a curse (Prov 28:27).

The widows

Widows were also among those who always moved God to mercy. They were so easily taken advantage of socially, financially, and interpersonally. For that reason, Yahweh prohibited the oppression of widows and orphans, otherwise "I will kill you with the sword, and your wives will become widows and your children fatherless" (Exod 22:22–24). The echo of this Torah is heard in Proverbs as well.

You shall not pervert the justice due to the sojourner or to the fatherless, or take a widow's garment in pledge (Deut 24:17).

Cursed be anyone who moves his neighbor's landmark (Deut 27:17; 19:14).

The LORD tears down the house of the proud but maintains the widow's boundaries (Prov 15:25).

Do not move an ancient landmark or enter the fields of the fatherless, for their Redeemer is strong; he will plead their cause against you (Prov 23:10–11).

The courtroom

This is the skeletal structure from which the body of society obtains its stability! Concerning this as well, Yahweh gave instruction in his evangelical Torah, for he is "a God of faithfulness and without iniquity, just and upright is he" (Deut 32:4). He did not want to see any oppression among his people (cf. Lev 19:13; Deut 24:14). It is the Lord who enforces the rights of the poor and the oppressed. Also, with respect to jurisprudence, the wise men have confessed that the fear of the Lord is the beginning of all *judicial* knowledge.

You shall not be partial in judgment. You shall hear the small and the great alike. You shall not be intimidated by anyone, for the judgment is God's (Deut 1:17; cf. 16:19; Exod 23:3; Lev 19:15).	Partiality in judging is not good (Prov 24:23).
	He who justifies the wicked and he who condemns the righteous are both alike an abomination to the Lord (Prov 17:15).
You shall not spread a false report. You shall not join hands with a wicked man to be a malicious witness. You shall not fall in with the many to do evil, nor shall you bear witness in a lawsuit, siding with the many, so as to pervert justice (Exod 23:1–2).	A man who bears false witness against his neighbor is like a war club, or a sword, or a sharp arrow (Prov 25:18).
	A truthful witness saves lives, but one who breathes out lies is deceitful (Prov 14:25; cf. 19:5, 9).

These were but a few examples of the close connection between the Torah and Proverbs. We could also have pointed to equivalent commands and counsels regarding protection of animals, taking pledges, marital life, raising children, one's attitude toward the king, issues involving requiring interest, and the like.

What we have assembled above, however, has focused adequate attention on *the echo of Moses* in Proverbs, as we also heard in the Psalms.[1]

---

1. See van Deursen, *Psalms I*, 32–38.

2. Learning wisdom from the prophets

Israel's sages were students not only of Moses, however, but also of the prophets. We could see that in the proverbs already quoted, which warned against evil business practices, social oppression, stealing land, and corrupt jurisprudence. In those maxims we hear in the book of Proverbs the echo of the prophets as well.

We know the tragic history that these books narrate. Israel repeatedly abandoned God and his Torah. In so doing, they robbed the poor of their protective shield and overturned the foundations of their society (Ps 11:3). For that reason, Yahweh arose in wrath and struck his unfaithful covenant partner all the more harshly.

The eyes of the wise men were certainly made more keen to these facts by the prophets. "Where there is no prophetic vision the people cast off restraint, but blessed is he who keeps the law" (Prov 29:18). That is the lesson of the prophets, one that the wise men have illuminated and imprinted by means of many *mashals*. In this way, wise men and prophets together called Israel back to the Torah. (Therefore we should not inflate the distinction between the sages and the prophets into a contrast.)

The wise men of this world analyze the situation in the world largely apart from the light of God's Word. But the fear of the Lord is the beginning of knowledge also for the wider arenas of human living. Therefore the sages consulted the prophets. Let's mention an example of that. Are you seeking wisdom with regard to civic and social matters? Do you want to discern the times in which you are living? Then do just as the sages did, and listen respectfully to the voice of Yahweh's prophets, and to its echo in Proverbs.

That is how the fear of Yahweh nurtures us unto wisdom (Prov 15:33).

3. Learning wisdom from Christ and his apostles

But no matter how much wisdom is to be learned from Moses, Solomon, and the prophets, the greatest wise one of all is our Lord Jesus Christ. For the kings of the South came from the ends of the earth to learn wisdom from Solomon, but Christ said, "Behold, something greater than Solomon is here" (Matt 12:42). Here on earth he supplied the loftiest example of a meek and wise walk of life. Upon him rested the Spirit of Yahweh, the Spirit of wisdom and understanding, the Spirit of counsel and might, the Spirit of knowledge and the fear of the Lord (Isa 11:2). That Spirit put the stamp of perfect wisdom upon all his comings and goings, his speaking and his silence.

We can see this in the Gospels. He never transgressed the boundaries of his authority. He always remained humble within the space that his Father gave him to act. He never functioned autonomously. He never forced anything. He never allowed others, not even his mother, to direct him in terms of his mediatorial office. He realized that he had been sent, and he did only what the Father told him.

How much wisdom, then, could ministers of the Word and other workers in the kingdom of God learn from Jesus' conduct for their own methods of activity! How calmly and how completely he did his work. Reverend J. van Andel pointed to that in his pastoral manual.[2] Van Andel wrote that Jesus never stacked one task upon another, and he never proceeded to a new task until he had finished the previous one. In van Andel's modest opinion, every preacher who encounters similar difficulties and is placed before the same issues as his Sender, on account of the breadth and the field entrusted to him for cultivation, could profit from Jesus' example. God never gives us a task without giving us the time for it; if we have more work than time, then we should investigate seriously whether we have overloaded ourselves, or allowed others to overload us, forgetting that a servant has only one employer: God.

This was only one sample of Jesus' wisdom: How did he organize his work? In the same way, one could ask: How did he behave as a child in his parental home? How did he talk about money and material possessions? How did he teach? When did he pray? How did he respond to enemies and to opposition? In all these things he lived out the wisdom of Proverbs, a book that he must have loved deeply.

In the teaching of the apostles as well, we hear the voice of the Master. All their commandments were motivated by the same Spirit of wisdom that had inspired Solomon. In the apostolic writings, you can draw wisdom galore for marital life, church life, living as a slave, guidelines for child-rearing, government, citizenship, and so much more.

In this way the fear of the LORD can lead a person to knowledge, as long as one shows respect for the *Word of God*, for Moses and the prophets, for Solomon, and for the one greater than him, our chief prophet and wisdom teacher, Jesus Christ. This Word of God is the preeminent source of wisdom. Perhaps it is the case with you, "how from childhood you have known the sacred writing that are able to instruct you for salvation through faith in Christ Jesus" (2 Tim 3:15). May the respectful handling of the Word continue to make many people "wise in what is good" (Rom 16:19).

---

2. Van Andel, *Vademecum Pastorale*, 212–15.

4. DRAWING WISDOM FROM GOD'S WORK

"The fear of the Lord is the beginning of knowledge" (Prov 1:7); that is the subject of this chapter. One who fears Yahweh can come to this knowledge along two paths. First, if one listens believingly to the wisdom of *God's word*. Second, if one uses the spectacles of God's Word to look at the multicolored wisdom in *God's creational works*.

For God has revealed wisdom in his Word, but (indissolubly connected with that word-*revelation*) also in his works. The psalmist sang about that, "O Lord, how manifold are your works! In wisdom you have made them all" (Ps 104:24). It is especially the numerous ordinances that God has instituted for his creatures that constitute an inexhaustible source of wisdom.

1. *Drawing wisdom from the ordinances of heaven and earth*

When Holy Scripture uses the word *statute* (Heb., *khoq*), it is referring not always exclusively to Yahweh's ordinances in his *Word*, but occasionally to the ordinances in his *creation*. Scripture uses the same Word to refer to both of those kinds of ordinances. We will mention a couple of examples of this; then it will automatically become clear how we can draw wisdom from God's creation works as well.

Psalm 148 praises Yahweh because he "fixed their bounds [Heb., *khoq*], which cannot be passed." In Job 38:33 such ordinances are called "the ordinances of the heavens." Scripture uses the same Hebrew Word *khoq* as elsewhere for the ordinances relating to Israel's life. So not only Israel's conduct but also the courses of the sun, moon, and stars were tied to divine ordinances (Heb., *khuqqot*).

Indeed, where in fact do we not observe this? The fixed season of harvest rests upon divine ordinances (Heb., *khuqqot qatsir*; Jer 5:24; cf. Gen 8:22). The same applies to the light of the sun, moon, and stars, as well as to the waves of the sea: "If this fixed order [Heb., *khuqqim*] were ever to cease from my presence," the Word of God says, "then . . ." (Jer 31:36).

For everything that God has created—people, animals, plants, and things—he has in his wisdom established "statutes and ordinances." In Jer 33:25 Yahweh calls them "the ordinances [Heb., *khuqqot*] of heaven and earth." In this context we would speak of natural laws, but let us not forget that these natural regularities do not exist autonomously. All of them are ordinances of our heavenly Father, whether or not people acknowledge that.

We have already seen what wonderful wisdom lies embedded in the statutes that Yahweh proclaimed in the Torah of Moses for Israel's life. But the ordinances of heaven and earth also radiate the wisdom of our Creator and Father. "When he gave to the wind its weight, and apportioned out the waters by measure; when he made a decree [Heb., *khoq*] for the rain, and a way for the thunderbolt; then he saw it [i.e., wisdom] and *declared* it; he established it, and searched it out. And he said to humankind, 'Truly, the fear of the LORD, that is wisdom [for you, people]; and to depart from evil is [for you, people] understanding'" (Job 28:25–28). There you see it being expressed in so many words: God's creation works (rain and wind, water and lightning) *proclaim* wisdom.

And they do so in such overwhelming measure! The psalmist confessed, "To all perfection I see a limit, but your commands are boundless" (Ps 119:96 NIV). This applies not only to God's ordinances in Holy Scripture but also to his "ordinances of heaven and earth." For one who fears God, these really do constitute an inexhaustible source of wisdom for a thousand and one things in daily life.

Let's look at three examples of that.

Our daily schedule

Our earth is subject to the rhythm of day and night. Here, too, we are standing before a divine ordinance (Gen 1:14–18). Every evening God "shuts off," as it were, "the greatest light" (Gen 1:16). One who fears God will respect this divine separation between day and night. He will not systematically go against that, but will schedule his day according to this divine ordinance.

In this way the fear of the LORD can be the beginning of knowledge with respect to a reasonable rhythm of working and resting. In this regard, we will experience the truth of the proverb "Fear the LORD and shun evil. This will bring health to your body and nourishment to your bones" (Prov 3:7–8; see our discussion of this *mashal* below).

Our eating customs

For these as well, God established ordinances (cf. Gen 1:29). In this connection we can see altogether clearly that the fear of the LORD is not exhausted by religious matters. This posture can also lead us to respect God's ordinances for eating and drinking, such as his statute that moderation is good for our health.

"Eat honey, my son," said the wise men, "for it is good" (Prov 24:13). But they took into consideration the wholesome ordinance about moderation and gave this advice: "If you find honey, eat just enough—too much of it, and you will vomit" (Prov 25:16; see our discussion of this proverb below). "It is not good to eat too much honey, nor is it honorable to search out matters that are too deep" (Prov 25:27). And don't drink a lot of wine: "Who has woe? Who has sorrow? Who has strife? Who has complaints? Who has needless bruises? Who has bloodshot eyes? Those who linger over wine" (Prov 23:29–35; see our discussion of this below).

In this way, the fear of the LORD can keep us from excessive eating, and, in the area of food and drink customs as well, it is the beginning of wisdom.

Our skills for craftsmanship

We have seen already that wisdom involves also the know-how of a craft or occupation, and is also a matter of taking into consideration God's statutes and ordinances for his creation works. Isaiah illustrated that once in terms of the work of the farmer.

> Give ear, and hear my voice;
> > give attention, and hear my speech.
> Does he who plows for sowing plow continually?
> > Does he continually open and harrow his ground?
> When he has leveled its surface,
> > does he not scatter dill, sow cumin,
> and put in wheat in rows
> > and barley in its proper place,
> > and emmer as the border?
> For he is rightly instructed;
> > his God teaches him.
> Dill is not threshed with a threshing sledge,
> > nor is a cart wheel rolled over cumin,
> but dill is beaten out with a stick,
> > and cumin with a rod.
> Does one crush grain for bread?
> > No, he does not thresh it forever;
> when he drives his cart wheel over it
> > with his horses, he does not crush it.
> This also comes from the LORD of hosts;
> > he is wonderful in counsel
> > and excellent in wisdom. (Isa 28:23–29)

In this way, the farmer takes into consideration God's ordinances regarding various times, measures, and methods in his occupation.

An outsider might well ask: How does he know all of this? To that question we heard just now Isaiah's answer that is so important for our topic. From this we learn that the simplest prescriptions of reason and sound understanding come from the only wise God alone. Isaiah apparently esteemed it as a gift from God when people pursue their occupation with understanding and prudence. Various kinds of professional competence also come from wisdom received from God. The same applies to the *gift of observation* whereby people acquire this wisdom. Thereby people are showing respect for "the ordinances of heaven and earth," and, alongside respect for God's Word, that is the second source from which we can draw wisdom.

As we have already noted in passing, these three examples can show us again that the fear of the Lord touches on not only the small sector of what belongs to "the religious" in our life, those few minutes and hours per week when we pray, read the Bible, and attend church. Nor is the fear of the Lord a matter only of the broad terrain for which God has given us ordinances in *his Word*. This attitude must truly govern us wherever we come into contact with *God's works*. To that immeasurable arena of "the ordinances of heaven and earth" applies the deep, all-inclusive introductory proverb at the opening of our Bible book: "The fear of Yahweh is the beginning of knowledge" (Prov 1:7).

2. *The fear of the Lord in proverbs that do not mention the name of the Lord*

Many have noted that many proverbs do not mention God's name. Even terms referring to God's pious people, like *righteous*, *discerning*, and similar words, do not appear.

In Prov 11:14–16 several such apparently "neutral" *mashals* are grouped together.

> For lack of guidance a nation falls,
>   but victory is won through many advisers.
> Whoever puts up security for a stranger will surely suffer,
>   but whoever refuses to shake hands in pledge is safe.
> A kindhearted woman gains honor,
>   but ruthless men gain only wealth.

Is this also real knowledge that begins with the fear of the Lord? Every allusion to such an attitude seems absent here, doesn't it? People have drawn all kinds of conclusions from that, as though we are encountering here the modern tension between faith and science, as though those who composed the proverbs would have been less godly than prophets and psalmists. If we look more closely, however, we perceive in the background behind all such proverbs a watermark consisting of the ground motive of this entire book: "The fear of Yahweh is the beginning of knowledge" (Prov 1:7).

In light of the preceding, this requires little further argument. Isaiah pointed us to the prudence with which a farmer conducts his work. He sows wheat differently than barley, he threshes dill differently than corn for flour. "Their God instructs them and teaches them the right way" (Isa 28:26). God gives the farmer an eye for the divergent characteristics that God has given to various kinds of grain. The occupation of farming is clearly a matter of showing respect for creation structures.

But, of course, a farmer is not the only one who is engaged with God's creation ordinances in his work. Each person confronts in every moment the boundaries and regularities to which God has subjected his creatures. A nation must be ruled with prudence, or else it will fall into ruin. Avoiding a handshake will spare much misery. The wise men observed legions of such regularities. Take, for example, the proverb "He who gathers crops in summer is a prudent son, but he who sleeps during harvest is a disgraceful son" (Prov 10:5). Here God's name is not mentioned. Nevertheless, the wisdom of this proverb begins with the fear of Yahweh! For the harvest time is one of God's ordinances, is it not? One who sleeps during this time is going against God's statute of "the regular weeks of harvest" (Jer 5:24). That is unwise. But one who works diligently is showing that he fears Yahweh as the one who, in view of the rhythm of the seasons, has also given his ordinances for the times of working and resting.

With the use of wine we discover the same thing. "Wine is a mocker and beer a brawler; whoever is led astray by them is not wise" (Prov 20:1). Here, too, we are definitely not receiving the wisdom of particular misfits among God's people, as some have argued. Nor do we have the insights of Israelite "humanists," but we do have knowledge whose ABC and XYZ is the fear of Yahweh. For it is God who has established the rule for using wine: too much will hurt you. The wise men respected this ordinance for using alcohol. For that reason, even without mentioning the name of the Lord, this proverb is speaking completely from the starting point of the fear of the Lord.

This applies to all the proverbs in which we don't find that name or an allusion to the fear of the Lord. All of them have sprouted forth from a believing respect for "the ordinances of heaven and earth" (Jer 33:25), which Yahweh has fixed. All of them constitute illustrations of the fundamental rule "The wise heart will know the proper time and procedure" (Eccl 8:5b NIV).

Such a "proper time and procedure" exists for sowing and reaping, for drinking wine and lending money—indeed, to what does this actually not apply? We are surrounded on every side by the boundaries and ordinances, the possibilities and impossibilities, to which God has subjected all his creatures. You cannot rule a nation without prudence. You cannot sleep during the time of harvest. These and innumerable other matters are what such apparently "neutral," more "worldly" proverbs teach.

But do not mistake the root from which this wisdom blossoms. There is no *mashal* in the book of Proverbs that speaks impiously or "humanistically." Why is this so? They teach us to discern every "time and procedure" to which none other than Almighty God binds all our actions. Without mentioning his name, they open our eyes to what God does or does not bring within our reach. They teach us what it means to submit to God's order as he has revealed that in his Word and in his work.

Really, there is no proverb in this Bible book that does not trace "the works of Yahweh" (Ps 111:2). The fear of Yahweh is the root of *all* knowledge that Proverbs teaches, no matter how "objective" and "nonreligious" it may appear. This fear is at its core a proof of deep respect for the will of the living God in every sector and in every aspect of life.

5. WISDOM AND DISCIPLINE: FOOLS DESPISE THEM

The book of Proverbs also says a lot about Israelites who do not fear Yahweh, however, but who nonetheless pretend to have deep insight. These were the wicked or fools whom we constantly encounter also in the Psalms.[3] Scripture even identifies fools among the prophets and Pharisees.

From this we see that in Holy Scripture, folly is not a question of limited intellectual ability and development, but a matter of despising wisdom and discipline. In Scripture the fool was an Israelite whose starting point, not in theory but in practice, was "there is no God" (namely, a God who does not require accountability; Ps 14:1, 53:2). Fools despise the discipline of their parents (Prov 15:5). They hate the knowledge and fear of Yahweh (Prov 1:29). They are "wise in their own eyes" (Prov 3:7; 12:15; 28:16). They do not acknowledge that Yahweh is sovereign over everything, and thereby they lack the beginning or root of all knowledge: the fear of the Lord. Although they are not stupid in the intellectual sense, such people behave like foolish people in a *chokma*-tic sense, because they refuse to take the first step on the path to wisdom.

---

3. See van Deursen, *Psalms I*, 93–96.

Wisdom and discipline teach a person to live in accordance with God's ordinances in his Word and other works. Many of wisdom's life lessons could be summarized with the words: never force anything! But that is precisely what a fool wants to do. Because he rejects wisdom and discipline, in contrast to the wise person, he does not respect the boundaries and limits of what is possible and impossible, and of what is permissible and impermissible. For that reason, he lacks the sense of reality that adorns the wise person with such elegance (Prov 17:24).

For that reason, so much in a fool's life ends up being a flop (Prov 14:8). Because he refuses to adapt to Yahweh's life-enhancing and life-protecting statutes, the fool's manner of life is deadly dangerous (Prov 10:21; 18:8). He continually collides with God's order, and such collisions destroy his life. Folly, then, is also in its deepest sense *dis-order*, conceit, the primeval human sin: declaring one's autonomy toward God by determining for oneself what is good and evil (Prov 24:9).

6. GOD'S WISDOM EXCLUDES AUTONOMOUS HUMAN KNOWLEDGE

One who fears God has taken the first step on the path to wisdom; one who refuses to fear God is a fool. With this, the wise men have expressed at the beginning of their book a confession that sounds to our ears almost offensive! They definitely did not choose as the starting point for their lessons the autonomy of human understanding and the human will. That is what they call leaning on one's own understanding (Prov 3:5, 7), trusting in one's own heart (Prov 28:26). No, they began with the humble confession: Our own understanding is absolutely subject to the Word of the only wise God. This is how God's people have made a courageous confession of their faith in various eras of church history, including over against the modern spirit of the times in church and world.

From the time of the Renaissance, already, but especially since the so-called Enlightenment, we stand as disciples of Jesus over against the powerful spiritual movement known as rationalism. This proceeds from the axiom that our understanding is our boss. Our human thinking is autonomous and sovereign. This dangerous enemy has invaded Christian territory as well, and for centuries it has slain its thousands. With demonic power it has taught that the authority of God's Word does not stand above that of human thought, but exactly the opposite: the authority of human thinking stands above that of Holy Scripture. This lie, which flatters our human pride so delightfully, has come to form the starting point of the reigning worldview and anthropologies among formerly Christian nations.

Does not Prov 1:7 come across in such a world almost as an offensive confession? God's Word recognizes no human knowledge that would stand independently apart from God and his Word. Solomon and the other wise men recognized no other reality than the one God created. He holds heaven and earth with all their fullness entirely within his power. With the light of this truth they viewed human living and composed their *mashals*.

They stuck closely to the Torah, or the instruction of God, and they bowed respectfully before his Word. To put it in the words of Vondel, they believed that "apart from God there is safety nowhere, and his exalted command is holy."[4] Therefore, for them *all knowing* was a matter of *confessing Yahweh*. Therefore, for them the righteous person was the wise person, and the wicked person was the fool.[5] According to Proverbs, one can obtain true knowledge only by way of submissive concourse with the truth.

For that reason, Prov 1:7 is no threadbare notion limited to Christian usage, but a stick of dynamite beneath all forms of rationalism. With only two very comprehensive sentences, Holy Scripture teaches here that it recognizes no autonomous human knowledge. It is high time that we learn again to see these short sentences of Prov 1:7 in their antithetical sharpness!

Since the Enlightenment, many Christians also think that taking God at his Word hinders them in their attempts to learn and know reality. But here God's Word is teaching exactly the opposite: only through the fear of the LORD does a person end up in exactly the right place. Only the fear of the LORD can preserve the train of our human thinking from derailing.

For that reason, Prov 1:7 continues to be a stone of stumbling for the proud, through which the thoughts of their heart are disclosed. For this is how Wisdom speaks: "Pride and arrogance [also belonging to understanding that pretends to be sovereign] . . . I hate" (Prov 8:13). "Behold, the fear of the Lord, that is wisdom," said Job, "and to turn away from evil [i.e., all rebellion against God, including intellectual rebellion] is understanding" (Job 28:28).

7. GOD'S WISDOM IS ALSO SUPRA-SCIENTIFIC

On the earliest Christian school buildings in our county, people often put as an inscription the proverb "The fear of the LORD is the beginning of science

---

4. Translator's Note: Dutch: "Buiten God is 't nergens veilig. / Heilig is het hoog gebod." Vondel, *Lucifer*, lines 339–40.

5. See van Deursen, *Psalms I*, chaps. 3, 4.

[Dutch, *wetenschap*]." That is how Prov 1:7 was rendered in the Dutch States Translation of the Bible (SV). More recent Bible translations, both Dutch and English, now have the word *knowledge*. Does this rendering of "knowledge" help to clarify?

Certainly, the term *science* is an early Dutch word for knowledge. The key is that we must not conclude from whatever term is used that the fear of the LORD constitutes the beginning of only *one particular kind of knowledge*, referring, for example, to what people like to call "practical knowledge" or prescientific knowledge, the kind that peasants, or citizens, or children have. For one could also confidently place Prov 1:7 on the facade of a Christian institution for higher education. This verse was also placed above the entrance to the College of Calvin in Geneva. Properly so, for what gives us the right to exclude scientific or systematic knowledge from the force of God's Word in Prov 1:7?

Holy Scripture does not at all forbid us from distinguishing practical knowledge and scientific knowledge, but it does forbid us from placing them in contradiction. Scripture recognizes no knowledge, including systematic knowledge, that does not need to begin with the fear of the LORD. Similarly, Scripture does not teach us to look at the world in two ways: with the eyes of a heteronomous faith and with the eyes of autonomous understanding. On the contrary, the wisdom of God's Word is supra-scientific. For that reason, it is also true to say about scientific knowledge that those people are fools who, in connection with this knowledge, despise the wisdom and discipline of God's Word and his other works. Through their fault, regrettably, the world is full of scientific folly.

8. WISDOM AND FOLLY: THE AGE-OLD TWO PATHS

In terms of the foregoing, Prov 1:7 identifies at the beginning of the book of Proverbs, just as Ps 1 did at the start of the book of Psalms, the age-old two paths:[6] The path of the righteous, with their living according to the Torah, and the path of the wicked, with their own principles of living. Proverbs calls these two groups the wise and the fools, for the same reason as Ps 1 does: on account of their attitude toward God and his Word. Proverbs will portray both paths before the eyes of its readers in numerous *mashals*.

With these two paths the book of Proverbs at the same time shows its unique character. Without doubt, Holy Scripture acknowledges that, as a consequence of the residual influence of God's word, the pagan world also possesses a certain kind of wisdom (1 Kgs 4:30–33). In recent decades

---

6. See van Deursen, *Psalms I*, chap. 5.

people have excavated from the sands of the Near East many examples of such extrabiblical proverbs.

But in terms of what we have discussed above, one of the deepest differences between biblical and extrabiblical wisdom lies precisely here! Pagan wisdom books do know the difference between the "hothead" and the wise person, but they do not know the difference that governs all of Scripture: the line of demarcation between the righteous and the wicked.

This demarcation is uniquely biblical.

5

Proverbs 1:8–33

Listening Makes One Wise, and Wisdom Brings Life, but Then Listen Early

HOW DOES A PERSON obtain wisdom? One must begin with fearing Yahweh. That is the only attitude with which one can attain to pure knowledge (Prov 1:7). That is what we discussed in the previous chapter. But what else must one do? To this question Solomon provides an answer in his Instruction Manual for Proverbs: one must listen, for listening makes one wise.

This is even one of the main themes of that Instruction Manual (Prov 1–9), and Solomon does not tire of repeating it with a variety of expressions. In fact, the book itself begins with that. Proverbs 1:1–7 in a certain sense constitutes the preface, from which we discern what it is that the book has *to offer* us (wisdom), for whom it is *intended* (especially for young people), and its *starting point* ("the fear of Yahweh is the beginning of knowledge," v. 7). And what is the next admonition to which Solomon gives pride of place immediately thereafter, at the very opening of his book? The admonition to listen especially carefully!

For starters, listen carefully to your godly father and mother (Prov 1:8–9). Second, do not listen at all to sinners who want to lead you astray (Prov 1:10–19). And listen, thirdly, to Lady Wisdom, who sounds forth her salutary advice amid the daily turmoil of our lives (Prov 1:20–33). So Prov 1 immediately places us at the start of *the path* leading to wisdom.

But also with regard to the other main themes of the Instruction Manual—*the value* of wisdom—Prov 1 says remarkable things as well. Wisdom will adorn you, Solomon assures us. It will preserve your life and rescue it from corruption, in many cases even from death.

1. LISTEN WELL TO WHAT YOUR PARENTS TAUGHT YOU; THAT WILL ADORN YOU, YOUNG PERSON! (PROV 1:8–9)

All wisdom begins with the fear of the LORD, and believers first learned the fear of the LORD at home. For that reason, Solomon begins his book with a variation of the commandment "Honor your father and your mother." Obedience to that fifth commandment is the prerequisite for obedience to commandments six through ten. So it appears to have been hardly accidental that the first lesson that Solomon wrote on the board in his school of wisdom was this fundamental command:

> Hear, my child, your father's instruction,
> and do not reject your mother's teaching.

That is lesson number one in the book of life-wisdom known as Proverbs: in your youth, make it a habit to listen well to your God-fearing parents. Hold firmly throughout your entire life to "what father always taught," and when you are forty or fifty years old, repeat to yourself often, "Mother always said. . . ." That is the royal path toward wisdom: as a child, listen to father and mother. The school of wisdom begins *at home*!

Of course, Israelite youth were also supposed to listen well to the priest and Levite, who had been assigned the task of giving instruction in the Torah. And they were to list to the prophets as well, who appealed back to God's Torah (Isa 8:20). But long before a child hears anything from a priest or Levite, from a teacher or minister, a child learns to adopt God-fearing customs and attitudes already *at home* from his mother and father. Who can estimate the immeasurable influence that God's Word and Spirit can exercise on a person for the rest of their life due to a set of godly parents? This explains why lesson number one in Proverbs teaches us, "*Listen*, my son, to the instruction [the authoritative guidance through teaching and, if necessary, warning and discipline] of your father, and do not reject the instruction of your mother" (Prov 1:8).

Solomon himself did this. When he was king, he treated his mother with great respect: he stood before her and bowed down before her, and offered her a seat at his right hand (1 Kgs 2:19). Was not the wise Solomon thereby showing that he understood what he owed his mother, even as king? Later in Prov 4 he will tell us more about the school of wisdom that was his parental home. And although our Savior was the one greater than Solomon, indeed, he was God's very Son, he, too was subject to his parents. Immediately after reading about this, we read, "And Jesus increased in wisdom and in years, and in divine and human favor" (Luke 1:51–52). He, too, attained wisdom by listening humbly.

The book of Proverbs will be pressing this home often (see e.g., Prov 4:10–13; 12:15; 19:20; 23:19).

Teachers called their pupil "my son"

Notice how warmly such an Israelite wisdom teacher addressed his pupils. The boys he called "my son," and the girls he would have called "my daughter" (cf. Ps 45:10; Isa 32:9–15; Matt 9:22). For wisdom was not reserved only for boys. Otherwise, how could Solomon have spurred us not to forget "the instruction of *your mother*," if she had not been schooled in such wisdom during her growing up (cf. Prov 6:20; 23:25; 29:15; 30:17; 31:1; 31:26)?

Where in our huge secondary schools do we find as warm a bond as this between an Israelite wisdom teacher and his pupil? Such a lad addressed his teacher as "my father" (cf. 2 Kgs 2:12; 6:21; that was how youngsters generally addressed their superiors; cf. 1 Sam 24:12). Such a teacher introduced himself to his pupils as a kind of father, just as Paul was a spiritual father to Timothy, and Peter was to Mark.

Here in the first lesson of Proverbs we immediately encounter fundamental ordinances for all teaching activity and for the interaction between youth and their elders. Holy Scripture does not proceed from an equality like that decreed by the French Revolution, but from a certain kind of inequality. This too belongs to wisdom, namely, that one must respect the place and the dignity that each person has received from God. Thus, in the form of address, "my son," we hear a certain authority that the teacher has over his student and the parent over the young person. After all, a father stands not beneath, but above his son, by virtue of the authority that God grants to a father over his son.

This divine ordinance was maintained even in ancient pagan cultures. Egyptian wisdom teachers addressed their pupils with the phrase "my son." But within modern Christianity, such forms of address regrettably arouse irritation and opposition. In any case, let us not confuse or identify this with the old-fashioned academic distance between teacher and student, for those who wrote the proverbs are following an approach entirely in line with Moses and the prophets, according to whose instruction the feature of age should dominate. According to the Torah, the oldest men in the community should exercise leadership and the youth should submit to their leadership.[1]

The youth are not being denigrated with such an approach, but are being esteemed in terms of their proper dignity. For they are in many respects inexperienced and therefore in many respects "ignorant"; indeed, in some things, they border on being silly. This explains why the wise men focus on them especially, in order to endow them, as youth, as soon as possible with the wisdom of those who are older.

Regrettably, the spirit of these ground rules for a God-fearing upbringing clash directly with the spirit governing many young people in our revolutionary age. Among the youth who live in the atmosphere of apostate Christianity there is at work a demonic obstruction and recalcitrance (the fruits of revolutionary rules for raising children). Here, the book of Proverbs can be "profitable for teaching, for *reproof*, for correction, and for training in righteousness" (2 Tim 3:16). In light of their form of address as "my son," the wise men were not declaring their students *prematurely* to be mature. For the book of Proverbs, even one who was forty years old with several children belonged to the youth (Prov 1:4).

On the other hand, acknowledging the dignity and authority of the teacher did not exclude the mutual demonstration of upright cordiality. Is not such warmth automatic in a father-son relationship? If, with his teaching, such a teacher has in view nothing else than the well-being of his "son," then this "son" can also fully trust the teaching of his father. Blessed are the teacher and student who encounter each other in terms of the relationship of heartfelt trust that characterizes the father-son relationship!

Obedience adorns the youth

In the ancient East, a man, too, would wear a necklace, on which occasionally he would fasten his signet ring. Tamar asked her father-in-law Judah for his signet ring as a form of security deposit (Gen 38:18). Such a necklace identified its wearer as a refined gentleman, someone up to whom people looked with respect. In the same way, lifelong respect for the instruction of God-fearing parents and teachers would impart honor and respect to a person, according to Solomon.

> For they are a graceful garland for your head
> and pendants for your neck. (Prov 1:9)

---

1. Cf. 1 Pet 5:5; cf. a concordance for the use of "elder" in Scripture.

These are invisible, yet simultaneously visible, adornments. The composer of the proverb saw something lovely in that childlike attitude. Nothing adorns young people, according to Holy Scripture, more than respect for parental instruction in the fear of God. By comparison, an Olympic medal fades to nothing.

The book of Proverbs will return frequently to the need for obedience to parental discipline and to the lovely blessing that God has bound to that obedience. But it will also speak about the sorrow of parents whose child refuses to render such obedience (Prov 10:1; 15:20; 17:21; 27:11; 28:7; 29:3).

2. DO NOT LISTEN TO SINNERS, FOR THEN YOU WILL BE ATTACKING YOUR OWN LIFE (PROV 1:10–19)

Gangsters and predatory killers certainly do not constitute a guild that has only recently flourished in modern Europe and America. Isaiah prophesied the dissolution of Israelite society and foresaw that young people would rise up against their parents and would despise their elders (Isa 3:5). Hosea talks about a gang of bandits—note well: priests!—who lay in ambush along the road to Shechem. In fact, during this time Gilead was well known for its criminality (Hos 6:8–9). Notice that we are speaking here about Israel, who knew God's Word!

Already at Horeb, however, God had taken into account that some among his people would lapse into murder and homicide. This explains why he gave *his people* the sixth commandment: "You [Israel] shall not murder [each other]." The wise men adopted this sober scriptural view by including in their teaching a warning against juvenile criminality. Even young people who belong to a Christian church are sometimes exposed to temptation from gangsters. The police and legal authorities nowadays are not unfamiliar with young people who come from a Christian family, who have wound up associating with gangsters and ended up committing crimes of killing.

Solomon has a couple of imaginary youthful gangsters speak some words, the kind who are skilled at getting rich quickly without having to work.

> My son, if sinners entice you,
>   do not consent.
> If they say, "Come with us, let us lie in wait for blood;
>   let us ambush the innocent without reason;
> like Sheol let us swallow them alive,
>   and whole, like those who go down to the pit;
> we shall find all precious goods,
>   we shall fill our houses with plunder;

> throw in your lot among us;
>> we will all have one purse"—
> my son, do not walk in the way with them;
>> hold back your foot from their paths,
> for their feet run to evil,
>> and they make haste to shed blood.
> For in vain is a net spread
>> in the sight of any bird,
> but these men lie in wait for their own blood;
>> they set an ambush for their own lives.
> Such are the ways of everyone who is greedy for unjust gain;
>> it takes away the life of its possessors. (Prov 1:10–19)

Such gangsters are more stupid than birds. When birds see a snare spread for them, they take another route. But robbers and killers spread their own snare; they pursue their own death. Not too long ago that is exactly what they got, by means of the gallows or the electric chair. For the divine command to sentence murderers to death was not set aside all that long ago.

Therefore, do not listen to such sinners. Did your mother steer you toward such a group, or did she not warn you clearly about them? How many people sitting in prison—too late!—think of their mothers? They endangered their own lives (and in Proverbs, the term *life* is often another word for "happiness"). Did things have to go that way? Not at all, if only they had thought about lesson number one in Proverbs: Listen to your parents!

3. BETTER TO LISTEN TO LADY WISDOM, BUT DO IT EARLY! (PROV 1:20–33)

Listen to wisdom, and then you'll get wisdom! That is the connecting thread in Prov 1:8–33. But then that has to happen early, for one who begins too late is not yet grown up. That is what the warning comes down to that we get to hear in Prov 1:20–33.

Solomon clothed this admonition in an artistic manner. First, he cast it in the style of a beautiful poem. Next, he placed this didactic poem on the lips of wisdom itself. He introduces wisdom here in the form of a wise woman, one who calls to us and addresses us. We call this kind of stylistic device personification; the technical term is *prosopopoeia*.

The Israelite was fond of such personification

Presumably we have less affinity for such a stylistic technique than the Israelite readers of Proverbs. Modern Westerners, especially those with lots of letters behind their names, often talk and write with a dry and prosaic style. Our textbooks teem with general concepts, bloodless ideas that people describe as abstractions. Providentially, God did not give us his Word in the arid language of science, but in the lush and succulent language of home, garden, and kitchen, the kind used by Israelite farmers and housewives, and in the graphic expressions of the Israelite poets.

Take, for example, steadfast love, peace, truth, and justice. Don't think for a moment that the Israelite would have reduced these to dry and bleached concepts. On the contrary, he spoke of them as though they were people of flesh and blood. As we read in Ps 85:

> Steadfast love and faithfulness *meet*;
> > righteousness and peace *kiss* each other.
> Faithfulness *springs up* from the ground,
> > and righteousness *looks down* from the sky. (Ps 85:10–11)

The psalmist introduces steadfast love and faithfulness as two men who meet one another along the road, and greet each other in the ancient Eastern manner with a kiss.

Israelites loved talking this way.

This is how Isaiah describes the need of his time:

> Justice is turned back,
> > and righteousness stands far away;
> for truth has stumbled in the public squares,
> > and uprightness cannot enter. (Isa 59:14)

Of course, the prophet himself knew that truth and uprightness were not real people, but he portrayed lawlessness in Israel with such personalized images. Paul spoke in the same Hebrew manner about sin, as though it were a *king* that demanded obedience from his subjects (Rom 6:12). Or an employer who pays wages (Rom 6:23); cf. vv. 17–18. In this way the Israelite poet could talk about heaven and earth, the sea and trees, love and passion, as though they were living beings (cf. Job 28:14; Ps 96:11–12; 114:3–7; Song 8:6; Isa 1:2). In fact, don't we ourselves speak of Lady Justice? And about activities that exact a heavy toll?

In this genuinely Israelite manner, Prov 1:20–33 speaks about wisdom. Solomon introduces her to us as a speaking woman. It is true that the personification is further developed here than with examples mentioned above, but that does not contradict the fact that here wisdom is no less a real woman than, in Ps 85, the truth is a real man. Not to mention that wisdom would be a divine person. The poet introduces her here simply as a prophetess, someone like Deborah or the prophetess Hulda (Judg 4:4; 2 Kgs 22:14; cf. 2 Sam 20:16–22). So we meet for the first time Lady Wisdom, someone we'll encounter more often—in Prov 8, displaying her nobility, and in Prov 9, inviting us for dinner (cf. Prov 4:5–9; 7:4).

What reality should we think is being identified by means of this figurative woman? Of whom and of what is she a poetic personification?

Lady Wisdom as a street evangelist

How rich were the treasures of wisdom that an Israelite could obtain by taking in everything with his eyes and ears throughout the course of his life.

First of all, one obtains the treasures of wisdom, naturally, by opening his ears to the Torah, the instruction of *God's Word*. He got to hear that first and foremost from his father and mother (Prov 1:8). He also received this from the local Levite and priest, whose task it was to instruct Israel from the Torah (2 Chr 17:7–9). In addition, he could hear God's Word from itinerant prophets, since men like Samuel, Elijah, and Elisha traveled throughout the land. Moreover, he could also listen to the wisdom of older people, when they adjudicated matters at the city gates, for example. Would not their wise decisions be the subject of daily conversation (cf. 1 Kgs 3:28; 4:34; 2 Chr 17:7–9)? This, too, was a channel along which the wisdom of God's Word was dispersed.

And then the believing Israelite could also enjoy every day that incomprehensible arsenal of divine wisdom *in the creation*. Heaven and earth don't speak with words, says Ps 19, but nevertheless "their voice goes out through all the earth, and their words to the end of the world" (Ps 19:4–5). God's creation, so full of wisdom, "speaks" to us (Rom 1:20). To the degree that the unbeliever listens, he can observe a certain measure of wisdom.

All this divine wisdom, revealed in Scripture and creation, and accumulated in the experience of many generations, does in fact constitute an organic, indissoluble unity. This great entity of revelation and experience is introduced here in summary fashion as Lady Wisdom. In her figurative form, we are here addressed by the wisdom that is accessible to all people. She comes like a prophetess with a serious message for young and old. She comes to us in her very own person to bind upon our hearts the truth that interacting with her is not a hobby, but a matter of life and death. And time is running out! Listen:

> Wisdom cries aloud in the street,
> > in the markets she raises her voice;
> at the head of the noisy streets she cries out;
> > at the entrance of the city gates she speaks. (Prov 1:20–21)

Israelite life was lived for the most part under the open sky. Given that the streets were mostly narrow alleys that were seven or ten feet wide, you can imagine what a bustle and hubbub dominated the scene during the day. It is not accidental that the Hebrew language has no word for "square" or "plaza," for the only open areas were near the entrance of their villages, often in the actual gate area itself. There you encountered the heartbeat of Israelite public life. In the cool spaces of the gate areas sat Job among the elders (Job 29:7–10, 21–22). There the merchants advertised their wares (2 Kgs 7:1), and Boaz advocated for the interests of Naomi and Ruth (Ruth 4). There the day laborers offered their services (Matt 20:3). There you would bump into your friends and you could follow the news of the day.

And there the voice of Lady Wisdom has sounded forth! Could she have chosen a better place to address the city inhabitants than the busy gate areas? There she could reach everyone, young and old, with her message. Therefore, she lifted up her voice specifically there, above the hubbub of the haggling and hollering, above the shouts of the hawkers and the children at play (Matt 11:16).

This poetic portrait contains a twofold lesson.

> How long, O simple ones, will you love being simple?
> How long will scoffers delight in their scoffing
> > and fools hate knowledge? (Prov 1:22)

Notice that there were many in Israel who were naive when it came to life, just as today in the churches there are many who go about in the world without having a clue, even to the point of silliness. We looked at this gullible type earlier. How long will they continue to live so unsettled, blind to the dangers of their lack of life experience? Nevertheless, Lady Wisdom did harbor some bit of hope for them. At least she asks them directly how long they will allow her to speak.

But in Israel there were also those who were wicked, mockers and fools, as they are called here. They were such, not first of all because of their jokes about holy things or their intellectual stupidity, but on account of their *self-exaltation* and despising of God's Word. Scripture talks about foolish prophets, and Peter and Jude spoke of mockers *within* the Christian church (2 Pet 3:3–4; Jude 18–19)![2] Lady Wisdom does not address them directly.

---

2. You can read more about this in van Deursen, *Psalms I*, 93–100, 131–32.

Did she perhaps consider them irremediable (cf. our comments on Prov 9:7–8)?

Nevertheless, she does not yet lock the door for good. Anyone who wants to listen still gets a chance. For such a person Lady Wisdom pours out her spirit and she will drench him with her lifesaving knowledge as with a bursting fountain.

> If you turn at my reproof, behold,
> I will pour out my spirit to you;
>   I will make my words known to you. (Prov 1:23)

What will they do? Will they yet accept this offer? There is a pause between verses 23 and 24. Will people allow themselves to be instructed, or will they remain ill-disposed to such teaching?

Let's remember very clearly who is speaking here: the representative of a wisdom that is accessible to all people, both the wisdom we can obtain through *revelation* (in Scripture and creation) and the wisdom we can obtain through *experience*. In countless respects, this great body of wisdom points us to the right path. It can extend to you the best advice for every step you take on your life path. With invitation and admonition, Lady Wisdom extends her hands.

Regrettably, many walk past her with indifference.

> Because I have called and you refused to listen,
>   have stretched out my hand and no one has heeded,
> because you have ignored all my counsel
>   and would have none of my reproof. (Prov 1:24–25)

There you have the reaction of many Israelites, and regrettably, also of many in the Christian churches, to the glorious revelation of God's wisdom in his Word and works. Scripture here points us with its poetic language to a disturbing reality: many coldly shrug their shoulders in response to all that good counsel that their parents and God-fearing teachers passed along from Holy Scripture and the experience of the ages.

Terrible realities! In Israel there were, and in God's churches there are, wicked people who live according to their autonomous principles or counsels (Ps 1:1).[3] Among God's people there are mockers and fools who laugh at the order that God has made known in his Word and works. But that laughter will be their destruction!

> I also will laugh at your calamity;
>   I will mock when terror strikes you,

---

3. See van Deursen, *Psalms I*, 127–30.

> when terror strikes you like a storm
> and your calamity comes like a whirlwind,
> when distress and anguish come upon you.
> Then they will call upon me, but I will not answer;
> they will seek me diligently but will not find me. (Prov 1:26–28)

A person can despise wisdom only to his own injury. The poet sketches the consequences of such folly, using four words: calamity, terror, distress, and anguish. Proverbs 10–31 will be illustrating this with hundreds of examples. Although we note that Prov 5–7 also shows us a striking portrait in connection with this lesson: the ruin that enters the life of the adulterer. In this way, folly can thoroughly destroy a human life just as suddenly as a tornado. But anyone who at that point calls out to Lady Wisdom is doing so too late!

With this, Holy Scripture is identifying for us a terrible possibility. A person can seek God and his Word—and thereby the source and spectacles of wisdom—*too late* (cf. Isa 55:6; Amos 8:11–12)! Sometimes God says, "Though they cry to me, I will not listen to them" (Jer 11:11; cf. Ezek 8:18; Mic 3:4; Zech 7:13). Lady Wisdom is saying something similar to fools: You laugh at me, but then comes my turn to laugh at you.

Naturally, Lady Wisdom is speaking so threateningly in order still to press for conversion. For that purpose, those who composed the proverbs often use the tool of mockery. But a person can end up in situations in which he must really get the sense that everything belonging to wisdom is derisively mocking him.

For what is the depth of the responses of such fools?

> Because they hated knowledge
> and did not choose the fear of the Lord,
> would have none of my counsel
> and despised all my reproof. (Prov 1:29–30)

There you have the deepest motives of the wicked among God's people: they hate the knowledge of God and his service. They refuse to keep his covenant. They simply refuse to fear him in his Word and works. Therefore they shrug their shoulders in response to the warnings of Lady Wisdom. "Behold, they have rejected the Word of the Lord, so what wisdom is in them?" (Jer 8:9).

Here we observe a striking resemblance between the voice of wisdom and the voice of prophecy. How often had not Yahweh complained through the prophets, "Why, when I called, was there no one to answer?" (Isa 50:2; cf. 65:2, 12; 66:4; Jer 7:13; 13:10; Ps 81:11–13; Neh 9:17; Luke 13:34). And we hear Lady Wisdom here and in verses 24–25 utter the same complaint. God's people have not only killed the prophets perpetually but they have also persecuted the sages among Israel (Matt 23:34; cf. Eccl 9:13–16). No wonder that this didactic poem and lamentation of Lady Wisdom has such an explicit *prophetic ring*!

Groen van Prinsterer characterized this wicked behavior with the word *revolution*. By that word he understood not only particular political events but a negative *life attitude* toward God and his Word, something that attacks the entirety of human living at its root. In his work, *Unbelief and Revolution*, van Prinsterer described in a classic and prophetic manner the comprehensively destructive effects of revolution in European history.[4] Revolution always swallows up its own children. That applies particularly to the mother of all revolutions: the great rebellion against God and his Word.

Lady Wisdom puts it briefly this way:

> Therefore they shall eat the fruit of their way,
>   and have their fill of their own devices.
> For the simple are killed by their turning away,
>   and the complacency of fools destroys them. (Prov 1:31–32)

In Prov 8, Wisdom will address us personally once more, and there Wisdom will conclude with a similar expression as here:

> For whoever finds me *finds life*
>   and obtains favor from the LORD,
> but he who fails to find me injures himself;
>   all who hate me love *death*. (Prov 8:35–36)

There you hear one of the keynotes, perhaps even the primary one, of the entire book of Proverbs. This is what Prov 10–31 shows in hundreds of proverbs: all evil *does* evil to a person! No wonder that the Instruction Manual (Prov 1–9) focuses our attention on that immediately in Prov 1: "Whoever is steadfast in righteousness will *live*, but he who pursues evil will *die*" (Prov 11:19). In fact, the entire book of Proverbs is embroidered with this pattern. Or as Paul would later express it, "Whatever one sows, that will he also reap. For the one who sows to his own flesh will from the flesh reap corruption, but the one who sows to the Spirit will from the Spirit reap eternal life" (Gal 6:7–8).

For this reason, mockers and fools are not victims of an angry fate, but facilitators of their own destruction (Prov 16:22; 19:3). Rebellion against God and his wisdom ends literally and figuratively in death. In this light we

---

4. Van Prinsterer, *Unbelief and Revolution*.

must recall that once God had to address *his entire people* as "[those who] turned away" (Jer 8:5).

But whoever does listen is well off. Lady Wisdom lets him know—as the Instruction Manual for Proverbs will soon repeat again and again—that wisdom or the fear of the Lord is the best life insurance program in which one can enroll. To a large extent, wisdom functions preventively. It is remarkable how much evil it can prevent and how much rest it can provide its students! In the coming chapter we will get to see sufficient examples of that. Lady Wisdom concludes her speech with this:

> But whoever listens to me will dwell secure
> and will be at ease, without dread of disaster. (Prov 1:33)

Listening to Lady Wisdom—that is, fearing Yahweh—or simply to let her *go on talking*, that is the difference between the stillness and the storm, between rest and panic, between security and disaster. To "dwell secure" was one of the promises that Yahweh had connected with observing his commandments. And that Torah expression Lady Wisdom is taking upon her lips here. (This is yet one more proof of the intimate connection between wisdom and the fear of the Lord.)

Listen early, for your life is at stake

Proverbs opens with this poem in which Lady Wisdom herself addresses us. For we must of course read her speech with an eye to its canonical place: it is found on page 1 of Proverbs, *as the introduction* to this Bible book, in fact, as the introduction to the Instruction Manual for using this Bible book. In this recommendation of the wisdom of these proverbs, we hear the same earnestness we find in other parts of God's Word: "And whether they hear or refuse to hear (for they are a rebellious house) they will know that a prophet has been among them" (Ezek 2:5). It will continue accusing the fools among God's people in this way, by reminding them that there has been a Solomon among them! Could he have put into words any more attractively than this beautiful poem the vital importance of this Bible book? Lady Wisdom as a street evangelist!

You encounter her every day. Especially when you read the Bible, you hear her speaking. But also, when you look at what God has made, at the divine order in his creation, and the statutes and ordinances that he established for everything he has made. What you can and cannot do in your vocation is related to that. Interaction with other people. Donating money. Marital life. Health. Strength to do your work. Purpose in life. Various periods in life. With respect to all those matters, Lady Wisdom wants to speak her redemptive word.

No one can ignore her with impunity, for she is the personification of all the humanly accessible wisdom in Proverbs, indeed in all Scripture and the entire creation. Therefore, listen *early* to her. All who despise that wisdom love death (Prov 8:36). Let's listen to her *from now on*. For that will do us good, in every respect!

6

Proverbs 2

The Treasure Hunter Looking for Wisdom
Discovers Life-Insight and Life-Preservation

WHEN ACHAN HID HIS stolen gold and silver in the ground, he was doing nothing unusual for that time and place (Josh 7:21). The same was true of the lazy slave in the parable who buried his talent in the ground (Matt 25:18). Often the owner of such a hidden treasure would not tell even his wife where he had hidden it. But if such a person were to die suddenly, then he would take his secret to his grave. For that reason, people in the Middle East still believe, and with good reason, that in many places the ground still preserves hidden treasure (cf. Job 3:21; Isa 45:3; Jer 41:8; Matt 13:44). Many have devoted heaps of time and trouble looking for treasure. In this context we might recall the gold prospectors of an earlier century.

Something of that obsession and gold fever on the part of treasure hunters is what Solomon would like to see applied by his students in their quest for wisdom! But whereas the gold digger often digs in vain, those who seek wisdom are richly rewarded by the discovery of incalculable treasures.

1. QUARRY FOR WISDOM LIKE A GOLD DIGGER (PROV 2:1–4)

Just as in Prov 1, here in Prov 2 Solomon is pushing strongly for *seeking* wisdom. Given the location of Prov 2—in the Instruction Manual for Proverbs—this stimulus should make us think of the words and commands that we find in Prov 10–31. There the treasures of wisdom and insight lie hidden. But then you must indeed quarry them and dig into them. That takes effort and tough perseverance, not because God has buried wisdom so deeply—note well that it calls out in the middle of daily life (Prov 1:20–33)—but because by nature our heart loves folly. Providentially we don't have to go searching in the wild for these treasures. Solomon is referring to his words and commands; there we can discover insight and discernment.

> My son, if you receive my words
>   and treasure up my commandments with you,
> making your ear attentive to wisdom
>   and inclining your heart to understanding;
> yes, if you call out for insight
>   and raise your voice for understanding,
> if you seek it like silver
>   and search for it as for hidden treasures. (Prov 2:1–4)

When you think of the highly expensive search for minerals and fuels in our own day (oil rigs in the ocean, earth orbiting satellites for soil research), then Solomon is certainly not using antiquated imagery here. That is how earnestly we must seek wisdom! We must turn our ears and focus our hearts on this quest. Practically this means that we must read and reread the book of Proverbs often and diligently. We should be reading preferably with a pencil in hand for underlining what strikes us in a special way, and then preserve that in our heart like a treasure (Ps 119:11; Prov 10:14; Isa 33:6). We should be mindful as well of the apostolic admonition, "If any of you lacks wisdom, let him ask God" (Jas 1:5).

But such explorers receive wonderful promises from Solomon: Their wisdom will, first, lead them to *understand* many things, and, second, provide *protection* in many respects. The only thing to notice is that he indicates these advantages somewhat less explicitly than we will in our discussion below.

2. THEN YOU WILL DISCOVER INSIGHT FOR YOUR LIVING (PROV 2:5–10)

"Those who seek me diligently find me," wisdom says (in Prov 8:17; cf. Matt 7:7; Jas 1:5). Those who read Proverbs with a kind of gold fever will always have their thirst quenched. For, by means of this book, divine wisdom enters our heart and enlightens our eyes, so that we see and understand more and more. We learn to distinguish and discern, which is such a desperately needed gift for God's children. We learn to see how we can put into practice our love toward God and the Lord Jesus:

> Then you will understand the fear of the LORD
>   and find the knowledge of God.
> For the LORD gives wisdom;
>   from his mouth come knowledge and understanding;
> he stores up sound wisdom for the upright;
>   he is a shield to those who walk in integrity,
> guarding the paths of justice
>   and watching over the way of his saints.
> Then you will understand righteousness and justice
>   and equity, every good path;
> for wisdom will come into your heart,
>   and knowledge will be pleasant to your soul. (Prov 2:5–10)

Proverbs can teach you what the fear of the LORD means in the entirety of life. As we will see later, Solomon shines the light of wisdom not only on strictly personal life but also on social, political, and economic life. What is just? What is social justice? What does the knowledge of God mean for practical living? Proverbs can teach to *understand* this with the use of hundreds of examples, so that you set out on the proper path.

And you will find that knowledge-of-God-in-practice to be so very lovely! We will discuss this further in connection with Prov 3:17. This involves the initial treasure that those hunting for wisdom will dig up: *insight for living*. And that will guarantee that they discover the second treasure: *protection of their lives*.

3. THEN YOU WILL DISCOVER THE PROTECTION OF YOUR LIFE (PROV 2:11–22)

We have already heard Lady Wisdom calling out, "Whoever listens to me will dwell *secure*" (Prov 1:33). That is one of the greatest advantages that wisdom can supply a person if one listens to her: wisdom can prevent such unspeakable evil. Proverbs 1–9 will return to this repeatedly, for it is one of the main themes of the Instruction Manual that comes with the book of Proverbs: wisdom is more beneficial. Proverbs 2 emphasizes that as well: Yahweh "watch[es] over the way of his saints" (v. 8). He is their shield (v. 7), which makes us think of either an ordinary shield or perhaps of the title of a suzerain who signed a treaty with a vassal. Israel's saints were under Yahweh's covenantal protection.

God does this, however, also directly.

> Discretion will watch over you,
>> understanding will guard you. (Prov 2:11)

God protects his children by giving them discretion. Then that godly discretion and that God-fearing life-insight together guard them from various forms of evil and misery. Proverbs illustrates this life lesson of the highest rank with innumerable examples. You could summarize this entire Bible book with this proverb: "The teaching of the wise is a fountain of life, that one may turn away from the snares of death" (Prov 13:14; cf. 4:6–7; 14:26–27; Eccl 7:12). Here Solomon goes on to mention two of these death traps.

> Delivering you from the way of evil,
>> from men of perverted speech,
> who forsake the paths of uprightness
>> to walk in the ways of darkness,
> who rejoice in doing evil
>> and delight in the perverseness of evil,
> men whose paths are crooked,
>> and who are devious in their ways. (Prov 2:12–15)

In Proverbs you will encounter such dark figures in various forms. Predatory murderers, black marketers, wicked potentates, unjust judges, false witnesses, land robbers, drunkards, scammers, adulterers, blackmailers, sloths, blasphemers, and those who incite quarrels. And notice the people often approve of such evil practices (v. 14). Isaiah was familiar with them, too: "Woe to those who call evil good and good evil, who put darkness for light and light for darkness, who put bitter for sweet and sweet for bitter!" (Isa 5:20; cf. Rom 1:32; 2 Thess 2:12).

How often do we see such fools destroying their own lives? By contrast, wisdom can offer protection. Those who take courses with the wise men will not need to come into contact with the judge, or crash into a tree through alcohol abuse, or be fired on the spot for forgery. Against all of these God has given us his redemptive proverbial wisdom that "*deliver[s] you from the way of evil*" (v. 12). God saves not only from eternal perdition but also from all kinds of temporal destruction. Like the terrible consequences of adultery:

> So you will be delivered from the forbidden woman,
>> from the adulteress with her smooth words,
> who forsakes the companion of her youth
>> and forgets the covenant of her God;
> for her house sinks down to death,
>> and her paths to the departed;
> none who go to her come back,
>> nor do they regain the paths of life. (Prov 2:16–19)

Here you see a very fatal death trap: the temptations of the adulteress. In Prov 5–7 Solomon will return to discuss this living snare extensively. Then he will have us hear her "smooth words" and see how all those who have sexual relations with her ("go to her," v. 19) are heading to their own destruction. At that time, we will discuss this dangerously lethal temptress in greater detail.

At this point she is led on stage as an example of what Solomon said earlier in verses 1–4: My words provide insight for living and for protection of life. Every man or lad who listens to those words need never fall into the snares of such a woman, who is unfaithful to God and her husband by breaking the seventh commandment of the Horeb covenant (Exod 20:14; Mal 2:14). Both literally and figuratively she can cost you your life (the Torah threatened capital punishment for adultery)! So you had better be hunting for wisdom like a gold prospector hunts for gold! Wisdom supplies you with preventive marriage protection, and protection against other evils, for nothing works as powerfully as unchastity to destroy one's taste for God's will.

> So you will walk in the way of the good
>   and keep to the paths of the righteous.
> For the upright will inhabit the land,
>   and those with integrity will remain in it,
> but the wicked will be cut off from the land,
>   and the treacherous will be rooted out of it. (Prov 2:20–22)

When an Israelite circumcised his son, he took the required oath of loyalty on behalf of that newborn covenant child of God. By cutting off his son's foreskin, this father was swearing on behalf of his boy: I am now cutting off a piece of skin from my body, but may I be entirely cut off from the covenant fellowship with Yahweh if I do not serve him loyally. What happened if someone refused to take this oath? Such a deserter "shall be cut off from his people; he has broken my covenant" (Gen 17:14). The text says, in other words, that such a person had to be circumcised (cut off) from Israel.

Is Solomon here making an associative wordplay in terms of this oath of self-malediction? In any case, verse 22 does speak literally of the wicked being *cut off* (circumcised) from the land. Here we are listening to *covenantal language* (cf. Exod 12:15, 19). Woe to the wicked in Israel in the Christian church! Not only the prophets but also the wise men warn such a person for the sake of his life (Deut 4:26; 11:17; 30:18; Ps 1:4–6; Ps 37; Ps 104:35; Prov 10:30).

But the upright shall dwell in the land (v. 21). In that connection we think no longer of Palestine, for our Savior has taught us that the promises given to the righteous extend further than that ancient promised land.

Believers will inherit the new *earth* (Matt 5:5; cf. 1 Tim 4:8). Wisdom that comes from fearing the Lord protects us not only in this life but keeps us on the path toward eternal life. With this second promise as well, Solomon was enticing us in Prov 2 to dig like tireless treasure hunters for the gold of wisdom stored in Prov 10–31.

7

Proverbs 3

In keeping God's Commandments Lies Rich Reward for Our Entire Life

NOTHING IS AS SALUTARY for a person as loving God and keeping his commandments. That is the crowning argument with which Solomon arouses his youthful readers to pay attention to God's ordinances. Especially in the introduction to his books, he continually hammers on this anvil: "If you are wise [i.e., fear Yahweh], you are wise *for yourself*" (Prov 9:12). We have heard these notes before. In Prov 1, Lady Wisdom held before us, "But whoever listens to me will *dwell secure*" (v. 33). To this Prov 2 adds, "Discretion will *watch over you*" (v. 11). But Prov 3 will hold before us in greater detail how beneficially that wisdom operates that proceeds from the fear of the LORD. When you apply it to your life, you find yourself on the best pathway toward receiving the following blessings:

> Wisdom can extend your life. (vv. 1–2)
> Wisdom makes you sympathetic to God and others. (vv. 3–4)
> Wisdom leads to the least amount of misery in this world. (vv. 5–6)
> Wisdom promotes your health. (vv. 7–8)
> Wisdom increases your possessions. (vv. 9–10)
> Wisdom teaches one to bow under God's discipline. (vv. 11–12)
> Wisdom is more valuable than jewels. (vv. 13–15)
> Wisdom lends wealth and honor. (v. 16)
> Wisdom bestows loveliness and peace. (v. 17)
> Wisdom lets you eat from a tree of life. (v. 18)
> Wisdom lies at the foundation of heaven and earth. (v. 19)

Wisdom makes alive, adorns you, and protects you. (vv. 21–23)
Wisdom benefits your sleep. (v. 24)
Wisdom preserves you while the wicked are perishing. (vv. 25–26)
Wisdom does not abuse trust. (v. 29)
Wisdom makes you peaceable. (v. 30)
Wisdom leads you into intimate interaction with God. (vv. 31–32)
Wisdom draws God's blessing to your dwelling. (v. 33)
Wisdom acquires God's good pleasure through its humility. (v. 34)
Wisdom makes you to inherit honor. (v. 35)

We may take this as practically as though it were said, "In the fear of the LORD one has *strong confidence*" (Prov 14:26). No one need wonder about the fact that Solomon works this out in Prov 3 so soberly and concretely. After all, in his covenant Yahweh troubles himself not only with Israel's religious life but also with this kind of everyday living. Therefore he spoke in the Torah not only about bringing sacrifices but also about picking grapes and paying day laborers. Regarding the keeping of all these good statutes Moses said back then, "That is your life" (Deut 30:20 NASB marg.).

The echo of this instruction in the Torah that is so curative for all of human living reverberates throughout the Psalms and Proverbs. The composer of Ps 19 also had this kind of open-eyed wonder for that life-advancing working of God's Word. Anyone so wise that he takes the God of life at his Word will enjoy the same experience as this psalmist: "The rules of the LORD are true [firm].... Moreover, by them is your servant warned; in keeping them there is *great reward*" (Ps 19:9, 11). In this same spirit the apostle Paul wrote, "Godliness is *of value* in every way, as it holds promise *for the present* and also for the life to come" (1 Tim 4:8). A bit later he wrote, "Godliness with contentment is *great gain*" (6:6). Proverbs 3 shows us what that reward and that life consists of.

We want to alert the reader in advance that in this passage of Scripture, Solomon does not present ironclad principles. He does not come with rules that operate all the time and everywhere, but he comes to us with *mashals*. These do indeed contain *rules*, but in order to apply them, one needs to know the manner of speaking unique to a *mashal*. Otherwise, as one reads Prov 3, one can easily be snared by various misunderstandings. As we proceed to discuss this chapter of Proverbs, we are assuming that the reader has become familiar with chapter 1 above, especially all of section 6, "A *mashal* occasionally contains a blunt formulation." That can perhaps spare the reader unnecessary sadness when Solomon is talking about blessings that he or she has never received.

So keep that *mashal* character clearly in mind.

1. WISDOM CAN EXTEND YOUR LIFE (PROV 3:1–2)

All of Proverbs provides instruction in the practical consequences of the fear of the LORD. "That your trust may be in the LORD, I have made them known to you today, even to you" (Prov 22:19). "My son, if you receive my words . . . then you will understand the fear of the LORD and find the knowledge of God" (Prov 2:1, 5). So when, in the proverb below, Solomon talks about his commandments and instruction, then he is of course referring also to his lessons about the practice of godliness. What means does he employ to entice his spiritual children to that practice? He uses the assurance that with wisdom arising from the fear of the LORD, they can extend their lives!

> My son, do not forget my teaching,
>   but let your heart keep my commandments,
> for length of days and years of life
>   and peace they will add to you. (Prov 3:1–2)

A long and happy life! Who does not hold that up as a wonderful ideal? But what do we as persons have to contribute to realizing that ideal? Surely we cannot contribute anything, can we? Surely we cannot add one day to our lives, can we? We will return to these cautious objections below. First, though, we want to establish that according to Prov 3:1–2 a person can extend his life, by years, even. As long as he is willing to serve and love God. This is not the only Scripture passage that makes this claim. We read in Prov 4 that Solomon himself had learned this already as a child while living at home with his father David: "Hear, my son, and accept my words, that the years of your life may be many" (Prov 4:10). Lady Wisdom opened up the same prospect: "For by me your days will be multiplied, and years will be added to your life" (Prov 9:11). "Long life is in her right hand" (Prov 3:16). However, we need to understand what Proverbs means by "length of days." What age should we have in mind?

Before proceeding, we wish first to answer these questions.

1. *What is "length of days"?*

Throughout the centuries, people did not always reach the same age. The mighty generations before the flood reached lifespans of more than nine hundred years, but after the flood lifespans decreased more and more (Gen 11:10–32). Shem reached six hundred years, but Terah only two hundred five; Abraham, one hundred seventy-five; Aaron, one hundred twenty-three; Moses, one hundred twenty; and Joshua, one hundred ten. Most of the kings of Judah did not get all that old, measured by our standards. Rehoboam lived to be fifty-eight; Jehoshaphat, sixty; Jehoram, forty; Ahaziah, twenty-three; Amaziah, fifty-four; Azariah, sixty-eight; Jotham, forty-one; Ahaz, thirty-six; Hezekiah, fifty-four (including the extra fifteen years that God added); Manasseh, sixty-seven; Amon, twenty-four; and Josiah, thirty-nine. The average lifespan of these rulers was forty-seven years. Other Scripture passages indicate lifespans that were not much longer.

A Levite was supposed to perform his full service until his fiftieth year (Num 4:3; cf. 8:25; 1 Chr 23:24). After that he could still lend assistance if he wished, but he was no longer obligated to serve (Num 8:23–26). May we deduce from this that people considered someone in his fifties to have reached old age? In Lev 27:1–8 we read a list of tariffs for redemption of vows; there, the oldest age class was sixty years and older. Barzillai was eighty years old, and for that reason was described as being "very old" (2 Sam 19:32). Did this mean that the average life expectancy at this time was not much beyond sixty?

What is "length of days"? We see that this is not a very simple question. In every country and in every era, the answer is not the same. Perhaps the wish expressed in Ps 128:5–6 can help us in this connection: "Yahweh bless you from Zion! . . . May you see you children's children!" For grandchildren are called "the crown of the aged" (Prov 17:6; cf. Job 42:16–17). In terms of Israelite thought, then, one was considered old who had grandchildren and great-grandchildren. In that connection, we do well to remember that the Israelite would have married at a younger age than is our custom, and thereby could have been a grandparent at forty and a great-grandparent already at sixty. For that reason, we are inclined, in connection with the phrase "length of days and years of life," to think not of extraordinarily long lifespans. Perhaps the wise men had in view someone approaching seventy as having reached a "ripe age," especially if God had blessed them with children and (great-)grandchildren. Does not this situation compare favorably with the average lifespans in our country during the nineteenth century, and among those living in the Third World?

2. Why should you die before your time? (Eccl 7:17)

Has not God long ago determined the day of our death? "In your book were written every one of them, the days that were formed for me, when as yet there were none of them" (Ps 139:16). And did not the Preacher say, "No man has . . . power over the day of his death" (Eccl 8:8)? That is what the psalmist confessed as well: "My times are in your hand" (Ps 31:15). Does not Proverbs contradict all of these? It all depends on how you read Scripture:

as though it contains a system of thought declared in advance to be closed, or as the living Word of God.

If the Scripture verses cited have to serve as links in an *argument* or as building blocks for a closed *system*, then we would advise caution and warn against fatalism and a quest for a rigid system. For one runs the risk of reading the passages mentioned through foggy spectacles without noticing, hindered by the steam and vapor of Greco-Roman or Muslim paganism. Those forms of paganism believed that necessity or fate stood above their supreme deity, whether Zeus, Jupiter, or Allah, and not even the supreme deity could oppose that. In their thinking, some Christians have also placed above our heavenly Father such a fate, something they call his eternal decree. And God was also bound to that, so that praying does not help "if it does not correspond to God's counsel." In this kind of thought system, the fear of the LORD ultimately has no influence at all on your lifespan. Did the aphorism "If it's not your time . . ." perhaps germinate in this fatalistic climate?

Scripture, however, does not speak in fixed, scientific terms, but with living words. It is not familiar with that caricature of God's decree, but is familiar with *the comfort*: "My times are in your hand" (Ps 31:15). This is not a proposition belonging to a theological system, but a faith confession that happily it is God who determines our lifespan and not our persecutors (see the context of this scriptural statement).

Certainly, "no one has power . . . over the day of his death" (Eccl 8:8). That is God's decision. Though remember that this same Preacher also points out that regarding that death, God has indicated a specific period that is the most appropriate. "For everything there is a season, and a time for every matter under heaven: a time to be born, and a time to die" (Eccl 3:1–2). Old age is the appropriate time for dying. This explains Hezekiah's lament, "I am consigned to the gates of Sheol for *the rest* of my years" (Isa 38:10). This is not a fatalistic expression. Hezekiah apparently did not think his time to die had yet arrived. Nor did the wise Preacher see such a fate above Yahweh, as we see from his remarkable question: "Why should you die *before your time*?" (Eccl 7:17). Such a thing can happen, according to Holy Scripture!

Proverbs teaches us as well that, up to a certain point, those with understanding can escape such a premature death and postpone their burial. The book speaks frequently about "turning away" death (cf. Prov 13:14; 14:27; 21:16). In Prov 15:24 we read very clearly, "The path of life leads upward for the prudent, that he may turn away from Sheol beneath." Regrettably, many do not take this wisdom to heart, and they *needlessly* die a premature death. If they had feared Yahweh, they would not have died "before their time," but "at a ripe old age." Instead, they pass away before that appropriate "time to die" has dawned in their life.

We will mention some examples of that.

3. *They could have lived longer.*

We need not think in this connection first of all of men like Saul, Ahithophel, and Judas, who took their own lives, for a person can sin fatally in so many ways. We must restrict ourselves to only a few examples. If you want, you can expand the list yourself in various ways.

Revolution devours its own children

Recall the clever prince Absalom! He is a striking example of someone who died "before his time." Eventually he became the victim of his own rebellion against his father, King David (2 Sam 15–19). Absalom is not the only victim of a revolution whom Scripture mentions. Sheba, Prince Adonijah, and Shimei owed their premature deaths to the same evil (2 Sam 20; 1 Kgs 2). The Northern Kingdom was especially plagued with revolutions. One general after another murdered the king and seized his throne. Revolutionaries like Zimri and Pekah fell victim to the sword after their regicide (1 Kgs 16; 2 Kgs 15). Surely such revolutions cost the lives of bystanders.

Wise Israelites warned people about this lethally dangerous evil, and in so doing, they provided life-extending advice, advice that is relevant to our own day. In many countries, anyone who stays away for God's sake from revolutionary demonstrations can avoid the lethal machine gun bullets of the police and thereby postpone his burial (Rom 13:1–7). Here are some pieces of advice whereby we can extend our lifespan:

> The terror of a king is like the growling of a lion;
> whoever provokes him to anger forfeits his life. (Prov 20:2)

> My son, fear the LORD and the king,
> and do not join with those who do otherwise,
> for disaster will arise suddenly from them,
> and who knows the ruin that will come from them both?
> (Prov 24:21–22)

Sexual sins

Prince Amnon, a son of David, violated his half-sister, Tamar. As a result of that folly, he was murdered by her brother Absalom (2 Sam 13). So David had three sons who could have lived longer if only they had kept God's commandments: Amnon, Absalom, and Adonijah. In the same way today, various extramarital love relationships can lead someone to find his premature end; the newspaper supplies examples almost every day. But, here as well, one can extend his life if he fears the Lord. God forbids extramarital sexual relationships, and whoever obeys him in this regard stays protected against the lethal shot or deadly knife of the jealous third party: "For jealousy makes a man furious, and he will not spare when he takes revenge" (Prov 6:34).

Drunkenness

The wisdom that the fear of the Lord supplies a person can extend his life by protecting him from the lethal consequences that often accompany drunkenness. Here we will omit mention of how alcohol abuse can undermine our health (we will say more about this in connection with Prov 3:7 and 23:29–35). But how many people meet a premature end in connection with drunken quarrels or drunk driving, each of which has well-known lethal consequences?

You may well think of such things when you consider proverbs like these:

> The fear of the Lord prolongs life,
>   but the years of the wicked will be short. (10:27)

> Whoever is steadfast in righteousness will live,
>   but he who pursues evil will die. (11:19)

> The light of the righteous rejoices,
>   but the lamp of the wicked will be put out. (13:9)

Capital punishment

In the Torah, Yahweh stipulated capital punishment for an assortment of crimes, such as murder, kidnapping, serious sacrilege against God and his covenant, crimes against parents, adultery, various forms of bloodshed, sodomy, and bestiality (cf. Exod 21–22; Lev 20, 24; Num 15, 25, 35; Deut

19, 22, 24). Anyone who loved God and did not commit such evil thereby escaped capital punishment for these wrongdoings. This is but one more illustration of the manner in which the wisdom of fearing the LORD could extend a person's life. In fact, was it not the case that for centuries capital punishment for murder and manslaughter was properly enforced in Europe and America? But surely no one who served God ended up on the gallows or in the electric chair because of these crimes.

You may well think of such things when you read these proverbs:

> The path of life leads upward for the prudent,
>   that he may turn away from Sheol beneath. (15:24)

> Gray hair is a crown of glory;
>   it is gained in a righteous life. (16:31)

> Whoever keeps the commandment keeps his life;
>   he who despises his ways will die. (19:16)

> If one curses his father or his mother,
>   his lamp will be put out in utter darkness. (20:20)

> If one curses his father or his mother,
>   his lamp will be put out in utter darkness. (21:16)

A sensitive subject

Regrettably, pious children of God also die, people who did not "live out half their days" (Ps 55:24). The son of Jeroboam died young, and Scripture says specifically about him that he was the only one in Jeroboam's house in whom Yahweh, the God of Israel, found something good (1 Kgs 14:13). Godly Israelites were tormented with the riddle of the prosperity and long lifespans of the wicked (Ps 37, 73). So we are indeed discussing a sensitive subject.

Especially with a view to those who mourn for the *godly* whom God has taken out of this life while they were young, we have pointed earlier to the fact that here Solomon is teaching in the form of *mashals*. Statements in this genre shed light on the rule without mentioning the exceptions. But even though such exceptions do exist, they do not vitiate the rule that *in many cases* the service of the LORD can protect us from a premature burial.

"There is *a time* to die," namely, old age. Wisdom has extended the lives of many to that period. Folly has robbed many of their old age. Precisely when God in his inscrutable wisdom does not follow this rule, such a premature death affects us all the more painfully. At that point may he supply us with the grace to bow under his hand and to trust in his goodness and wisdom, which infinitely surpasses our own.

2. WISDOM MAKES YOU SYMPATHETIC TO GOD AND OTHERS (PROV 3:3–4)

Who does not like to receive appreciation? Who does not like to be loved? The feeling of being ignored, unwelcome, or inferior can seriously undermine our happiness in life. Every person wants to be attractive in a particular way. But how? "Improve your looks, and that will make you attractive," say the clothing and cosmetics advertisers. Followers of Jesus Christ, however, must not seek their strength in outward adornment, but pursue piety and good works (1 Tim 2:9–10). That is a better way and on that pathway Solomon places the prospect of the approval of God and people (Prov 3–4).

> Let not steadfast love and faithfulness forsake you;
> > bind them around your neck;
> > write them on the tablet of your heart.
> So you will find favor and good success
> > in the sight of God and man.

In Scripture, love and faithfulness are genuinely *covenant words*. They always have the ring and tone of fellowship, whether between God and humans, or between a person and his neighbor, but always in one or the other relationship. You cannot capture both of these words with two equivalent English words. Older Bible versions speak of lovingkindness or benevolence and mercy rather than love, but you could easily render the Hebrew with loyalty or solidarity. Here especially, Scripture is not making an appeal to some vague, humanistic humanitarianism, where everyone follows what feels good, but is encouraging us to obey the central commandment: "You shall love the Lord your God with all your heart and with all your soul and with all your mind. This is the great and first commandment. And a second is like it: You shall love your neighbor as yourself. On these two commandments depend all the Law and the Prophets" (Matt 22:37–40).

By nature, however, this commandment appeals so little to us that we risk the danger that love and faithfulness do indeed "forsake" us. They simply forget us! This explains the crass encouragement: bind them as a cord around your neck (in Israel this was worn by men as well; cf. Gen 28:18; Song 8:6). Did the name "Anakim" perhaps mean "the people of the necklaces"? In that case, people needed to keep that in mind. Even more strongly, write them upon the tablets (we would say, notepad) of your heart, for everything we do proceeds from there (Prov 4:23). Let your heart be ruled by love, and everything you do will be dominated by love.

Then God and others will love you, and see in you someone "*with good understanding*." At least as a rule, for here too we are dealing with a *mashal* that, as usual, does not mention the exceptions. Paul writes, "*If possible*, so far as it depends on you, live peaceably with all" (Rom 12:18). "Indeed, all who desire to live a godly life in Christ Jesus *will be persecuted*" (2 Tim 3:12). But this is not to deny that with the proverb cited above, Solomon is teaching a rule that many children of God have seen operate in their own lives, people like Joseph, Samuel, and Dorcas.

Joseph had inscribed on his heart, "I must be loving, loyal, and benevolent in my interactions. Not haphazardly, but continually." That is what he practiced. Although Potiphar's wife tried "day in and day out" to seduce him, he refused any kind of sexual contact with her, with the words, "Behold, because of me my master has no concern about anything in the house, . . . nor has he kept back anything from me except you, because you are his wife. How then can I do this great wickedness and sin against God?" (Gen 39:8–10). By means of this attitude of "love and faithfulness," the slave Joseph had earned the affection and approval of his master. Even more importantly, he has acquired God's affection and approval, for God showed to Joseph reciprocal steadfast love "and gave him favor in the sight of the keeper of the prison" (Gen 39:21–23).

As a small boy Samuel lived in the corrupt town of Shiloh, but he practiced what his mother had taught him. He loved Yahweh and showed deep respect for him. And then God and others loved him more and more: "Now the boy Samuel continued to grow both in stature and in favor with the Lord and also with man" (1 Sam 2:26). In the same way, a school child can be viewed by God with increasing pleasure if such a child demonstrates "love and faithfulness" in his or her small corner.

Dorcas's Christian love also came to expression in benevolence. When she had died, the widows showed Peter the garments with which Dorcas had shown her "love and faithfulness" (cf. 1 Pet 3:3–6). With these kindnesses she had captured the heart of the church in Joppa (Acts 9:36–39). In so doing, she was following her Master, who had supplied the most beautiful example of this proverb: "And Jesus increased in wisdom and in stature and in favor with God and man" (Luke 2:52). (We find additional examples in Eccl 10:12; Dan 1:9; 3:30; and Acts 2:47.)

Here are similar proverbs:

What is desired in a man is steadfast love,
    and a poor man is better than a liar. (19:22)

He who loves purity of heart,
    and whose speech is gracious, will have the king as his friend. (22:11)

3. WISDOM LEADS TO THE LEAST AMOUNT OF MISERY IN THIS WORLD (PROV 3:5–6)

God's people possess in Holy Scripture an immeasurable wealth of divine insight regarding the real condition of things in God's creation. But from paradise onward, Satan has been putting everything in the service of making God out to be a liar, and of seducing people to distrust God's Word and to overturn his insights. In so doing, he is sowing the seed of what Groen van Prinsterer called "Unbelief and Revolution." Satan is the arch-revolutionary, the arch-disrupter of everything that God has revealed. Time and again, his ideas invaded God's church so that, there as well, people began to live according to unbelieving insights and deceptive notions regarding the condition of things in God's creation.

Faithfully and graciously, however, God always preserved a remnant of believers, both in Israel and in Christianity. They have constituted the anti-revolutionary movement in church history and world history. Israel's wise men also belonged to this movement. They described the only adequate means for countering revolution, as we read in Prov 3:5–6:

> Trust in the LORD with all your heart,
>   and do not lean on your own understanding.
> In all your ways acknowledge him,
>   and he will make straight your paths.

How many contemporary Christians do precisely the opposite? They do not trust in God and they lean on their own understanding. Whether this involves religion or performing justice, having children and nurturing them, spending money or ruling a nation, clothing or pursuing science, everywhere we meet among such Christians the autonomous person (2 Thess 2:5–6) with the "I'll do as I please" attitude.

That is what people in Calvinist circles understand by *revolution*. This word describes not only a political and civil overthrow, like the French Revolution of 1789, when countless citizens were beheaded at the guillotine. No, from of old, revolution has been understood among Calvinists to refer to "the reversal of attitudes of thought and disposition manifested throughout all of Christian living." At its deepest, revolution is rebellion against God. It is doing exactly what Solomon is forbidding here: leaning on our own understanding. But revolution teaches: You yourself need to be ruler! God's Word teaches us: Holy Scripture stands as the truth above human understanding. But revolution teaches: human understanding stands above God's Word.

Groen van Prinsterer characterized revolution this way:

> The Revolution ought to be viewed in the context of world history. Its significance for Christendom equals that of the Reformation, but then in reverse. The Reformation rescued Europe from superstition; the Revolution has flung the civilized world into an abyss of unbelief. Like the Reformation, the Revolution touches every field of action and learning. In the days of the Reformation the principle was submission to God; in these days it is a revolt against God.[1]

In our own countries throughout the West, this means rebellion against the God and Father of our Lord Jesus Christ, who has shown his grace and reconciliation virtually nowhere in the world as richly as he has in those countries, through the proclamation of his Word and the establishment and preservation of his church.

This revolution encompasses, as we said, our entire life. For just as God in his Word requisitions for his service the entire life of his people, so, too, revolution draws the entirety of human living away from obedience to God. And this ancient paradise revolution appears during recent centuries to be gaining in strength among Christianized nations. "Let us burst their bonds apart!" (Ps 2:3). That is gradually becoming the device employed by baptized Christians, who perhaps for centuries have been elevated by God's Spirit as high as heaven itself, but who are now throwing off the bonds of God's covenant and the yoke of his commandments.

To their own immeasurable unhappiness!

For the very best insight that he supplies in his Word—regarding good and evil, reconciliation and sanctification, justice and injustice, money and possessions, wisdom and discipline, young people and old people, working and resting, love and loyalty, and everything else—is all directed to *our wellbeing*. Everything that God holds out before us is good for us. But everything that Satan places before us to delude us drives the world to the abyss, puts the pry bar beneath church and state, leads society to dissolution, loosens the bonds of marriage and family, takes the sword from the government,

---

1. Van Prinsterer, *Unbelief and Revolution*, 44.

and severs jurisprudence from its root. As Groen van Prinsterer put it, "That is why there rages again today one universal war in church, state, and the world of learning, one holy battle over the supreme question: to submit unconditionally to the law of God, or not."[2]

You can find the only adequate means against this comprehensive revolution in the proverb cited above, which can be summarized this way: *trust in God; do not lean on your own insight; acknowledge him in all your ways.* The three commands boil down to the same. To acknowledge Yahweh is to trust in him, to subject your own insights to his Word. To love him is to show holy reverence for him and to live humbly with him. Then we will no longer lean on our own rebellious insights regarding the reality of God's creation, but then we will believe with our whole heart that God's Word provides us with the correct insights about that reality.

For us, then, all knowledge of God's entire creation is in the first place a matter of faith or trust in God (and all revolutionary insights belonging to the children of this world are a matter of deep suspicion). In this way, in literally every area of life, we are anti-revolutionary in the deep and broad sense of the word: we are principled opponents of all rebellion against God. For the believing practitioner of science, even scientific knowledge is never autonomous, not even neutral, but a matter of believing subjection to the authority of the sovereign God.

On this point as well, Solomon saw a reward connected to the fear of the LORD: "*and he will make straight your paths*." That is a genuinely ancient Near Eastern metaphor. For in those regions they were unfamiliar with those smooth paths we know. Rather, their paths could be strewn with stones, so that they had far greater difficulty walking than we do today with our sidewalks. To smooth a path meant, then, to clear away the stones to make it passable. This is what God is promising here: If you acknowledge me in all your paths, then I will see to it that you will be able to walk much more easily.

Here again you have a variation on the basic theme of Proverbs: one who keeps God's commandment has the least misery in this miserable life. In this way, you contend against revolution in the broader sense of the word as it was used by Groen van Prinsterer, in your personal life and further in your family, church, state, and society. We need only to listen to our Creator, keeping his commandments and ordinances in Scripture and creation. Thereby paradise does not yet descend to earth, but this is certainly the best life attitude that provides the least amount of misery in our sinful world. This includes the area of our health, as the next proverb teaches us.

---

2. Van Prinsterer, *Unbelief and Revolution*, 44.

4. WISDOM PROMOTES YOUR HEALTH (PROV 3:7–8)

Have you ever pondered the claim that fearing God is also healthy for us? That it is good for one's heart and blood vessels, and beneficial for one's stomach and nerves? Or do you automatically think, in connection with the fear of the LORD, of religious things (praying, reading the Bible, going to church)? Then it is good that in his Instruction Manual for Proverbs, Solomon draws our attention to this fruit of wisdom as well. A life of faith lived according to God's commandment can especially benefit us *also physically*.

> Be not wise in your own eyes;
>   fear the LORD, and turn away from evil.
> It will be healing to your flesh
>   and refreshment to your bones. (Prov 3:7–8)

1. *To prevent misunderstanding*

This subject is just as sensitive as claiming that the fear of the LORD can extend your life (Prov 3:1–2). Just as with that proverb, here as well the question arises: Does this always happen? Do faith in God and good health go hand in hand *always* and *for everyone*? The answer must be: Regrettably not! Many godly people died much too young, at least according to our reckoning. Does this mean, then, that they have not feared God? This question could be torturous for believers who are sick. In order to protect them from that, let's consider the following.

Some "faith healers" dare to claim that sick people were not healed because they did not have true faith. Scripture speaks a different language. It testifies of Job, "That man was blameless and upright, one who feared God and turned away from evil" (Job 1:1). So there you find someone who did what the proverb cited above commands: "Fear Yahweh and turn away from evil," but despite that, he sat covered with sores from head to toe (Job 2:7–8). The Lord Jesus said about the man born blind, "It was not that this man sinned, or his parents" (John 9:3). Yet from his birth, this man had not been able to see anything. These examples could be multiplied easily. But the experiences of Job and the man born blind can protect those who are chronically ill and who love God uprightly in the face of this oppressive question: "I have been sick for so long; do I really believe God?"

They can be protected from this all the more if we recall once again the manner in which we are being taught here, namely, *in the form of a mashal*. We cannot repeat this in connection with every proverb, but in connection with this sensitive subject we want to recall what we wrote earlier about the somewhat blunt expression of a *mashal*. Of course Solomon was also acquainted with people who suffered, like Job and the man born blind. But he omitted mention of such tragic situations (for which God has given us the book of Job). Solomon wanted to point out the truth that the fear of the Lord is beneficial for our health as well. In so doing, he provides a rule whose truth many have experienced firsthand. But in so doing, he did not want to press the conclusion upon those who are an exception, which suggests that "I am sick and *therefore* I have not feared God." Familiarity with the typical form of a proverb can protect ailing believers from drawing that conclusion.

Moreover, we live in a broken world, in which the following applies also to the righteous: "You are dust, and to dust you shall return" (Gen 3:19). God implements this universal human judgment every day, in part by using various illnesses as causes of death. Illnesses will indeed continue to bring people to the grave until the last day, including God's own children.

2. Health and obedience

Without detracting at all from the foregoing, God's Word does teach us, on the other hand, that there is some causal connection between the fear of the Lord and our health, or between sin and sickness.

Already in the Torah, Yahweh taught that the degree of Israel's national health would depend on the measure of their obedience to God's commands. Yahweh *promised*, "If you will diligently listen to the voice of the Lord your God, and do that which is right in his eyes, and give ear to his commandments and keep all his statutes, I will put none of the diseases on you that I put on the Egyptians, for I am the Lord, your healer" (Exod 15:26).[3] But he *threatened* all kinds of bad and chronic illnesses in case Israel did not keep God's commandments and ordinances (cf. Lev 26:25; Deut 28:20–21, 27, 35, 60). Take careful note that Yahweh promised and threatened these things to Israel *as a people*. In that context he talked about pestilence (all kinds of epidemics?), tuberculosis, fever, inflammation, incurable Egyptian sores, boils, rashes, madness, blindness, and dementia. In so doing, Yahweh was reminding his people in advance that he possessed the power to establish a causal connection between the rejection of Yahweh and sickness, or between the people's obedience and the people's health.

Did not Christianity discover the truth of the foregoing threat when covenant-forsaking Europe was afflicted with cholera and plagues? During the black death of 1348–1351, entire regions were depopulated. Everywhere

---

3. Vonk, *Exodus*, 79–80.

people found a so-called emptied homestead: an entire farming family had died, and the cattle were wandering about without provision. Ships whose mariners had died floated without steerage. Three-fifths of the Dutch population died. Nijmegen and Zwolle were dead cities. In the Frisian monasteries monks died by the hundreds. Groen van Prinsterer speaks often in his survey of the history of our fatherland, in connection with similar catastrophes, of *God's judgments*. As believers, should we not view the increase of tuberculosis, inflammation, infections, boils, and scabies during the war years of 1940–1945 in this light? God continues to be able, in connection with ruling his people, to connect sin with sickness, and obedience with health.

In fact, does not sin as such already endanger our health?

This brings us back to Proverbs.

3. *Health and wisdom*

Proverbs, which is a textbook about fearing Yahweh, is also occupied with the connection between sin and sickness. Naturally we should not expect here any scientific perspectives setting forth concepts that function in modern medicine. Holy Scripture is not a book of science—it transcends science—and those who wrote the proverbs were not doctors but sages who supplied those life lessons for God-fearers. We can still learn a lot from them, lessons that are salutary for our own health. Concerning many a proverb, the modern doctor will have to admit: This is excellent advice for your health!

For what does someone who fears God do? Such a person is so wise as to honor the ordinances that God has revealed in Scripture and in nature. Those ordinances are good for us as well, for they were instituted by the God of life, who likes nothing better than to grant life to his people. How often do we not read in the Torah that he gave Israel his ordinances "that you may live, and that it may go well with you" (Deut 5:33; cf. 4:1; 8:1; 16:20; 30:16, 19; Lev 18:5)? In saying this, he was referring not only to what we are accustomed to calling "spiritual life" but to the entirety of Israelite human life, including their health.[4]

This claim should not surprise us. Would the God and Father who himself has made us to be physical beings not be interested in our bodily well-being? After all, he promises us "the redemption of our bodies" (Rom 8:23; cf. v. 11; 1 Cor 15:35–49; Phil 3:21). As long as this remains a wonderful but unrealized expectation for the future, he teaches us in his Word what is the best lifestyle here and now for experiencing the least misery in this

---

4. See van Deursen, *Psalms I*, 32–34.

broken world. This includes the area of our health. You can count on it that his ordinances in Scripture and in nature are salutary! Would the one who himself formed us and blew into our nostrils the breath of life (Gen 2:7) not know best what is good and bad for our heart and nervous system, our stomach and intestines, our physical strength and nightly sleep?

This is what Solomon meant when he taught, "Fear the LORD, and turn away from evil. It will be healing to your flesh and refreshment to your bones" (Prov 3:7–8). The same goes for when he called his own commandments "life to those who find them, and healing to all their flesh" (Prov 4:22). Those who composed these proverbs saw sharply that evil practices also do evil to a person. Sin can make a person sick, just as avoiding evil can be medicine for someone's flesh (heart and blood vessels, nervous system and intestines, etc.). Anyone who does not stubbornly oppose God's ordinances but arranges his life in faith according to them, as he walks this path, he can spare himself much misery in respect to his physical well-being.

Obeying God's law leads a person also into favorable conditions for his health. The man who in Prov 5:11 moans about his flesh and his body wasting away as a result of a sexually transmitted disease contracted through relations with a strange woman clearly had only himself to blame for his disease. (Here, then, is a case where it is indeed meaningful to ask: I am sick; is this perhaps the result of a particular sin?)

It would lead us too far afield to illustrate any further the connection between health and wisdom. Such reflection is presented in various ways in Prov 10–31. In those chapters, we encounter various proverbs that treat directly the connection between the fear of Yahweh and our health. "A tranquil heart gives life to the flesh, but envy makes the bones rot" (Prov 14:30) is one of them. Others do not speak directly about this connection, although their counsel includes the promotion of our health. In this context we might think about those proverbs that warn against excessive use of alcohol, and also of words that recommend discipline. After all, an undisciplined life can bring injury to our health in various ways.

We cannot discuss every proverb, and with those that we do discuss, we cannot always focus attention on this aspect of wisdom. We will do so in connection with Prov 11:17, 12:25, 13:12, 14:30, 15:13, 15:15, 15:17, 16:24, 17:22, 18:1, 19:11, 25:16, and 29:15. In any case, Solomon has focused our attention on this important aspect of wisdom. You can take note of this for yourself in connection with those proverbs that we are unable to discuss. For this is true of the fear of the LORD in all its aspects: it can benefit your health as well!

5. WISDOM INCREASES YOUR POSSESSIONS (PROV 3:9–10)

The fear of the Lord also entails a rich reward with regard to our material wealth. This is the fifth reason why Prov 3 urges us to be so wise as to fear Yahweh. Earlier Moses had pointed to the rain that Yahweh had promised to Israel if they would keep his commandments: "Blessed shall you be in the city, and blessed shall you be in the field. . . . Blessed shall be your basket and your kneading bowl. . . . The Lord will command the blessing on you in your barns and in all that you undertake . . . [so that] you shall lend to many nations, but you shall not borrow" (Deut 28:1–12; cf. Lev 26:3–13). The prophets, too, from Joshua to Malachi, proclaimed that God is the one who can bestow or withhold wealth. He can send rain, so that the earth yields its fruit; but he can also send the "devourers" (Mal 3:11), which destroy the harvest (or devour the value of the money for which it is sold).

The echo of this instruction of Moses and the prophets reverberates in Proverbs. This book, too, contains wholesome wisdom for economic life, and is the ABC of that life: fear the Lord when you spend your money. Proverbs 3:9–10 stands at the head of all the financial wisdom, offering this counsel: *Give to Yahweh and you will receive!* This is the fundamental principle for prudent use of money and possessions. In the kingdom of God, giving is the path to getting, and sharing is the path to receiving more.

> Honor the Lord with your wealth
>   and with the firstfruits of all your produce;
> then your barns will be filled with plenty,
>   and your vats will be bursting with wine.

It was harvest time. The Israelite had once again brought in his new wheat and barley. The grapes and olives had been picked, calves and lambs were again romping in the meadow, and once more the cellar held a supply for eating and drinking that would last several months. What was supposed to happen now? He was to acknowledge the rights of Yahweh! To do that, the Israelite was to take a month's worth of all his produce—wheat, barley, grapes, and olives—and bring this to the nearest sanctuary, where the priest serving for that month had to take it from him and put it before the altar of Yahweh. Then the farmer was supposed to declare, "A wandering Aramean was my father. And he went down into Egypt and sojourned there, few in number, and there he became a nation, great, mighty, and populous. . . . And he brought us into this place and gave us this land, a land flowing with milk and honey. And behold, now I bring the first of the fruit of the ground, which you, O Lord, have given me" (Deut 26:5, 9–10; see the whole passage at vv. 1–11).

In the Torah, this sacrificing of firstfruits is discussed seven times as a divine ordinance for Israel. This kind of farmer appeared before Yahweh to offer his month's worth of harvest, not with a little present that he could have just as easily kept for himself, and he appeared at the sanctuary to acknowledge Yahweh's *right* as Israel's God and Savior. "The land is mine," Yahweh had stated clearly (Lev 25:23). This included the entire harvest! That is what the Israelite was acknowledging with his firstfruits: "I am coming before you with *one month's* harvest, but in fact *the entire harvest* is yours. You are the landowner, my Suzerain, to whom I owe tribute." Yahweh had an automatic right to those firstfruits. First, because he was Israel's God, but even more because he was Israel's Deliverer. That was evident from the farmer's verbal confession. At the foundation of all his prosperity was that matchless deliverance from Egypt. Without Yahweh's intervention, Israel would have been exterminated.

This was the ABC of the Torah for Israel's economic life: First acknowledge the rights of Yahweh! The wise men echoed that: "*Honor Yahweh with your possessions,*" and especially with "*the firstfruits of all your earnings.*" Instead of "firstfruits" you could just as easily read: the first, the best, the fattest of all your wealth or produce. Scripture speaks in this connection about the tithe. Whether this was always ten percent is a different question. In any case, it involved *the best portion* of someone's capacity and what one initially set aside before thinking about other payments. This was because Yahweh had a right to that, and because *his* right to that preceded the rights of anyone else.

When, in the days of Malachi, Israel neglected to pay Yahweh's tithe, the prophet asked, "Will man rob God?" And then Yahweh challenged his people, "Bring the full tithe into the storehouse. . . . And thereby put me to the test . . . if I will not open the windows of heaven for you . . . [so that] your vine in the field shall not fail to bear" (Mal 3:8–11). That was a test *of faith* by means of a test *of God*! Proverbs 3:10 gives us the same promise: "Then your barns will be filled with plenty, and your vats will be bursting with wine."

Nowadays we no long live under the Horeb covenant with its altars, priests, and prescribed firstfruits. This does not mean, however, that the measuring cup of obedience has been downsized. On the contrary, it has been enlarged! If God expected from Israel their firstfruits, the best of their capacities, then he is asking from us an even deeper acknowledgement of that right (Matt 5:20; 23:23). "But seek first his kingdom," the Lord Jesus said (Matt 6:33). To that belongs also the acknowledgement of God's kingship over all our possessions. One does not perform one's duty then by giving a tip, but by giving him the *first*, the *best*, the *fattest* of one's income, because the earth and its fullness belong to him (Ps 24:1). This is also because we can confess, "My father was a pagan, who lived in fear of thunderstorms and omens. But you have called us by your Word and Spirit out of that pagan darkness into your wonderful light (cf. 1 Pet 2:9). Therefore the best of what I possess belongs to you. For it all comes from you and we are giving it to you from your hand (cf. 1 Chr 19:14)."

With this, the Instruction Manual for Proverbs has given us to see the fundamental principle of its economic and financial wisdom. *"First acknowledge the rights of Yahweh, then you will behold something wonderful!"* From this principle proceed all the proverbs about caring for the poor and spending our money. Anyone who follows this wisdom will experience that this is the surest and safest method to obtain wealth. And it is the best way to turn a little into a lot.

6. WISDOM TEACHES ONE TO BOW UNDER GOD'S DISCIPLINE (PROV 3:11–12)

God-fearing life-wisdom also includes the need for people to adopt the proper attitude toward the discipline that God sends to us throughout our entire life. Happily, this pertains once again to those who fear God! Such a man or woman knows that they should bow humbly under God's discipline and chastisement. They believe that the love of their heavenly Father is the overtone and that God is not wishing to pester them with his discipline, but to save them for his kingdom. This is the sixth reason why Solomon counsels us in Prov 3 to fear Yahweh, as we learn from verses 11–12.

> My son, do not despise the LORD's discipline
> or be weary of his reproof,
> for the LORD reproves him whom he loves,
> as a father the son in whom he delights.

1. *The discipline of Yahweh*

When God places a person under his discipline, what is he actually doing? We have met many Christians who think exclusively of *chastisement*. They understand this to refer to all the suffering that a person bears throughout life. But is that really correct? Is God's discipline entirely equivalent to chastisement? And does all suffering in the lives of God's children bear the character of paternal punishment, so that in connection with all their distress and sorrow they must sigh, "Ah, does not the Lord chastise those whom he loves?" Occasionally in that context we hear the undertone "at least now I know that he loves me." Must we talk about God's discipline this way? To us this seems less than correct.

For starters, the word *discipline* includes more than just chastisement or punishment. The book of Proverbs itself is designed, among other things, "for attaining wisdom and discipline" (Prov 1:1 NIV). Clearly we should not think in that connection merely of a rod and a physical blow, for one doesn't administer that by means of a written document. Those who composed the proverbs understood by discipline the *authoritative guidance* that God gives us in various ways. For that, he uses initially our God-fearing parents, and later various teachers. Through them God causes us to be *instructed* initially in a friendly manner. In that context, he does not entirely exclude our own understanding and insight, but constantly includes it. Proverbs continually tells us why this is good and that is evil.

Included in the "discipline of Yahweh" is also *the admonition* if we proceed against his leading and if we do not take to heart his *correction*. This too comes by means of his Word and from those who seek to bind this upon our heart. If we don't listen to that or if we fall into serious evil, then God will have us *chastised*. All of this—discipline, admonition, correction, and chastisement—is what Proverbs has in view when it talks about *"the discipline of Yahweh."*

"My son, do not despise those!" Solomon says in the proverb cited above. Let us read it, however, in its context. It is found in Prov 1–9, the Instruction Manual for Proverbs. And that Instruction Manual points out, as we have already observed, the great blessing that the wisdom of *this book* in particular (Prov 10–31) can extend. So then, should we not think, in connection with "the discipline of Yahweh" in Prov 3:11, first of all of the discipline, the admonitions, and corrections in Proverbs itself?

What a powerful piece of divine discipline this book contains!

But one must be willing to bow before that! Does a person have a weakness for strong drink? Then let him not turn away in disgust when Proverbs warns him about excessive use of wine. Is another person easily seduced by a strange woman? Then let him not shrug his shoulders when Prov 5–7 describes the destruction that one can bring into his life through adultery. All of that, too, is the discipline of Yahweh! Administered not first as chastisement, but first through instruction and warning. Blessed is the one who fears the LORD and thereby is so wise as to suffice with Yahweh's discipline-through-words.

But if God's people, or a single member of his people, do not *listen* to his discipline-through-words, then God causes them to *feel* it. Then he supplements his discipline-through-words with a tangible chastisement. The only question is what we must understand by that. Fatherly discipline? Or can one say, somewhat inappropriately, "The Lord chastises those whom he loves?" Here again proper distinctions are necessary and illuminating.

2. *Not all suffering is God's chastisement.*

All suffering on earth is a result of sin (cf. Gen 3:16–19), but all the results of sin must not serve as personal punishment. There is also a kind of suffering "without cause" (cf. Ps 25:3; 35:7), which happens not because we have forsaken God, but precisely because we are holding fast to him. Psalm 44 calls that suffering *"for your sake"* (v. 22). Peter talks about suffering not as an evildoer but "for righteousness' sake" (1 Pet 3:14; 4:15–16). The Lord Jesus called that kind of suffering "taking up one's cross" (cf. Matt 16:24; John 15:18; 16:33). For that reason alone, people cannot claim that all suffering signifies fatherly chastisement on account of our sin.

Furthermore, Scripture also knows of suffering whereby God is not so much punishing our sins as he is testing our faith, in order to purify us (Ps 66:10–12; 119:67; Jas 1:2–4; 1:12–18; 1 Pet 1:6–9). About the man born blind, the Lord Jesus said, "It was not that this man sinned, or his parents, but that the works of God might be displayed in him" (John 9:3). In this way, the suffering of Job served the honor of God (Job 1:9–12). Through this suffering, Yahweh was vindicated over against Satan. In all such suffering, without cause, for the righteousness and honor of God, our patience, forbearance, and fortitude are fitting responses. At that point, God's power is perfected in our weakness (cf. 2 Cor 12:9). One day all this suffering will receive a just reward (Jas 5:7–11; Rom 8:17).

There is one more reason why we would not dare to call all suffering a fatherly chastisement. Here Solomon is comparing God's manner of action with that of an earthly father. Both apply chastisement in the context of nurturing their children, but then surely there must be a *reason* to do so, or not? What normal father administers physical discipline to his child without reason? Then people may not claim that our heavenly Father is doing so, either. When he disciplines his people or his children, he always does so *on account of their sins* (cf. Lev 26:14–46; Deut 28:15; and throughout the prophetic books). Here, too, in connection with the proverb under discussion (3:11), we are dealing with *chastisement on account of sin*. That is clearly evident from the additional explanation that Heb 12:4–11 provides.

Scripture contains many examples of such chastisements. All the prophetic books, from Joshua through Malachi, show us the severe blows with which Yahweh chastised his unruly people. The arrival of the new covenant has altered nothing in that regard. Paul indeed saw a cause behind the many cases of death in the church of Corinth (1 Cor 11:30). God also chastises his children individually. The aged Miriam became a leper because she sought to push Moses out of leadership (Num 12). Moses himself was not permitted to enter the promised land because he had not sanctified Yahweh (Num 20). David lost four sons and observed adultery on the part of three of them because he had killed Uriah and had committed adultery with Uriah's wife (2 Sam 12). In Ps 6 he prays for healing from his sickness, in which he had observed God's chastisement (v. 1). Jeroboam received a withered hand because he had made Israel to sin (1 Kgs 13).

3. *Don't despise, but let yourself be blessed.*

How then must we behave under God's hand of discipline and punishment? Not as Israel so often behaved. When Yahweh disciplined Israel for their sin, they sought to avoid any pain. Rather than humbling themselves under the mighty hand of God (1 Pet 5:6), they hardened themselves. People can react to God's chastisement in that way, too, by continuing to stand tall, refusing to be broken, refusing to acknowledge shame and humiliation, approving sin. Or people can resort to erudite logical ploys by taking refuge in the claim that the connection between sin and punishment is rather controversial, so that we should really be careful with that alleged connection. As though Amos 3:6 had not spoken clearly enough about this. In this way, humbling under the hand of God is absent, and God's chastisements are dubbed a "problem" about which we can theologize informally. In this way, we are not being "trained" by those chastisements (Heb 12:11), in order that we might bow penitently under God's hand and break with evil.

That is the goal to which Proverbs seeks to nurture its readers.

Those who followed Solomon's counsel always began by examining their way in times of unusual adversity, in order to see if there was any *cause* of their adversity. Job did that, but came to the conclusion: "With my hands, feet, knees, eyes, ears, and heart I have done what Yahweh commanded me and refrained from doing what he forbade me" (cf. Job 31). And the Spirit of God testifies that Job was speaking the truth (cf. Job 1). Those who suffer "without cause," or suffer "for God's sake," like the church of Ps 44, can muster the same confession: Why I am suffering, I do not know. Perhaps for God's honor or my faithfulness to him. The problem of this suffering I need not solve. But it is not on account of my unrighteousness, or because I have forsaken God (Ps 26).[5] How magnificent when God's suffering children are privileged to confess that!

It is also possible, however, that they are unable to say this. Then they will be able *to determine for themselves* whether particular difficulties have overtaken them as a fatherly chastisement. In this way David accepted a serious illness as divine chastisement (Ps 6:1; cf. Job 33:16–33). If we must come to that conclusion, then let Solomon's maxim show us the way: My son, it is my love that is disciplining you. Then may the fear of the Lord lead us not to despise the chastisement, but to accept it humbly, thankful that in his love God did not want us to stray from him. And thankful that we may believe "he disciplines us for our good, that we may share his holiness. For the moment all discipline seems painful rather than pleasant, but later it yields the peaceful fruit of righteousness to those who have been trained by it" (Heb 12:10–11). Righteousness, since once again we walk humbly with the Lord our God, and peaceful, because we have rediscovered peace with God.

7. WISDOM IS MORE VALUABLE THAN JEWELS (PROV 3:13–15)

Gnostic Christians pull up their nose with regard to earthly possessions, but Holy Scripture does not. Paul wrote, "Everything created by God is good, and nothing is to be rejected if it is received with thanksgiving, for it is made holy by the word of God and prayer" (1 Tim 4:4). God blessed Abraham, Isaac, and Jacob, and many other godly people with a wealth of earthly possessions (Prov 22:4). Anyone who thinks, however, that money and material possessions provide a person with supreme happiness is sadly mistaken. For people obtain supreme happiness when they have found wisdom, the saving knowledge of God and of his Christ, and when they live by his Word (Phil 3:8). In this respect, who can possibly talk from experience more extensively then the very wise Solomon? With all of his gold and silver, he knew very well:

> Blessed is the one who finds wisdom,
>   and the one who gets understanding,
> for the gain from her is better than gain from silver
>   and her profit better than gold.
> She is more precious than jewels,
>   and nothing you desire can compare with her. (Prov 3:13–15)

---

5. See van Deursen, *Psalms I*, 249–76.

Here Solomon presents us with a genuine beatitude: "Blessed are the wise in heart, for theirs is the greatest wealth!" It is the most expensive pearl in the world (cf. Matt 13:45–46). Whoever has it is far richer than a multimillionaire without it. Even for him, it is priceless. A Talmudic proverb goes like this: "If you lack wisdom, then what do you have? If you have wisdom, what do you lack?" Gold and silver, expensive chrysoprase or lazurite, mother-of-pearl and crystal sink in value to nothingness (see Job 28:15–19; cf. Prov 16:16: "How much better to get wisdom than gold! To get understanding is to be chosen rather than silver!").

This is the seventh reason why Prov 3 recommends reading this Bible book. Proverbs teaches you to fear the LORD and to submit to his wise government; that is more valuable for you than all the British crown jewels. Of course, one who has money can lend it out at interest, and with property one can make a profit. But no one obtains such immeasurable profits like the one who has found wisdom. Imagine the happiness of such a person! His capital yields immeasurable profit—in a word: Life (Prov 14:27; 19:23)!

8. WISDOM LENDS WEALTH AND HONOR (PROV 3:16)

Of course, the wise men had their eyes open for *the dangers* of wealth. They warn about that more than once (Prov 11:16; 14:20; 18:23; 23:4; 30:7–9; cf. Matt 19:23; 1 Tim 6:9). But in doing so they were not condemning *all possession* of earthly goods! On the contrary, in such earthly goods they could also see the blessing of Yahweh bestowed upon a person's God-pleasing conduct. Otherwise Solomon would not have put in the mouth of Lady Wisdom these words: "The reward for humility and fear of the LORD is riches and honor and life" (cf. Prov 22:4). Here in Prov 3:16 he makes a similar statement:

> Long life is in her right hand;
> in her left hand are riches and honor.

We have already seen, in connection with Prov 3:1–2, how the fear of the LORD can extend our life. We will not discuss that any further at this point. And in connection with Prov 3:9–10 we saw that this fear of the LORD can also increase our wealth. We want to make a few additional observations about this. We are limiting ourselves to two of the three aforementioned benefits: along the route of wisdom that comes through the fear of the LORD many people receive *wealth* and *honor*.

But how does this work? How can wisdom benefit materially the one who listens to it? In connection with Prov 3:9–10 we observed that wisdom levels the path for the *blessing* of Yahweh. To that we now add: it does this also through the *instruction* that it provides in Proverbs! Notice how much this book praises zeal and how much it denounces the sloth: "A slack hand causes poverty" (Prov 10:4). Sleeping during harvest time? Shameful (10:5)! "The slothful will be put to forced labor" (12:24). "Love not sleep, lest you come to poverty" (20:13; cf. 20:4; 21:5; 28:19). But "the hand of the diligent makes rich" (10:4); indeed, those hands will rule (12:24). For "in all toil there is profit" (14:23). All of this belongs to discerning conduct! Along this path God will often crown wisdom with wealth.

But we must not exaggerate this picture. It is true according to Prov 12:27 that "the diligent man will get precious wealth," but other proverbs talk of having "food to spare" and having "abundant food" (20:13 NIV; 28:19 NIV). Perhaps we could best describe the "wealth" of Prov 3:16 by saying that thanks to wisdom, a person has "a full stomach."

The Israelite sages attached great value to our human honor. "A good name is better than precious ointment" (Eccl 7:1). "A good name is to be chosen rather than great riches, and favor is better than silver or gold" (Prov 22:1). More than once, Proverbs mentions riches and honor in the same breath (3:16; 8:18; 22:4). Now it is true that the vanity of this dispensation includes the reality that the wise and discerning do not always strike it rich (Eccl 9:11). We cannot always be repeating this, but in connection with all the proverbs we must consider the unique mode of speaking in a *mashal*. Nevertheless, the exceptions do not invalidate the rule that along the path of God-fearing wisdom a person can also be *honored*. "The wise will inherit honor" (Prov 3:35; 4:8–9).

How does this happen? Wisdom adorns its possessors and places something like a halo atop their head (see our comments on Prov 1:9). "A man is commended according to his good sense" (Prov 12:8). "Good sense wins favor" (Prov 13:15). The fear of the LORD places a stamp on the entirety of one's conduct, however, and that total behavior can make a person honored in his surroundings. This is especially true of the most basic and fundamental virtue of God's children: their humility and modesty. "He who is lowly in spirit will obtain honor" (Prov 29:23). "Humility comes before honor" (Prov 15:33; cf. 18:12). Wisdom makes a person industrious, magnanimous, and communicative. These and other good qualities that wisdom fosters provide its possessors the respect of their surroundings (cf. Acts 2:47; 1 Tim 3:7).

Once again, we find an important clue that the Instruction Manual for Proverbs gives us: the wise counsels of this Bible book cost you no money. On the contrary, in addition to all the other advantages that it offers you, it can also help you to increase your wealth and enlarge your reputation.

9. WISDOM BESTOWS LOVELINESS AND PEACE (PROV 3:17)

To that aspect of wisdom, the Instruction Manual points in the ninth place. Concerning every counsel that Proverbs offers, one could ask: Does not this also advance loveliness and peace in our lives? The entire pattern of living that Proverbs prescribes—"all her ways"—causes us to behold God's loveliness and beautiful service (Ps 16:11; 27:4; 90:17). Solomon says it this way:

> Her ways are ways of pleasantness,
> and all her paths are peace. (Prov 3:17)

Take, for example, our tongues. A tongue that is used foolishly is "a restless evil, full of deadly poison" (Jas 3:8). It is a fortress of violence from which all kinds of calamity can come forth (Prov 10:11, 14). But when wisdom governs that tongue, it is a fountain of loveliness. What the meadow is for cattle, and what medicine is for a sick person, that is what a wise use of our capacity for speech is for our surroundings. In a phrase, it is "a fountain of life" (Prov 10:11; cf. 10:21; 12:18; 15:4; 16:24). When parents and children take to heart that wisdom of Proverbs regarding speaking and being silent, then they will enjoy nothing but a lovely family life where lovely peace rules.

In this way people can mine from Proverbs life lessons galore, rules that will lend to our living a glow and harmony. Think in this context of the God-fearing woman portrayed in Prov 31. What loveliness such a woman suffuses in her surroundings! Wisdom also makes a person long-suffering, so that one is not annoyed by every offense (19:11) and is honored by keeping aloof from strife (20:3). In this way as well, wisdom promotes peace and loveliness!

In short, in his Instruction Manual Solomon wants to draw our attention to this: the entire mode of living embodied in Proverbs is directed also toward *loveliness* and *peace*. Read this book from beginning to end once in terms of this aspect, and it will show you a hundredfold how lovely it is to fear God. (See our comments in connection with Prov 10:11 and 18:17 as well.)

10. WISDOM LETS YOU EAT FROM A TREE OF LIFE (PROV 3:18)

All the fruit trees in paradise were "good for eating," but the fruit of the tree of life must have possessed extraordinary nutritional value and healing power. God would have created those elements that would have enabled Adam and Eve to continue living had they eaten from them (Gen 3:22).[6]

---

6. Vonk, *Genesis*, 129–34.

To this best of all trees in the entire garden of Eden the writer compares wisdom. Whoever seeks and practices wisdom is picking, as it were, fruit from a tree of life (cf. Prov 11:30; 13:12; 15:4).

> She is a tree of life to those who lay hold of her;
> those who hold her fast are called blessed. (Prov 3:18)

But what must we understand here by the word *life*? We can learn this wonderfully from Moses in Deut 28 and 30:15-20. There we see that, in the language of Scripture, *life* includes more than simply "existence," or even something like what we call "spiritual life." For Moses, life was another word for *the good* or for God's blessing, and death was another word for *the evil* or God's curse (Deut 30:15, 19). And you can read in Deut 28 all that Moses understood to be included in "the good and in life." Of course, it included breathing, but it also included your spouse and your children, your cow and your donkey, your wheat and your olive trees, your basket and kneading bowl, your land and your freedom. An Israelite farmer was talking about "living" when his wife and children were healthy, olives were hanging from his trees, his wheat was waving in the breeze, when the rains fell on time, and when he with his boys could bring in the harvest without fear of invading bands of robbers.

In fact, *life* is then another word for *happiness*.

We continue to speak of life as long as a person is breathing, but an Israelite spoke of life only when he was enjoying the *values* of life. Proverbs 3 summarizes them in a list: to receive many days for enjoying the good (Prov 3:1; cf. Ps 34:12), enjoying affection and approval in the eyes of God and people (v. 4), walking the right paths (v. 6), enjoying good health (v. 8), having full cupboards and vats (v. 9), enjoying peace (v. 17), honor (v. 16), security (v. 23), and intimate interaction with Yahweh (v. 32). We should have these things in mind when we meet the word *life* in Proverbs more than forty times. At those points the wise men were thinking of the happy life of a godly Israelite, as he lived it each day with his entire house under the blessing and lovingkindness of Yahweh.

This good life—naturally, to the degree that it can still be good on this accursed earth—you can pluck from the tree of life known as wisdom. With this, Prov 3:18 is in fact summarizing in two lines the main theme and primary intention of all of Prov 1-9, indeed, of this entire Bible book. Choose life by being so wise as to observe Yahweh's ordinances (cf. Deut 30:19-20). That is what the Instruction Manual for Proverbs is seeking to imprint upon us: Wisdom is the best life insurance that you can obtain (cf. Prov 3:33; 4:4, 13; 7:2; 8:36; 9:6)! "The fear of Yahweh is a fountain of life" (a fountain of profit for living a full life) (Prov 14:27). And behold what a multiplicity of subjects from the full Israelite life the wise men broach! In that, too, you can see how broadly they understood the word *life*, when they said they wanted to promote life. Whoever takes to heart their life lessons will eat from the *tree of life*, will drink from the *fountain of life*, and will walk on the *path of life*. Those are three images for their instruction (cf. Prov 5:6; 6:23; 10:11, 17; 11:30; 13:12, 14; 14:27; 15:4; 16:22).

In the verse cited above, Solomon is congratulating all those who lay hold of this tree of life (notice the parallel: life // happiness). Its fruit makes the users increase in vitality, so that they grow in the strength and skills of life, in understanding and discernment. For the tree of life that is wisdom offers restorative power and the capacity to resist the poison of foolishness that brings human life to the dissolution of death.

11. WISDOM LIES AT THE FOUNDATION OF HEAVEN AND EARTH (PROV 3:19–20)

Solomon is in fact aiming in Prov 3 at nothing other than imprinting upon his pupils the lesson that wisdom has *inestimable value* for you. We have heard him furnish one proof after another of this truth. Wisdom can extend your life, can promote your *health*, can increase your *possessions*; in short, it can give you life. Now follows once again a powerful reason that will win hearts to wisdom: no one less than God himself has made widespread use of wisdom in connection with creating heaven and earth (vv. 19–20):

> The LORD by wisdom founded the earth;
> > by understanding he established the heavens;
> by his knowledge the deeps broke open,
> > and the clouds drop down the dew. (Prov 3:19–20)

That is what the poet sang in Ps 104: "O LORD, how manifold are your works! *In wisdom* have you made them all; the earth is full of your creatures" (v. 24). He showed this from what God had made on each of the six creation days.[7] In the verses cited above, the writer speaks more concisely and mentions only the establishing of the earth, the separation of seas and dry land, as well as the miracle of the "number." Most translations speak here of "the dew," but then we should not imagine what we usually understand by dew, but think of the heavy evening mist that, during the dry Palestinian summer and autumn, descended on the fields like a very light drizzle, and every night moistened the earth.

---

7. See van Deursen, *Psalms II*, 255–75.

In this way, both heaven and earth bore witness ten thousandfold in both large and small phenomena that God had created everything *with wisdom*. The earth hangs from nothing, floats like a ball through space, turns upon its axis, and orbits around the sun, and nevertheless it is not shaken. With great wisdom God has given it stability. To the same divine insight, the seas bear witness, those waters that do not flood the land, along with the water management throughout the earth, like the heavy night dew, whereby the produce of the fields is kept from withering. The entire creation teaches "his understanding is unsearchable" (Isa 40:28).

The prophetic books often point to the creation in order to comfort God's people with the *power* with which God created everything; by contrast, Proverbs does so in order to point God's people to the *wisdom* with which he created everything. They do so in order to lead them to this conclusion: if in connection with his work of creating, God needed wisdom, then do you think that *you* can get along without it? Proverbs 3:19–20 does not draw this conclusion in so many words, but Prov 8:22–30 does. There Solomon addresses us once again with a reference to God's work of creation, focusing with great emphasis on the immeasurable value of wisdom. It has value for God himself, because through wisdom God created heaven and earth. It has value for heaven and earth, because an immeasurable quantity of wisdom lies at their foundation.[8] And it has value for us people, because without wisdom, we have no life.

12. WISDOM MAKES ALIVE, ADORNS YOU, AND PROTECTS YOU (PROV 3:21–23)

Wisdom adorns those who have it, and makes them live. We discussed this earlier in connection with Prov 1:9, 3:3, and 3:18. Solomon points, however, to one other advantage of wisdom that comes through fearing the Lord. It can *protect* those who have it against unspeakable evil. Through wisdom, one can *prevent* so much misery:

> My son, do not lose sight of these—
>   keep sound wisdom and discretion,
> and they will be life for your soul
>   and adornment for your neck.
> Then you will walk on your way securely,
>   and your foot will not stumble. (Prov 3:21–23)

---

8. See van Deursen, *Psalms II*, 262–66.

In his book, Solomon returns often to this. In speaking about wisdom, he says among other things, "Do not forsake her, and she will *keep* you; love her, and she will *guard* you" (Prov 4:6). "When you walk, your step will not be hampered, and if you run, you will *not stumble*" (4:12). "In the fear of the Lord one has *strong confidence*, and his children will have a *refuge*" (14:26; see our comments on 2:1 as well).

Dozens of proverbs illustrate this preventive function of wisdom with practical examples. There is much evil in the world, about which we can say with the Preacher, "The one who fears God shall come out from both of them" (Eccl 7:18). At that point wisdom functions like a shield. You can spare yourself much suffering that fools needlessly bring upon themselves. This too is a serious reason for taking to heart the wisdom of Proverbs. It is altogether true "the teaching of the wise is a fountain of life, that one may turn away from the snares of death" (Prov 13:14). There is much lacking in this twisted life (Eccl 1:15), but wisdom teaches us the life attitude that gives us the least amount of misery.

13. WISDOM BENEFITS YOUR SLEEP (PROV 3:24)

A physician has written that sleep is one of the essential laws of good health. No one knows this better than our heavenly Father, who created us and bestowed upon Adam a restful dwelling place. He heartily grants us our rest as well. This appears no more clearly than from the Sabbaths that he gave Israel, whereby he *commanded* his people to take periodic rest: one day each week, several weeks each year, and, after every six years, an entire year. From him came the ordinance that after a day of work, a person must have a night's rest, because we need sleep as essentially as we need food.

But who pauses nowadays to ponder the truth that a good night's rest is promoted by wisdom that comes to a person who fears the Lord? Nonetheless, this is the case. In seeking to teach us to fear Yahweh in all of life, Proverbs talks about something as ordinary as our night sleep. And we are assured that fearing Yahweh benefits our sleep as well:

> If you lie down, you will not be afraid;
>   when you lie down, your sleep will be sweet. (Prov 3:24)

1. *God gave us the night for resting.*

But *how* can the fear of the Lord benefit someone's nightly rest? It can do so, because someone who fears God, if things are well, is showing respect not only for God's regulations in Scripture but also for those in creation. To such divine statutes belongs the night (Gen 1:4; 8:22). People in Israel praised God for the night (Ps 19:2; 74:16; 104:20). Pathways part, however, between divine wisdom and human folly also in connection with this ordinance.

What a benefit God prepares for humanity by granting us in his favor each evening again the darkness (Ps 104:20). To a certain degree he makes it impossible to work on account of the darkness. From this our Lord Jesus Christ derived a metaphor, "Night is coming, when no one can work" (John 9:4). God gave the day for working and the night for sleeping (Ps 104:23; 1 Thess 5:7). The night darkness is a blessing for humanity, given as a soft blanket that God spreads out across the earth in order to provide humanity the opportunity to rest from its fatigues of the day. Whoever respects the night as a divine ordinance will be wise enough to use it as much as possible for the purpose for which God created it. Doing this is already one of the ways in which the fear of the LORD can benefit someone's nightly rest.

Regrettably, modern life prevents us in various ways from observing this wholesome ordinance. Bright artificial light gives us the ability to turn the night darkness into day, by this it means that many allow themselves to be tempted to work or to go out long into the night. The fast tempo of our lives, the many sources of noisy distraction, together with the hunger for news, rob many harried Westerners of the blessing of nightly quiet and evening darkness, and thereby of an undisturbed sleep. But people cannot transgress any of God's ordinances, including that of a night's sleep, with impunity. Many whose nights are short are already well aware of the damage done by a constant shortage of sleep. Our constant stress keeps us from falling asleep. Our proverbs talks in this context about "being afraid"! Here too one can see how foolishness can damage our life, extending to our nightly rest.

But the matter has even more dimensions.

2. Sin and insomnia

"I can remember my astonishment and even my indignation as a doctor," Dr. Paul Tournier wrote,

> on hearing a lady remark, a few years ago, that insomnia was a symptom of sin. My experience of these last few years has led me to realize how much truth there is in this assertion. Doubtless there are exceptions, nor is the relation always direct; and it would be wrong to suggest that a person who sleeps well is less sinful than one who suffers from insomnia. But I cannot keep count of the number of patients I have seen rediscover the habit

of sleep as a result of the transformation of their lives brought about by submission to Jesus Christ.[9]

We can agree that some things lie far beyond the reach of usual calming medicines, in connection with which sin and foolishness impair someone's nightly rest.

Consider the many forms of *hatred* that can dominate a person. Scripture says, "Do not let the sun go down on your anger" (Eph 4:26), but suppose a person takes it to bed? He lies awake restlessly throughout the night thinking of what someone has done or said toward him. He gets wound up about it and throws another log on the fire of his resentment and vindictiveness. The wise men knew well: "From the fruit of a man's mouth his stomach is satisfied; he is satisfied by the yield of his lips" (Prov 18:20; cf. 13:21; 14:14). The hateful thought, "I'll get him!" has cost many a person hours of their night's sleep. In the same way, still more sins can keep a person awake at night.

3. *Our walking with God and our nightly rest*

The entire *manner of life* that Proverbs wants us to adopt is an excellent preventive for insomnia. For it promotes in every respect our peace with God and with our neighbor. If someone has done an injustice to us, and we react foolishly to that, then we run great risk that our desire for revenge will keep us awake. But our Savior was speaking as one who personified wisdom, entirely in the spirit of Proverbs, when he taught, "And if anyone would sue you and take your tunic, let him have your cloak as well" (Matt 5:40). That is indeed crippling to our pride, but efficacious for our nightly rest. Solomon said, "Good sense makes one slow to anger, and it is his glory to overlook an offense" (Prov 19:11). "If your enemy is hungry, give him bread to eat, and if he is thirsty, give him water to drink, for you will heap burning coals on his head, and the Lord will reward you" (Prov 25:21–22). He does that by protecting in this way our nightly rest against the damaging consequences of all kinds of feelings of hatred, and also by improving the quality of our sleep: "You will lie down and your sleep will be sweet," our proverb promises.

In addition, wisdom promotes our nightly rest by teaching us to *surrender* our life and our affairs into God's hands. Thereby David could say, "I lay down and slept; I woke again, for the Lord sustained me" (Ps 3:5). The superscription above that psalm reads, "A Psalm of David, when he fled from Absalom his son." "In peace I will both lie down and sleep; for you

---

9. Tournier, *Healing of Persons*, 119.

alone, O Lord, make me dwell in safety" (Ps 4:8). Was it not through that faith that our Lord Jesus could sleep in a boat during a storm at sea (Matt 8:24)? And was not Peter, when he was bound in prison between two soldiers, so fast asleep that an angel had to shake him awake (Acts 12:6)?

The uncertainty of life, however, leads many people into the grip of fear that often gives them a lot of stress and sleeplessness. The Preacher complains about the man who sweats in his work so intensely that "neither day nor night do one's eyes sleep" (Eccl 8:16; cf. Gen 18:1; 2 Sam 4:5; Eccl 5:11). The manner in which we perform our work can also be crippling for our rest (cf. Eccl 10:10). What a relaxing enjoyment, then, comes from the following of this advice: "Commit your work to the Lord, and your plans will be established" (Prov 16:3; cf. 10:3). "Better is a handful of quietness than two hands full of toil and a striving after wind" (Eccl 4:6). Child of God, dare to get your rest! That is also what our Master did with his disciples, didn't he? "And he said to them, 'Come away by yourselves to a desolate place and rest a while.' For many were coming and going, and they had no leisure even to eat" (Mark 6:31).

Unconfessed sins can also keep us awake. That is what David experienced when he kept silent about his sin (with Bathsheba): "For when I kept silent, my bones wasted away through my groaning all day long" (Ps 32:3). Anyone, however, who has poured out his heart from the depths to God and to the one to whom he owes confession, and who confesses everything that has caused him to suffer fear and torment, will be dumbfounded at the rest and relaxation this provides (Jas 5:16). In this way, too, wisdom can promote nightly rest. "Whoever conceals his transgressions will not prosper, but he who confesses and forsakes them will obtain mercy" (Prov 28:13).

Do not God's promises also give us rest (Jer 31:26)?

We readily admit that here, again, we are dealing with *mashals* that, in terms of their nature, cannot be said *always* to apply to *everyone*. The wise men were surely familiar with sleeplessness due to church struggles, or because of a foolish son (Prov 10:1). This does not mean, however, that Prov 3:24 does not continue to hold its full value for everyone who suffers sleeplessness. Unrighteousness leads to unrest, but righteousness supplies rest, also during the night. God's Word says this not only in the proverb cited above but also in this one: "The fear of the Lord leads to life, and whoever has it rests satisfied; he will not be visited by harm" (Prov 19:23; cf. Job 11:18–19).

14. WISDOM PRESERVES YOU WHILE THE WICKED ARE PERISHING (PROV 3:25–26)

And still the wicked who are mighty and wealthy walk with their unbelieving principles down dead-end paths! With this explicit faith-expectation Ps 1 had introduced the Writings. This faith-expectation wafts throughout Proverbs as well. The lives of the wise or righteous are like fruitful *trees*, but those of the foolish godless are like useless *chaff* that is blown away by a sudden gust of wind. Proverbs shows that continuously. And the Instruction Manual for this book briefly summarizes how we must view that ancient contrast between the righteous and the wicked among God's people.[10] This appears in Prov 3:25–26:

> Do not be afraid of sudden terror
>   or of the ruin of the wicked, when it comes,
> for the Lord will be your confidence
>   and will keep your foot from being caught.

Of course, people can understand the phrases "sudden terror" and "the ruin of the wicked" here to be referring to the final judgment.[11] After all, the apostle did write, "For you yourselves are fully aware that the day of the Lord will come like a thief in the night. While people are saying, 'There is peace and security,' then *sudden destruction* will come upon them as labor pains come upon a pregnant woman, and they will not escape" (1 Thess 5:2–3). Oh, how terrified the wicked will be! Our Lord Jesus foretold "*distress* of nations *in perplexity* because of the roaring of the sea and the waves, people *fainting with fear and with foreboding* of what is coming on the world. For the powers of the heavens will be shaken" (Luke 21:25–26; cf. Matt 24:30; Rev 1:7). But precisely at that time the godly must lift up their heads, because their salvation has drawn near (Luke 21:28).

Scripture and history show, however, that, even before then, God prepares for many wicked people a quick and unexpected demise. Suddenly the ground split open and swallowed Korah, Dathan, and Abiram, and their families, and suddenly a divine flame engulfed their entire entourage (Num 16). Suddenly, Nabal's heart "died within him, and about ten days later the Lord struck Nabal, and he died" (1 Sam 25:38). Suddenly, Joab stood before the wicked prince Absalom, when the latter was hanging by his hair from a tree, and Joab pierced him dead (2 Sam 18:14). Suddenly an arrow pierced between the scale armor and the breastplate of Ahab, and by nightfall the wicked ruler was dead (1 Kgs 22:34–36). Suddenly Jezebel was grabbed by

---

10. See van Deursen, *Psalms I*, 47, 83–118.
11. See van Deursen, *Psalms I*, 139–40.

a pair of palace officials and thrown from her window, such that her blood splattered on the wall, horses trampled her and wild dogs ate her flesh (2 Kgs 9:30–37).[12] And should we not also surmise behind many a news report nowadays the sudden demise of the wicked?

On the other hand, in times of judgment when many wicked perished, Yahweh worked to protect the godly. Elijah and a hundred other prophets survived the famine (1 Kgs 17; 18:4). And when in AD 70 the city was once again besieged, this time by the Romans, many disciples of the Lord Jesus escaped with their lives to Pella (Luke 21:20–21). Anyone in our day who prays with Habakkuk about judgments upon apostate Christianity, "O Lord, I have heard the report of you, and your work, O Lord, do I fear," may also beseech the Lord on behalf of the godly remnant in our day, "In wrath remember mercy" (Hab 3:2).

With the use of many examples, Proverbs also shows that the wicked are exposed to various terrors, because evil always afflicts the evildoer. This demise has come upon innumerable lives of those practicing unrighteousness. But the wisdom that learns the fear of Yahweh is the means whereby the Lord keeps the feet of the godly from the snares of sin. The suffering and shame of an adulterer, which is portrayed so poignantly in Prov 5–7, need not describe the discerning. Thus, godliness or wisdom can protect a person from numerous snares. This is one of the main themes of this Bible book, to which it constantly returns: wisdom *protects*, godliness is *preventive*! (See our comments on Prov 1:20–33.)

15. WISDOM MAKES A PERSON HELPFUL AND BENEVOLENT (PROV 3:27–28)

The wisdom teachers certainly did not ignore the poor in Israel. How many proverbs speak about the burdens and dangers of poverty (cf. Prov 10:15; 13:8; 14:20; 19:4; 22:7; 30:9)? How often do they not urge us to stand up for the poor? Proverbs 3:27–28 constitute a remarkable introduction to that subject, because they proceed so clearly from the unique *judicial basis* upon which care for the poor, indeed, all generosity and neighborly love in Israel, ought to rest, namely, on the mutual solidarity toward one's neighbor to which every Israelite was called by virtue of the covenant of God. In verse 27, we read,

> Do not withhold good from those to whom it is due,
>   when it is in your power to do it.

---

12. See van Deursen, *Psalms I*, 138–40.

Of course, pagans also legislated their social actions, just as unbelieving governments do today. But in Israel all the laws, including those relating to caring for the poor, were covenant stipulations, which people could keep only out of grateful fear of Yahweh. For Israel constituted one huge family, in which every brother was a covenant partner of Yahweh, and wherein the required loyalty toward Yahweh and the neighbor was supposed to govern everyone's actions. For that reason, the Lord Jesus called alms a matter of *righteousness* (Matt 6:1–2; cf. Dan 4:27; 2 Cor 9:9; Ps 112:9). And righteousness in Scripture is the usual term for the obedience of believers to God's covenant. This pertained also to the ordinances of that covenant legislation with respect to those needing assistance. For that reason, one can clearly see from someone's attitude toward the poor what that person's attitude toward God is.

Proverbs 3:27 breathes the spirit of the Torah entirely. Perhaps that appears even more clearly when we translate the verse a bit more literally this way: "Never withhold something good from one who is *the lord* of it." The Dutch States Translation (SV) reads, "Do not withhold the good from *its masters*." Here, then, those who need help are called, somewhat crassly, the lord or master of the good. They can make a kind of legal appeal for that help. So when we are able to do something good, something that is precisely what our neighbor needs, who then is lord and master of that good? To that question the wise men answered: Those needing help!

They had learned this in turn from the Torah, that standard work for living in God's covenant. In the Torah, Yahweh, Israel's great King, had stipulated that all deeds of generosity and charity should rest, not first of all on the subjective basis of our feelings of sympathy but on the objective basis of righteousness, which he required from his people as a *covenant demand*.

Clearly, only wisdom that comes from fearing the LORD makes a person generous and benevolent. For thereby one is acknowledging the *right* of the poor, by virtue of God's covenant (Prov 29:7). This righteousness is what the wise men wanted to teach the young people in Israel (Prov 1:3). This pertains to the needy in God's church as well. They provided the elementary education in this regard. Assistance and sharing among God's people are benefits, to the giving of which *the giver is obligated* and to the receiving of which *the receiver has a right* (cf. Gal 6:10; Heb 13:16).

One may not seek to escape this, according to Prov 3:28:

> Do not say to your neighbor, "Go, and come again,
>   tomorrow I will give it"—when you have it with you.

Here as well, the echo of the Torah is heard clearly.[13] "You shall not oppress your neighbor or rob him. The wages of a hired worker shall not remain with you all night until the morning" (Lev 19:13). "You shall not oppress a hired worker who is poor and needy, whether he is one of your brothers or one of the sojourners who are in your land within your towns. You shall give him his wages on the same day, before the sun sets (for he is poor and counts on it), lest he cry against you to the LORD, and you be guilty of sin" (Deut 24:14–15). Otherwise you are sinning against the eighth commandment. The same is true when your neighbor's ox is straying about or falls down, and you don't lend a helping hand (Deut 22:1–4). By procrastinating with your laborers, you are also sinning against the sixth commandment, for in so doing you are attacking his *nephesh* or life. With such examples God taught the Israelites to adopt a helping, generous attitude toward their neighbor (cf. Deut 15:11).

The wise ones wanted to teach this evangelical social institution to young Israel as well. Do not withhold grain in the face of threatening famine (Prov 11:26). Do not close your eyes to another person's misery (Prov 28:27; cf. 11:24–26; 14:21; 19:17; 22:9; 29:7). But you must help your neighbor as soon as possible. That means not only that we pay the accounts of our suppliers and our tax assessments on time but also that we loyally fulfill this entire "debt" to which God's covenant obligated every Israelite, to say nothing of us under the new covenant: "You shall love your neighbor as yourself" (Lev 19:18). To which the wise men added, entirely in the spirit of Moses: Do not procrastinate, do not invent excuses, but help! Later they will point out that God will also reward the benevolent giver for doing so (Prov 11:24, 25, 26; 14:21; 19:17; 22:9)!

This, then, is how wisdom teaches someone to render speedy benevolence, as you can see from the godly man Job, who could honestly declare his innocence in these terms: "If I have withheld anything that the poor desired, or have caused the eyes of the widow to fail, ... if I have seen anyone perish for lack of clothing, or the needy without covering, if his body has not blessed me, and if he was not warmed with the fleece of my sheep, ... then let my shoulder blade fall from my shoulder, and let my arm be broken from its socket" (Job 31:16–22).

In this respect as well, our Lord Jesus Christ fulfilled the Scriptures in word and deed: "Give to the one who begs from you," he taught, "and do not refuse the one who would borrow from you" (Matt 5:42; cf. Matt 25:40–45; Luke 6:38). He did not avoid providing teaching to the Samaritan woman

---

13. See "Learning wisdom from the Torah of Moses" in chapter 4 above; see also van Deursen, *Psalms I*, 32–38.

by saying, "I am too tired" (John 4). Even when someone asked him for help on a Sabbath, Jesus did not refuse him by saying, "Come back tomorrow, or else I will get in trouble with the Pharisees and scribes" (cf. Matt 12:1–14). And as a genuine disciple of this Master and of Prov 3:28, James wrote, "So whoever knows the right thing to do and fails to do it, for him it is sin" (Jas 4:17; cf. Matt 25:41–46; Rom 13:8; 2 Cor 9:6; Jas 2:15–16).

16. WISDOM DOES NOT ABUSE TRUST (PROV 3:29)

> Do not plan evil against your neighbor,
> who dwells trustingly beside you.

David was sitting before Saul, playing the lyre, with full trust, until suddenly the king hurled his spear at him to kill him (1 Sam 19:9). But for a long time, Saul had been plotting evil against the unsuspecting David (1 Sam 18:21–25). Later David's trust was shamed maliciously by his son Absalom and his counselor Ahithophel (2 Sam 15). In Ps 55 David tells how this kind of treachery can wound and injure someone. "For it is not an enemy who taunts me—" he complains, "then I could bear it; it is not an adversary who deals insolently with me—then I could hide from him. But it is you, a man, my equal, *my companion, my familiar friend*. We used to take sweet counsel together; within God's house we walked in the throng" (vv. 12–14). Regrettably, David himself fell into this sin, against Uriah, when this man was sitting by him with fervent trust (2 Sam 11:8–13).

Many have shared this sorrow with David. Abner walked along, without any suspicion, when Joab took him aside at the gate "to speak with him privately," and there Joab killed Abner (2 Sam 3:27). In the same way, the men of Anathoth plotted evil against their fellow villager Jeremiah, who was living among them in full trust. "But I was like a gentle lamb led to the slaughter," the prophet assures us. "I did not know it was against me they devised schemes, saying, 'Let us destroy the tree with its fruit, let us cut him off from the land of the living, that his name be remembered no more'" (Jer 11:19; cf. v. 21).

This suffering of the righteous is something our Lord Jesus also fulfilled, when he was betrayed by one of his disciples, one who ate with him (Ps 41:9). "He who has dipped his hand in the dish with me will betray me," the Lord foretold (Matt 26:23). And do we not hear the pain of Ps 55:12–19 in Jesus' question when he was arrested: "Judas, would you betray the Son of Man with a kiss?" (Luke 22:48)?

But by means of the fear of God a person comes to the realization that trust forms the foundation of society (Pss 11 and 12). Anyone who violates trust, the wise men said, is a no-good, a deceiver (Prov 6:14, 18; 12:20). The apostles taught the same heavenly wisdom, when they summoned us to "*sincere* brotherly love" (1 Pet 1:22; cf. Rom 12:9; 1 Tim 1:5).

17. WISDOM MAKES ONE PEACE-LOVING (PROV 3:30)

> Do not contend with a man for no reason,
>   when he has done you no harm.

In this context, one might think first of all of quarreling, where people occasionally know how it began but not where it's going to end. "The beginning of strife is like letting out water, so quit before the quarrel breaks out" (Prov 17:14). Even better is the example of our Lord Jesus Christ, who said, "Take my yoke upon you, and learn from me, for I am gentle and lowly in heart, and you will find rest for your souls" (Matt 11:29). When he was reviled, he did not revile in return, but surrendered himself to him who judges righteously (1 Pet 2:23; cf. Matt 5:25, 40–42; Rom 12:18).

But the Hebrew word for quarrel (*rib*) can also refer to a lawsuit (for example, God's quarrel with or lawsuit against Israel, about which the prophets speak so extensively). In connection with this kind of process, wisdom teaches us moderation. Of course, we may seek justice for ourselves when someone has committed wrong against us, "either by means of the Magistrate, or to bring him to an acknowledgement of his fault by the Ecclesiastical power, or other private admonition, and that without desire of revenge, and scandal, Exod 22 verse 8. Mat. 18.15, 16, 17. 1 Cor 6.4. Eph 4.26."[14]

For this, God administered justice to Israel in the wilderness already, and Proverbs discusses this very often. It is even one of the main purposes of this book, namely, to teach God's people to love *justice* (Prov 1:3). But the fear of the Lord can impart to a person wisdom not to run to a judge to file a lawsuit against his neighbor for every little dispute. And surely not to pick a quarrel with someone who has not done us any harm. Wisdom makes a person peace-loving.

This comes out in the following proverbs as well: "It is an honor for a man to keep aloof from strife, but every fool will be quarreling" (Prov 20:3). "Do not hastily bring into court, for what will you do in the end, when your neighbor puts you to shame?" (Prov 25:8).

---

14. Schuringa, *The Wisdom Literature*, 644 (on Prov 3:30).

In the fear of Yahweh there is rich reward, also with respect to this. People spare themselves all the misery that comes from quarrels and needless lawsuits. Again, this is medicine for our body (see our comments on v. 8) and promotes our nightly sleep (see our comments on v. 24). People then rejoice in the promise of the Lord: "Blessed are the peacemakers, for they shall be called sons of God" (Matt 5:9).

18. WISDOM LEADS YOU INTO INTIMATE INTERACTION WITH GOD (PROV 3:31–32)

The righteous and the wise often—or mostly—constituted a minority in Israel and in Christianity. At that point, the wicked called the shots,[15] who usually belonged to the wealthy, and despite their pious exterior were often people of real violence and men of blood.[16] This often seemed to provide them many advantages, at least at first glance. And this to the sorrow of many a godly person. In Ps 73, Asaph acknowledges that he was embittered when he saw the prosperity acquired by many wicked people. He viewed them getting their way as luxuriously and richly fed people, while they had big mouths toward God and others (Ps 73:2–12). This problem tormented him, one he worried about for some time: "All in vain have I kept my heart clean . . . for all the day long I have been stricken" (Pss 13–14; cf. Eccl 7:15; 8:10, 13–14; 9:2).

This wrestling between the righteous and the wicked among God's people finds an echo in Proverbs. This Bible book continually urges us to remain on the good side in this battle, staying close to God and his Word. It also gives instruction on the basis of the firm faith with which Ps 1 introduces the Writings: those powerful wicked people, like false witnesses, unrighteous judges, and malicious land robbers, are nothing but worthless chaff that the wind of God's judgment will nevertheless cause to be blown away (Ps 1:4).[17] From this conviction comes Solomon's powerful assurance in Prov 3:31–32, given to the godly poor, that no one needs to be envious of those apparently successful wicked.

> Do not envy a man of violence
>   and do not choose any of his ways,
> for the devious person is an abomination to the LORD,
>   but the upright are in his confidence.

---

15. See van Deursen, *Psalms I*, chap. 4.
16. See van Deursen, *Psalms I*, 109–13.
17. See van Deursen, *Psalms I*, 138–39.

We called this assurance powerful because the writer is using very graphic language to express Yahweh's revulsion of those who commit violence. Before God they are an *abomination*. The Torah uses this term with reference to what is unclean, to everything that smells of Canaanite wickedness and was therefore inadmissible into fellowship with God! Psalm 37, which provides us with the most wonderful explanation of this proverb, tells us what it means that God abominates those oppressors. God laughs about those bigwigs at whom David was looking, "for he sees that his day is coming" (Ps 37:13). Just a little while yet, and God will uproot them, so that they will no longer be found (v. 10). And then he will give the land (the Lord Jesus said, the earth) to the meek (vv. 11, 29; Matt 5:5)! What a terrifying future for wicked church members! After all, they belonged to God's people, had even received in their circumcision and baptism the sign and seal of God's covenant, but they sinned against God's grace and drew his curse down upon them.[18] This is what eliminated Asaph's bitter disgust from his heart: he considered their end (Ps 73:17).

Meanwhile Yahweh lives intimately with the upright. With them he keeps *sod*. This Hebrew word made an Israelite think of the convivial group of men who, each evening, after a day's work was finished, would sit around talking in the gate. Jeremiah lamented that God's hand had always kept him outside "the *sod* of revelers" (Jer 15:17; cf. Job 19:19; Ezek 13:9). David felt betrayed by a friend with whom he had enjoyed *sod*, intimate concourse (Ps 55:14). The proverb writer uses this ordinary word to tell us: This is how heartily and intimately God wants to interact with his upright children! As with friends in a *sod* or group. Today, of course, by means of his holy Word. But in view of the context of our proverb, we naturally think especially of that treasure house filled with pieces of friendly counsel, which this Bible book offers us. In this book, God is speaking intimately with us about the greatest and least things in our life, just as someone giving his friend good advice during an intimate conversation. In this way, in addition to giving us many other advantages, wisdom puts us on familiar terms with God (Ps 25:14; Gen 18:17; Job 29:4; John 15:14–15). Does anyone know of a greater honor? Asaph comforted himself later with this as well: "But for me it is good [already in this life] to be *near God*" (Ps 73:28). Living very intimately with God, like friends in their *sod*.

---

18. See van Deursen, *Psalms I*, 83–90.

19. WISDOM BEHOLDS ITS DWELLING BLESSED BY GOD (PROV 3:33)

God's blessing is a salutary power that can bring our life to full bloom in every respect. If Israel would fear Yahweh, then he promised them blessing in the fruitfulness of the maternal womb, the birth of cattle, in the harvest of the fields, and the security of public health.

By contrast, God's curse is a destructive power, whereby he can poison our life in all its components, so that death enters into everything, and the Israelite experiences in this empty kneading trough and unproductive field and livestock that Yahweh has turned against him and has destroyed his peace.

Moses gives a broad summary of blessing and curse in Lev 26 and Deut 28. But Proverbs is, in fact, talking about this on every page. Solomon summarizes briefly all that proverbial instruction about blessing and curse in Prov 3:33 this way:

> The LORD's curse is on the house of the wicked,
>   but he blesses the dwelling of the righteous.

The wise men show the dreadful reality of God's curse on the house of the wicked in dozens of *mashals*. Let us make a random selection from them: his name will rot away (10:7); his years will be shortened (10:27; cf. our comments on 3:2); his hope will perish (10:28); his profits will not thrive (11:18); building on his wealth, he will fall (11:28); there will be shouts of gladness (11:10). He may well pretend to be religious,[19] but Yahweh despises his sacrifice (15:8). He will not continue to dwell in the land (10:30). In short, Yahweh is far from him (15:29). And that last reality is the worst.

But the righteous stand as a lasting foundation (10:25) and in eternity will not be moved (10:30; cf. Ps 15:5).[20] That, too, can be read on every page of Proverbs. He gets what is coming to him, he is recompensed on earth (Prov 11:31). He eats until he is satisfied (13:25). And even at death he finds a refuge (14:32).

Regrettably, life does not always allow all of this to be seen clearly. "There is a vanity that takes place on earth," says the Preacher, "that there are righteous people to whom it happens according to the deeds of the wicked, and there are wicked people to whom it happens according to the deeds of the righteous. I said that this also is vanity" (Eccl 8:14). It seems that the writer of our proverb has seen this as well. He talks at any rate about the *house* of the wicked; that sounds like something solid. But for the dwelling

---

19. See van Deursen, *Psalms I*, 84–90.
20. See van Deursen, *Psalms I*, 220–21.

of the righteous he uses a word that refers to a simple abode, a settlement, originally pointing to a meadow. Do you sense the contrast? Proverbs speaks in fact also about the *distresses* of the righteous (Prov 11:8).

But in the proverb under discussion, as in the previous one, we hear the sounds of faith language! Here the writer is speaking in the unity of true faith with the Preacher, who wrote, "Yet I know that it will be well with those who fear God, because they fear before him. But it will not be well with the wicked, neither will he prolong his days like a shadow, because he does not fear before God" (Eccl 8:12–13). Suddenly God's curse will break that apparently unshakable *house* of the wicked, and his blessing will bring the *tent* of the righteous to great flourishing (cf. Prov 14:11).

20. THROUGH ITS HUMILITY WISDOM OBTAINS GOD'S GOOD PLEASURE (PROV 3:34)

Repeatedly throughout the Psalms and Proverbs we encounter the scoffers. With this term you must not think only of unsavory characters who pass along coarse jokes about God and his commandments, for scoffers often surround themselves with an aura of religiosity. For that reason you must look for them not only in the world but especially in Israel, and now in God's churches. Their most essential feature, in fact, is not their mockery but their audacity, their self-aggrandizement and unfathomable arrogance toward God and his Word (Prov 21:24). The scoffer is the self-declared autonomous person whom you can observe everywhere within Christianity. Not only are they the fringe church members, to be sure, but not infrequently they are prominent figures in the ecclesiastical and theological world. We can see the biblical portrait of the scoffer sketched elsewhere.[21] There, too, we devoted some attention to the proverb:

> Toward the scorners he is scornful,
>   but to the humble he gives favor. (Prov 3:34)

One such "pious" scoffer, whom Yahweh in turn mocked, was King Jeroboam, whom he made to look foolish by giving him a stiff arm—and doing that, note well, at a religious feast, at an altar that was torn down (1 Kgs 13). And as far as the worldly scoffers are concerned, see Rom 1:18–32. There in the background we hear the rumble like a drum beat: What? You mock me? Then I will mock you!

---

21. See van Deursen, *Psalms I*, 96–99.

Who the scoffer is also appears clearly from his counterpart: the humble person (the *ani*, also translated, the afflicted or the poor).[22] He fears God and therefore people find wisdom with him. Wisdom gradually makes a person more humble (Prov 11:2). Wisdom teaches a person to remain humble with the limits of God's ordinances. To humbly submit to living with the space that God grants. To humbly accept the reach that God has fixed for him (see our comments on Prov 1:2–3). To acknowledge humbly what fits and does not fit. Just as pride is the scoffer's *attitude of life*, so humility is the wise person's attitude of life. The former bursts with conceit, the latter praises God as the Almighty and the all-wise one.

It is exactly those who are humble before God who are "those with whom he is pleased" (Luke 2:14). Upon them he pours out his grace or favor. Of such humble ones the godly remnant in Luke 1 and 2 consists.[23] To them God makes known the birth of the Messiah. In their midst God's Spirit caused the most beautiful prophecies to be heard. But he passed by the proud Jerusalem priestly aristocracy. When Mary saw how God had exalted her circle and had entirely bypassed the religious bigwigs, she said, "My soul magnifies the Lord, . . . for he has looked on the humble estate of his servant. . . . He has brought down the mighty from their thrones and exalted those of humble estate; he has filled the hungry with good things, and the rich he has sent away empty" (Luke 1:46–55; cf. 1 Sam 2:1–10).

People in Israel had been singing that for centuries: "For though the LORD is high, he regards the lowly, but the haughty he knows from afar" (Ps 138:6; cf. Ps 18:27). This is the essence of Holy Scripture. To put it in the words of our Savior, "For what is exalted among men is an abomination in the sight of God" (Luke 16:15; cf. Matt 23:12; Luke 18:14; Jas 4:6; 1 Pet 5:5).

21. WISDOM MAKES ONE INHERIT HONOR (PROV 3:35)

Wisdom lends its possessors capacities whereby they can acquire *the respect of their surroundings* (Acts 2:47; 1 Tim 3:7). Solomon talks about this in Prov 3:16, and returns to this once again in Prov 3:35:

> The wise will inherit honor,
> but fools get disgrace.

This occurs because fools despise wisdom and discipline (see our earlier comments on Prov 1:7). Part of their disgrace comes from their feigned

---

22. See van Deursen, *Psalms I*, 55–57, 65–67.
23. See van Deursen, *Psalms I*, 40–41, 74–76.

religiosity. Often the notion of shame applies to them, as we will see in proverbs such as those in 11:2, 12:18, 13:5, 17:7, 19:10, 26:1, and 26:7–8.

The Preacher saw, however, that in this world, those who are wise hardly ever receive the honor they deserve. He saw in a besieged city, for example, a poor, wise man who could have rescued the city by his wisdom, "Yet no one remembered that poor man. But I say that wisdom is better than might, though the poor man's wisdom is despised and his words are not heard" (Eccl 9:13–16; cf. 6:8). What he saw even more clearly in this context is evident still today: "Folly is set in many high places" (Eccl 10:6). Honor before God and honor before people seldom go together. Often the believer must choose between them and for the sake of his honor before God he must take up his cross and suffer reproach (Matt 5:11–12). Is Solomon therefore teaching that the wise will *inherit* honor? For one can make an appeal to an inheritance, even though he does not yet possess it.

However, as long as fools continue to occupy eminent positions of honor in this world—even though this is as inappropriate as snow in summertime (26:1)—we can hear in this proverb the familiar promissory and believing language of Holy Scripture. "Those who honor me I will honor, and those who despise me shall be lightly esteemed" (1 Sam 2:30). But this proverb-like prophecy was not fulfilled on that very same day in Eli's house. Just as with so many other promises, like the promise of eternal life, the righteous possess their honor before God in the present time for the most part in the form of a promise. But even though many wise people receive today far too little of the honor due to them, and even though many fools are sitting prominently in places of honor, nevertheless the promise of our Lord Jesus will not fail: "If anyone serves me, the Father will honor him" (John 12:26). One day God will definitively reverse the roles and allow the wise to inherit their promised honor intact. "And many of those who sleep in the dust of the earth shall awake, some to everlasting life, and some to shame and everlasting contempt. And those *who are wise* shall shine like the brightness of the sky above" (Dan 12:2–3); indeed, "Then the righteous will shine like the sun in the kingdom of their Father" (Matt 13:43; cf. Ps 84:12; 1 Cor 15:42; 2 Cor 3:18; Phil 3:21).

22. WISDOM ENCOMPASSES AND BLESSES OUR ENTIRE LIFE

"If you are wise, you are *wise for yourself*" (Prov 9:12). The Instruction Manual for Proverbs (Prov 1–9) continually hammers on this anvil. We saw the impressive list that Solomon connected to living in the fear of Yahweh. As we conclude this chapter, we will review this series once more. The wisdom that one can obtain through the fear of the Lord really encompasses and blesses our entire life:

> Wisdom can extend our life.
> Wisdom makes us sympathetic to God and others.
> Wisdom leads to the least amount of misery in this world.
> Wisdom promotes our health.
> Wisdom increases our possessions.
> Wisdom teaches us to bow under God's discipline.
> Wisdom belongs to our most valuable possessions.
> Wisdom lends wealth and honor.
> Wisdom bestows loveliness and peace.
> Wisdom lets us eat from a tree of life.
> Wisdom lies at the foundation of heaven and earth.
> Wisdom makes alive, adorns us, and protects us.
> Wisdom benefits our sleep.
> Wisdom preserves us while the wicked are perishing.
> Wisdom makes us helpful and benevolent.
> Wisdom does not abuse trust.
> Wisdom makes us peace-loving.
> Wisdom leads us into intimate interaction with God.
> Wisdom brings blessing into our dwelling.
> Wisdom acquires God's good pleasure through its humility.
> Wisdom makes us inherit honor.

As we will observe, in Prov 4–9 we frequently encounter the same reasons for seeking wisdom that we have read in Prov 3. We can refer the reader at those points to our discussion in this chapter. One thing Solomon brings into view with abundant clarity in Prov 3 is this: wisdom obtained through the fear of the Lord in this broken human life provides the least amount of misery, and is the best way to taste as much pleasure as possible and to avoid as much distress as possible.

8

Proverbs 4

What Solomon Himself Learned as a Child from His Father David

AT THIS POINT, SOLOMON gives us a glimpse into his parental home, with his father David and his mother Bathsheba. You can understand why he affords us this glimpse into his private life. Solomon is writing an Instruction Manual to accompany his book Proverbs, in order to impress on young and old alike the immeasurable *value* of wisdom. At the same time, he wants to strongly urge them to *take that wisdom to heart*. In that context, a recollection from his parental home could strengthen his appeal. If his readers could hear how Solomon's famous father, King David, had pointed him toward wisdom already when he was a young prince, then they would surely esteem its value even more highly. This explains these royal recollections from his youth in the Instruction Manual for Proverbs (1–9).

One might well be wondering: To what extent is Solomon citing his father David here, and when is Solomon himself speaking as he turns toward his own pupils? This is a difficult question! But does it really matter? Could not Solomon have learned from his father David everything that he teaches us in Prov 4, for David had also composed a number of *wisdom* psalms (cf. Ps 34)?[1] Why would Solomon have preserved what he had learned from his father only for his biological sons and not have readily passed it on to his spiritual sons?

---

1. See van Deursen, *Psalms II*, chap. 4.

1. LISTEN TO WISDOM

From these recollections of his youth on the part of wise Solomon, you can see clearly what in fact Proverbs understands by "discipline." Regrettably the view is widespread that those who composed the proverbs were such callous pedagogues. After all, they dared to advise the use of *the rod*! But from Prov 4:1–2 you can see for yourself how mistaken this viewpoint is.

> Hear, O sons, a father's instruction,
>   and be attentive, that you may gain insight,
> for I give you good precepts;
>   do not forsake my teaching.

Apparently, Solomon believed that discipline surely should not begin with a rod and a beating, but with *words* that people can *hear*. For that reason, he would later tell about how his own father *instructed* him as a child. As you can see, Solomon readily uses as a substitute for "discipline" the word *teaching* (Heb., *torah*).

Solomon, who was the preeminent author of Proverbs, saw discipline as referring in the first place not to a physical beating but to instruction. This was naturally accompanied with the exercise of authority over their pupils that was bestowed upon parents and other God-fearing pedagogues. According to Solomon, one can very easily provide someone written lessons in discipline. What else than this is he doing in this Bible book? The book of Proverbs itself must serve "to know wisdom and instruction [discipline]" (Prov 1:2). Only when children refuse stubbornly to *hear* this authoritative and guiding instruction does Proverbs advise that they need to feel that discipline. In serious cases one may need to go as far as picking up the rod; see our comments in connection with Prov 13:24, 22:6; 22:15, 23:13, and 29:15. But, once again, Solomon began his "discipline" with recalling his parental home, where father David *talked* so intimately with his son. We see this in verses 3–4a:

> When I was a son with my father,
>   tender, the only one in the sight of my mother,
> he taught me and said to me . . .

Is this not a powerful stimulus for all fathers today for paying close attention to their duties? Undoubtedly there were many things outside the home that required David's attention. God has called him to govern a great nation. Nevertheless, he did not view this public calling as giving him any reason to neglect his domestic calling and to shift the nurture of his son Solomon entirely to educators. This royal father obeyed God's command:

"You shall teach them diligently to your children" (Deut 6:7; cf. Eph 6:4; Col 3:21). In fact, "if someone does not know how to manage his own household, how will he care for God's church?" (1 Tim 3:5).

One cannot communicate the incalculable benefit of the life-wisdom-through-fearing-the-LORD in any better way than father David did. He did so by way of the natural channels of the affinity that a child has for his or her father, and a grandchild for his or her grandpa. No wonder that Holy Scripture portrays the ideal teacher-student relationship as a father-child relationship.[2] Even Solomon, that universal genius, the wisest man after the Lord Jesus, did not esteem it to be beneath his dignity to emphasize his instruction by recalling what his father David had taught him, when Solomon was still at home with his mother Bathsheba.

For that matter, life *lessons* obtain even more authority for an ear that loves wisdom when the teacher appeals in connection with them to the life *experience* of the preceding generations. "For inquire, please, of bygone ages, and consider what the fathers have searched out" (Job 8:8–10; cf. 15:10). Later, Prov 8 will illuminate the excellence of wisdom by a broad explanation of its awe-inspiring age!

What did father David hold before the young Prince Solomon during that time? That he had to fix the words of his father in his ears and remember them throughout his entire life, because his entire life-happiness depended on that! As an aside, we would mention how beautifully this Scripture passage brings together a grandfather, a father, and a grandchild through the fear of Yahweh. In this way, wisdom can bind various generations to one another, whereas folly often divides them by means of generational chasms. If only parents will lovingly instruct, and young people willingly listen to them! For a lot depends on whether young people will listen! It is surprising how often Solomon dares to repeat that. Our chapter contains about fifty lines, and no fewer than sixteen of them express a summons to *listen* to the lessons of wisdom. Here they are:

> Hear, O sons. (v. 1)
> Be attentive. (v. 1)
> Do not forsake my teaching. (v. 2)
> Let your heart hold fast my words;
>   keep my commandments, and live. (v. 4)
> Do not forget,
>   and do not turn away from the words of my mouth. (v. 5)
> Do not forsake her,
>   Love her. (v. 6)

---

2. See van Deursen, *Psalms II*, 97–99, and our comments on Prov 1:8 above.

> Hear, my son, and accept my words. (v. 10)
> Keep hold of instruction . . . ; guard her. (v. 13)
> My son, be attentive to my words;
>   incline your ear to my sayings. (v. 20)
> Let them not escape from your sight;
>   keep them within your heart. (v. 21)

We recognized all of these statements from Prov 1–3. But these are precisely the familiar truths on which our life depends. Therefore, the Instruction Manual for Proverbs dares to restate repeatedly what it had already stated repeatedly, that a person must especially *listen* wisely, with an attention that never flags, and with boundless *esteem* for wisdom. One must love wisdom (v. 6) and value it highly (v. 8).

Could the secret of Solomon's prayer for wisdom lie here? When he was permitted to make a wish to Yahweh, he asked for "an understanding mind" in order to "discern between good and evil" (1 Kgs 3:9). Did not this request itself proceed from wisdom? Wisdom begins with acquiring wisdom. That is the most important. For that, everything that this life has to offer must come in second place, as father David had taught his son. "The beginning of wisdom is this: Get wisdom, and whatever you get, get insight" (Prov 4:7). The king had formulated it for the ears of young people in this wonderful way: Let wisdom become your young lady whom you take in your arms and who weaves a wedding wreath for you (v. 8).

Even though we have the Proverbs of Solomon printed in our Bibles, his appeal that we *listen* in order to become wise remains valid. Especially while we are still young, living with father and mother, the formula is this: Open your eyes and ears! Remember that this is about happiness or unhappiness! In addition, in the appeals mentioned we must also sense the urgency to *read* this Bible book frequently, to read and reread it, throughout our entire life, every day for a year. With pen or pencil in hand to underscore what speaks most directly to our situation. In this way, as we read, our heart will preserve this divine wisdom and put it into practice. Then we cannot help but experience that whoever takes this wisdom to heart can avoid much distress and taste much happiness.

2. WISDOM MAKES ALIVE

The wise men of Israel did not give their students commands that they had to observe blindly. It is precisely one of the attractive features of their instruction that in Prov 1–9 they constantly tried to lead their students to this insight: I cannot act with more understanding than what wisdom and its teachers hold before me. "Be attentive, that you may gain *insight*," Solomon said, "for I give you *good* [beneficial] precepts" (vv. 1–2; cf. vv. 5, 7). After this he identifies extensively why his instruction is so beneficial. The reasons he adduces for that we have already learned from Prov 1–3. Since we have discussed them rather extensively there, at this point we will limit ourselves to providing here, for the sake of summarizing, a list of those benefits, together with the references where you can find a discussion of these advantages of wisdom.

"I am giving you *beneficial* knowledge," Solomon said, for:

> It can *promote your life*. (vv. 4, 13, 22; see 2:11; 3:21)
> It can *preserve you from much misery*. (v. 6; see 2:11; 2:21)
> It can *exalt you and lead you to honor*. (vv. 8–9; see 2:9; 3:16; 3:33)
> It can *extend your life*. (v. 10; see 3:2)
> It leads you to *walk in right paths*. (v. 11; see 3:5–6)
> It can *protect you from stumbling*. (v. 12; see 3:21–26)
> It *benefits your nightly rest*. (v. 16; see 3:24)
> It lends you *increasing vitality*. (v. 18; see 3:18)
> It can *promote your health*. (v. 22; see 3:7–8)
> It preserves you from *the way of the wicked*. (v. 19; see 3:25)

Whoever wants to enjoy these benefits should, before everything else, exercise the most extreme carefulness with respect to his heart. There is where we must be most scrupulous, for, according to Holy Scripture, everything a person does proceeds from his heart. Therefore, in Prov 4:23 Solomon emphatically impressed upon his young readers this:

> Keep your heart with all vigilance,
>   for from it flow the springs of life.

Preserve my words *at the very center* of your heart—this is what he himself had learned at home from his father David (v. 21; cf. 23:26). For with your heart you feel, you think, you remember, and you desire. "For from within, out of the heart of man," said the Lord Jesus, "come evil thoughts, sexual immorality, theft, murder, adultery, coveting, wickedness, deceit, sensuality, envy, slander, pride, foolishness" (Mark 7:21–23). That is, unless we fear God, and unless his wisdom is sitting there on the throne!

Was our Savior perhaps thinking of Prov 4:23 when he said, "Whoever believes in me, as the Scripture has said, 'Out of his heart will flow rivers of living water'" (John 7:38; cf. 4:14)? When through his Word and Spirit, Christ governs our heart, then he governs the power station or headquarters of our life, and thereby all of our actions. And then no living death emerges, as the Lord described in Mark 7:21–23, but streams of living water flow forth from that heart. This describes the kind of life that Solomon was promising in Proverbs. This life alone deserves the name of life, life that is simply another word for happiness, life that later leads to eternal life (John 4:14; 17:3).

Then we will be speaking aright, and then we will be looking aright, and then we will be walking aright (Prov 4:24–27). Then our eyes will be looking ahead. Proud people look upward, dissolute people look down, deceitful people look around, but upright people look straight ahead (v. 25). Their feet travel the path of God's commandments (v. 26). That is the path that leads to life (John 17:3; Matt 7:13–14).

Please do not call this instruction of Solomon "Old Testament-ish," for the apostle Paul taught substantially the very same thing when he wrote, "Godliness is of value in every way, as it holds promise for *the present life* and also for the life to come. The saying is trustworthy and deserving of full acceptance. . . . The living God, who is the Savior of all people [if they want to derive profit from his wisdom], especially of those who believe" (1 Tim 4:8–10).

9

Proverbs 5–7

Adultery and Prostitution: Folly Is Crowned

ONE OF THE WORST missteps you can make as a man or lad is sexual intercourse with a prostitute or the wife of another man. For then you become guilty of what Prov 5:23 literally calls a "great folly," which can destroy the life not only of a man but also that of his wife and children. Concerning this, Prov 5–7, the chapters under discussion here, place in our hands salutary wisdom. They do so not abstractly, but bluntly, and with a poignant example from experience.

As disciples of Jesus Christ, however, please let us not feel that we are above this lesson, for then in our own estimation we would presume to stand more strongly against this temptation than God teaches us in his Word (Mark 7:21; Rom 7:21; Gal 5:19–20). He does not consider us too good for such a lesson. Otherwise he would never have laid down the commandment for *his own people*: "You [!] shall not commit adultery"! For that reason, it was far from determined in advance for Israel's wise men that the young men of God's people "naturally" would never go to a prostitute or enter into a sinful relationship with another man's wife. On the contrary, there is no sin against which Proverbs warns so extensively as that of sexual immorality and adultery. Virtually the whole of Prov 5–7 is devoted to a discussion of this wickedness.

The form in which Solomon does this is as fascinating as it is educational. He meets his (mostly young) readers not with a boring sermon about morals but, among other things, with a real historical narrative that he himself had seen as he looked through his own window. A thickheaded young man was hooked by a slut of a woman. He narrates this true story so vividly that we can almost see ourselves sitting in front of that window. You can savor the atmosphere of the growing evening darkness. You see the woman all dolled up, walking restlessly to and fro. You hear how she wins over her victim with seductive words, and you are horrified as you watch how, with open eyes, the fool walks into her trap. In Prov 5 you hear the wail with which the folly of such men ends and the remorse with which they cry out, "If only I had listened to my teachers!" (v. 13). So graphically does Solomon illuminate this perpetual threat to our marital happiness. Preachers could hardly find a more gripping text for a sermon about the seventh commandment.

The wisdom that Solomon provides here about marital and sexual life is worth its weight in gold, even after so many centuries have passed. Especially because greater similarity exists between the situation in which ancient Israel lived and the situation in which we live in the present day than the historical distance might lead us to assume. Israel lived in the ancient Near East, in a world that was at least as sexualized as ours.[1] Israel lived with the Word of God about the man-woman relationship in the same isolation as we live. Therefore, his wisdom-from-the-Word fits so appropriately in our contemporary society, in which a spirit of "do what you want" (the spirit of permissiveness) continues increasingly to undermine good morals.

In this chapter we wish to investigate, in terms of Prov 5-7, first, how the folly of adultery and prostitution always *begins*; second, how it usually *progresses*; and, third, how one can be *armed* against this folly.

1. HOW THIS FOLLY ALWAYS BEGINS

Evening is falling. In the Israelite town the boisterous activity that daily precedes the falling of darkness dominates the scene. The evening meal has been eaten. The men are still chatting at the village gate. The women are scrambling to finish their final activities before dark, and the children are playing in the square. A couple of travelers enter the city in order to spend the night behind its safe walls (Gen 19:1; Judg 19:11-21). A cool breeze is driving away the heat of the day. Oh, these were glorious evenings in Israel! Isaiah enjoyed them so much (Isa 21:4).

But who is that woman there, wearing such flashy clothes (7:10), walking around surveying the scene? Notice her shameless countenance and how noisy and restless she is, "now in the street, now in the market, and at every corner she lies in wait" (7:12). Look, there is a young fellow shuffling

---

1. See van Deursen, *Psalms I*, 279-80.

about near her house. Pay attention, she has noticed him, and she is approaching him. More than that, she grabs him and gives him a kiss! Quiet, listen to what she is telling him:

> "I had to offer sacrifices,
>   and today I have paid my vows;
> so now I have come out to meet you,
>   to seek you eagerly, and I have found you.
> I have spread my couch with coverings,
>   colored linens from Egyptian linen;
> I have perfumed my bed with myrrh,
>   aloes, and cinnamon.
> Come, let us take our fill of love till morning;
>   let us delight ourselves with love.
> For my husband is not at home;
>   he has gone on a long journey;
> he took a bag of money with him;
>   at full moon he will come home."
> With much seductive speech she persuades him;
>   with her smooth talk she compels him.
> All at once he follows her,
>   as an ox goes to the slaughter,
> or as a stag is caught fast
>   till an arrow pierces its liver;
> as a bird rushes into a snare;
>   he does not know that it will cost him his life. (Prov 7:14–23)

Solomon saw this happening with his own eyes, when on a given evening he was sitting behind the wooden latticework of his window looking out. It was almost three thousand years ago, but from this example you can see that the world has not changed substantially. Such scenes are played out every day around the whole world. And if you look past the incidentals of time, place, and custom, dramas like this continue to be played out in terms of the pattern portrayed by Solomon in Prov 5–7.

First of all, with regard to the manner in which you as a man arrive at such a misstep: to do that, you don't have to be what people call "a bad fellow." You need think only of godly brothers like Samson and David, each of whom had slain a lion, but succumbed to the charm of a woman! Solomon is definitely not portraying here a young man with a depraved character, but rather one who is naive, thickheaded, who looked at life far too innocently. He was a genuine fool (Prov 7:7; Heb., *peti*, simple one; for this type, see our comments on Prov 1:4 and 14:15).

Her house, her clothes, her mouth, and her eyes

What, then, was his first stupidity? That he came too close to her neighborhood. Why did he need to "pass along the street near her corner" (Prov 7:8)? Rather than fleeing the temptation, he purposely searched her out, and that was his mishap. Therefore Solomon gave this advice, "Keep your way far from her, and do not go near the door of her house"(Prov 5:8). Never walk unnecessarily through seedy neighborhoods.

In addition, her provocative clothes could have alerted him. In any case, her shameless words should have done so. What decent woman starts talking with an unfamiliar young man or with a strange man about her bed that smells so wonderful, and about her husband who will not be coming home for the time being? You should never start up a conversation with such a person. Keep walking! And please walk fast.

It is striking how emphatically the wise men warn about the tongue of the "strange woman" or the wife of another man, with whom one may not have sexual intercourse. They talk about her in Prov 2:16–19, 5:1–23, and 6:20–7:27—very extensively—and in each of these passages they refer to her smooth tongue. She is "the adulteress with her smooth words" (2:16). "For the lips of a forbidden woman drip honey" (5:3; at this time people were unfamiliar with candy as a delicacy). O she can talk so nicely. Of course, she "understands" you much better than your own wife, and she looks far more "attractive." "Her speech is smoother than oil" (5:3). Her words drip with seductive security: "I have been looking everywhere for you . . . I am so lonely . . . My bed smells so wonderful . . . Do you love 'making love'?"

Indeed, she approached him with even more refinement, for she presented herself as being religious! For this reason, she was so glad to have "found" him (7:15), because this was such a special day for her. She had made a vow to God and he had satisfied her wish. She had brought to him her peace offerings (to which belonged the votive offerings, according to Lev 3 and 7:11–21). The one bringing the sacrifice was permitted to eat from what was offered. In this way, she was attracting him with the prospect of a delicious meal of sacrificial food. Surely he could not refuse such an invitation?

What an impudent woman! For an Israelite brought a *peace* offering only when everything was well between Yahweh and him. And she dared to mention that sacrifice which was stipulated for when nothing was wrong! An adulteress who was, in fact, specifically forgetting the covenant of her God (Prov 2:17). For the rest, Scripture warns more often against unchastity under the guise of religion (Jer 29:21–23; Rev 2:20–23).

The young man need not be afraid of being discovered, for the coast was clear. "The old man," as she poignantly and almost hatefully spoke of him, was not at home for the time being. In view of her luxurious bed we may well think of him as a wealthy merchant who was gone on a business trip. And besides, darkness had fallen so who would see them?

That is how she attempted to seduce the young man.

Nevertheless, at the very moment when she was talking to him and directing her seductive words to him, he was not yet lost. A young man like Joseph resisted this temptation, although the wife of Potiphar shamelessly invited him, "Lie with me!" She said that not once, but day in and day out. Nevertheless, Joseph resisted and refused each day anew to come lie with her and have sexual relations with her (Gen 39:7–10). But here our young man fell from one folly into another. He looked at the woman and listened to her "lovely" words. Meanwhile she worked intensely with her eyes, another feature that Solomon talks about with such sobriety: "Do not let her capture you with her eyelashes" (6:25). But he did fall for her charms and allowed himself to be taken in by her ogling.

At that point the arrangement was quickly settled. We get the impression that he was still conflicted, because he made his decision "suddenly" (7:22). Her smooth and saccharine words, which she had made to drip into his heart, had broken his resistance (7:21). Like an ox going to slaughter, the dope went with her.

Four rules of thumb

We are living almost three thousand years after this incident, but the pattern of adultery and prostitution has hardly changed since then. This folly constantly begins in the manner sketched above. To start with, the young man should not have come near her house, just as we should not be walking unnecessarily through seedy areas, and could better avoid certain women. Next, her clothing should have alerted him, just as that feature can still alert young men today. Next, he should have seen through her words, which in similar instances today have the same content: "My husband is not home . . . Good to see you . . . Enjoy making love . . ." Finally, her manner of looking at him should have deterred him.

Although we will later investigate more extensively which weapons Solomon offers against this temptation, from what we have read up to this point, we can draw the preliminary conclusion that, between the lines, Proverbs was warning us about four dangers: first, about her *house*; second, about her *clothes*; third, about her *mouth*; fourth, about her *eyes*. From this, God-fearing men and lads should derive four rules of thumb:

- Stay as far away from her neighborhood as possible.
- Don't be fooled by her clothes.
- Don't be taken in by her mouth.
- Don't be ensnared by her eyes.

2. HOW THIS FOLLY PROGRESSES

How many have not thought in their stupidity that they could have sexual relations with a prostitute or with another man's wife without experiencing bad consequences from that? At an ill-fated hour, however, they get to find out. Even though such a woman may well have tasted like honey, "in the end she is bitter as wormwood," Solomon said, "sharp as a two-edged sword" (5:4). But this is obvious, isn't it?

> Can a man carry fire next to his chest
>   and his clothes not be burned?
> Or can one walk on hot coals
>   and his feet not be scorched?
> So is he who goes in to his neighbor's wife;
>   none who touches her will go unpunished. (Prov 6:27–29)

An Israelite carried burning coals in a brazier, but not in his "bosom," a term referring to the excess fabric of his garment above his belt, which he often used as a kind of sack (Exod 4:6). We would put it this way: Who carries fire in his pants pocket? Did you really think that your pants would not catch fire? Just as stupid is someone who has sexual relations with the wife of another man ("go in to her," Gen 16:2–4; 20:6; 30:3; 1 Cor 7:5), and then thinks that in doing so, he is not taking any risk. Such a man is playing with fire; indeed, he is embracing fire! The life experience of many generations is able to tell about the terrible burns that a man and his family can incur through this embracing of a strange woman. Solomon's comments about this could well have been written in our day.

If we were to summarize that Solomon is describing for his readers the damage that the strange woman can cause you, then it would be this warning: Stay away from her neighborhood, for she will cost you your *strength*, your *health*, your *honor*, perhaps even your *life*, and much *heartbreak*.

Let's consider this warning in greater detail.

1. *She costs you your strength.*

Adultery and chasing prostitutes often causes the perpetrator great financial damage. For such a woman is not satisfied, of course, with sexual relations. Whoever goes to her, like the man in Prov 5, will pay handsomely for every visit. And if she becomes a firm "friend," like the type of fellow in Prov 7 perhaps wanted, then you will be enriching with your money and possessions another household. She desires expensive luxuries, and now and then you'll need to bring along something for her family. You may well be happy that she does not fall into the hands of a pimp, who will extort money from you to remain a "friend" who will not tell your wife and acquaintances about your indiscretions. Such bribes can cost you dearly.

For that reason, these sweet-talking women are ruthless! Ruthless women, who are able to watch a man abandon his wife and children for her, in order to bring his hard-earned money into the house of strange women. For that reason, adultery is the crown of folly. Anyone who walks on coals will burn his feet, and anyone who commits adultery is driving himself into the ground. That is what Proverbs is holding clearly before its mostly young readers (Prov 6:32; cf. Luke 15:30).

> Keep your way far from her,
>   and do not go near the door of her house,
> lest you give your honor to others
>   and your years to the merciless,
> lest strangers take their fill of your strength,
>   and your labors go to the house of a foreigner. (Prov 5:8–10)

She presented herself as such a soft woman, but she turned out to be a tough woman. Unmercifully she forsook "the companion of her youth" (2:17). Unmercifully she robs you of your "radiance," your "years," your "fortune," and your "hard earned money." Here, the one explains the other. What else should a man's "radiance" be than his youthful vigor and vitality, his élan, the best years of his life, the accomplishments of his study and his professional skills, in short, everything that supplies him with prestige in society and for which he has labored for years? This is what the strange woman demands ruthlessly from the man's lawful wife and children, to devote them to herself and her coterie. Solomon was right: "For a prostitute can be had for a loaf of bread, but another man's wife preys on your very life" (Prov 6:26 NIV).

2. *She costs you your health.*

Throughout the entire world, health authorities are witnessing with concern the phenomenon that the classic venereal diseases of syphilis and gonorrhea are coming back with intensity. In the United States, gonorrhea stands near the top of the list of the most widespread infectious diseases, and its victims number in the millions. In the Netherlands, the number of gonorrhea cases has risen so sharply that experts are talking of an epidemic. One can point to various causes for the renewed rise of these terrible sexual diseases.

The new morality, pornography, and sex tourism

First of all, consider the new morality, with its permissiveness toward growing promiscuity. Away with the unbearable prescriptions of the Bible and of religion! Away with the constraining tradition and the antiquated legislation from a Victorian period, which provided a person with only unhealthy inhibitions! Do what you want, follow your sexual impulses, no matter how strange and wild they may be. With this seductive flute music today's prophets of "everything is okay" have lured innumerable young people to the utopia of their sexual "freedom." In increasingly broadening circles, people begin to find it normal that a young man has multiple liaisons with various hastily chosen women, and that a man has sexual encounters with various "strange women."

Furthermore, in this context we may think of the increasing practice of bizarre and unusual forms of sexual experiences, promoted by pornographic materials.

Finally, modern mass tourism also plays a significant role here. Large groups of people move about nowadays throughout the world, and as they travel across the border, many a person forgets all too easily the norms that he observed at home.

Groaning when your flesh and body are consumed (Prov 5:11)

Seldom, however, do we ever hear the advocates of such sexual "freedom" talk about the terrible consequences of this new morality. To learn about those, you need to turn to Holy Scripture, which is thoroughly honest about these things, and, in particular, to the book of Proverbs, which is so faithful to reality. Here our compassionate God gives us the salutary warning that the brief enjoyment of unchastity can very easily change into long-term groaning: "At the end of your life you will groan, *when your flesh and body are spent*" (Prov 5:11).

In saying this, Solomon was likely pointing to the gruesome consequences that prostitution and adultery can have for the health of those committing these acts, for he could certainly have observed these results in his own day. When the Canaanites celebrated their Baal festivals, they committed massive prostitution, whereby everyone had sexual relations with everyone else. One need not doubt that this ancient Near Eastern promiscuity also had catastrophic consequences for public health. And that was a time when penicillin had not yet been discovered! Every popular medical encyclopedia can inform you about the horrible character of the classic sexual diseases. At that point, one can do nothing other than admit that Solomon was not exaggerating when he talked about "*groaning* when your flesh and body are spent" (Prov 5:11).

Gonorrhea, or the clap

Anyone who contracts gonorrhea, or the clap, through sexual intercourse with a "strange woman" may not necessarily notice anything during the weeks following. And that is the time when the disease can be treated in its beginning stages. Thereafter with the male it can spread through his urethra to his bladder and eventually impede his ability to beget children. At the same time, this disease can lead to arthritis and intense pain in his abdomen.

For women, gonorrhea advances more treacherously, because with her the infection in many cases does not appear immediately. Thereby the disease can penetrate the uterus almost unnoticed, and, once it has settled there, it prevents many victims from being able to have children.

If a mother who is infected with gonorrhea does give birth, then there is a great chance that the eyes of her child will be infected during the birth. Africa and Asia are well acquainted with thousands of blind beggars, most of whose blindness is attributable to the gonorrhea of their mothers. Their only food is the crumbs that among poor people seldom fall from the table. When they ask for bread, they can receive a couple of stones thrown their way, or be chased away by mangy dogs. Although we don't see this in our own country, it was not that long ago that institutions for the blind were populated largely by victims of gonorrhea.

Syphilis, the curse of Venus

Syphilis, the other classic sexual disease, progresses even more horribly, if that's possible. Within a few weeks the infection can be stopped with the use of antibiotics, but how long have these been available in human history? It is shocking to consider that the great mass of the world population never knew about these means, to say nothing of possessing them and needing the rudimentary principles of enlightenment in this field.

After two months the disease enters its second stage, where various skin lesions can appear and one's hair can fall out. Next, the disease can lead the victim to think that he or she is healed, but only now does the treacherous character of the disease appear! Like a lethal time bomb, it remains ticking for years in the body of the person infected, only to explode after five years, but sometimes even thirty years later. What awaits the poor sufferer is absolutely atrocious.

In this third stage, syphilis can manifest itself in the following phenomena: unsightly skin conditions (bumps, ulcers in the oral mucus); inflammation of the periosteum; deterioration of the bones and joints; changes in the heart and the aorta, whereby even after twenty years one can suffer a syphilitic heart attack; damage to the liver, testicles, and the inner ear. In fact, there is no organ that might never be affected. Fifteen years after the infection, the disease can still develop into a syphilitic disease of the central nervous system, with bad effects on the brain and spinal cord. In connection with this, sicknesses relating to cerebral damage can appear, whereby delusions of grandeur and amnesia can be the accompanying mental disorders. The damage to the nervous system can result in paralysis of feeling and of movement. No wonder people call syphilis *Lues Venerea*, the curse of Venus, or Cupid's disease!

One who fears God escapes all of this (Eccl 7:18)

Needless to say, we would note that we must not view everyone who manifests one of the phenomena mentioned above as a victim of gonorrhea or syphilis. We have mentioned these phenomena as a warning and as an illustration to accompany the words of Solomon: "Groan *when your flesh and body are spent*" (Prov 5:11).

One can think of such misery also when we read in Prov 7 about those young men, "All at once he follows her, as an ox goes to the slaughter, or as a stag is caught fast till an arrow pierces its liver" (Prov 7:22–23a). Not to mention the various neurotic phenomena that result from sinning against the seventh commandment; these can in turn cause various psychosomatic illnesses.

But the person who is pleasing to God escapes the snares of such a woman (Eccl 7:26). For the fear of Yahweh is unto life, not in a vaguely spiritual sense but in a sense that is able to be felt physically. In many cases it keeps you out of the doctor's office and the psychiatrist's waiting room.

The fear of the LORD *is healthy*

With all of its knowledge, medical science cannot solve the worldwide problem of sexual diseases. Its antibiotics are beginning to fail, and its information remains inadequate to stem the rising flood. There is only one effective means against this evil and that is the fear of the LORD. For living according to God's commands is healthy! We discussed this already more extensively in connection with the proverb "Be not wise in your own eyes; fear the LORD, and turn away from evil. It will be healing to your flesh and refreshment to your bones" (Prov 3:7–8).

For Adam, God created *one* woman, and the Lord Jesus taught, "Therefore a man shall leave his father and mother and hold fast to his wife" (Mark 10:7; cf. Gen 2:24). Pay attention to those *two*! One stranger between both of you can bring you into lethal contact with ninety (!) other people. In this respect, some pagans are even wiser than modern Westerners.

Approximately three thousand years before the invention of the microscope and the discovery of the gonorrhea gonococcus, Yahweh knew that dangerous world of microbes and gave his people the only preventive commandment to keep these mass murderers and life destroyers away from your body: "You shall not commit adultery." One man and his wife, and only *those two* shall "become one flesh." For a healthy husband and a healthy wife who demonstrate marital faithfulness to each other cannot possible contract a venereal disease. To say it with a variation on Prov 14:30: "Marital fidelity gives life to the flesh, but unchastity makes the bones rot."

3. *She costs you your reputation.*

Unchastity and adultery can also rob you of *your reputation*, at least in a healthy society. But that was not present in Israel in every century. Through Jeremiah, Yahweh complains about the men of Jerusalem, "When I fed them to the full, they committed adultery and trooped to the houses of whores. They were well-fed, lusty stallions, each neighing for his neighbor's wife" (Jer 5:7–8; cf. 6:15). Before that time Jeremiah had also lived in a time of terrible covenant forsaking among Israel. Does this not apply to Christianity in our century as well? Can we not discern this from the changing judgment about various forms of unchastity and prostitution that one hears proclaimed in ever wider Christian circles? We presume that many from these circles would find the portrait of Prov 5–7 to be a gross exaggeration or even ridiculous. In our view, the permissive public opinion about these matters constitutes a proof and an expression of the general apostasy in every sphere of life on the part of previously Christian people groups.

Providentially one also still finds groups everywhere that believe that prostitution and adultery undermine the foundations of family, church (1 Cor 5:1; 6:12–20), and society. They believe that these practices signify the deathblow for marital love and the shattering of children's happiness. When people in such healthy groups hear that married Mr. So-and-so has forged a relationship with the also married Mrs. So-and-so, then they continue to use the word *scandal*. Solomon knew that years later this would not have ended up in the book of forgotten words and ideas:

> He will get wounds and dishonor,
> and his disgrace will not be wiped away. (Prov 6:33)

This is certainly the case when the enraged spouse of the unfaithful woman initiated a lawsuit against her lover, as could happen in Israel. Then one stood publicly shamed, "in the assembled congregation" (Prov 5:14). Then this sin could even cost you your life, as we will see later (Lev 20:10; Deut 22:22–24; John 8:5).

Also, in the Christian church that maintains the discipline of God's commandments, even though she believes in the forgiveness of sins, it is still considered shameful when someone falls into the sin of adultery, to say nothing of someone who lives in that sin. It belongs to this "folly in Israel" that it costs you your reputation, certainly with your wife and children, toward your friends and acquaintances, and toward the church. What a bitter experience!

Proverbs 5–7 wants to preserve you from that.

4. *She can even cost you your life.*

Nowadays people laugh about adultery and punish thievery, but God had taught his people to think differently about that! Among Israel, people viewed someone's invasion of another man's marriage far more seriously than an invasion of another man's house. One who had stolen did not go to prison but had to repay what was stolen, several times its value (Exod

22:1-4; Prov 6:31). With this you can help rid the world of the matter. And surely if someone had stolen because he was hungry, he was certainly punished but not despised. But someone who had sexual relations with another man's wife must, according to the Torah, be put to death!

The Torah prescribed capital punishment for adultery

Adultery was the purest form of Canaanitism and had to be exterminated from among God's holy people. Otherwise people would erase the dividing line that Yahweh had drawn between his holy people Israel and the surrounding pagan Canaanite world. Indeed, then Israel would be bringing down upon her own neck the judgment it was called to execute against Canaan. Although in other cases the Torah could judge mildly, for this sin the Torah knew no pardon. Because it touched the foundation of Israel's existence as God's holy people, God required the death penalty in such cases: "So you shall purge the evil from Israel" (Deut 22:22; cf. Lev 20:10). God esteemed marriage to be so holy and righteous, and of such fundamental importance, that he wanted to see the breaking of marriage in Israel punished with the ultimate punishment. A thief who was caught had to restore, but an adulterer who was caught must bleed. This was so, first of all, because God demanded it, and, in the second place, because the cheated spouse demanded it.

Jealousy makes a man furious

A man generally reacts more mildly when someone has stolen his bread to allay his hunger than when someone has stolen his wife to allay his passion. "For jealousy makes a man furious," said Solomon, "and he will not spare when he takes revenge" (Prov 6:34; cf. 27:4).

Consider the merchant mentioned in Prov 7, whose wife lured a young man into her marriage bed while her husband was absent. At full moon he came home (7:20). Had his wife been unfaithful during that time? She denied it most vigorously. Nonetheless he could not shake his suspicion. In that case, by virtue of the "law of jealousy," he could go with her to a priest, who would then place her symbolically and provisionally under Yahweh's curse (Num 5:11–31). If there were witnesses of her misdeed or if she had been caught with the young man, then "the day of vengeance" dawned when the cheated spouse went to the judges at the city gates (Prov 6:34).

There they stood, the adulterer and the adulteress, "in the assembled congregation" (5:14). At that point the most expensive gift no longer sufficed as a means of atonement. At that point the desperate young man, who was perhaps married himself, could make whatever excuses he wished—"She began to kiss me, she lured me inside"—but her husband was relentless and did not give in. "He will refuse though you multiply gifts" (6:35). "You," Solomon says to his readers, whereby he wished to say, This can happen to you, if you do not remain vigilant.

There was no doubt about the sentence, for the judges knew the Torah: "If a man commits adultery with the wife of his neighbor, both the adulterer and the adulteress shall surely be put to death" (Lev 20:10; cf. Deut 22:22; Ezek 23:45–49). In this way Yahweh protected not only his own holiness and that of Israel but also the existence of marriages among his people, and thereby the existence of society.

Solomon taught the same in the form of *mashals*:

> People do not despise a thief if he steals
>   to satisfy his appetite when he is hungry,
> but if he is caught, he will pay sevenfold;
>   he will give all the goods of his house.
> He who commits adultery lacks sense;
>   he who does it destroys himself.
> He will get wounds and dishonor,
>   and his disgrace will not be wiped away.
> For jealousy makes a man furious,
>   and he will not spare when he takes revenge.
> He will accept no compensation;
>   he will refuse though you multiply gifts. (Prov 6:30–35)

This was referring to a man who brought the matter before the judges. Presumably, however, many a cheated spouse took justice into his own hands and killed his wife's lover in blind rage. "For jealousy makes a man furious" (6:34). This is how Prince Amnon met his end. He had raped his half-sister Tamar. Two years later he was murdered by his enraged brother Absalom (2 Sam 13). Should we not think of such tragically shortened lives of adulterers when we hear the Preacher ask, "Why should you die before your time?" (Eccl 7:17)? How many men and lads would have met a premature end as a result of a triangular relationship? This is almost a daily part of our news.

Proverbs warns often, not without reason, that anyone who has sexual relations with another man's wife is walking along the edge of his grave. Literally (through the capital punishment in Israel or being killed by her husband) and figuratively.

Adultery is deadly, literally and figuratively

As we saw above, adultery can lead literally to someone's death. But in Proverbs, the terms *life* and *death* can also have a broader meaning. Your *life* is often a different word for your happiness. And *death* is often the destruction of your happiness. This comes to expression in our terms this way: if your marriage is broken, and irreparable damage is done to your fatherhood and paternal happiness, if your children are assigned to your wife and you are burdened down with exorbitant legal costs and alimony payments, if later you, perhaps, must live out your old age without children and grandchildren, then the wise composer of proverbs calls this "death," already while you are living! At that point you may still talk of happiness, that you have not fallen by a murderer's hand or your health was not destroyed by a terrible sexual disease.

God wants to protect the members of his church from that, and for that reason he gave the book of Proverbs, with its life lessons, especially for young people. For that reason he warned so often against this evil. Think of death, both in a literal and in a figurative sense, when Holy Scripture warns us,

> So you will be delivered from the forbidden woman,
> > from the adulteress with her smooth words,
> who forsakes the companion of her youth
> > and forgets the covenant of her God;
> for her house sinks down to death,
> > and her paths to the departed;
> none who go to her come back,
> > nor do they regain the paths of life. (Prov 2:16–19)

> Her feet go down to death;
> > her steps follow the path to Sheol;
> she does not ponder the path of life;
> > her ways wander, and she does not know it. (Prov 5:5–6)

> For many a victim has she laid low,
> > and all her slain are a mighty throng.
> Her house is the way to Sheol,
> > going down to the chambers of death. (Prov 7:26–27)

> For a prostitute is a deep pit;
> > an adulteress is a narrow well.
> She lies in wait like a robber
> > and increases the traitors among mankind. (Prov 23:27–28)

5. *She costs you a lot of heartbreak.*

All this misery was avoidable. If only one had listened to God and his Word, and had taken to heart Solomon's wisdom, then nothing would have happened. Thereby adultery and prostitution can provide their perpetrators with such heartbreak, when one comes to the insight that one has destroyed his life through this sin. One moment of carelessness can produce years of weeping. Also, on account of the remorse that can continue to gnaw for the rest of one's life:

> How I hated discipline,
> and my heart despised reproof!
> I did not listen to the voice of my teachers
> or incline my ear to my instructors. (Prov 5:12–13)

3. HOW TO ARM YOURSELF AGAINST THIS FOLLY

The best cure is prevention. That notion undergirds Solomon's broad admonition of Prov 5–7, the full-disclosure description of the misery that adultery and fornication occasionally yields can serve to deter readers and to spare them this misery.

Do not infer from this, however, that Holy Scripture thereby wishes to minimize our marital happiness, or to restrict a person's sexual enjoyment. On the contrary, those who proclaim sexual "freedom" apart from God and his Word are leading their devotees straight into the most severe slavery and robbing them of pure marital happiness. Just like cows break through the hedge of a juicy meadow to seek starvation rations in a cactus field. What God holds before us in his Word, by contrast, is not designed to *reduce* our marital joy as much as possible but to *enlarge* it as widely as possible between two sinful people!

In this context Solomon supplies in Prov 5–7 a number of worthwhile hints as to how people can prevent marital *misery*, and can increase their marital *happiness*:

- Remember the teaching in the fear of the Lord.
- Stay away as far as possible from her neighborhood.
- Do not desire her beauty in your heart.
- Consider the outcome of such a relationship.
- Enjoy the love of your own wife.
- Remember that God sees you everywhere.

1. *Remember the teaching in the fear of the* LORD.

Observing the seventh commandment depends, according to Proverbs, on observing the fifth commandment (see our comments on Prov 1:8). "Honor your father and your mother" lends the requisite power for "You shall not commit adultery." This assumes, of course, that one's parents were God-fearing. Such godly nurture can equip and arm a young heart against various threats to his future happiness, including those of adultery and fornication.

But then, of course, one must indeed listen to one's parents! No wonder that each of the three segments about the strange woman in Prov 5–7 begins by emphasizing that: *Listen up!* It is not the smooth words of that strange woman that must charm your heart, but what you heard at home from your God-fearing parents.

For then you will have in hand a powerful weapon for protecting your happiness. "My godly mother always said . . . . My believing father never wanted . . ."; that is what you must keep before your eyes day and night. How they inculcated childlike respect for the Word of God, and taught you to believe that only serving him would be able to make you happy. Hang this teaching on your neck like an expensive signet ring. Let that be your adorning, your bodyguard, the guide that goes ahead of you, and the lamp with which you walk down a dark path (cf. 1:8; Exod 13:9; Deut 6:6–9). Then you will be armed by their godly words against her sinful words, and you won't walk around naively with her, straight to your destruction. Your parental discipline keeps you on the path of life.

Solomon taught this concisely in these *mashals*:

> My son, keep your father's commandment,
>   and forsake not your mother's teaching.
> Bind them on your heart always;
>   tie them around your neck.
> When you walk, they will lead you;
>   when you lie down, they will watch over you;
>   and when you awake, they will talk with you.
> For the commandment is a lamp and the teaching a light,
>   and the reproofs of discipline are the way of life. (Prov 6:20–23)

God not only caused you to be instructed in his Word in your parental home, however,—although he assigned that first of all to fathers and mothers (Deut 6:7; 11:19; Ps 78:3–4; Eph 6:4)—but also in the "schoolhouse." In Israel, it was the task of the priests and Levites to instruct the people in the Torah (Deut 33:10; Jer 2:8; Mal 2:7; Neh 8; Luke 2:40–52; 4:16). In addition, many proverbs of Solomon and other wise men were circulating. In the same way, we too are familiar with more teachers of God's Word than only our parents. To the extent that they taught us to know Holy Scripture, they emphasized to us that we must love our heavenly Father and walk in his ways. This pertains as well to the husband-wife relationship and the boy-girl relationship. Moreover, they can also hand down to us the teaching of our Lord and his apostles (cf. Matt 5:27–32; Rom 1:24–32; 1 Cor 6–7; Gal 5:19; 5:22–33; Col 3:18–19; Heb 13:4; 1 Pet 3; 2 Pet 2:14; Rev 22:15). Rich blessings along this line can also be harvested from daily Scripture reading in the home.

But the best warning does not help if one does not listen to it, and, for that reason, the wise men pressed strongly that you apply their lessons about the strange woman to your lifestyle from your heart. What they held before you about her in Prov 5–7 you must preserve just as carefully as "the apple of your eye" (7:2). You must be very familiar with Lady Wisdom, but not with the strange woman. You must be as intimate with Lady Wisdom as with your bride, whom people in Israel would call "my sister" (Song 4:9–10; 5:1–2). In short, make these life *lessons* your life *habits*! Bind them on your fingers—a genuine Torah expression—so that you see them constantly:

> My son, keep my words
>   and treasure up my commandments with you;
> keep my commandments and live;
>   keep my teaching as the apple of your eye;
> bind them on your fingers;
>   write them on the tablet of your heart.
> Say to wisdom, "You are my sister,"
>   and call insight your intimate friend. (Prov 7:1–4)

2. *Stay away as far as possible from her neighborhood.*

Another helpful hint from Solomon goes like this: "Keep your way far from her, and do not go near the door of her house" (5:8). Do not pursue the temptation. Do not fly like a moth to the light. Offer no place in your heart to sinful sexual thoughts and desires. Avoid books and pictures, websites and other tools that stimulate your imagination and drive it in a wrong direction. Flee from this evil. Not very heroic advice? The Lord and his apostles have often repeated it another way: "If your right eye causes you to sin, tear it out and throw it away" (Matt 5:28–30). "Flee from sexual immorality" (1 Cor 6:18). "Flee youthful passions" (2 Tim 2:22; cf. Sir 9:1–9).

3. *Do not desire her beauty in your heart.*

"You have captivated my heart with one glance of your eyes," we read in Song 4:9. But there a *bridegroom* is whispering in pure love into the ear of his own *bride*. By contrast, bad women use their eyes as a snare for catching strange men (Eccl 7:26). "The haughty stare betrays an unchaste wife; her eyelids give her away," says Sir 26:9 (NRSV). In his day, Isaiah watched them walking the streets of Jerusalem with their wanton eyes (Isa 3:16). Therefore, Solomon warned about the *eyes* and *eyelashes* of the strange woman, in fact, about all her charms:

> Do not desire her beauty in your heart,
> and do not let her capture you with her eyelashes. (Prov 6:25)

A different translation of this verse reads like this: "Do not lust after her beauty" (NKJV). Sirach teaches something similar: "Turn away your eyes from a shapely woman, and do not gaze at beauty belonging to another; many have been seduced by a woman's beauty, and by it passion is kindled like a fire" (Sir 9:8; cf. 9:3–9). For from the heart bubble forth both the adulterous leers of feminine eyes and the lecherous glances of masculine eyes (Mark 7:21).

Therefore, the proverb writers said: Listen to those who nurtured you, for then at such dangerous moments you will recall what you learned at home and in church: "You shall not *desire* your neighbor's wife" (Exod 20:17). And then you will fight against rising unchastity already in your heart. Our Lord Jesus fulfilled the law on this point as well, with his instruction, "But I say to you that everyone who looks at a woman with lust has already committed adultery with her in his heart" (Matt 5:28).

4. *Consider the outcome of such a relationship.*

"Better is the end of a thing than its beginning" (Eccl 7:8). For that reason, the wise men constantly teach us to evaluate things in terms of their *progress* and *end*. Thus, joy can end up in sorrow (Prov 14:13). What appears to be a good path can end up being a bad path (16:25 [= 14:12]). Listening to wisdom can ultimately make you wise (19:20). A fortune initially gained hastily can in the end remain unblessed (20:21). The enchanting wine can in the end sting (23:32). Hasty lawsuits can yield acid (25:8). Pampered when young, unruly when old (29:21; cf. 19:20; 23:18; 24:14, 20). The same is true regarding the strange woman: your final impressions teach you far better who she is than your first impressions.

> For the lips of a loose woman drip honey,
> > and her speech is smoother than oil;
> but in the end she is bitter as wormwood,
> > sharp as a two-edged sword. (Prov 5:3–4)

As we have already seen, it can cost you your fortune, your honor, your health, and in some instances, even your *life*. But whoever is wise enough to listen to Holy Scripture, and courageous enough to row against the current of permissiveness, is walking along the safest path for sparing oneself all those miseries we have mentioned. This includes the misery of sexual disease.

5. *Enjoy the love of your own wife.*

But my beloved young man, it is entirely unnecessary, isn't it, for you to go to a strange woman when you have such a lovely wife at home? Why not enjoy love with the one who is lawfully yours? This is perhaps the finest advice that Solomon provides to prevent going to the strange woman (Prov 5:15–20). "Rejoice in the wife of your youth" (v. 18). Men who have been married somewhat longer could well take this to heart, as well as the inexperienced young men (1:4; 7:7), many of whom were already married. For in Israel, men likely married before reaching twenty, at which point one cannot boast in having a lot of life experience. The undiscerning lad who we saw in Prov 7 going to bed with the wife of another man was, as we suggested, himself married.

Now a husband can occasionally act as though there is something deficient about his own wife, and that's why he looks at another woman. It seems as though, in Prov 5, Solomon grabs such a blockhead by the shoulders in order to warn him with very clear imagery not to stare himself blind at the beauty of a strange woman, but rather to enjoy the charm of his own wife. The poet compares masculine passion with thirst, which in the arid Near East was a poignant image of sexual desire. He compares the lawful spouse and her charms to an expensive well, from which the husband can quench the thirst of all his senses.

> Drink water from your own cistern,
> > flowing water from your own well.
> Should your springs be scattered abroad,
> > streams of water in the streets?
> Let them be for yourself alone,
> > and not for strangers with you.
> Let your fountain be blessed,
> > and rejoice in the wife of your youth,
> > a lovely deer, a graceful doe.

> Let her breasts fill you at all times with delight;
>   be intoxicated always in her love.
> Why should you be intoxicated, my son, with a forbidden woman
>   and embrace the bosom of an adulteress? (Prov 5:15–20)

Of course, Solomon is not sketching a complete portrait of the place of the wife in marriage. Proverbs 31 will add a lot to that picture. What is in view, however, is the need to arm his readers as powerfully as possible against the seduction of the strange woman. This explains his bold imagery, which strongly resembles that of the Song of Solomon.

It seems that, with a certain mischievous cunning, he is trying to make such a floundering man jealous. Why would you actually quench your thirst with public women ("streams of water in the streets"), when you have at home, with the sweetheart of your own wife, a private fountain from which you can drink to your heart's content (Prov 5:15–16)? Or must she perhaps, because you have neglected her, provide satisfaction to other men and not to you alone? You can interpret verse 16 in this way as well. Then she is not only your own cistern but really a fountain for the town, whose water runs across the public square. You must have a wife for yourself, young man (v. 17; Song 4:12). Come on, let her hear your words of praise—that young maiden from the years of your youth—and not the wanton woman (Prov 5:18). Or is she perhaps not worthy? Is your own wife perhaps not a lovely deer or a gracious gem? Let her breasts continually make you satisfied with joy, rather than those of an unchaste woman! Be intoxicated with her caresses and not with those of a strange woman (v. 19)!

Between the lines we can hear the warning of the wise proverb writer: Away with that smoldering dissatisfaction in your heart! Smother that fire! Make room again for real happiness and be deeply grateful for the wife God has given you, when she was still a young maiden and you were a young man (cf. Eccl 9:9). And remember that whoever reaches for *the forbidden* always shoves aside *the best*.

The watchword for a happy marriage

Solomon is in fact relating the admonition we hear later in Scripture: "Husbands, love your wives" (Col 3:19; cf. Eph 5:28). With those words, Holy Scripture simultaneously points married people to the secret of the ultimate in sexual joy. The "everything goes" prophets of the new morality accuse those who teach "godliness according to Holy Scripture" of having obstructed for a long time the development of sexual expression. But experience proves that sex without love is merely a short-term connection hardly deserving of the name "marriage." Moreover, it provides many with much less joy than it had promised them. You need only believe Scripture: everything that you subtract from God and his Word, from your wife and your family, these are the enemies of your sexual happiness. The watchword for a happy marriage is this: *together*! "Husbands, love your wives" (Col 3:19). "And *those two* shall be one flesh" (Matt 19:5).

Paul arms the church with the same wisdom

In the cosmopolitan port of Corinth, men went as easily to a brothel as people today go to the cinema. At that time, the apostle Paul pointed in 1 Cor 7 to the same means as Solomon identifies in Prov 5: "But because of cases of sexual immorality, each man should have his own wife and each woman her own husband" (1 Cor 7:2). People should satisfy their sexual needs within marriage and not in a brothel. But then husband and wife may not withhold their body from one another, for sexual hunger must also be satisfied in its time. In this context, the apostle talked about marital "obligations" (1 Cor 7:3–6; cf. 1 Thess 4:4).

Elsewhere the apostle had to warn against gnostic heretics. They taught that God prohibited the enjoyment not only of foods but also of sexual intercourse in marriage. According to them, sexuality was displeasing to God. This despite the fact that everything God created is good. Timothy was supposed to communicate this courageously (1 Tim 4). In doing so, he could naturally appeal in the first place to the Torah (Gen 2:24; 2 Tim 3:16), and, in addition, to the book of Proverbs. For in that latter book, the wise man Solomon had clearly identified with practical imagery this act of marriage as a sovereign means against extramarital sexual relations (Prov 5).

By means of this openhearted instruction, Holy Scripture gives us, not in a prudish but in a delicate manner, the requisite wisdom for navigating between the shoals of gnostic contempt for marriage and libertine practices of "I'll do as I please."

6. *Remember well that God sees you everywhere.*

Adultery and prostitution belong to the "works of darkness," also in a literal sense (Rom 13:12–13; Eph 5:11; 1 Thess 5:4–7). Those practicing this unrighteousness easily arrive at the notion: Who can see me in the darkness? "The eye of the adulterer also waits for the twilight, saying, 'No eye will see me'; and he veils his face" (Job 24:15; cf. Sir 23:18–21). But Solomon warned: Do not forget that Yahweh sees everything; "There is no gloom or deep darkness where evildoers may hide themselves" (Job 34:22; cf. Ps 139:1–12; 2 Chr 16:9; Zech 4:10). He sees you going to that strange woman and lying with her; don't forget that!

Proverbs 5 concludes with that serious warning:

> For a man's ways are before the eyes of the LORD,
>   and he ponders all his paths.
> The iniquities of the wicked ensnare him,
>   and he is held fast in the cords of his sin.
> He dies for lack of discipline,
>   and because of his great folly he is led astray. (vv. 21–23)

In a manner of speaking, God doesn't need to punish adulterers at all, for this evil punishes itself. We have seen that extensively. This sin can cost you your fortune, your health, your good name, and perhaps even your life. Adultery itself is the undoing of its perpetrators. And in one sentence, what is their fundamental flaw? Lack of discipline! Great foolishness or wickedness (v. 23).[2] One senses that Solomon wants to engrave in the palm of every man and boy, "Who, O fool, chooses death instead of life?"

7. Six rules of thumb

These were the six rules of thumb that Prov 5–7 puts in the hand of the God-fearing man and boy:

- Remember the teaching in the fear of the LORD.
- Stay away as far as possible from her neighborhood.
- Do not desire her beauty in your heart.
- Consider the outcome of such a relationship.
- Enjoy the love of your own wife.
- Remember that God sees you everywhere.

But the woman is not always the one who is primarily guilty

Some have observed that Solomon speaks exclusively about the seduction of a man by a woman. Adultery and prostitution are sins of which, by the nature of the case, *two* people are culpable, such that the initiative can proceed, of course, from the man as well. Holy Scripture tells the story of the

---

2. See van Deursen, *Psalms I*, 93–96.

cunning princess Tamar, who was disgraced by her half-brother (2 Sam 13). And among the social oppressions occurring in the time of Amos, Yahweh identified this one: "A man and his father go in to the same girl" (Amos 2:7; perhaps a defenseless servant girl?).

That results from Israel forsaking Yahweh, for in the Torah Yahweh raises up a shield over Israelite women and maidens (see, e.g., Deut 22:13-30). Woe to the newly married young man who lied in saying that, on her wedding day, his bride was not a virgin. He would be beaten publicly and pay a hefty fine (Deut 22:13-21). Woe to the man who assaulted a betrothed girl in the open field, where nobody had heard her cry for help. He was condemned to death (Deut 22:25-27). Nonetheless, Yahweh did distinguish compassionately between such men and an unmarried young man who had seduced a girl; he received much more grace (Deut 22:28-29).

But in Prov 5-7 Solomon was warning young men about the wicked woman. Believing women and girls can draw from this the requisite teaching in order to be armed against being seduced by an evil man.

But with you there is forgiveness, that you may be feared (Ps 130)

In order to bring an accusation against the Lord Jesus, one day the Pharisees and scribes brought a woman to him. She had been caught in adultery and Moses had commanded, "Such a man or woman must be put to death by stoning." But what would Jesus say about that? Initially he did not answer, but drew some kind of drawing in the sand. When they continued to press him, however, he stood up and said, "Let him who is without sin among you be the first to throw a stone at her." Then he bent down again and wrote some more on the ground. But when these men heard this, they went away one by one, "beginning with the older ones."

This was a telling sequence!

"And Jesus was left alone with the woman standing before him. Jesus stood up and said to her, 'Woman, where are they? Has no one condemned you?'"

"No one, Lord," she replied.

Then Jesus said to her, "Neither do I condemn you; go, and from now on sin no more" (John 8:3-11).

10

Proverbs 8

A Canticle Celebrating Wisdom

WE ARE REACHING THE end of the Instruction Manual for Proverbs (Prov 1–9). As you have seen, it has shed light in various ways on the profit of wisdom, and has prodded us in a variety of ways: "Take wisdom to heart, for then you will taste the greatest possible happiness and you will experience the least possible misery." Of course, in saying this, it was pointing especially to the life lessons that we will be reading later in Prov 10–31, which is the actual book of Proverbs. Proverbs 8 comes along, however, to underscore once more the life importance of those lessons.

It does this in a poetic and fascinating manner. The author places wisdom itself on the stage as though it were a speaking person (vv. 1–3). Wisdom points to its own honesty (vv. 6–13); to the power and profit that goes forth from it (vv. 14–21); and to its longevity (vv. 22–31). Therefore, young and old must listen to wisdom every day; their happiness in life is at stake (vv. 32–36).

In the course of time, however, people have offered various perspectives on Prov 8. It was as though here Scripture was not supplying a poetic description of wisdom, or a personal representation, but that it had in view a real *living person*, perhaps even a divine person. The apocryphal book Jesus Sirach (ca. 180 BC) differs on this point from the canonical book of Proverbs. Later in history, the apocryphal book of Wisdom of Solomon and Gnosticism twisted the explanation of Prov 8:22–31 even more.

Arius used this passage to prove his error that our Lord Jesus Christ was ultimately a creature as well, the highest creature, to be sure, but still a creature. His proof? Proverbs 8:22, where we read clearly, "The LORD possessed me at the beginning of his work, the first of his acts of old." According to Arius, that referred to God's Son, for in Scripture he is called "the wisdom of God" (1 Cor 1:24, 30; Col 2:3; cf. 1:15). As if a creature could save us (cf. Heidelberg Catechism, Lord's Days 5–6)![1]

We will leave aside these questions surrounding Prov 8:22–31 in order to provide our own explanation of Prov 8. In our view, this Scripture passage definitely does not create for us penetrating theological or philosophical problems. On the contrary, it lets us hear a wonderful canticle celebrating wisdom, one that climaxes in the urgent appeal: take wisdom to heart! Afterward, in a separate section, we will return to consider the explanation of Arius and his sympathizers.

1. LADY WISDOM STANDS WITHIN ALL OF LIFE, READY TO HELP EVERYONE WITH COUNSEL (PROV 8:1–5)

Do you still know Lady Wisdom? We met her earlier in Prov 1:20–33. She is not a living person, but rather meets us as a poetic personal representation. You need only recall all the wisdom that God has deposited in his Scripture and in his creation; that is what Prov 8 is now setting before us like a wise woman (Joab once sent such a woman to David to plead for Absalom [2 Sam 14:2; cf. 20:16–17]).

To make it even more concrete for you: perhaps you already owe a lot of your life-insight to Holy Scripture. You are amazed at the reason and logic with which God has created everything; to see that, you need look only at your own body. You have mastered a subject; this too is a matter of wisdom. You know that living a life worthy of the name is also an art that you can practice only if you respect God and his order (see chapter 4). For that, you can learn a lot from nature, but never as well as when you look at nature through the spectacles of Scripture. And in that connection, the Proverbs of Solomon constitute the standard work in the area of wisdom. So then, that entire ocean of wisdom contained in divine *revelation* and in human *experience* is what Solomon is setting before us here as though it were a living person.

The Israelites loved such personal representations. We see this from the book of Proverbs. Occasionally it presents wisdom as a bride or spouse (4:6–9; 6:22); at other times, as a companion or bosom buddy (7:4); again, as a builder (9:1); and here in Prov 8 as *a wise woman*. A prophetess or street preacher. In her "person," all the wisdom in the world turns to speak to us.

---

1. Dennison, *Reformed Confessions*, 2.773.

Does not wisdom call?
Does not understanding raise her voice? (Prov 8:1)

For the sake of convenience, in what follows, we will call her Lady Wisdom. We capitalize this title because this is a personal name, even though it is a fictitious person. We could speak just as easily of Lady *Insight* or Lady *Understanding*. Such names would then have been less susceptible to the strange speculations or representations that people have given to Prov 8:22–31 (see below).

No, Prov 8 will not be exhausting us with any philosophical problems. Rather, this poem will later reach the climax of "in the beginning," when God created the heavens and the earth with wisdom. But where does the poet place his refined Lady Wisdom in the opening scene? On the street! Don't read past this. This canticle, which later will be looking back to a point beyond the creation of the world, begins on the street! In so doing, the poet is adding a significant feature to the portrait of his main character, from which we get to know her even better:

On the heights beside the way,
    at the crossroads she takes her stand;
beside the gates in front of the town,
    at the entrance of the portals she cries aloud. (Prov 8:2–3)

Lady Wisdom does not shrink back from mingling with ordinary people. She does not lift up her voice in a sacred space, far away from the noise of the street, but she chooses to stand at the gate. The Israelite can find her at the heart and focus of social life. Where he conducts his business, talks with his friends, defends his right, makes agreements, pursues his civic interests, seeks companionship, and enjoys his small pleasures, precisely there stands Lady Wisdom on the platform.

After all, wisdom is not something for which you sense a need only a few times in your life. This, too, Prov 8 teaches in a poetic manner. When does Lady Wisdom demand attention? Specifically when the merchants are standing around the payment scales, when the elders have to render a legal judgment, and when women are chatting together. Lady Wisdom lifts up her voice not in a quiet corner where nothing is happening but amid the noise of "the marketplace of life," in a lively open-air gathering. She interrupts her audience in their *daily activities*, because it is exactly in those activities where she can provide so much good counsel.

She wants to help everyone, even the biggest blockhead. That appears from her activity at the gate. For she is not standing in a cellar whispering, but on a promontory proclaiming her insights loudly (v. 3). So nobody needs to make do without her counsel. We see that even more clearly in her appeal:

> To you, O men, I call,
>   and my cry is to the children of man.
> O simple ones, learn prudence;
>   O fools, learn sense. (Prov 8:4–5)

She is not delivering a lecture to a select company of scholars, but issues an appeal to everyone: "My appeal applies to *the children of men*," she says, without any exception. She is talking to every John Doe—to every one of us. It's possible that she is looking somewhat more intently at the undiscerning, the naive ones. No wonder, for they are so defenseless against various cunning temptations. Often they act so immaturely and allow themselves to be taken in so easily by various follies. There is only one medicine that will be effective against that: acquiring wisdom. *Discernment*. That is what you need, the first thing in the morning and the last thing at night. You need to be able to see through everything. That is what Lady Wisdom teaches. She wants to inculcate that into fools, if only they give her their heart (v. 5).

Do you not consider it to be a friendly gesture that Lady Wisdom seeks us out? According to this poem, the initiative proceeds from her. She is standing in the marketplace of life calling out. That is true, isn't it? Is it not the case that from Holy Scripture there goes forth a world embracing appeal for wise living, according to God's order? As people live according to that Scripture, they can say, "Does not nature itself teach you to live wisely?" Do you not hear that *appeal* going forth throughout the entire creation?

Therefore, in Prov 8, Lady Wisdom may well be a fictitious person, but at the same time she is the poetic image of a *cosmic reality* (cf. our comments on Prov 1:20)! Later, all that wisdom in nature and in Scripture will declare from her lips, "I love those who love me, and those who seek me diligently find me" (Prov 8:17). That is simply bound to happen.

2. LADY WISDOM, WHOSE COUNSEL IS THOROUGHLY HONEST, YOU WILL FIND NOWHERE ELSE (PROV 8:6–13)

In such a city gate, however, could be found on occasion a merchant with a fraudulent scale. And false witnesses came there, and on occasion unrighteous judges rendered their verdict there. You could find false prophets and priests there who twisted God's Word. Listen to the prophets rage against this evil (Isa 30:9; 59:14; Hos 4:2). Listen to the psalmists complain about "lying lips."[2] "Save, O LORD," they would call out, "for the godly one is gone. . . . Everyone utters lies to his neighbor; with flattering lips and a double heart they speak" (Ps 12:1–2).

No, listen then to Lady Wisdom!

> Hear, for I will speak noble things,
> and from my lips will come what is right. (Prov 8:6)

Notice the word *noble*, which reflects the Hebrew accurately. Lady Wisdom comes—also in Proverbs—to speak of matters that princes and other high officials definitely need not consider as being beneath them (see our comments on v. 15).

> For my mouth will utter truth;
> wickedness is an abomination to my lips. (Prov 8:7)

In Scripture, truth is often another word for steadfastness, fidelity. You can trust Lady Wisdom 100 percent. She is a thoroughly reliable counselor, whose advice will never lead you astray into deception. You can look high and low for even one proverb that will provide you with catastrophic advice. Her words derive their solid character from her aversion to all forms of wickedness (the rebellion against Yahweh that may or may not be clothed with piety). She hates that wickedness like an abomination (*to'abah*), the word forged in the Torah to describe Canaanite paganism.

> All the words of my mouth are righteous;
> there is nothing twisted or crooked in them. (Prov 8:8)

Lady Wisdom is always on point. She does not embellish things, but shows them in their true extent and form. She does not close her eyes to the conjunction of sin and misery in which we must live, and for that reason, she does not treat us to dreamy fantasies that have nothing to do with the real world. She does not throw a smokescreen in front of us with complicated lines of reasoning that will drive you nuts. Whether she addresses you from God's creation or from God's Scriptures, everything is saturated with *righteousness*—completely permeated with loyalty toward God and his order for living. In a book like Proverbs absolutely nothing is twisted in a deceptive manner.

The more you get to taste wisdom, the more readily you will endorse the sayings of this book.

> They are all straight to him who understands,
> and right to those who find knowledge. (Prov 8:9)

---

2. See van Deursen, *Psalms I*, 113–18.

Knowing wisdom leads us to recognize wisdom (cf. Matt 11:19; 13:12). Unspiritual people often view wisdom as foolishness (1 Cor 2:14–15), but whoever is "of God" (1 John 4:1–6) or "of the truth" (1 John 3:19) teaches discernment (see our comments on Prov 8:5). Once we are on that path, we endorse the words of Lady Wisdom with increasing heartiness: She is right!

> Take my instruction instead of silver,
> and knowledge rather than choice gold,
> for wisdom is better than jewels,
> and all that you may desire cannot compare with her. (Prov 8:10–11)

Precisely because Proverbs can value precious gems, you are able to see how highly it values wisdom. Whoever "eats" Proverbs and learns the art and discipline of living from it, wears more beautiful jewelry than if he or she wore choice gold (v. 10). Really, in this life, nothing compares to the value of wisdom that comes through fearing Yahweh; we have heard Solomon say that more often (cf. 2:4; 3:14; 8:19; 16:16). Although wisdom is, in fact, priceless, it is obtainable for everyone (see our comments on Prov 8:1–5).

> I, wisdom, dwell with prudence,
> and I find knowledge and discretion. (Prov 8:12)

When you invite Lady Wisdom, she brings along her daughter, Shrewdness, for they dwell together and accompany each other throughout life. How can you derive profit from them in your daily living? By regularly reading and rereading the book of Proverbs, of course, preferably with pencil in hand for underlining what impresses you as you are reading. But if you are dealing with a particular problem, you could read only this book about that topic. Then you'll be reading with a focus on your questions, and you will discover *well-considered* knowledge. Someone has observed that a good proverb contains an entire book squeezed into one sentence.

And where lies the secret of this counselor who is much more precious than gold and thoroughly reliable? Why do the sayings of Lady Wisdom fit so well in such different situations like a key in a lock? Because she has but one quest that completely dominates her: "I love Yahweh and I *hate* evil (rebellion against him)." Pay careful attention to the fact that in the next verses, she uses the idea of "hate" twice.

> The fear of the LORD is hatred of evil.
> Pride and arrogance and the way of evil
> and perverted speech I hate. (Prov 8:13)

All true wisdom begins with humble respect for God's revelation in Scripture and creation (bound together indissolubly). We discussed this extensively in connection with Prov 1:7; we even devoted a separate chapter to that (chapter 4). Wisdom is nothing other than the applied fear of the LORD (Prov 2:5). Put another way, wisdom is humility in practice.

God has tied our happiness to the order of his ordinances in both Scripture and nature. He specified the boundaries of our power and the breadth of our calling. In so doing, he measured out for us a certain space for living and working. Those who are godly and wise adapt themselves to that space, unto their own happiness (Ps 19:7–11). The proud and those with lying lips, by contrast, rise up in sharp rebellion against God and his order (evil is rebellion). In so doing, they are bringing about their own unhappiness. They twist the entire truth about God and his creation, and for this they even use religious and scientific terms. I hate that arrogance and I hate that revolution, says Lady Wisdom (Ps 19:13; see our comments on Prov 3:5).

3. LADY WISDOM ALWAYS KNOWS WHAT TO DO AND THEREBY SUPPLIES HER FRIENDS WITH POWER AND PROFIT (PROV 8:14–21)

Lady Wisdom stands ready throughout all of life to help everyone with counsel (Prov 8:1–6). She does that with thoroughgoing honesty (vv. 7–13). And she is able to help everyone, because she always knows what to do (vv. 14–21). If you are wondering, "Where should I start?" she answers quietly, "I will give you insight to see through your situation." In this way, you will no longer stumble blindly into your troubles, but with her help you will resolve them carefully and properly. Not that your path will immediately be a bed of roses—were you perhaps expecting that in this world?—but her advice does provide you the least amount of misery and often the most profit. That is what she is pointing to in the next few verses.

> I have counsel and sound wisdom;
>   I have insight; I have strength.
> By me kings reign,
>   and rulers decree what is just;
> by me princes rule,
>   and nobles, all who govern justly. (Prov 8:14–16)

"Do not give your strength to women," said the mother of King Lemuel. Rather, defend justice and righteousness, for those affect the order of life with which a people stand or fall (Prov 31:1–9). Therefore, a king, a cabinet member, a judge, or a legislative representative cannot function for a day without wisdom. Such a person stands every day before questions like: What should I do about that? (So he needs good *counsel*.) How should I approach this? (So he needs *caution*.) What is involved with this? (He must possess *insight*.) How can I master this matter? (He needs *strength*, referring to strength for endurance.) No one other than I can give him all of this, says Lady Wisdom with emphasis.

The young Solomon knew what he was doing when, at his coronation, he asked God for wisdom (1 Kgs 3:9). Only wisdom can equip a person for the difficult art of ruling. Only wisdom supplies the statesman with the needed counsel, caution, insight, and political perseverance. You can count on this: wherever good rule occurs, people are governing with wisdom. There you'll find advisors who are giving good counsel. There you will find people with an understanding of time, manner, and place, such that they act carefully. There you will find people with insight into the problems and strength to deal with them.

Regrettably, the wise ones are not always sitting in the seats of government and on the judges' benches (Eccl 9:13–16). Often it is the fool who occupies the highest position (Eccl 10:6). Unwise rulers implement "iniquitous decrees" (Isa 10:1). The histories of Israel and of Christianity show innumerable examples of that. And this despite the fact that, in the Torah of Moses, God had supplied such salutary foundational instruction about what is just and righteous in his eyes. But who today is inquiring after that in politics? During election campaigns you never hear the word *wisdom* mentioned at all. The ancient pagans may well have had more of an eye for that. Nowadays we can often sigh with the Preacher as we learn the world news, "Woe to you, O land, when your king is a child" (Eccl 10:16).

This catastrophic lack of wisdom leads us to yearn more intensely for the kingdom of God. In this kingdom peace will finally rule, in part because we will then get a perfectly wise king: "And the Spirit of the LORD shall rest upon him, the Spirit of wisdom and understanding, the Spirit of counsel and might, the Spirit of knowledge and the fear of the LORD" (Isa 11:1–10; 32:1–8).

We will return to Prov 8:14–16 later.

> I love those who love me,
>   and those who seek me diligently find me. (Prov 8:17)

How must you do that? First acknowledge that you need Lady Wisdom every day. Next, fall to your knees with your hand on God's promise: "If any of you lacks wisdom, let him ask God, who gives generously to all without reproach, and it will be given him" (Jas 1:5). As a rule, God supplies wisdom in an indirect way.

For that, you will have to sit at Solomon's feet and read and reread his proverbs. As we have said more often, with a pencil in your hand in order to imprint in your memory later what you have underlined. You will need to seek out the company of wise people, for "whoever *walks* with the wise becomes wise" (Prov 13:20). Investigate how the Lord Jesus went about his work; he is ultimately the one greater than Solomon (Matt 12:42). Look especially through the spectacles of Scripture to God's wisdom in his creation. In short, our entire life attitude must become: What is wise in this situation? If you seek her carefully, Lady Wisdom will guarantee that you will find her!

> Riches and honor are with me,
>   enduring wealth and righteousness.
> My fruit is better than gold, even fine gold,
>   and my yield than choice silver.
> I walk in the way of righteousness,
>   in the paths of justice,
> granting an inheritance to those who love me,
>   and filling their treasuries. (Prov 8:18–21)

About these verses we can be brief. Wisdom can provide you with tangible wealth and honor. We have already discussed this extensively in connection with Prov 3:9–10, 3:13–15, and 3:33–35.

4. LADY WISDOM SHOWS HER NOBILITY CREDENTIALS (PROV 8:22–31)

All life *wisdom* is based partly on life *experience*. That includes the wisdom of Proverbs. For that reason, people say: A proverb is a short expression that arises from lengthy experience. Those who composed these proverbs were speaking what they "received from their fathers" (Job 15:18 NIV). No wonder! Wisdom and age go hand in hand more often with age than with youth. That is why Rehoboam acted so stupidly when he followed the advice of his young counselors. What had they acquired by experience? For the same reason, Eliphaz thought that Job was speaking far too rashly for a middle-aged man. What was Job thinking? Maybe that he was the oldest man? "Both the gray-haired and the aged are among us, older than your father" (Job 15:7–10).

What is true of wisdom is true also of nobility. The older the noble person, the greater his respect. The older the wise person, the greater his authority. This is so because wisdom can boast of such long experience. For that reason, Lady Wisdom concludes by displaying her advanced age. Here in Prov 8:22–31 she is showing her nobility credentials. "Were you brought forth before the hills?" asked Eliphaz ironically of Job (15:7). Lady Wisdom could answer that question truthfully: "Indeed, I am older than the hills and the mountains, than the rivers and the seas, than heaven and earth."

With this, Prov 8 is supplying an important tone to the songs of praise that the Instruction Manual for Proverbs is singing to wisdom. The main theme of these praise songs was clearly "wisdom preserves the life of him who has it" (Eccl 7:12). At this point, Lady Wisdom praises this important life quality of wisdom, by referring to her advanced age.

The intention of this reference is clear to us. Before we proceed to read the book itself (Prov 10–31), Prov 8:22–31 imprints firmly on our mind and heart *how old* the wisdom is that is speaking to us here, and *with what great authority* wisdom is teaching us. Proverbs 8:32–36 supplies us with the reading guide for verses 22–31 when it draws the conclusion from these verses: "And now, O sons, listen to me." No one can speak with as much authority as Lady Wisdom, for she is older even than heaven and earth, as we will read in a moment. Owing to her advanced age, she has at her disposal the life experience of all humanity. Therefore, you cannot choose a better advisor than her.

We believe this is the basic tone of Prov 8:22–31. That is why we feel justified in bringing into consideration the practical conclusion that verses 32–36 draw from all of Prov 8 in connection with verses 22–31. Later we will provide further explanation about why we view wisdom here as a personification, a poetic personal representation, and not as a (semi-)divine being. But first, we will provide our own explanation of verses 22–31, then of verses 32–36, and then we return to devote a separate section to verses 22–31.

> The Lord possessed me at the beginning of his work,
>   the first of his acts of old. (Prov 8:22)

The first line of this proverb could be translated in three ways: (1) Yahweh has *created* me at the beginning of his ways; (2) Yahweh *acquired* me; (3) Yahweh *possessed* me. There is little substantive difference, however, if we read that he created wisdom or acquired wisdom: in any case, he *possesses* wisdom and that is what the poet wants to say.

God and wisdom are inseparable. He is the only wise God (Rom 16:27; cf. 1 Tim 1:17 KJV; Jude 25 KJV). He did not begin creating heaven and earth apart from wisdom. On the contrary, he considered wisdom to be indispensable and of fundamental importance in that connection. If you have in the back of your mind the conclusion of Prov 8:32–36, then you sense the unexpressed purpose of this proverb. If God the Creator could not do without wisdom for *making* the world, then we absolutely cannot do without wisdom for *living* in that world.

This will impact you all the more when you recall how broadly Scripture uses the word *wisdom* (*chokma*). It uses this word not only for our life wisdom but also for various professional skills, artistic skills, technical ability, and handiness. With that wisdom, taken now in the widest sense of the word, but of course in divine measure, God created the heavens and the earth. But that divine wisdom with which he *created* the world differs in degree but not in principle from the wisdom with which we may *use* the earth. We see that from verse 32: "And now, O sons, listen to me." The same Lady Wisdom is speaking there as in verse 22. Exactly the same wisdom that tells us in verse 22 that God created the world through wisdom calls us in verse 32 to listen to her. (We are not capitalizing the word *wisdom* here because we do not have in mind a cocreating demiurge.)

Verse 22 is teaching us a profound life lesson: the order according to which we live must adapt itself to the order that God revealed in Scripture and in nature. Life wisdom, then, is also submitting yourself to God's creational wisdom. Our happiness and success in every moment depend on that.

> Ages ago I was set up,
>   at the first, before the beginning of the earth. (Prov 8:23)

When an Israelite used the word *eternity*, he usually meant simply this: far ahead into the future, or far back into the past. Lady Wisdom points back to the beginning, "before the beginning of the earth." At that time God formed it. You could also read, anointed it. With the latter reading we are led to think of a ceremonious installation (cf. Ps 2:6).

Naturally she is not saying this so we can rack our brains trying to solve a profound problem. She is seeking to lead us to recognize the *authority* with which she is speaking. For that reason, in this verse she is inculcating within us respect for her advanced age. That is the connecting thread of verses 22–31.

> When there were no oceans, I was given birth,
>   when there were no springs abounding with water. (Prov 8:24 NIV)

To an Israelite, the Mediterranean Sea was the "ocean." Who can recall the time when it did not exist? When the springs did not exist, where the women and maidens for centuries had gone each evening to fill their vessels

(Gen 24; Exod 2:16–20; 1 Sam 9:11; John 4)? All those generations Lady Wisdom had observed. She was older than the seas and the springs. What experience that Lady must have!

> Before the mountains had been shaped,
>   before the hills, I was brought forth,
> before he had made the earth with its fields,
>   or the first of the dust of the world.
> When he established the heavens, I was there;
>   when he drew a circle on the face of the deep. (Prov 8:25–27)

Do you think this is expressed a bit strangely? But if you look up, don't you see the sky that looks a lot like a giant half-bowl suspended above the earth? When you are standing on the beach, doesn't the horizon look like a half circle, an arc stretching from the beach on your left across to the beach on your right? When you look out of an airplane down on an island, doesn't it look like a saucer floating in the water? As modern people, let's not smirk and drag up the term *worldview* in order to rescue Scripture from embarrassment. In this and subsequent verses, Scripture is speaking in the language of ordinary experience to describe the optical phenomena. Just as we do, when we say, "The sun is setting."[3]

The intention of these verses is clear to us. Who can remember when those unshakable mountain peaks did not exist? Or when the plains did not lie outside the city and the sky did not hover above the earth? Only Lady Wisdom can remember this. When God began to create all of this, "I was there" (v. 27). God didn't make a single clod of dirt without using wisdom. That is how fundamentally important he considered wisdom to be. Wisdom lay at the foundation of the entire cosmos, from the greatest to the least part of creation.

Psalm 104:24 said this without using metaphor: "How many are your works, O Lord! In wisdom you made them all" (cf. Prov 3:19). The writer of this proverb is saying the same thing in a poetic way. He has wisdom tell about it like a fictitious person: God created nothing apart from me. This comes down to the same thing the psalmist was saying. For that reason, people should not find material here for any theological or ontological speculations about the "birth" (eternal generation) of wisdom (seen as Son-of-God-before-his-incarnation). Does not Scripture speak poetically about the "birth" of the mountains and the sea (Ps 9:2; Job 28:8–9)?

> When he made firm the skies above,
>   when he established the fountains of the deep,

---

3. See van Deursen, *Psalms II*, 262–63, 275–78.

> when he assigned to the sea its limit,
>> so that the waters might not transgress his command,
> when he marked out the foundations of the earth,
>> then I was beside him, like a master workman,
> and I was daily his delight,
>> rejoicing before him always,
> rejoicing in his inhabited world
>> and delighting in the children of man. (Prov 8:28–31)

Lady Wisdom had quite some experience at that first light of the golden days of the world! Perhaps you recall from your own youth how you stood wide-eyed as a child while watching your father tinker with a toy he was assembling for you. Now and then you clapped your hands in pure delight in his ability. This is what Lady Wisdom experienced during the six days of creation. As a beloved child in her father's workshop, she looked through eyes full of wonder at how wisely God created everything: what insight, what logic, what skill, what ability he displayed! Wisdom could not get enough of that and clapped her hands in pure delight.

Take the rain clouds above our head. Notice the efficiency that God embedded in them; we discussed this in our commentary on Ps 104:24.[4] And Wisdom loves *efficiency*! Consider God's ordinances for the seas: here you have water, there you have dry land. Obediently that majestic sea observes that commandment. And Wisdom loves *obedience* to God's commandments! Consider the foundations of the earth and the order in all of God's creation. And Wisdom loves *order* so much! Can you understand why she never tired of watching, and like a child she clapped her hands in delight? Will we ever finish observing God's creational wisdom with respect to human beings and animals and plants (Ps 111:2)? So much wisdom to observe in one flower, one finger, one fly leg.

But "my delight was in the children of men," says Lady Wisdom in verse 31b (literally, "I was delighting"). What a creation: man, woman, child! The crown of God's creational work. The medical specialist needs half a life before he comes to know so very little. You can walk—what divine wisdom lies in that capacity: your muscles, your joints, the gravity of the earth that is exactly right. Oh, how much Wisdom loves human beings! She loves us human beings most of all. Not only Jewish people—as the apocryphal wisdom books suggest—but all people. Not only people from the upper classes, the little sons of kings and high officials—as we read in the Egyptian wisdom books—but all people, rich and poor, young and old. Wisdom enjoys their

---

4. See van Deursen, *Psalms II*, 272–73.

friendship! She enjoys showing them the good path; you cannot hear that as clearly in any other passage as in Prov 8.

But God loves her dearly. She was his beloved child, his darling during those six days of creation. They rejoiced with each other: Wisdom was intoxicated with joy in God's work, because God enjoyed so intensely making everything with wisdom.

5 LADY WISDOM PROVIDES YOU LIFE (PROV 8:32–36)

Are you holding on firmly to the thread of the entire chapter? In Prov 8 we read a canticle celebrating wisdom. The poet introduces her as a woman. And she is the best counselor a person could choose. For

- She is prepared to assist everyone throughout all of life with counsel and advice (vv. 1–5);
- She is not pulling your leg, but is speaking the honest truth (vv. 6–13);
- She always knows what to advise and she gives her friends strength and profit (vv. 14–21);
- She is taken into consideration by God himself in connection with everything he created (vv. 22–31).

How does this praise song end, that exalted section (vv. 22–31) about the role of wisdom in connection with the creation of heaven and earth? With this practical application:

> And now, O sons, listen to me:
> > blessed are those who keep my ways.
> Hear instruction and be wise,
> > and do not neglect it.
> Blessed is the one who listens to me,
> > watching daily at my gates,
> > waiting beside my doors.
> For whoever finds me finds life
> > and obtains favor from the Lord,
> but he who fails to find me injures himself;
> > all who hate me love death. (Prov 8:32–36)

This is the conclusion of Prov 8:8–31. When we commented on verses 22–31, we touched on this in a sense, in order to point out how you must read the passage about the role of wisdom in connection with the creation. Don't read it as a piece of theological or philosophical reflection about the preexistence of the Second Person of the Trinity, but as a piece of instruction about the age and resulting authority of wisdom.

All the power and beauty of this canticle—including the terrific scene in verses 22–31—leads to the warning cited above: Listen to her. Do what she says. If, at creation, God created nothing without her, how then could *you* live on that earth apart from her? Whoever lacks her is committing suicide. You would destroy your life. But if you allow yourself to be directed by her and submit to her discipline, then you will obtain God's pleasure and life, both for now and for eternity. We heard this last note back when we discussed Prov 1–8 (see our comments on Prov 3:1–2, and Prov 4).

How must you do that? We discussed that in connection with verses 1–5. Open your heart fully for wisdom. She is speaking to you everywhere. God's Word is full of wisdom and all God's creation rests upon wisdom. Therefore, our use of creation, then, also depends on wisdom. Whoever lives wisely lives most functionally and rationally.

In the preceding, we observed somewhat incidentally that it is one and the same Lady Wisdom who watched as God created, and was his beloved companion, and who at the end of Prov 8 summons you to listen to her. So it is one and the same wisdom that God took into consideration and that you can apply. God "confirmed it and tested it," something we cannot do. But to us he said, "The fear of the Lord, that is wisdom, and to shun evil is understanding" (Job 28:27–28).

The more we fear God in everything, the more we will experience that this is also the wisest course of living. And the best. This is because a believing attitude of life provides us with the best chance, in this broken life, for some happiness, and gives us the least possible misery, universal human misery (we are not talking about the kind of cross-bearing that Christ desires).[5] For wisdom—and this was the lesson of Prov 8:22–31—is the foundation of everything valuable and joyful. Blessed is the one who believes (vv. 32, 34)!

If this explanation of Prov 8 finds your agreement, then you can skip the next section, if you want. For in the next section we want to investigate the suspicious origin of the explanation that in Prov 8:22–31 we are reading reflections about the preexistence of God the Son as personified wisdom. To do that, we will need to get into the apocryphal books and into church history. If this does not interest you, you can move on to chapter 11, which deals with Prov 9.

---

5. See van Deursen, *Psalms II*, 62–63.

6. LADY WISDOM IS NOT A DIVINE BEING

We heartily believe that our Lord Jesus Christ is the Son of God, who could say, "Before Abraham was, I am" (John 8:58). We fully accept the apostolic testimony that, "In the beginning [i.e., at creation (see Gen 1:1)] [he] was the Word, and the Word was with God, and the Word was God. . . . All things were made through him" (John 1:1–3). As a human being, he descended from Israel, but, for the rest, he is "God over all, blessed forever" (Rom 9:5; cf. Matt 3:17; 16:16; 26:63–64; John 1:14, 30; Rom 1:4; 8:32; Phil 2:6; 1 John 2:23).

But it is another question whether *this* is to be read in *Prov 8*. Many believe so, and saw the wisdom in Prov 8 not as a poetic personal representation—as we, together with others, have understood, as we explained above—but as a real person, even a divine person, a mediator between God and the world. According to some Christians, this is about the Son of God, who would later become man.

You can find this opinion already in the apocryphal wisdom books of Ecclesiasticus, which is also called by its author "The Wisdom of Jesus [the son of] Sirach," and in the apocryphal book "Wisdom of Solomon." We wish to devote some attention to these writings.

1. *The apocryphal books Jesus Sirach and Wisdom of Solomon*

Just like the canonical book of Proverbs, these books also contain hymns in praise of wisdom. They were apparently motivated by Prov 8:22–31, and offer a significant expansion of those verses. Scripture tells us that, like a beloved child, as it were, wisdom was *present* at creation. But the apocryphal books mentioned tell us much more. According to them, wisdom functioned like a real person to co-*create* the world. We are afraid that, in so doing, these writings have opened the door to deadly Gnosticism, which is filled with pagan wisdom speculations.

Jesus Sirach

This book tells us that wisdom is from eternity, "created before all other things" (Sir 1:4 NRSV; cf. Prov 8:22). God has poured out wisdom "upon all his works" (Sir 1:9 NRSV; cf. 1:14). According to 24:3, wisdom even "came forth from the mouth of the Most High and covered the earth like a mist" (NRSV). A mist aids fertility and causes the crops to grow. With these notions, Sirach is alluding to a kind of *cooperation* that wisdom exercised at creation, and is thereby offering a point of contact with the later Logos speculations.

Wisdom of Solomon

To estimate the value of the claims presented in this writing, we must first set forth something about the author of this apocryphal wisdom book. Presumably he was a Greek-speaking Jew who lived about 100 BC in Alexandria. At that time this city was renowned for its scholarship and as the center of Hellenism. As with many Jews at that time, this author was influenced by the intense attraction of Greek morals and customs. Though it was also the case that, like Philo, he wanted to remain a good Jew.

But could he do that with a good conscience? He did not need to suppress the Jewish wisdom entirely in the face of the Greek wisdom of that day, did he? That is what he wanted to prove to the proud Greeks and the wavering Jews. Jewish wisdom was far superior! The wisdom of Israel could easily surpass the logos of the Stoics, and more easily satisfy the heart, and better confirm morals than that Greek philosophy. The wisdom of Israel originated in God, and had demonstrated its power throughout all of history, especially the history of Israel.

Regrettably, as he wrote, this opponent of Greek philosophy fell under its spell. How often had that philosophy done this throughout the centuries? It fantasized that between the lofty deity and the lower, material world, one or more *intermediaries* existed. One such intermediary—its varying representations were called the *logos*—supposedly created this world. The Epicurean and Stoic philosophers whom Paul met at the Areopagus spoke of such a logos (Acts 17). These pagan fantasies apparently played a role in the book of Wisdom. How else would the author have come to write about wisdom as a divine intermediary? Where else would he have obtained all those details about that being? He must have obtained them from Greek philosophy. Meanwhile he could set forth quite a number of features of that so-called divine person called Wisdom:

- It is a *divine being*, a "holy spirit" (Wis 1:5 NRSV), "a breath of the power of God, and a pure emanation of the glory of the Almighty" (7:25 NRSV).
- As a divine being, it lives in communion with God (8:3) and sits next to him on the throne (9:4, 9–10). It even possesses an immaterial spirit (cf. 7:22). Accordingly, wisdom is clearly more than a personification; it is a living being.

- As such, wisdom has *divine attributes*: it is almighty (7:23, 27), omniscient (9:11), and holy (7:22). Wisdom has been initiated into the knowledge of God (8:4). "I learned both what is secret and what is manifest" (7:21 NRSV). (This goes further than Job 28:28 and the wisdom of Ecclesiastes, which remains limited to things "under the son" [cf. 8:8; 9:9]).

- Wisdom is a partner in God's works, and thus his *collaborator* (Wis 8:4) (this in contrast to what Prov 8:27–31 says, namely, that wisdom was *present* at creation).

- Wisdom is even the *fabricator* of everything. It is "their mother" (Wis 7:12 NRSV). (This is something different than saying that *God* created everything by his wisdom and almighty power [Prov 3:19].)

- Wisdom now *governs* everything, "all-powerful, overseeing all, and penetrating through all spirits" (Wis 7:23 NRSV). "She reaches mightily from one end of the earth to the other, and she orders all things well" (8:1 NRSV).

- Wisdom provides a person with "immortality" (6:19; 8:13 NRSV). "In kinship with wisdom there is immortality" (8:17 NRSV). (By contrast, Scripture teaches that God alone possesses immortality (1 Tim 6:16), and that we will put on immortality for the first time at the resurrection (1 Cor 15:54).

With these observations we have given you an impression of the ways in which the Jews have speculated about a fictitious "Wisdom," already before the New Testament era. These reflections have not only hampered the proper understanding of Prov 8:22–31 but have also fostered errors in the early Christian church about the deity of our Lord Jesus Christ.

2. *Logos and Wisdom identified*

"In the beginning was the Word," John wrote in the prologue of his Gospel (John 1:1). In Greek we read, "In the beginning was *the Logos*." The apostolic fathers (ancient Christian writers from around AD 150) drew from this the conclusion that the Wisdom of Prov 8 had to be the same as the Logos of John 1. How did they arrive at this conclusion? Possibly by means of a certain similarity between various phrases. The phrase "in the beginning of his way" of Prov 8:22 (KJV) sounds like "in the beginning" of John 1:1. Perhaps their Greek philosophical training played a role here; we cannot overestimate its power among the early Christians. Perhaps they were under the influence of Philo. This Jewish writer had called the Logos by the name Wisdom. Perhaps the book of Wisdom and its notions exercised some influence as well. Finally, Gnosticism must have been a significant factor. Every gnostic system was familiar with the myth of Sophia (wisdom), a divine being that can deify its friends. Perhaps a specific correspondence in wording between Col 1:15 and Prov 8:22 also influenced these notions.

Whatever the reason, around AD 300 many in the Christian church were certain that the Wisdom of Prov 8 was a divine person: the same person as the Logos in John 1 and thus the Son of God, our Lord Jesus Christ.

At that time the Arian struggle erupted.

3. Arius appeals to Prov 8: God's Son is created

According to Arius, our Lord Jesus Christ was not the eternal Son of God, but was the first and highest creation of God. "There was a time when he was not," Arius said. God had created his Son first, and through him created the heavens and the earth. As you can see, in this system of thinking our Deliverer resembled in many ways the logos demigod of Greek philosophies. This was the intermediary through which God supposedly created the world. The gnostic also proclaimed these ideas.

With this set of ideas, paganism entered into the Christian church in a threatening way. For how can a mere creature bear for us the burden of God's eternal wrath against sin, and save other creatures (cf. Heidelberg Catechism, Lord's Day 5)? The burden of God's wrath required the power of Jesus' deity (as we confess in subsequent Lord's Days).

Did Arius appeal to Scripture in defense of his error? Indeed he did, to Prov 8:22, among other passages. Both Arians and non-Arians agreed that here Wisdom is the same as the Logos of John 1, namely, our Lord Jesus Christ. What, then, does this Wisdom say about himself? "Yahweh has *created* me as the beginning of his way, before his (other creation) works from of old." That is what they read in the Septuagint, the Greek translation of the Old Testament and apocryphal books. And, indeed, you could translate this verse this way. So people could see in the very text of Scripture: Wisdom (God's Son) is God's *first creation*.

Let us not bother with the artificial attempts that orthodoxy tried to employ in order to escape the force of this Arian Scripture proof. But one element deserves mention: in the footsteps of Athanasius, people argued for a long time that the "creating" of wisdom in Prov 8:22 referred to Christ's taking on human nature from the virgin Mary. The phrase "the beginning of his works" would then refer to God's redemptive work through the incarnate Son (as though this work began first after his incarnation).

The Arian struggle has influenced the interpretation of Prov 8:22–23 for centuries. Subsequent Judaism pulled back from its speculations about a Wisdom-hypostasis. If only people had read Scripture carefully and had not gone in search of "deep" truths behind the glorious truth it presented: Yahweh has made everything with wisdom and now his people must also live with wisdom. That seems to be the main point of Prov 8: "For the sake of your life, listen to the age old wisdom!" If at the creation of the world, God made use of wisdom, shall we despise wisdom as we live in that world?

Apparently, people did not consider this to be profound enough. Wisdom was a hypostasis, not a personification; a living being, not a poetic personal representation. In our view, however, we believe that the least tortuous reading of Prov 8:22–31 requires seeing wisdom as a *fictional* person, a poetic stylistic figure, the poetic designation of all wisdom in Scripture and in creation.

In what follows we shall summarize our reasons for this view.

4. Why a personification but no hypostasis

We have been reading and interpreting Prov 8 as a canticle about wisdom, one that incites us to become imitators of God by doing everything with wisdom, as he does. We did not view wisdom as a living being, but as a developed personification of all the wisdom that God has set forth in his Word and in the rest of his work.

We did that on the basis of the following arguments.

The Israelites loved to speak in personal metaphors

Proverbs is a poetic book. It swarms with figurative language. Moreover, the Israelites loved to talk about abstract things as though they were persons. In this way, Proverbs introduces wisdom in so many different ways: as a street preacher (1:20); as a bride and spouse (4:6–9; 6:22); as an intimate companion and confidant (7:4); as a builder (9:1); and in Prov 8 as a prophetess or street preacher. Why should we view only that last identification as a hypostasis (divine being)? After all, nowhere does Proverbs *call* wisdom a divine person in so many words. It simply portrays wisdom in a poetic manner.

In fact, fifteen hundred years before Solomon was born, people throughout the entire ancient Near East were using such personification in their speaking and writing. The personification of wisdom in Prov 8 and 9 therefore has nothing to do with Greek influence—that was read into the text later—but belongs to the same category as personifications of truth, righteousness, and other similar matters. You encounter them all over the entire ancient Near East. Do we ourselves not say things like, "The flu *is winning*"?

The Hebrew text

The original text does not compel us to render it as "Yahweh has *created* me as the beginning of his ways" (v. 22). We could translate it just as properly to read, "Yahweh *acquired* me" or "Yahweh *possessed* me." In verse 30, the Hebrew word *amon* can just as properly be translated with "beloved child" as with "supervisor." The entire hypostasis theory surrounding Prov 8 rests, in fact, on words that are capable of multiple interpretations.

The canonical place of Prov 8

Pay attention to the text, the context, and the canonical place! We saw that this golden rule of Scripture interpretation was not always taken into consideration in connection with Prov 8. This chapter, Prov 8, is located in the Instruction Manual for Proverbs (which consists of Prov 1–9), and seeks to do nothing other than sing the praise of wisdom. In that connection, as was fitting for Israelite sensibilities, a reference to wisdom's advanced age was appropriate. That would serve to confirm wisdom's authority. An allusion to the Second Person of the Trinity in this context strikes us as being both unexpected and entirely incomprehensible for the first readers.

Christ's deity nowhere proven with Prov 8

Nowhere do the apostles clearly appeal to Prov 8:22–23 to prove that Jesus Christ is the Son of God. Even Col 1:15 ("He is the image of the invisible God, the firstborn of all creation") shows at most terminological points of contact. To be sure, the apostle writes that Christ has become to us "wisdom" (along with other gifts) (1 Cor 1:30; cf. 1 Cor 1:24; 2:6; Col 2:3). But that is entirely different from identifying Christ with a preexistent wisdom figure. In fact, precisely at the point where one would have expected this identification, we find not even a whisper about Wisdom, namely, in Colossians (1 Cor 8; 2 Cor 4). As Herman Ridderbos observes, "There is no proof that [Paul] himself views Jesus Christ as the preexistent Wisdom of Proverbs 8."

He continues, "This ought to make us very careful not to posit a connection between Proverbs 8 and Colossians 1, too eagerly and too easily."[6]

The Old Testament does not equate the form of wisdom in Prov 8 with the Messiah either. Do you not find that striking? Even subsequent Judaism does not do that.

We do not need such complicated speculations at all in order to know that Jesus Christ is the Son of God, and that he is the wisest man, far surpassing Solomon. Holy Scripture teaches us that clearly enough elsewhere. Nor do we need Prov 8:22–23 in order to talk Christocentrically about the wisdom of Proverbs, for this entire book *proceeds from* God's redemption through his Son and envisions nothing other than to govern us by the Spirit of wisdom. Proverbs offers us, so to speak, "skills for redeemed living." How could that happen apart from our Redeemer?

Wisdom presented as a playing child

The apocryphal book Wisdom of Solomon said that Wisdom (viewed as a divine being) *created* this world (7:12, 22; 8:4). But Proverbs said that wisdom was *present* at creation, like a playing, wonder-filled *child* (Prov 8:30). How could this be? At creation, God's Son was not a playful *child*, was he? He did indeed collaborate in creation (Heb 1:1–2; John 1:1). Moreover, in these verses in Proverbs it is a *woman*—Lady Wisdom—who is speaking in verses 22–23 about her youth. Proverbs 8:30–31, then, is in fact talking about a playful *girl*.

Why is folly not viewed as a real person?

Later, in Prov 9, the poet will bring Lady Folly on stage as a person. If one views wisdom in Prov 8 as a living being, one can just as legitimately view folly in Prov 9 as a real person. Perhaps the devil? Then why not explain every passage where Proverbs talks about wisdom as though it were talking "messianically" about a person (e.g., 1:20–33; 4:6–9; 6:22; 7:4; 9:1)?

Proverbs 8 is too early to have been influenced by Greek thought

It was not too long ago that people claimed a post-exilic date for the longer sections of the book of Proverbs (Prov 1–9). In that period Greek influence entered Israelite thought, and along with it came the notion of wisdom as a

---

6. Ridderbos, *Paul and Jesus*, 126.

hypostasis. The excavations of recent decades, however, have rendered this view outdated and untenable. Proverbs 8 and 9 could not have been written later than the seventh century BC (one hundred years before the Babylonian captivity), according to the famous archaeologist William Albright.[7] At that time there was no Greek influence upon Israel. According to this authoritative expert on the ancient Near East, Canaanite literature contained hymns in praise of wisdom when Israel was still sitting in Egypt!

We should be cautious with the apocryphal book of Wisdom of Solomon. Should that teach us how to read Prov 8? The author was an early gnostic, and Gnosticism is one of the deadly enemies of the Word of God.

By me kings reign (Prov 8:15)

"By me kings reign, and rulers decree what is just; by me princes rule, and nobles, all who govern justly" (Prov 8:15–16). Just as in all of Prov 8, here too we heard the voice of *fictitious* Lady Wisdom, who taught by means of poetry: government personnel cannot work a day without wisdom. More often, however, we saw these words of Scripture cited to prove that all kings and governments on earth stand in service to *Jesus Christ*. Was he not the Wisdom that addressed us in Prov 8? Well, now you heard it from his own mouth: "Through me [Wisdom = Jesus Christ] kings rule." This accounts for expressions like "As Head of the church Christ is also the supreme Ruler over the life of the state."

In this way we would fall back into the Roman Catholic doctrine of the two swords: as the lieutenant of Christ on earth and as head of the church, the pope would possess both worldly and ecclesiastical ruling authority. But Scripture teaches us clearly that the kingdom of Christ comes through his Word and Spirit. As a *servant of the gospel* Paul calls himself a servant of *Christ Jesus* in Rom 15:16, when he had a short while earlier called the *government* the servant of *God* (Rom 13:6). Are we exaggerating when we savor some difference between these?

We may refer the reader to the discussion of this matter in Leviticus. The entire issue turns on the foundation of papal claims to worldly supremacy. Such an authoritative "lieutenant of Christ" cannot validate his demands any more powerfully than by means of the fiction of a Christ who is already supreme on earth. An earthly pope with both ecclesiastical and worldly authority calls for a heavenly pope with all ecclesiastical and worldly authority.

---

7. Albright, *From the Stone Age to Christianity*, 368.

At the present time, Christ has received "the name that is above every name" (Phil 2:9), and the place of honor "at the right hand of the Majesty on high" (Heb 1:3). But he is seated there "*waiting* from that time until his enemies [including those on earth] should be made [by God the Father (Heb 1:13)] a footstool for his feet" (Heb 10:13). At the present time, Christ is not yet the sovereign of all the kings on earth. To defend the notion that he is such a sovereign in the present time, one cannot appeal to Prov 8:15–16 without first reading into those verses an identification between Wisdom and Christ. But that is incorrect.

Proverbs 8:15 teaches simply that all good rulers can rule well only thanks to wisdom. As far as governments are concerned, they stand in the service of God (Rom 13:1–6). As far as Jesus Christ is concerned, at the present time he is still an *heir* of the world, and all authority over the world has been given to him in promise form. At the present time, he does not yet rule with an iron rod (Ps 2:9),[8] but by his Spirit, who is spreading the gospel of Christ throughout the world, and by his intercession. Let us, then, be careful that we do not, by means of a mistaken interpretation of Prov 8:15, promote any Roman Catholic notions of an imperious church.

These were the reasons why we have read Prov 8 as we did, as a canticle celebrating wisdom. This provides a wonderful, poetic, personal representation with this life lesson: Wisdom is older than the world. God used wisdom in connection with his creation work. Should you, then, not use wisdom daily in all of your activities?

---

8. See van Deursen, *Psalms I*, 174–76.

11

Proverbs 9
Which Invitation Will You Accept?

WE COME NOW TO the conclusion of the first section of Proverbs! What is the bottom line of that entire practical Instruction Manual for Proverbs? It comes down to a choice that everyone must make in his life: Whom will I choose to be my *companion*? Wisdom or folly? On this choice depends everything, for time and for eternity. This is a life-and-death question, in the broadest sense of those words. Proverbs 1–8 has already bound this upon our hearts in a variety of ways. Proverbs 9 now comes along to place an exclamation point at the end in order to conclude the Instruction Manual. We will then be fully instructed so we take up the book of Proverbs (Prov 10–31).

As a real Israelite wisdom teacher, however, Solomon does not supply the conclusion of his unforgettable introduction in a couple of dry formulas but in the form of a couple of wonderful metaphors. He introduces us to wisdom and folly as two women, both of whom invite us in for a meal. You may choose for yourself which invitation you want to accept.

Lady Wisdom you know, of course, from Prov 8. She represents all the wisdom that God has set forth in Scripture and in creation. No wonder that the author portrays her as a real lady, a noblewoman who dwells in a royal house. Her counterpart is Lady Folly. She is the poetic personal representation of all foolishness in the world. The poet describes her as a bad woman who walks the street like a prostitute.

You may take the time to reflect carefully as to whose dining invitation you will accept. That is the counsel of Prov 9. Lady Wisdom is offering you the food of life. Lady Folly is serving deadly poison.

1. LADY WISDOM AND HER GUESTS EAT LIFE-FOOD (PROV 9:1–6)

You learn quite a bit about Lady Wisdom from her house. The house of an ordinary laborer did not have a courtyard with columns. That was something for King Solomon (1 Kgs 7:2–7) and for Lady Wisdom!

> Wisdom has built her house;
>   she has hewn her seven pillars. (Prov 9:1)

Without doubt Lady Wisdom lived in a royal house. That appears initially from what a distinguished lady she is. Stated without metaphor: Wisdom always has a regal character. Wisdom bestows on her friends an unmistakable allure. Wisdom exalts a person, just like a gold chain distinguishes an Israelite from the masses (see our comments on Prov 1:9).

Why is she living in a house with seven columns? Behind this number, some have sought various secret notions, but this seems mistaken. Was it the case that the ordinary Israelite, who was very alert for symbolism, should have heard here in the number seven a refined reference to God's covenant with Israel? In Hebrew, "to swear" sounded like "to seven" something.[1] And obedience to God's covenant was the ABC of Israel's wisdom (Prov 1:7; cf. our comments below on Prov 9:10).

Whatever the case, Wisdom lives in a regal dwelling, one that is solid and spacious. It was very suitable, therefore, for hosting many guests. You could always find lodging there; she had room enough to receive you. And then you would be in a solid environment. Indeed, what Wisdom *builds* is spacious and solid, and what she *provides* is regal and beneficent.

> She has slaughtered her beasts; she has mixed her wine;
>   she has also set her table. (Prov 9:2)

Israelites did not eat meat every day, so what Wisdom is offering here is a real feast. This metaphor is something Scripture uses more often to refer to God's promises (cf. Josh 25:6–7; Matt 19:28; 22:21; Luke 14:16–17; 22:16, 20; Rev 19:7, 9). Here the metaphor is referring to the blessings that Wisdom has in store for her friends.

Her table is decked out. When we read this in its context, then Prov 9 functions as the transition from the Instruction Manual for Proverbs to the actual book itself (Prov 10–31). Do these chapters not in fact consist of a table decked out with costly fare? Everyone who wants may come and eat from this table.

---

1. See Vonk, *Exodus*, 198–99.

> She has sent out her young women to call
>> from the highest places in the town. (Prov 9:3)

For an Israelite, something like this was as ordinary as a wedding invitation in the mailbox is for us. In those days, it was very stylish to send a servant around with invitations. The Lord Jesus once used this metaphor from daily life in one of his parables. "See, I have prepared my dinner," a king announced through his slaves, "my oxen and my fat calves have been slaughtered, and everything is ready. Come to the wedding feast" (Matt 22:4; cf. Luke 14:17; Esth 5:4; 6:14).

The poet has Lady Wisdom functioning here in the same manner as we saw in Prov 8:1–3; she is speaking in public, openly and passionately to everyone who would like to eat with her. She is not a voice crying in the wilderness but a counselor standing amid the bustle of the city. Wisdom is a matter for daily living. No one needs to be ashamed of needing her every day, for she invites with kindness.

> "Whoever is simple, let him turn in here!"
>> To him who lacks sense she says. (Prov 9:4)

Here again, Israel's wise men indicate what it is that they are primarily interested in: winning the hearts of the youth. Proverbs is directed especially to young people, say, from fourteen to forty years old, with the aim of giving the *youth* knowledge and prudence. But in Prov 1:4 they are mentioned in the same breath as the *peti*, a Hebrew word that is difficult to translate. The word refers to those who are innocent, naive, inexperienced, undiscerning, simple.

Because of their *age*, young people often lack the needed life *experience*. Because of that, they encounter life too naively. Lady Wisdom makes good use of that phenomenon; with such people she has the best chance. Keep that in mind when you read that Lady Wisdom addresses these undiscerning people with her invitation. She is definitely not the only one working to get their attention; Lady Folly is also trying to get them into her house.

So it is especially the youth who constantly face the choice: Wisdom or folly, with whom will I travel? The authors of these proverbs want to help them with that choice. In order to ensure that in their innocence they do not lodge with Lady Folly, Lady Wisdom calls out to those inexperienced youth, "Come here! You need to enter here. I have life-food ready on my table!"

> Come, eat of my bread
>> and drink of the wine I have mixed.
> Leave your simple ways, and live,
>> and walk in the way of insight. (Prov 9:5–6)

For an Israelite, table fellowship was life fellowship. We realize this somewhat in our symbol-impoverished Western world, where we sit together for a meal at weddings and funerals. Israelites must have experienced this far more intensely; for them, eating together meant living together. When Wisdom and Folly each invite us to her meal, each is proposing that we enter into an intimate relationship with her.

In fact, where do we experience more intimate contact with people than when we eat and drink with others? In its figurative language, Scripture uses this metaphor frequently. "For they *eat* the bread of wickedness and *drink* the wine of violence" (Prov 4:17; cf. 5:15). Thus, you can eat God's Word, as Jeremiah and John did (Jer 15:16; Rev 10:10). The Lord Jesus said that it was his *food* to do God's will (John 4:34). He called himself "the bread of life," which we must "eat" (John 6:22–59). One who believes in him "feeds on [his] flesh and drinks [his] blood" (John 6:56). This is how wisdom must become our food and drink. We must live just as intimately with wisdom as we do with food in our stomach.

In view of the canonical place of this Scripture passage, we think first of all of Prov 10–31. There we find an abundant dinner of wisdom prepared for us. Whoever sits down at her table will eat life-food. With this, Prov 9 is once more drawing our attention in a poetic manner to one of the main themes of the Instruction Manual for Proverbs: *Wisdom leads to life!* Not only to life in the hereafter but also to life here and now. Proverbs 3 in particular has shown us this extensively (cf. chapter 7).

2. LADY WISDOM REFUSES TO CAST HER PEARLS BEFORE SWINE (PROV 9:7–12)

In verses 7–12, Lady Wisdom gives her servants further instructions about her invitation. This seems to us to be the most suitable explanation of the intention of these verses in this context. Otherwise they would sound a discordant note.

Lady Wisdom definitely does not commission her servants to speak to everyone without exception. They may surely invite those who are foolish or simple. But mockers and the wicked, they could better ignore. For the foolish have not yet made a firm choice, but mockers and the wicked have. Those latter are unruly characters on whom wisdom makes no impression at all. If the messengers do invite them, that will lead only to sorrow and regret.

For what is a mocker? An Israelite or Christian who is so immeasurably proud that they consider themselves above God and his Word (with or without an appearance of piety[2]). And what is a wicked person? An Israelite or Christian who may well appear religious, but who refuses to fear God in humility. In fact, the term *wicked* is a collective term for sinners, perpetrators of unrighteousness, enemies of Yahweh.[3]

Lady Wisdom speaks about them to her servants.

> Whoever corrects a scoffer gets himself abuse,
>   and he who reproves a wicked man incurs injury.
> Do not reprove a scoffer, or he will hate you;
>   reprove a wise man, and he will love you. (Prov 9:7–8)

This is also what the Lord Jesus did. "Do not give dogs what is holy, and do not throw your pearls before pigs, lest they trample them underfoot and turn to attack you" (Matt 7:6). He definitely did not engage all the (trick) questions that his opponents set before him. "And he said to them, 'Neither will I tell you by what authority I do these things'" (Matt 21:27). He was silent before Pilate, and when Herod interrogated him "at some length," "he made no answer" (Luke 23:9). Herod had already heard quite enough from John the Baptist about the kingdom of heaven.

He advised his apostles to do the same. When he sent them out to proclaim the Word of God—including the wisdom of Proverbs, of course—he prohibited them from applying every form of nagging pressure. "And if anyone will not receive you or listen to your words, shake off the dust from your feet when you leave that house or town" (Matt 10:14). This is also what Paul and Barnabas did before the hostile Jews in Antioch (Acts 13:51). They did not continue speaking endlessly in the hearing of these mockers.

In doing this, the Lord and his apostles were acting in the spirit of Prov 9: "Direct your teaching to those who *want* to listen," Wisdom was saying to her messengers. "Others will simply laugh at you." "Bind up the testimony; seal the teaching among *my disciples*" (Isa 8:16). Jeremiah did not enter into endless discussions with the false prophet Hananiah. "But Jeremiah the prophet went his way" (Jer 28:11).

Overseers in a Christian church can draw wholesome pastoral advice from these verses. There may well come an end to our admonition, especially when we are dealing with deaf people who have become unapproachable by us (Isa 6:9–10; Matt 13:14–15). At that point, the time will have come for us to be silent (Eccl 3:7). Whoever at that point continues to speak is running the serious risk of experiencing the truth of the proverb cited above: "He who reproves a wicked man incurs injury." He is laughed to scorn.

---

2. Cf. van Deursen, *Psalms I*, 96–100.

3. See the list in van Deursen, *Psalms I*, 92; we discussed these wicked people and mockers extensively in *Psalms I*, chap. 4.

God is specifically not demanding that we walk through walls to spread the truth. On the contrary, Prov 9 teaches us that it is a sign of our wisdom (humility) when we respect walls. In this way, the sharp line dividing the righteous and the wicked among God's people can be manifested more clearly.[4]

This does not mean, however, that the wise and the righteous are supposedly perfect.[5] On the contrary. "Who can bring a clean thing out of an unclean?" asked Job. "There is not one" (Job 14:4). Therefore, it may be necessary that a generally wise person needs to be corrected. But what the mocker stubbornly refuses is what the wise person acknowledges: "Let a righteous man strike me—it is a kindness; let him rebuke me—it is oil for my head; let my head not refuse it" (Ps 141:5). This was how Peter humbly accepted the correction given by Paul, and for that reason received all the more affection from his brother (Gal 2).

> Give instruction to a wise man, and he will be still wiser;
> teach a righteous man, and he will increase in learning.
> (Prov 9:9)

You don't become wise or foolish in one afternoon. This is a process of growing and maturing. The one who is becoming more foolish will increasingly stumble over the admonitions of the God-fearing wise ones. Whereas the one who is becoming wiser prefers to listen more and more to them, thereby to obtain insight (Rev 22:11). In the background, the question arises as to whether one fears Yahweh and knows the Holy One, but we will come to that in connection with verse 10.

Our Lord Jesus Christ pointed out the same development in the Israel of his day, as we mentioned earlier. Many a Jew did not *want* to see in him the Messiah in his messianic glory. "They have shut their eyes; so that they might not look with their eyes, and listen with their ears, and understand with their heart and turn—and I would heal them" (Matt 13:15 NRSV). They consciously turned against Jesus. But the disciples had opened their hearts to his teaching.

At that point the offended King said, "For to the one who has [namely, believing insight in the gospel of the kingdom], more will be given, and he will have an abundance [namely, faith-insight], but from the one who has not [because he closed his ears and eyes to Jesus], even what he has [in terms of insight] will be taken away" (Matt 13:12). For that reason, the Lord spoke to them in the form of puzzling parables. They were supposed to believe

---

4. See van Deursen, *Psalms I*, 125–33.
5. See van Deursen, *Psalms I*, 253–54.

in him, but that would have constituted their sin! From that time forward, the preaching of the Lord made many Jews even more blind than they had already wanted to be. In that way, the pure preaching of the Word can make Christians who have hardened their hearts even more blind and deaf.

But when we humbly listen to him and do not plug our ears to the admonitions of Proverbs and do not harden our hearts, then we can attain "the knowledge of the Son of God," said the apostle, "to mature manhood, to the measure of the stature of the fullness of Christ, so that we may no longer be children, tossed to and fro by the waves and carried about by every wind of doctrine, by human cunning, by craftiness in deceitful schemes. Rather, speaking the truth in love, we are to grow up in every way into him who is the head, into Christ" (Eph 4:13–15; cf. Phil 1:9–11).

So everything turns on the question whether our heart is thoroughly humble toward God. Then we acknowledge that by nature we are filled with darkness and foolishness. Then we break radically with the illusion of the unbelieving world that our understanding can stand in judgment over the Almighty. Then we cast ourselves down to the dust under him and his Word.

Wisdom always begins at that point. "We destroy arguments and every lofty opinion raised against the knowledge of God, and take every thought captive to obey Christ" (2 Cor 10:5). The Instruction Manual for Proverbs begins with that in Prov 1:7, and ends with that in Prov 9:10. Since we have devoted a separate chapter (chapter 4) to this fundamental declaration in connection with Prov 1:7, we may refer the reader to that discussion and be more brief in connection with the repetition of this verse here.

> The fear of the LORD is the beginning of wisdom,
> and the knowledge of the Holy One is insight. (Prov 9:10)

True wisdom begins with acknowledging that as creatures, human beings possess no wisdom in themselves. All our wisdom comes from the "only wise God" (1 Tim 1:17 KJV). "For the LORD is a God of knowledge" (1 Sam 2:3). Solomon acknowledged that. Especially when he asked God for wisdom, he was acknowledging his own lack of wisdom (1 Kgs 3:7–9). He admitted humbly that discovering the right path for him and his people was beyond his ability. That is always the starting point for wisdom: "If any of you lacks wisdom, let him ask of *God*" (Jas 1:5). Wisdom is a gift that God desires to give his people as part of his covenant, including the wisdom in the book of Proverbs.

One could just as easily say, "*Humility* is the beginning of wisdom." For the humility of wisdom leads us to honor our Father as the God who reveals himself to us in his Word, and who made a covenant with Israel and with all believing Christians and their children. The humility of wisdom leads you to honor God as the Creator, and fills you with respect for the ordinances that were appointed for all his creatures. Therefore, we could perhaps better translate Prov 9:10 this way: "and *the respect* for the Holy One is insight."

This is the basis of all wisdom. When people forsake that foundation, their wisdom disappears irretrievably. "Your word is a lamp to my feet and a light to my path" (Ps 119:105). That is the nutrient soil of wisdom, in which it cannot die, but from which it receives grace upon grace. As an example of that, Lady Wisdom mentions our longevity.

> For by me your days will be multiplied,
>   and years will be added to your life. (Prov 9:11)

Wisdom can protect you from a *premature* death. We have discussed this more extensively in connection with Prov 3:1–2. But you can experience the blessings of wisdom far more broadly, spread over your entire life. Proverbs 3 explains that extensively, and Prov 9:12 summarizes this in two lines.

> If you are wise, you are wise for yourself;
>   if you scoff, you alone will bear it. (Prov 9:12)

This is what the Instruction Manual for Proverbs has trumpeted forth in every musical key. Later in Prov 10–31 you can see illustrations galore. Wisdom places you under the favor of the LORD. It makes you to be a joy to your parents and a blessing for your surroundings. It protects your marital happiness from being crushed by unchastity. It forms you into the ideal wife who is the crown of her husband. It makes your family flourish. It blesses your labor with profit and prosperity. It makes you endearing and supplies you with a good name. It protects your health and promotes your nightly rest. For it teaches us to know God's ordinances for our living and to pay attention to them every day.

But the mocker refuses this and must experience this recklessness firsthand (Prov 21:24). This, too, Prov 10–31 will illustrate with numerous examples. A person does not sin cheaply and freely. As Ps 32:10 puts it, "Many are the sorrows of the wicked." Because he despises the rails of God's ordinances, the train of his life's happiness must necessarily run off the rails (cf. Prov 1:24–33). Sin is an attack upon one's own life.

"Do not be deceived: God is not mocked, for whatever one sows, that will he also reap. For the one who sows to his own flesh will from the flesh reap *corruption*, but the one who sows to the Spirit will from the Spirit reap *eternal life*. And let us not grow weary of doing good, for in due season we will reap, if we do not give up" (Gal 6:7–9).

3. LADY FOLLY AND HER GUESTS EAT A DEADLY MEAL (PROV 9:13–18)

At this point, Proverbs introduces to us Lady Wisdom's counterpart, Lady Folly. Like Lady Wisdom, she is not a real person, of course, but she too is a personal *representation*. Just as Lady Wisdom is the personification of all wisdom that God has deposited in his Scripture and his creation, so too Lady Folly is the imaginary figure representing all possible human foolishness.

You need to see her as representing all the sins that we human beings commit, for in Holy Scripture foolishness has a religious tint. The fool is another term for the wicked, the person whose life attitude is one of living everyday as though there is no God who is paying attention to you.[6] You can see that characterization also from the synonyms that Proverbs uses for folly, such as *stupidity, hating knowledge, mockery, stubbornness,* and *sin*. In fact, all of these different expressions point to one and the same thing: forsaking God in word and deed. Rather than speak of Lady Folly, we could also speak of Lady Sin, Lady Wickedness, etc.

We begin first with her portrait.

> The woman Folly is loud;
> she is seductive and knows nothing.
> She sits at the door of her house;
> she takes a seat on the highest places of the town. (Prov 9:13–14)

Clearly this is a portrait of an ancient Eastern prostitute. This is how Tamar sat near the entrance of Enaim (Gen 38:14; cf. Jer 3:2; Ezek 16:31). Such a shallow, shameless creature is supposed to represent sin and folly. Is not sin occasionally boundless superficiality and frivolity? Is not interaction with a prostitute a fitting metaphor for the thoughtlessness, the stupidity, and the carelessness that characterizes every sin?

Lady Folly has absolutely no knowledge of the essential things in life. She is stupidity personified. She is also shameless in her foolishness. Reverend J. C. Sikkel formulated it strikingly in his address delivered at the prayer convocation on June 26, 1889, for the Free University of Amsterdam (founded 1880). Speaking about wisdom and folly, Sikkel said about the latter,

> *Here* you have the withered, the nebulous, the hopeless, and the joyless scientific knowledge [Dutch, *wetenschap*]. The scientific knowledge that brings pain; that extinguishes the final spark; that yields exhaustion in living; that fails to satisfy the abiding

---

6. See the portrait of the fool sketched in van Deursen, *Psalms I*, 93–94.

quest for wisdom; that has no other answer to the question of origin, essence, and purpose than a fantasy, a hypothesis, a presupposition, which ascribes to itself no essential value; that has nothing to predict but the silent grave; that, in service to the depraved heart, is enmity against God as the carnality of the flesh; that renders itself serviceable to *opposing God's will and wisdom*; that seeks every cause and purpose in the *creature* alone and thereby fuels pride and arrogance through its labor; drives everything from the good path; teaches one to despise his God and corrupt himself; and in the end is capable of speaking one boisterous claim, of providing but one solution, which must rescue its own illusory value and satisfy the depraved heart, that word of foolishness, that "wisdom" which says, "There is no God!" This is the false, so-called scientific knowledge. "Claiming to be wise, they became fools" (Rom 1:22; cf. 1 Tim 6:20; Col 2:8; Rom 1:18–32).[7]

The poet is portraying Lady Folly living in an *Israelite* city, of course. In so doing, he is telling us that foolishness and apostasy from God attempt to win followers from among God's own people as well. She appears in public just like Lady Wisdom. Stated concisely, wherever God's Word is known, there you can encounter sin and folly every day and be exposed to her seduction.

This is true especially for young people.

> Calling to those who pass by,
> who are going straight on their way,
> "Whoever is simple, let him turn in here!"
> And to him who lacks sense she says. (Prov 9:15–16)

Daily, every Israelite, just like every Christian, was exposed to the seduction of folly. Amid the bustle of your activities, as you are walking on the good path with all good intentions, Lady Folly can confront you impolitely. Especially if you are still young and have little life experience, she thinks she has found you to be easy prey.

We have already heard how Lady Wisdom commissioned her messengers: "Do not invite the mockers and the wicked; they won't follow you anyway." Lady Folly doesn't need to say this, for she has the mockers and the wicked already under her spell. The struggle between Wisdom and Folly involves *the youth*, the "inexperienced" (or the foolish or ignorant or naive). They have not yet made the decisive choice, and therefore remain open to various influences. Just as Wisdom, so too Folly goes especially after

---

7. Sikkel, *Het Beginsel der Wetenschap*, 11.

the youth. And with the *same words* that Lady Wisdom used: "Whoever is simple, let him turn in here!" (Prov 9:4). Has not Satan used this tactic ever since paradise? Did he not boldly say the same thing God had said: "If you do what I tell you, you will be happy" (cf. Gen 3:5–6)?

> Stolen water is sweet,
>   and bread eaten in secret is pleasant. (Prov 9:17)

Occasionally, "to eat" and "to drink water" can refer to sexual pleasure (Prov 5:15–20; 7:18; 30:20; Song 4:13–15). If that is the intention here, then the poet is having Lady Folly talk like a real, loose woman. Although, to be sure, we can hardly call this a speech, since she is merely suggesting something. With intense passion she is giving her hearers the impression that she has something very desirable to give them, something that will make them very happy. But has not sin done this from the time of paradise, as well? Sin always introduces itself as more desirable than obedience to God's commandments.

No wonder that the poet has chosen the metaphor of a prostitute to represent foolishness. She derives her devilish power of attraction especially from what is forbidden, from what is secret, from what is unknown. To our evil nature sin appears so pretty and seductive. One who sits down to "eat and drink" with her—literally and figuratively—is surrendering his body and soul to her. Lady Wickedness will not rest before she has all of you in her possession.

Surely the difference in the menu has caught your attention? Lady Wisdom invites us to a regal meal of meaty delicacies in a royal house. Lady Folly grabs us on the street to come enjoy *bread and water* with her. The only attractive feature of her menu consists in the forbidden, the secret. But what she does not tell us is what our wise teacher adds: whoever accepts her invitation is sitting down to his last meal.

> But he does not know that the dead are there,
>   that her guests are in the depths of Sheol. (Prov 9:18)

In Prov 7:27, Solomon says about the strange woman, "Her house is the way to Sheol, going down to the chambers of death." But here his formulation is more severe. One who endeavors *to live together* with Lady Folly or with Lady Sin (which is not the same as *falling* into sin), should remember that her house is an apartment of death. Her guests are dead while they breathe. They supposed that they would receive a delicious meal, but instead ate deadly poison.

Later the apostle wrote substantially the same thing: "For the wages of sin is death" (Rom 6:23). In Proverbs, as happens more frequently in

Scripture, "death" means more than breathing one's last breath. "Death" can also refer to the dissolution that our human life can experience even while we are still walking about and being active: "Dead in your trespasses and sins" (cf. Eph 2:1). For some, this means encountering a premature death (see our comments on Prov 3:1) and later facing the second death, "the lake of fire" (Rev 20:14). "Her guests are in the depths *of hell*," is the King James rendering of Prov 9:18.

The two ways

Proverbs 9 sets before us the age-old choice between the two ways, before which the Torah, the Prophets, the Psalms, and our Lord Jesus Christ continually place God's people.

Moses had said to Israel, "I have set before you life and death, blessing and curse. Therefore choose life, . . . loving the Lord your God" (Deut 30:19–20). Joshua confronted the people with the same decision: "Choose this day whom you will serve" (Josh 24:15). Psalm 1 opens the third section of Scripture with a description of the two ways: the way of the righteous and the way of the wicked (cf. Jer 17:5–8). And our Lord fulfilled the Law and the Prophets with his teaching about "the wide gate and the broad way that leads to destruction" and "the narrow gate and the small way that leads to life" (Matt 7:13–14).

Proverbs 9 is also setting this age-old choice before us. Thereby it summarizes the entire Instruction Manual for Proverbs. What is the bottom line of part 1 of this Bible book? It comes down to this question: What will be your food and drink? Wisdom or foolishness? Food for life or deadly poison? Which meal will you choose?

Part 2

Proverbs 10–31: The "Real" Book of Proverbs

12

Some Proverbs of Solomon and of Other Sages

A Selection from Proverbs 10–31

NOW WE ENTER THE throne room! If we may compare the Instruction Manual (Prov 1–9) to a majestic lobby, then in Prov 10:1 we are opening the door to the throne room and to the corridors of the great palace of Proverbs. In a certain sense, Prov 10–31 constitutes the actual book of Proverbs. How shall we now proceed to read it?

The arrangement of this series of volumes, entitled Opening the Scriptures, is such that we are not writing a commentary, not even on the book of Proverbs. Our goal is to help you find your way around in the world of this book (and what a *world* it is!). Therefore, we have devoted the largest amount of space to Prov 1–9, since this is where Solomon has introduced his book in such an attractive manner. In view of the arrangement of our work, we had to devote that amount of attention to that section.

But now we are opening the "actual" book of Proverbs. We have been instructed by the author himself about how we must read this portion, namely, as a book full of life-wisdom, intended especially for the as yet inexperienced youth. This wisdom has been cast in the concise and figurative form of the *mashal*, a form that can occasionally be somewhat crass and one-sided. This is a book of lessons from real life. As you read it you must constantly remember: This book speaks everywhere with wholesome counsel. It can benefit my entire life: my marriage and family, my health and nightly rest, my money and my possessions. We flatter ourselves with the hope that our extensive discussion of Prov 1–9 has somewhat sharpened your view of the beneficent power of wisdom in Prov 10–31.

We offer the following comments about our method of discussing various proverbs in what follows.

Since, as we indicated, we are not writing a commentary, in what follows you will not find a treatment of each proverb in the remainder of the Bible book, but merely of selected proverbs. Naturally, this is somewhat limited and rather arbitrary, even though we have tried as much as possible to introduce variety, and have intentionally quoted many similar proverbs in full. We hope that the discussion of those proverbs we have selected will shed some light on those similar proverbs that we have not discussed. For that reason, we have included them in our subject index, which may render a favor to some of our readers.

Many a proverb resembles a thick book that someone has summarized in two lines. Who would be able to explain such comprehensive sayings exhaustively? For that reason, we have for the most part limited ourselves to providing some examples in connection with a proverb. If you'd like, you yourself could multiply these with many other examples. Try to do this; that is a good way to make this wisdom your own.

Regarding the nature of our examples, we preferred to choose them from Scripture. We did so because the God-fearing heart readily bows most easily before Scripture, and because Scripture can best be explained by Scripture. But we have done this also being mindful of the adage "There it is *written*, and there it has *happened*," so that, now and then, we have chosen an example from history, which also naturally offers many illustrations in connection with the wisdom of Proverbs.

We make one final comment about the teaching form of this Bible book. "*Mashals* of Solomon" is the heading above Prov 10–31. In chapter 1, we discussed extensively the uniquenesses of this form of poetry and teaching. We did so especially to prevent misunderstanding of the concise manner of speaking used by Solomon and others who composed *mashals*. In what follows, we will assume that readers are familiar with that chapter.

1. SOME PROVERBS OF SOLOMON (PROV 10–22)

As the reader knows, our Bible book of Proverbs consists of selections from various collections. These include several larger collections from Solomon himself, together with a couple of smaller appendices from other wise men. For the most part we have selected proverbs from the collections of Solomon, of course, because those constitute the lion's share of the book.

Proverbs 10:1

> A wise son makes a glad father,
> but a foolish son is a sorrow to his mother.

"I have gotten a man with the help of the LORD!" Eve exclaimed joyfully when she became a mother (Gen 4:1). Later it became evident, to her great sorrow, that she had given birth to a murderer. Rebekah complained to Isaac about their son Esau, "I loathe my life because of the Hittite women. If Jacob marries one of the Hittite women like these, one of the women of the land, what good will my life be to me?" (Gen 27:46; cf. 28:8). Scripture mentions a number of other wise fathers who had foolish sons: Noah, Samuel, David, Jehoshaphat, and Hezekiah. Even Solomon himself!

In the proverb quoted above, we hear a twofold challenge. First, to Solomon's young readers: "Be careful, my son, do not be so foolish that you forsake God and his Word. Spare your mother that heartache and give your father the best present possible: your wise, God-fearing walk of life." This is certainly similar to what the apostle John wrote: "I have no greater joy than to hear that my children are walking in the truth" (3 John 4).

This proverb should prod parents not to neglect their children but to nurture them in the discipline and correction of the Lord (Eph 6:4). Should their children not listen to that teaching, then, despite their pain, such a father and mother will be spared the recrimination of "We gave him food and clothes, but withheld from him the bread of life."

There is almost no more important work than that of nurturing children in the fear of the LORD. Is it not remarkable that Solomon begins not only his Instruction Manual for Proverbs but also the book of Proverbs itself with a proverb about the family? No wonder that the family is the nuclear cell and supporting pillar of church, state, and society. Solomon will come back to this repeatedly (see our discussion of Prov 13:24; 19:18; 22:16, 15). In connection with this proverb, see also Prov 13:1; 15:5, 20; 17:21, 25; 19:13, 26; 20:11, 20; 28:7; and 29:3.

Proverbs 10:2

> Treasures gained by wickedness do not profit,
> but righteousness delivers from death.

At the start of the sixteenth century, Spain was a wealthy country. The famous "silver fleet"—part of which Piet Hein captured in 1628—carried shiploads of valuable cargo each year. But these were really "treasures gained by wickedness," as Solomon expresses it in this proverb. The Spaniards had not earned their wealth honestly, but had robbed the mines and treasuries of the conquered nations in Central and South America. For that reason, what God's Word teaches us in this proverb applied to them: "Treasures gained by wickedness do not profit." At the end of the sixteenth century, the same nation of Spain had suffered various financial disasters.

The large increase in types of currencies coming from South America, strange as it may sound, had not benefited the Spanish economy. On the contrary, the stolen treasure had disastrous effects on the Spanish domestic economy. The king and his high-ranking friends could adopt a standard of living that was far too high. The excessive supply of money put them in a position to drain more and more labor resources from farming and manufacturing. But as a result, these important means of economic existence increasingly ended up in foreign hands. Thanks to silver from the Americas, Spain could pay for its ongoing wars, but did not succeed in meeting its wide-ranging need for war materials on its own. As a result, the stolen money flowed without restraint to foreign countries that were producing the needed mercenaries and war materials.

The wise statesman, Solomon, had warned about this course of events: "Treasures gained by wickedness do not profit." This includes a nation's domestic economy. Rather than enriching the country, the stolen silver from the Americas impoverished Spain and slowed its economic development for centuries. Just as with Egypt earlier in history, so too Spain, ever since the day of its "silver fleets," has descended from being a world power to becoming a backward country that has begun to recover somewhat only in the twentieth century. History shows us repeatedly, in fact, that a nation never acquires lasting prosperity by robbing and extorting other nations.

But why did Spain's "treasures gained by wickedness" provide no profit? This was due to its own self-directed religion, whereby Spain failed to take into account God's command for economic and political life. God had commanded Israel and Christianity, "You shall not steal." A nation must earn its bread through honest labor. That is God's order (cf. Prov 28:19; Eph 4:28; 1 Thess 4:11; 2 Thess 6:6–12). Lasting economic development and prosperity exist only through industriousness, normed by God's commandments. That is why the silver stolen from the Americas did Spain no good in the long run, because it had acquired these treasures *through wickedness*. The nation's suppliers, by contrast, became rich, because they had worked for their wealth.

That is how God's commandments function practically in life, including the life of a nation. The Spaniards could have read the constitution for economic life in their Bible: "You shall not steal." By transgressing this commandment, they had imported death or dissolution into their domestic economy. This applied, of course, to their personal lives as well, but we chose the example of the entire nation. What Solomon is teaching in this proverb is echoed in our common adage "Something stolen does not satisfy," and in the saying "Easy come, easy go."

This matter has another side, however, and Solomon pointed to that as well. "But righteousness delivers from death," he added to his warning. Righteousness or obedience to God's covenant and God's words can rescue someone's economic life, indeed even that of an entire nation, from death (i.e., from dissolution, fruitlessness, destruction). This happens when people respect God's order—"You shall not steal, but earn your bread with your own hands." In the same century when Spain went broke with its American silver for which it had not worked, the Netherlands was entering its golden age, in part because feverish efforts were being put forth.

Here, then, are several similar proverbs: "Wealth gained hastily will dwindle, but whoever gathers little by little will increase it" (13:11). "The plans of the diligent lead surely to abundance, but everyone who is hasty comes only to poverty" (21:5). "In all toil there is profit, but mere talk tends only to poverty" (14:23). "Whoever works his land will have plenty of bread, but he who follows worthless pursuits will have plenty of poverty" (28:19).

Proverbs 10:4

> A slack hand causes poverty,
>   but the hand of the diligent makes rich.

Many diligent hands make an entire nation rich, as you can see from the Netherlands in the seventeenth century. At that time, people in the Netherlands worked hard, and, according to God's order, that is the condition for economic prosperity: "You shall not steal, but earn your bread with your own hands" (cf. Prov 28:19; Eph 4:28; 1 Thess 4:11; 2 Thess 3:6–12). The "most vital gold mine" was, contrary to what people think, the fisheries, followed by the cargo trade, especially on the Baltic Sea and further throughout Eastern Europe and the East Indies. Do not underestimate agriculture, animal husbandry, and finishing industries. Along that route of diligence and entrepreneurship, God made the Dutch in the seventeenth century a prosperous nation. The wisdom that comes from the fear of the LORD includes the promise of the increase of possessions. Solomon had repeatedly drawn attention to that in his Instruction Manual (see our comments on Prov 3:9–10 and 3:16).

Regrettably, these zealous workers were succeeded by lazy grandchildren, who preferred to rest on their laurels. In the eighteenth century, the entrepreneurial spirit subsided, and the Netherlands began living off its own accumulated wealth. The country became the banker of Europe. But one needs to work for money, otherwise it hardly sustains (see our comments on Prov 10:2; 11:18; 13:11). That is what Spain experienced with its "silver fleets" in the seventeenth century, and the Netherlands with its financial enterprises in the eighteenth century. Other nations advanced their position with the help of our money, while our own economy began to languish. For a nation's economy, just like a family's economy, cannot flourish without economic accomplishments. Our national life had to suffer the consequences of sloth in the eighteenth century, experienced well into the nineteenth century.

Here are several similar proverbs: "Whoever is slothful will not roast his game, but the diligent man will get precious wealth" (12:27). "Whoever is slack in his work is a brother to him who destroys" (18:9). "Slothfulness casts into a deep sleep, and an idle person will suffer hunger" (19:15).

Proverbs 10:7

> The memory of the righteous is a blessing,
>   but the name of the wicked will rot.

Names like Herod, Judas, Alva, and Hitler have been left to rot in history. But the memory of Solomon remains a blessed one to this day, for through him God gave us these treasures of proverbial wisdom. So too the name of David is indissolubly connected with the Psalms, which continue to dispense so much blessing. In the same way, the name of our God-fearing parents and teachers can continue having a wholesome effect for years after their departure, because their living close to God's Word stimulates us to imitate them. But whose remembrance is more precious and more blessed to us than that of the great righteous one, our Lord Jesus Christ? "May his name endure forever, his fame continue as long as the sun! May people be blessed in him, all nations call him blessed!" (Ps 72:17).

Proverbs 10:11

> The mouth of the righteous is a fountain of life,
> but the mouth of the wicked conceals violence.

How many mouths have unleashed violence upon God's destitute people! Think of Saul, Haman, and the members of the Sanhedrin, or those of the later Inquisition. And what about the mouth of the righteous! Here Solomon likens it to a water fountain, and what that signified for life was understood very well by people living in an arid land. A fountain—your life can depend on it, as Hagar and Ishmael experienced (Gen 16).

In that context, Israel sang to Yahweh, "For with you is the fountain of life" (Ps 36:9; cf. Jer 2:13; 17:13). For that reason, his Word is so very wholesome for our life. All the more now that God's Son has fulfilled and completed it through his teaching, so that with Peter we can ask, "Lord, to whom shall we go? You have the words of eternal life" (John 6:68). Having been instructed by those words, disciples of Jesus can now promote with their own words the life-happiness of their neighbor and point him to the path of eternal life. This life is not simply a one-time deal, but an unlimited life. Such a mouth resembles a continuously bubbling fountain, like the kind that kept Israel alive every day.

Here are a number of related proverbs: "The tongue of the righteous is choice silver; the heart of the wicked is of little worth" (Prov 10:20). "The teaching of the wise is a fountain of life" (13:14a; cf. 10:14, 21; 14:27; 16:22; John 7:38–39; see also our comments on Prov 3:17; 15:1; 16:24; and 18:7).

Proverbs 10:14

> The wise lay up knowledge,
> but the mouth of a fool brings ruin near.

A fool spews forth his foolish ideas all the time, with all the bad results that they produce. But wise people preserve their knowledge for the right moment, when the *opportunity* to speak arises. They do not offer their teaching indiscriminately, for they know "a word in season, how good it is!" (Prov 15:23; cf. Eccl 3:7, 11; Matt 7:6; see our comments on Prov 18:7).

Proverbs 10:15

> A rich man's wealth is his strong city;
> the poverty of the poor is their ruin.

Riches are certainly not the highest good. Righteousness, understanding, and a good name are worth far more. But we must not move in the opposite direction of despising money and possessions as improper. Sometimes people do this from a sense of idealism and romanticism, or simply out of laziness. Proverbs frequently acknowledges that, in addition to their many dangers, money and possessions also have advantages, and lack of money is painful and often harmful.

Money offers its possessors a certain measure of protection against the uncertainties of life (Eccl 7:12). The rich man is surrounded by his possessions like a strong fortress, Solomon says, even though that protection is relative, of course (Prov 18:11). The poor man, by contrast, can trace much of his misery to his lack of money. Solomon characterizes personal poverty literally as "his ruin" or "his reproach" (the same word that we find in Ps 89:41). This is a poignant contrast to the wealthy man! Where this latter person is living safely behind a high wall, thanks to his wealth, the poor man lives, as a result of his poverty, on a heap of ruins, exposed and naked, so that everyone can push him around.

Other proverbs show us something of the calamity that poverty brings. For example, it can cost you friends: "The poor is disliked [passed by, ignored] even by his neighbor, but the rich has many friends" (Prov 14:20). "All a poor man's brothers hate him; how much more do his friends go far from him!" (19:7). Poverty can also injure one's self-esteem: "The poor use entreaties, but the rich answer roughly" (18:23). Deprivation leads to despondency. "The rich rules over the poor, and the borrower is the slave of the lender" (22:7). These are simply the harsh facts, which Solomon is not evaluating but merely observing.

Remember as well that often in Scripture, the poor refer to the godly and the rich refer to the wicked.[1] In Israel, poverty was often the result of forsaking the covenant, for in the Torah Yahweh had raised up a protective shield over the poor. But what if that shield were broken? Elsewhere we discussed the calamity that could befall Israel's poor godly ones.[2] No wonder that Agur prayed for protection from poverty (Prov 30:8; see our comments on that verse).

No, we must not despise owning some possessions.

---

1. See van Deursen, *Psalms I*, 55–57, 66, 109–10.
2. See van Deursen, *Psalms I*, 57–66.

Proverbs 10:16

> The wage of the righteous leads to life,
> the gain of the wicked to sin.

How do we spend our money? That too is a matter of wisdom and part of fearing the Lord. Boaz permitted two poor widows to share in his wealth. Nabal refused to allow David and his beleaguered companions to share any of his abundance. Here we have two wealthy farmers, one righteous, the other wicked, displaying two attitudes toward money and property, indeed toward God, as the owner of all money and property. Solomon identifies the difference as being "unto life" (in Proverbs this is another phrase for prosperity and happiness) or "unto sin" (that is, against God's purpose).

Has not that distinction continued to characterize the approach toward money on the part of the righteous and the wicked? The righteous ones—who were often poor—were dealing with God and his Word when it came to their spending. And that benefited their life and the life of their neighbor, including even their health (we will say more about this in connection with Prov 11:17; cf. Eph 4:28; 1 Tim 6:17–19). But the wicked were often the wealthy extortioners, the skinflints, robber barons, those who oppressed widows, harsh creditors, and financial tyrants. With icy arrogance they ignored the fact that all money and property belonged to God (Ps 24:1), and instead boldly devoted them to their own sinful purposes—to satisfy their thirst for money and other fleshly lusts (Jas 5:4–6).[3] "Unto life" or "unto sin"—that is indeed the great distinction. (See our comments on Prov 11:18 as well.)

Proverbs 10:17

> Whoever heeds instruction is on the path to life,
> but he who rejects reproof leads others astray.

This is what Israel experienced with King Jeroboam. He appeared to be a very religious man, but he despised the warnings of the prophets (1 Kgs 11:29–39; 12:33—13:34). As an ominous refrain we read in the books of 1 Kings, "Jeroboam, the son of Nebat, who made Israel to sin" (1 Kgs 22:52). This was how the Pharisees and scribes despised the warnings of John the Baptist and Jesus, so that finally the Lord had to warn them, "Let them alone; they are blind guides" (Matt 15:14; cf. 23:16–17).

---

3. See van Deursen, *Psalms I*, 124.

Nowadays, many politicians and social reformers prefer to call themselves progressive. But here Solomon teaches us that anyone who despises the discipline of God's Word leads people astray. This is altogether different from progress or advancement; it often signals regression. "O my people, your guides mislead you and they have swallowed up the course of your paths" (Isa 3:12). Whoever has eyes to see can discover facts in the daily news that can establish and illustrate the truth of this proverb.

But one who does not exalt himself sovereignly above God's Word is a "path to life." Here and there he can clean up this miserable life under God's blessing. For only the fear of the Lord can lift humanity out of the morass, as the history of Israel's godly kings shows. But all who turn away from God are shown ultimately to be false guides with corrupt judgment. They injure both themselves and their families, sometimes even entire churches, schools, and nations.

Proverbs 10:19

> When words are many, transgression is not lacking,
>   but whoever restrains his lips is prudent.

"Many words, many slips," says one proverb, but Solomon digs more deeply: With much speaking comes much sinning. How many sins are tied to words? Cursing, lying, mocking, hating, committing injustice, unchastity, false testimony, dishonest business practices, self-directed religion, hypocrisy, disobedience. By contrast, silence rarely does damage.

For that reason, Proverbs so often praises silence as one of the finest fruits of wisdom. To mention but a few: "Whoever restrains his words has knowledge, and he who has a cool spirit is a man of understanding" (17:27). "Even a fool who keeps silent is considered wise; when he closes his lips, he is deemed intelligent" (17:28). The wise apostle James agrees with this: "Know this, my beloved brothers: let every person be quick to hear, slow to speak, slow to anger" (Jas 1:19; cf. 1:26; 3:2–12).

Even pagans were somewhat familiar with this. A father asked the philosopher Cleanthes, "What must my son learn?" The answer he received was this: "Teach him above all to be silent." Pythagoras said, "In my school they learn to listen and to be silent; in other schools they learn to speak." Egyptian and Babylonian wisdom books also emphasize silence: "Sleep (on it) before speaking."[4] In the proverbs of Amenemope the term for the wise or pious person is *the silent one*.

---

4. Gemser, *De Spreuken van Salamo*, 145.

What impresses us the most, however, is the warning of our Lord and Master: "I tell you, on the day of judgment people will give account for every careless word they speak, for by your words you will be justified, and by your words you will be condemned" (Matt 12:36–37). Therefore, we may pray often, "Set a guard, O Lord, over my mouth; keep watch over the door of my lips!" (Ps 141:3).

Proverbs 11:2

> When pride comes, then comes disgrace,
>   but with the humble is wisdom.

Isaiah proclaimed this very graphically in Isa 2–4. How proudly the men of Judah looked at their horses and chariots, their ships and art treasures. Their wives and daughters looked around with equal arrogance. Haughtily and with outstretched necks, they strutted down the street, with jingling ankles. Ostentatiously they displayed their headbands, earrings, ornamental belts, veils, scarves, coats, bags, undergarments, and outerwear (Isa 3:16–23). Exactly what the Lord abhors so intensely: haughty eyes and proud hearts.

To the eye it perhaps appeared as though the church of Judah was still serving Yahweh, but in fact it had been thoroughly influenced by the world of the ancient East (Isa 2:6). The men betrayed this by trusting their fortresses and pushing aside Yahweh as their Protector. The women showed this by their charms and jewelry. For they liked to wear a crescent, symbol of the ancient Easter moon god (Isa 3:18).

That is, until God came with his judgments upon his arrogant church and the entire welfare society of Judah, which he caused to disintegrate under the violence of war. Young boys and hoodlums stormed against old and respected men. Numerous young men perished, and the chances for many young women getting married went up in smoke. Many fashionable ladies were put in a prisoner of war camp, where there was inadequate water for bathing, such that the scent of perfumes was replaced with the odor of foul stench. The ornamental belt was replaced with a rope, the beautiful shawl with a sack, which was the ancient mourning garb. The golden headband disappeared, replaced by a prisoner tattoo. Pollution brought scabies. Isaiah had said, "For the Lord of hosts has a day against all that is proud and lofty, against all that is lifted up—and it shall be brought low" (Isa 2:12).

In the same way, during the German occupation of the Netherlands, professors and bankers, notaries and parliament members—though they had recently been on the top rung of society—were completely humiliated as skinny prisoners behind barbed wire. In the Far East, impoverished and spoiled European ladies sat in Japanese camps All of this resembled Isa 2:17: "And the haughtiness of man shall be humbled, and the lofty pride of men shall be brought low, and the LORD alone will be exalted in that day." Was that fate or judgment? And will our generation escape? Pride is an unmistakable prelude to an imminent fall.

So pride is folly. But Isaiah and his group humbled themselves under the mighty hand of God. Therefore they were wise. Only then does one see the reality in which God allows us to live at a given moment, and only then can one take appropriate measures for each situation. For pride blinds, but wisdom clarifies one's vision. (See also our comments on Prov 3:34; 15:33; 16:18; 18:12; and 22:4.)

Proverbs 11:4

> Riches do not profit in the day of wrath,
>   but righteousness delivers from death.

Zephaniah saw this "day of wrath" coming upon Israel, and he warned, "Neither their silver nor their gold shall be able to deliver them on the day of the wrath of the LORD" (Zeph 1:18). What good was the money of the wealthy residents of Jerusalem when in 586 BC Nebuchadnezzar stood at the city gates? Ezekiel had seen it coming: "They will throw their silver into the streets, and their gold will be an unclean thing. Their silver and gold will not be able to save them in the day of the LORD's wrath. They will not satisfy their hunger or fill their stomachs with it, for it has made them stumble into sin" (Ezek 7:19 NIV; cf. Isa 2:20–21; 10:3).

What good was the gold of the wealthy Jews when in AD 70 Titus lay siege to Jerusalem and the word of the Lord Jesus was fulfilled: "There will be great distress in the land and *wrath* against this people. They will fall by the sword and will be taken as prisoners to all the nations. Jerusalem will be trampled on by the Gentiles" (Luke 21:23–24 NIV; cf. Matt 3:7). At that point no bank balance or personal residence will benefit you. Just like the rich fool had no benefit from his new barns when God took his life one night (Luke 12:16–21; cf. 16:19–31; 2 Kgs 1; Ps 49).

This history of Israel and of Christianity has since those days often seen such a "day of wrath," when God's wrath fell upon those who forsook his covenant. At that point there is only one means of rescue: righteousness. Doing the righteousness of the Lord. Having shown covenantal obedience. Having displayed loyalty to the God who made a covenant with us, and in that covenant provided us the blood and Spirit of his Son. In general, the following applies already now: "The truly righteous man attains life" (Prov 11:19). In various ways, righteousness can prevent the dissolution of life, something that Solomon has demonstrated extensively in the Instruction Manual (Prov 1–9). But in the proverb cited above, he is pointing more to its value in times of judgment. At that point, righteousness can rescue a person from death.

Biblical history shows this here and there. Frequently God indeed preserved the life of the righteous in a "day of wrath." In this connection we might think of Joshua and Caleb, Rahab, Elijah, Jeremiah and his secretary Baruch, and the Christians who in AD 70, in obedience to the Word of the Lord (Luke 21:20–21), left Judea and Jerusalem in time and fled to safety.

Undoubtedly, we may appeal to this proverb when God's judgments come upon the earth; on the other hand, let us not turn this into an insurance policy that guarantees us as the righteous that, in such times, *no evil at all* will come to us. For Scripture also shows that God allows the good to suffer along with the wicked (Joshua and Caleb, Jonathan, Hosea, Ezekiel, Daniel and his friends).

In this context, it is good to listen once again to Zephaniah. When he saw a "day of wrath" approaching, he cried out, "Gather together, gather yourselves together, you shameful nation, . . . before the Lord's fierce anger comes upon you, before the day of the Lord's wrath comes upon you. Seek the Lord, all you humble of the land, you who do what he commands. Seek righteousness [!], seek humility; *perhaps* you will be sheltered on the day of the Lord's anger" (Zeph 2:1–3 NIV; cf. Lam 3:29, "there *may* yet be hope"; Amos 5:15 NIV, "*Perhaps* the Lord God Almighty will have mercy on the remnant of Joseph").

This "perhaps" does not apply, of course, to eternal salvation—for at that point Scripture never talks about "perhaps"—but to rescue in times of judgment. For then people must fall to their death, like Jonathan as part of an army under God's judgment, or like the prophet Uriah who was killed for the sake of the Word of God (Jer 26:23; cf. Rev 2:13). We point out these events so that you don't turn this proverb into an ironclad rule to which we might bind the Lord.

But this word of Solomon will be completely fulfilled only on that day when many rich and mighty people will call out to the mountains and the rocks, "Fall on us and hide us from the face of him who sits on the throne and from the wrath of the Lamb! For *the great day of their wrath* has come, and who can stand?" (Rev 6:15–17). With this in view, all those who have pursued righteousness (Deut 16:20) may firmly trust that such righteousness will surely rescue them from death. "Therefore, since we have been justified through faith, we have peace with God through our Lord Jesus Christ" (Rom 5:1). "He who overcomes [he who practices righteousness] will not be hurt at all by the second death" (Rev 2:11; cf. 20:6).

Proverbs 11:11

> By the blessing of the upright a city is exalted,
> but by the mouth of the wicked it is overthrown.

If Israel would fear Yahweh uprightly, he promised to bless their kingdom. This blessing was not only for their "spiritual life" but also for their family life, their marital life, their economic life, their social life, and their political life. The Israelites could observe God's blessing in terms of the fertility of the womb, the productivity of their animals, the harvest of their fields, and peace within their borders. Yahweh would regulate the world situation in such a way that Israel would enjoy such peace and possess so much wealth that Israel could function as the World Bank in making loans to their neighbors (Lev 26:1–13; Deut 28:1–14).

Does not biblical history happily show us many among God's people who were upright? We might think in this connection of Boaz, Hannah, Samuel, David, Solomon, and numerous upright in the land. They appealed to God's covenant promises when, in the spirit of 1 Kgs 8 or Ps 72, they prayed for his blessing upon their "city" (but with that word we may also include the nation). In this proverb one could render the Hebrew, in place of "the *blessing* of the upright," as the "*prayers* for blessing" or "*wishes* for blessing." At many times throughout Israel's history, God was indeed willing to hear such prayers, so that the promised showers of blessing did indeed descend upon Israel.

During the reign of David and Solomon—genuinely upright believers—the posterity of the slaves from Egypt ascended to the level of a first-rank nation. In Jerusalem the temple was built. The queen of Sheba came to listen to Solomon's wisdom. So much gold streamed into the country that people hardly counted out silver. "The people of Judah and Israel were as numerous as the sand on the seashore; they ate, they drank and they were happy" (1 Kgs 4:20). We read nothing about catastrophic drought, like that experienced under Ahab, or about invading Syrians, as in the time of Elisha. God held Israel's enemies in check. When Judah later served Yahweh uprightly under Jehoshaphat and Hezekiah, God gave revival everywhere. Revival of national power, revival of jurisprudence, revival of the economy, revival of worship. God also gave Hezekiah material benefits. He owned precious stones, spices, grain, and oil in abundance (1 Chr 32:27–29).

Can we too not observe that blessing upon the upright in the rise of our own nation? How fervently those martyrs in the sixteenth century loved the Lord Jesus, and honored God and his Word! They went to the stake for their loyalty. Would they not have beseeched God for his blessing upon their descendants, and has God not heard them? In connection with the "exalting of the city" we might think of Amsterdam, which was just beginning to flourish. Did not God send showers of blessing in the golden age upon the descendants of the martyrs who had honored his covenant so faithfully? To be sure, not every Dutchman did so, but God wants to allow worldly people to profit as well from his blessing upon the upright in their midst. In this way he blessed Laban for the sake of Jacob, and Potiphar, along with all of Egypt, for the sake of Joseph (Gen 30:27; 39:5; 41:46–57; 47:25).

We see the blessing of God's covenant, of course, also in the religious life of the seventeenth century. After several decades, the strength of medieval scholasticism and mystical religiosity was broken. The annotations to the Dutch States Translation of the Bible (SV) testify to a deep insight into Holy Scripture. But God also blessed business and industry, literature and statecraft, the arts, and sciences. God supplied that generation with a comprehensive worldview and clear insight into every arena of life. Indeed, "by the blessing of the upright a city is exalted." You can still see this in the houses lining the Amsterdam canals and in the historical world atlas.

But by the mouth of the wicked it [the city, the land] is overthrown. That is what Solomon points to in the second line. The wicked here refers to Israelites or Christians who supposedly know better than what God has revealed in his Word. These are the members of God's people who, often despite having a religious exterior, follow their own "counsel" or live according to their own principles.[5] Such "pious" covenant breakers have caused the greatest damage to the Israelite—and our own—"city."

Moses had warned: if you forsake God, he will forsake you and visit his curse upon you. His curse is just as concrete as his blessing. You will see that curse in your grain basket and your livestock, in the womb of your wife and in the defeat of your army, in your body and in your business, and finally in your utter ruin as you are carried captive from your land. Israel did indeed experience this covenant curse with increasing severity. Gideon was threshing grain in a winepress, afraid of a Midianite raid. Under Ahab, the ground had cracked open from drought. Under Elisha, an Israelite slave girl

---

5. See van Deursen, *Psalms I*, 129–30.

was serving the foreigner Naaman in Damascus, kidnapped from her land, to the grief of her parents.

All of this, however, was not the result of autonomous political and economic powers, operating beyond the control of Yahweh, but the result of the ruin brought about by "the mouth of the wicked." By this means, Israel was led to forsake God's covenant, at which point the curse sanctions of the covenant were enforced. The "mouth," the *ideas*, the unbelieving *principles*, the *false prophecy*[6] of wicked Israelites demolished Samaria and Jerusalem, when the Assyrians and Babylonians literally turned them into rubble.

Was not the Dutch Republic, also known as the Republic of the Seven United Netherlands, destroyed in the same way? "Our human understanding stands not under, but above Holy Scripture." That was not being claimed by pagans, but by sons of Reformed churches in the Netherlands. Many rulers and patriots, whose mouths (!) were spouting the ideas of the so-called Enlightenment, were members of the national Reformed church. That is forgotten sometimes. It was the mouth of wicked Reformed people, who were stirred up on behalf of ideas arising from the French Revolution.

Through "the mouth" (i.e., the doctrine, the ideas, the slogans) of these wicked people, Reformed churches forsook God's covenant in the eighteenth century, despite all their activist, subjectivist religiosity. At that point, God forsook them, just as concretely and comprehensively as he had blessed their ancestors. Thus, not only in the area of religion but in every arena of life, in art, in science, in morality, in jurisprudence, even in physical and psychological respects. When you compare the portraits produced in the seventeenth century with those of the eighteenth century, you will see men with brighter eyes next to sophisticated and effeminate figures who kept tranquilizers on hand for their nerves.

With their mouth ("Liberty, Equality, and Fraternity!"), wicked religious people helped destroy the Dutch state. In 1795 many Reformed people were dancing around the Liberty Tree. But their boys were drowning in the battle of Berezina or were creeping on their bellies in the Russian snowfields like cannon fodder for Napoleon, the whip God used for chastisement. It was the compassions of the Lord (Lam 3:22) that our Dutch "city" at that time was not permanently destroyed by the mouth of the wicked.

But perhaps this signified merely the postponement of execution?

---

6. See van Deursen, *Psalms I*, 115–18.

Proverbs 11:14

> Where there is no guidance, a people falls,
> but in an abundance of counselors there is safety.

In view here, of course, are good advisors. Even Solomon with all his wisdom did not govern without advisors (1 Kgs 12:6)! His son Rehoboam rejected their advice and, due to this lack of guidance, he forced the division of his kingdom. Moreover, one might think, in connection with this proverb, of the saying of the Preacher: "Woe to you, O land whose king was a servant and whose princes feast in the morning. Blessed are you, O land whose king is of noble birth and whose princes eat at a proper time—for strength and not for drunkenness" (Eccl 10:16–17).

Proverbs 11:16

> A gracious woman gets honor,
> and violent men get riches.

Both are irresistible and often undeserved.

Proverbs 11:17

> A man who is kind benefits himself,
> but a cruel man hurts himself.

When he was fifty years old, John D. Rockefeller Sr. was the wealthiest man in the world and the only multimillionaire.[7] But to achieve this, he had mercilessly worked himself and others to death. He allowed himself no rest in his chase after continually greater profits. Many who were financially weaker were destroyed by him and driven into the ground. He was hated so intensely in the oil fields of Pennsylvania that people hung on a gallows a doll that resembled him, and he needed a bodyguard day and night.

In so doing, however, the unmerciful Rockefeller had damaged himself. He was as lonely as he was rich. He yearned for love, but failed to realize that to receive love one must give love. When he turned fifty-one he looked old and worn out. He suffered from alopecia, a disease that causes one's hair to fall out, not only from one's head but also one's eyelashes and eyebrows. He looked like a mummy. He "earned" a million dollars a week, but slept

---

7. See McMillen, *None of These Diseases*, 128–32.

poorly and had such poor digestion that he could eat only crackers and milk. He was skin and bones, and people thought he would be dead within a year. Journalists had already prepared his obituary. Lovelessness had cut off the bloom of his life.

Until one sleepless night, when he came to realize that he should not hoard his money but distribute it on behalf of his weak fellow human beings. The next morning he began to do so. He established the Rockefeller Foundation and began to distribute his millions to missions, universities, hospitals, and institutions of mercy. The discovery of penicillin, which has saved numerous human lives, we owe, humanly speaking, to the millions of dollars that came from him.

Just as the unmerciful Rockefeller had damaged himself, so now the beneficent Rockefeller benefited himself. When he changed from an egoist to an altruist, his health improved as well. He could sleep again, eat normally, and enjoy life somewhat. His deadly selfishness and the accompanying bitterness and unmerciful attitude had made room in his heart for love and kindness. At that point, the benefactor was simultaneously refreshed by the fresh streams of mutual love and gratitude coming from those who were being helped.

But this lesson could be read in the Bible for a long time: "A man who is kind benefits himself, but a cruel man hurts himself" (Prov 11:17). Regrettably it cost Rockefeller fifty-three years—almost half a human lifespan—and much physical and spiritual suffering before he had learned this lesson. He could have learned this from the Lord Jesus as well: "*Give*, and it will be given to you. A good measure, pressed down, shaken together and running over, will be poured into your lap. For with the measure you use, it will be measured to you" (Luke 6:38; cf. Matt 5:7; 25:31–46; 1 John 3:14). Rockefeller's fifty-third birthday appeared to be his last one, but a life of giving did him so much good that he lived to be ninety-eight.

"So in everything, do to others what you would have them do to you, for this sums up the Law and the Prophets," taught the Lord Jesus (Matt 7:12 NIV). And that is healthy as well! Modern psychiatry has an eye for the wholesome influence that Christian neighborly love can have on our spiritual health. It too encourages patients not to live with an inward looking orientation, but to look outward! Don't stare at yourself until you become blind, but focus on your neighbor. But remember that your neighbor cannot supply you with drive and sufficient strength to remove all the obstacles along this path. For that to happen, you must love your neighbor, something that, like enduring friendship, is a fruit of the Spirit, which he works in our hearts through faith in the Word of God (Gal 5:22). That includes "healthy [health-giving] words" (1 Tim 6:3; cf. Prov 3:7–8; Isa 58:10–11; Jas 2:13).

The church in Jerusalem, whose members sold houses and fields for the sake of the poor, must surely have experienced firsthand the truth of this proverb (Acts 4:34–37)!

Proverbs 11:18

> The wicked earns deceptive wages,
> but one who sows righteousness gets a sure reward.

God blessed with great prosperity the diligence of our nation in the seventeenth century (see our comments on Prov 10:4). "People who want to get rich fall into temptation and a trap and into many foolish and harmful desires that plunge men into ruin and destruction. For the love of money is a root of all kinds of evil" (1 Tim 6:9–10a). Thereby the Republic, which was born amid the struggle for God's Word, began to enrich itself with means that God had forbidden or that were unacceptable to him.

They kept the monopolistic profits from spices artificially high by partially destroying the harvests of the people in India. Or those who farmed the interior were forced to produce crops in return for low prices. All this occurred at a time when Reformed people in the Netherlands could have known from the Torah that God hates oppression. In addition, the Republic profited, just as did France and England, from the slave trade, which often was far more ruthless than owning slaves. And then to recall that in the captain's quarters on every slave ship there was a Dutch Bible containing the verse "Anyone who kidnaps another and either sells him or still has him when he is caught must be put to death" (Exod 21:16).

The famous United East India Company, however, became aware that God's word through Solomon is true: "The wicked earns deceptive wages." For God's commandment applied to them as well: "You shall not steal"—and surely this included people! After two centuries, the company ceased to exist due to bankruptcy.

The United Stated acted more wisely after World War II. Rather than demanding reparations from those they conquered and refunds from their allies, they provided funding for repairs (the Marshall Plan). This wisdom corresponded to God's ordinance "You shall not steal, but give" (Deut 23–24; Lev 25:35–55). This economic righteousness was soon followed with the restoration of the global economy. Surely this statement applied to the United States: "But one who sows righteousness gets a sure reward" (See as well our comments on Prov 11:24, 25; and 15:27.)

Proverbs 11:22

> Like a gold ring in a pig's snout
> is a beautiful woman without discretion.

This discretion is to be understood as needed for the sake of fearing the Lord. Solomon is not claiming that a woman must possess a high IQ or must have obtained an advanced degree, but that she must be able to *discern*. He is talking literally about *taste*, the capacity to determine, among the thousand and one things that are part of daily life, what is good and bad. What Solomon desires here is *having sound judgment*; and does that not begin with the fear of the Lord (Prov 1:7)? What benefit comes from a clever woman if she has absolutely "no understanding" of God and his service? For then she lacks the love, the clear insight, and the sensitivity needed for discerning what is important in life (Phil 1:9–10; cf. Ps 119:66).[8] Without such a discerning interior, a beautiful exterior is like a ring in a pig's snout.

Here Solomon is teaching his young readers—and his book is aimed at them—about what kind of girl they should be seeking as a potential wife. Proverbs 31 paints for us the portrait of the ideal woman. It ends with the assurance "Charm is deceptive, and beauty is fleeting; but a woman who fears the Lord is to be praised!" (v. 30). Undoubtedly such a woman can also be pretty, like Abigail, of whom we read, "She was an intelligent and beautiful woman" (1 Sam 25:3). But those young men for whom outward beauty is decisive for choosing a woman could well be making an ugly mistake.

Proverbs 11:24

> One gives freely, yet grows all the richer;
> another withholds what he should give, and only suffers want.

In the kingdom of God, one can increase his possessions by sharing them. That contradicts the wisdom of this world, which teaches that you can share one dollar only one time, after which you have lost it for good. For that reason, many people close their hearts to the need of those in distress. Or people support the causes of the kingdom of God less generously than they are able. In this way, people keep for themselves more than is proper, for giving is the obligation of the rich and receiving is the right of the poor. People are afraid to dip into their savings. As a result, not only are the needy shortchanged but wealthy people hardly dare to enjoy with gratitude what

---

8. See van Deursen, *Psalms II*, 327–28.

God has provided in his kindness. In this way people suffer in many respects from voluntary "lack."

Others, by contrast, share generously, but receive still more in return. Perhaps you have experienced this yourself. Out of love for God you give one hundred dollars for a good cause, and then in one way or another the Lord gives you one thousand dollars in return. After all, his divine fatherly hand rules over all the gold and silver! When we "scatter" on behalf of his kingdom, and generously share with his children in distress, his favor can transform our subtraction into multiplication. But if we fail to recognize his kingship over our wallet, his disfavor can in various ways disrupt our greedy bottom line.

Our Lord and his apostles taught this as well. "Give, and it will be given to you. Good measure, pressed down, shaken together, running over, will be put into your lap. For with the measure you use it will be measured back to you" (Luke 6:38). "The point is this: whoever sows sparingly will also reap sparingly, and whoever sows bountifully will also reap bountifully" (2 Cor 9:6). "And let us not grow weary of doing good, for in due season we will reap, if we do not give up. So then, as we have opportunity, let us do good to everyone, and especially to those who are of the household of faith" (Gal 6:9–10). That is the financial wisdom that comes from above: God can transform disbursements into income (cf. Ps 112:9; Gal 6:7–10; 2 Cor 9:6–11; see also our comments on Prov 11:18).

Proverbs 11:25

> Whoever brings blessing will be enriched,
> and one who waters will himself be watered.

One of the initial fruits of the outpouring of the Holy Spirit was that people opened their wallets. Barnabas sold a field on behalf of the needy in the church. Indeed, "they were selling their possessions and belongings and distributing the proceeds to all, as any had need" (Acts 2:45). "No one said that any of the things that belonged to him was his own, but they had everything in common" (Acts 4:32). When need arose, neighbor love was stronger than possessiveness.

But these people who were blessing others were themselves "made fat," as the Greek literally expresses it, with the abundance of God's house. "And great grace was upon them all" (Acts 4:33). Is that not refreshing for a Christian? They were unified, they were joyful, and they were attractive to those around them (Acts 2:46–47). Have you ever experienced something of the opposite? Then you realize what refreshment this church received. (See also our comments on Prov 11:18.)

Proverbs 11:26

> The people curse him who holds back grain,
> but a blessing is on the head of him who sells it.

Naturally, business is not a form of charity, and scarcity determines value. But for a student of Scripture, the law of supply and demand is not the crowning economic wisdom. In times of acute food shortage, to ruthlessly hold back grain reserves until the prices have risen is absolutely godless. Withholding food from people is to withhold one of life's basic necessities, something people cannot live without! Such action of course destroys the poorest first. Amos knew such villains, people who profited exorbitantly from other people's need. On the Sabbaths they were hankering for the day's end, "that we may offer wheat for sale, . . . and deal deceitfully with false balances, . . . and sell the chaff of the wheat" (Amos 8:5–6).

Such unscrupulous speculators and profiteers are severely cursed by desperate fathers and mothers. And you can believe that the Almighty hears such curses! "He does not forget the cry of the afflicted" (Ps 9:12, 18). Amos proclaimed, "The LORD has sworn by the pride of Jacob: 'Surely I will never forget any of their deeds!'" (Amos 8:7; cf. Pss 10, 37).

Joseph acted differently. He too had mammoth grain reserves, but he sold them! "So when the famine had spread over all the land, Joseph opened all the storehouses and sold to the Egyptians, for the famine was severe in the land of Egypt. Moreover, all the earth came to Egypt to Joseph to buy grain, because the famine was severe over all the earth" (Gen 41:56–57). He sold grain to foreigners as well, such that his own brothers did not make a trip to Egypt in vain! He did not give the grain away, for business is business, but he did not hoard the grain in order to drive the price up. Joseph knew: Better not to take advantage of others than to suffer God's judgment!

People would have blessed him for that (Gen 47:25)! And God hears such benedictions as much as he hears maledictions. His good pleasure rests on anyone who shows compassion to the needy. "Blessed is the one who considers the poor! In the day of trouble the LORD delivers him; the LORD protects him and keeps him alive; he is called blessed in the land; you do not give him up to the will of his enemies" (Ps 41:1–2). (See also our comments on Prov 28:27.)

Proverbs 12:10

> Whoever is righteous has regard for the life of his beast,
> but the mercy of the wicked is cruel.

This occurs because the righteous know Yahweh and the wicked do not. The Torah of Moses taught that God's compassion extends not only to his people but also to the animal world. That is obvious, isn't it? He himself has made all the birds and fish, all the livestock and wild animals. When he was finished doing that, God blessed them and saw "that it was good" (Gen 1:21, 25). Therefore, he commanded Israel to love not only their neighbors but also their animals. One day each week the Israelite farmer was supposed to allow his draft and plough animals to walk about freely. "Six days you shall labor, and do all your work," Yahweh had required in the fourth commandment, "but the seventh day is a Sabbath to the LORD your God. On it you shall not do any work, you, or your son, or your daughter, your male servant, or your female servant, *or your livestock*" (Exod 20:9–10; Deut 5:13–14). Throughout the week, as well, he was supposed to treat them compassionately. "You shall not muzzle an ox when it is treading out the grain" (Deut 25:4). Who would have his animal walk all day, walking through the grain, and not allow it to grab a mouthful of food? Yahweh considered that cruel, just as he thought it was cruel to take young birds from their nest along with the mother bird. At least allow the mother bird to fly away, Yahweh commanded (Deut 22:6–7).

We know God's love for animals from the book of Jonah as well. God wanted Nineveh to repent on account of its appalling wickedness. But why did he eventually withhold his judgment? In part, on account of the small children and the *many animals* in the city. "And should not I pity Nineveh, that great city, in which there are more than 120,000 persons who do not know their right hand from their left, and *also much cattle*?" (Jonah 4:11). Those donkeys, camels, and oxen would have run around distraught through the choking smoke from the burning houses! Jonah never gave that a thought, but God did. "Man *and beast* you save, O LORD," sings Ps 36:6. All the animals eat from his hand daily (Ps 104:27; 145:15–16; Job 39:1–3). After all, does he not see to it that the cattle have grass to eat (Ps 104:21)? Birds "neither sow nor reap nor gather into barns, and yet your heavenly Father feeds them," said the Lord Jesus (Matt 6:26).

Therefore, the fear of the LORD is the beginning of wisdom also in the arena of animal welfare. Thereby the Israelite was protected, on the one hand, from false sentimentality, as though with the slaughter of every animal he would have been sinning. God's Word speaks sensibly about killing animals in cases, for example, where a person wanted to bring a sacrifice to Yahweh, or he needed the animal for food or for its hide, or simply because the animal had caused harm. Yahweh himself had eaten the meat of a calf when he was a guest of Abraham (Gen 18:7–8). David courageously killed a lion and a bear when they attacked his flock (1 Sam 17:34–35). On the other hand, however, the fear of the Lord is also the strongest motive for treating animals with gentleness.

In the proverb cited above, Solomon is literally saying, "Whoever is righteous has regard for the *soul* [Heb., *nephesh*] of his beast." One could also translate it: has regard for the appetite (for in the Bible, the soul can eat), the humor, the life, the desire, the nature of his beast. The righteous one "knows" this *nephesh* of his ox and donkey. He loves it, similar to when the Hebrew Bible says that a husband "knows" his wife. Perhaps this word includes the notion that such a godly farmer treats his animals *with loyalty*, as covenant partners should.[9] Do they work faithfully every day for him, and are they unable to find food on their own, like wild animals do? Then for his part, he must "know" them, show reciprocal faithfulness, by giving them food and rest in a timely fashion, protect them against cold and predators, not taunt them, not curse them, not hit them unnecessarily, as Balaam did to his donkey; in short, they are to treat them in every respect with gentleness.

In that connection, God's children would be aware that the animal world must also groan under the curse that rests upon the earth on account of our sin: "For we know that the whole creation has been groaning together in the pains of childbirth until now" (Rom 8:22). One who sees something of that groaning cannot find pleasure in taking the life of an animal with cruelty or bitterness. Even when it is necessary, it remains an inflicting of pain on our earth. As we do so, we groan together with all creatures and long for that time when people will not inflict pain anywhere on the earth.

In addition, in this context are we fully aware that we ourselves must live entirely from God's compassion? Then we would not so easily say about a harmless insect, "Just kill it!" Children must learn as early as possible that these matters also belong to the fear of the Lord, just as much as "You shall not steal." A powerful tool for avoiding cruelty is teaching them to admire animals. Teach them to see a butterfly as a beautiful artistic creation of their heavenly Father and a fellow creature of God's for which we praise him. Then they will not needlessly and easily squash the animal or insect to death.

But the wicked demonstrates his aversion to God and his Word in a *shortage of compassion*. "The mercies of the wicked are cruel" is another

---

9. See van Deursen, *Psalms I*, 140–42.

translation of Prov 12:10b. In that case, the proverb is telling us that even if a wicked person wants to be compassionate, he is in fact cruel. Viewed this way, the *mashal* is even stronger: the wicked have no capacity for compassion. You can see this in the "pious" wicked members of the Sanhedrin who had our Lord Jesus crucified and his apostles imprisoned. In the sixteenth century, their sympathizers led faithful believers to the stake. They could watch such a cruel scene, despite their "sensitive" religiosity.

Apart from God, however, our human sensitivity is hardly strong enough to prevent cruelty. History teaches us that even those who talk about the sovereignty of feelings later often practiced the most severe cruelties. As a young lawyer, Robespierre pleaded against capital punishment, but that same sympathy for suffering humanity drove him onward to establish with demonic results the utopia of Rousseau by means of the guillotine and mass riots. Lenin was also sensitive. He opposed vivisection. And precisely in order to construct a world in which no one would have any suffering, in 1918 he had thousands of people killed who refused to support this world renewal. But that is what God's Word had been saying all along in this proverb. When our inner self, the seat of our feelings, is not governed by God's Word, we can fall into the most severe cruelties.

That is why we said the fear of the LORD is the beginning of wisdom also in the arena of animal welfare. Godliness is the most powerful impulse in all works of mercy. Only someone who holds fast to Scripture acknowledges that God is sovereign over a human being and an animal, and that all of us must live here on earth out of his goodness. At that point we are listening to our Lord: "Be merciful, even as your Father is merciful" (Luke 6:36).

Proverbs 12:19

> Truthful lips endure forever,
> but a lying tongue is but for a moment.

The literal Hebrew formulation speaks of lips of truth and a tongue of lies. But what is truth? For us, it's a matter of dispassionate honesty with regard to brute facts. In Scripture, truth is a matter of passionate love toward God and our neighbor. Truth is showing *consistency* in those relationships, with word and deed. In the Bible, truth is another word for faithfulness or reliability.[10] You can depend on the truth. God's Word is *the* truth (John 17:17). Therefore, it will continue to exist eternally (Isa 40:8), together with everything that is

---

10. See van Deursen, *Psalms I*, 123–24.

said and done in obedience to the truth (1 Cor 15:58). "For we cannot do anything against the truth, but only for the truth" (2 Cor 13:8).

But with the lie you always trip. To lie means to be *inconsistent*. The lie is not solid, but looks like the kind of ice that has unfrozen water just beneath it: it appears firm, but you will fall through. People have echoed the truth of this proverb in the adage "Though falsehood fly ever so fast, truth catches it at last." The lying tongue lasts "but for a moment" (literally, the blink of an eye), says Solomon. As we find more often in these *mashals*, the matter is stated rather strongly. But even if one must often wait longer than "for a moment" before the lie is exposed, what the Germans say is true: Lies have short legs. In the long run, they cannot survive, surely not in the smelting furnace of the last day (1 Cor 3:13).

Proverbs 12:20

> Deceit is in the heart of those who devise evil,
> but those who plan peace have joy.

"Planning *peace*" involves more than settling quarrels and arguments, although that too provides much joy. With the word *peace* Scripture understands more than its negative import of "no fighting." "Peace" is another term for life-flourishing in the fullest sense of the word. Wherever God's kingship is acknowledged, there you find shalom or peace. In Scripture, peace always rests upon truth and justice. Everyone who defends these is "planning for peace." This is so even though one may be going against the humanistic ideal of peace that is so popular in public opinion, which in fact is so often tolerant of lies and injustice.

Often those who "plan for peace" encounter fierce opposition from "those who devise *evil*," which refers to rebellion against God and its accompanying disharmony and destruction of life. Such usually travels under false flags. That led the psalmist to complain, "I am for peace, but when I speak, they are for war!" (Ps 120:7). All the prophets could echo him. Jeremiah felt like "a man with whom the whole land strives and contends!" (Jer 15:10 NIV). And the Prince of Peace himself declared, "I have not come to bring peace, but a sword" (Matt 10:34). Nevertheless, these were people who pointed God's people to the path leading to true peace! Amid all the difficulty that this gave them, they were allowed to taste rich joy in the God of peace. That is what the Lord promised his disciples as well: "Blessed are the peacemakers, for they shall be called sons of God" (Matt 5:9; cf. Prov 10:23; 21:15).

Proverbs 12:21

> No ill befalls the righteous,
> but the wicked are filled with trouble.

The godly man Asaph experienced exactly the reverse of this proverb. He complained: the wicked have no difficulties, but I am being assaulted all day long (Ps 73). David said, "Many are the afflictions of the righteous" (Ps 34:19; cf. Ps 37). Our proverb, then, is definitely not the easiest one to understand. Apparently, it belongs to "the words of the wise and their *riddles*" (Prov 1:6).

Sometimes people solve this difficulty by adopting the view that the "optimistic" book of Proverbs was supposedly corrected at this point by the more realistic books of Job and Ecclesiastes. But this claim is not valid, for Proverbs itself also speaks on every page about calamity and adversity in the life of the righteous. Others seek the solution in the question: What are you calling an adversity in the life of God's children? "And we know that for those who love God all things work together for good, for those who are called according to his purpose" (Rom 8:28). This is a comforting word, but does it not presuppose various kinds of bad things in the life of God's people? We must take the words of this proverb as they stand: calamity is calamity, and adversity is adversity.

It seems best to us to recall the unique manner of speaking that characterizes a *mashal*, as we explained in chapter 1. In this unique form of instruction, Solomon gives us the promise—without mentioning the exceptions—that echoes throughout all of Proverbs: The righteous can avoid all sorts of adversity through their piety, while sin leads its perpetrators to fall irretrievably into adversity.

Proverbs 12:24

> The hand of the diligent will rule,
> while the slothful will be put to forced labor.

Cardinal Richelieu, a sixteenth-century French statesman, characterized the Dutch of his day as "a mass of people who own a piece of ground consisting of water and grass, and in spite the people of Europe, they provide the bulk of the goods needed by them."[11] In the span of several decades, the Almighty exalted our nation to a power of the first rank. The world map still shows

---

11. Van der Poel, *Hoofdlijnen der Economische en Sociale Geschiedenis*, 40.

traces of that. In the seventeenth century, little could occur in Europe apart from this Republic. That was God's blessing upon the diligence of our ancestors (see our comments on Prov 10:4).

"The hand of the diligent will rule." This divine ordinance exerts its wholesome influence even when the great Lawgiver himself is no longer acknowledged. Was not a poignant illustration of this to be seen in the "economic miracle" that occurred after World War II in industrial Germany? And what about the powerful position in the global market that has been acquired by industrious Japan?

"While the slothful will be put to forced labor"—these words certainly do not explain all forced labor throughout the world, but they do identify an important aspect of the social and political relationships involved.

Here are several related proverbs: "Go to the ant, O sluggard; consider her ways, and be wise. Without having any chief, officer, or ruler, she prepares her bread in summer and gathers her food in harvest. How long will you lie there, O sluggard? When will you arise from your sleep? A little sleep, a little slumber, a little folding of the hands to rest, and poverty will come upon you like a robber, and want like an armed man" (Prov 17:2).

Proverbs 12:25

> Anxiety in a man's heart weighs him down,
> but a good word makes him glad.

How can a person's heart weigh him down? Think about a broken engagement, financial troubles, marriage problems, the loss of a loved one, awareness of guilt, or fear of death or of God's judgment on one's nation and people. A concern that is both large and long-lasting can affect a person's health (Prov 17:22). One's appetite decreases. One takes his cares to bed at night and suffers insomnia. One feels inexplicably tired. Sadness and worry can cause stress and lead to high blood pressure.

But a good word can gladden such an oppressed heart. Of course, for that purpose one can also open the Bible, but an anxious heart wants to hear such encouragement once in a while from the lips of friends. For that to be helpful, wisdom is needed. For a good word testifies to empathy with someone's sorrowful heart. Christians will be led in this by the apostle: "Whoever speaks, [let him speak] as one who speaks oracles of God" (1 Pet 4:11). God's Word is such a gold mine of comforting words. With them we might not be able to remove the cause of someone's worry, but we may well provide strength to look at it clearly. This is what Jonathan did with his persecuted friend David. He "strengthened his hand in God. And he said to him, 'Do not fear'" (1 Sam 23:16–17a). For many centuries David has been able to do the very same thing by means of his psalms: strengthen the trust of many in God. "The Lord is my shepherd; I shall not want. . . . Even though I walk through the valley of the shadow of death, I will fear no evil, for you are with me; your rod and your staff, they comfort me" (Ps 23:1, 4).

It is glorious to know by heart several such Scripture verses, in order to use them to comfort our sorrowing brothers and sisters. Verses like these "good words" from the apostles: "And we know that for those who love God all things work together for good, for those who are called according to his purpose" (Rom 8:28). "[Cast] all your anxieties on him, because he cares for you" (1 Pet 5:7). "Do not be anxious about anything, but in everything by prayer and supplication with thanksgiving let your requests be made known to God. And the peace of God, which surpasses all understanding, will guard your hearts and your minds in Christ Jesus" (Phil 4:6–7; cf. vv. 13, 19).

But whether or not these encouragements are drawn directly from Scripture, the proverb is true: "Gracious words are like a honeycomb, sweetness to the soul and health to the body" (Prov 16:24; see our comments on this verse). This also ensures the health of our fear of the Lord, as Solomon said in his Instruction Manual for this book (Prov 3:7–8 [see our comments on these verses]; 4:22; Isa 26:3). "Blessed is he who has regard for the weak; the Lord delivers him in times of trouble" (Ps 41:1 NIV).

Proverbs 12:26

> One who is righteous is a guide to his neighbor,
> but the way of the wicked leads them astray.

A couple of times, the Lord Jesus gave way to evildoers, did he not? "So they picked up stones to throw at him, but Jesus hid himself and went out of the temple" (John 8:59). "When Jesus had said these things, he departed and hid himself from them" (John 12:36). This is also what he told his disciples: "When they persecute you in one town, *flee* to the next" (Matt 10:23; cf. 24:16). Paul and Barnabas did the same thing: "When an attempt was made [in Iconium] by both Gentiles and Jews, with their rulers, to mistreat them and to stone them, they learned of it and fled to Lystra and Derbe, cities of Lycaonia, and to the surrounding country" (Acts 14:5–6). Their Sender did not require that they *needlessly* die a "hero's death" for him, as would happen in subsequent history, when people sought martyrdom. But sheep may simply flee, if they have a chance. In fact, was not Joseph's flight from Potiphar's wife a hero's escape?

Proverbs 13:11

> Wealth gained hastily will dwindle,
>   but whoever gathers little by little will increase it.

"A slack hand causes poverty, but the hand of the diligent makes rich," we read in Prov 10:4 (see our comments on this proverb). Of course, a sluggard would also like to enjoy a good sandwich, but as long as he does not work for it, his desire is futile. We do not need to limit this proverb, however, to material things. One can desire a lot of things in vain, because he simply was too lazy to do anything to satisfy his desire. Here lies one of the causes of differences among people. What has the one person *done* for what he is enjoying, and what has the other person *done* for what he is lacking?

Proverbs 13:12

> Hope deferred makes the heart sick,
>   but a desire fulfilled is a tree of life.

Hope invigorates. But if it is deferred for too long, it can lead one to the brink of death, as we learned during World War II. At that time, there were allied prisoners of war in Japan who had enough to eat but still died. Their hope of liberation had been unrealized for so long that they became listless, hardly eating and drinking, and finally perished from despair and hunger for affection.

We need only recall that where the gospel disappears, no genuine hope survives (Eph 2:12; 1 Thess 4:13). It is inevitable that this should affect not only the spiritual but also the physical public health of a nation. One more proof that the fear of the Lord is healthy (cf. our comments on Prov 3:7–8; 11:17; 12:25; 14:30; 15:13, 15, 17; 16:24; 17:22; and 25:16).

Proverbs 13:14

> The teaching of the wise is a fountain of life,
>   that one may turn away from the snares of death.

Here you have the entire book of Proverbs summarized in two lines. For the first line, see especially our comments on Prov 3:18, and for the second line, our comments on Prov 3:21–23.

Proverbs 13:20

> Whoever walks with the wise becomes wise,
> but the companion of fools will suffer harm.

Reading widely in Proverbs is a form of interaction with wise people. Just as bad literature and television programs can put us in contact with fools.[12] A popular adage teaches: If you play in the mud, you'll get dirty. "Do not be deceived: 'Bad company ruins good morals'" (1 Cor 15:33). For that reason, Solomon also advised, "Leave the presence of a fool, for there you do not meet words of knowledge" (Prov 14:7; see our comments on Prov 8:17).

Proverbs 13:24

> Whoever spares the rod hates his son,
> but he who loves him is diligent to discipline him.

Many modern child-rearing experts reverse this: Whoever *uses* the rod hates his son, but he who loves him never spanks him. Of course, no one is longing to go back to the time when schoolmasters kept a running count of how often they used the rod and the strap. But have we not fallen into the other extreme today? Woe to the teacher who gives a naughty child a slap on the backside! The apostle's saying applies not only to Cretans, "for there are many who are insubordinate" (Titus 1:10; cf. v. 6). In the name of humanitarianism, and with an appeal to the dignity of the child, the stick has been banned everywhere as a tool of discipline. But this apparently is not based on the authority of Holy Scripture, for the Bible repeatedly recommends, especially in Proverbs, the use of corporal punishment as a tool of nurture (Prov 10:13; 18:6; 19:29; 20:30; 22:15; 23:13–14; 26:3; 29:15; cf. Deut 23:2–3; Luke 12:47–48).

In so doing, the wise men were following the example of our heavenly Father. He frequently called Israel his "son" (Exod 4:23; Hos 11:1), and how did he nurture this son? First by means of loving instruction, which clearly tops the list everywhere in Scripture. In Scripture, discipline is not first of all

---

12. For their portrait, see van Deursen, *Psalms I*, 93–96.

a slap but friendly instruction, leading and admonishing (see our comments on Prov 1:2–3 and 3:11–12). But when Israel refused to listen, then she had to feel it, although Yahweh did not initially apply the most severe blows. The prophetic books show how Yahweh's discipline became increasingly more severe throughout the centuries, until finally, after centuries of warning, he sent his son Ephraim out of the promised land. But this punishment was still wounding the divine heart of the Father after a hundred years (Jer 31:20)! So great was the love with which God had applied the rod.[13]

Here, too, we must be willing to be imitators of God.

Our discipline of our children must, just like God's discipline of us, consist first of all of lovingly guiding through teaching. For that reason, the staff of the word is the best tool of discipline at home and at school. Yahweh exercised discipline toward Israel in the first place by means of the instruction in God's Word given to fathers and mothers, priests and prophets. In this way, the daily reading and discussion of the Word of the Lord is the tool of discipline par excellence at home and at school. Thereby God's people acquire understanding of God and his covenant, as well as the rules and threats of that covenant, and it teaches them the true wisdom.

In addition, we will show ourselves to be imitators of God also by applying discipline in no other way than in love. "Let no one punish a child who himself would not wish to receive the punishment himself a thousand times rather than have another undergo it. Love will automatically provide the outer limit for punishment in general, and for physical discipline in particular."[14] But true love does not preclude using the rod! The proverb cited above is given to remind us of that.

True love cannot tolerate evil spreading insidiously and nestling within a child's heart. If words are ineffective, then a rod and punishment can inculcate wisdom (Prov 29:15; see our comments on that verse). Apparently in Israel some parents and educators spared the rod, perhaps because they thought that parental love and corporal punishment did not go together. But the wise men sharply condemned such a course of action, as perhaps appearing to be loving toward the child at the moment, but in fact proceeding from hatred. Such parents misperceive the power of sin in the hearts of children, and must pay closer attention to the example of Almighty God. He preferred to discipline his son Israel verbally, but if necessary he did not hesitate to use the rod. So should we, even though, like him, we ourselves will also feel its pain.

---

13. See van Deursen, *Psalms II*, 197–98.
14. Wielemaker, *Lichtstralen uit het Woord*, 77.

To these things as well, however, the scriptural maxim applies: "The wise heart will know *the proper time and procedure*. For there is a proper time and procedure for a way for every matter, though a person may be weighed down by misery" (Eccl 8:5b–6 NIV). For that reason, the wise men gave the advice of this proverb: One who loves his son disciplines him *early*. Little children enjoy hearing Bible stories. Make good use of that age! Once a child turns sixteen, the opportunity is gone. In our society we should be providing our "home catechism" by the time a child is about ten. But if a much younger child refuses to listen, such a child will not need much by way of harsh discipline and you can likely suffice with somewhat lighter chastisement. For that reason, the adage is correct: "The earlier the pruning, the better the fruit." The years when a child is a toddler and just beginning school are the best time for shaping character. Even in elementary school, when a child is between six and thirteen years old, they do not change significantly. The foundational elements of respect must be laid before school age. Then, during those years in elementary school, such well-nurtured children will be able to get along without corporal discipline. (Regarding using the rod in school, we offer additional comments in connection with Prov 22:15.)

For that matter, with the word *rod* Solomon is referring not only to the stick but to every tangible instrument of discipline whereby a discerning educator lets a naughty child know that he or she has sinned.

One who listens to Holy Scripture as the eternal and abiding Word of God hears in it God's ordinances for exercising authority over children, and receives divine principles for guiding youngsters in his paths. People should not dub this "Old Testament-ish," since Heb 12:5–11 communicates the same wisdom.

Without doubt there is a principled difference between this loving skill for nurture found in Proverbs and the callous method of the Pharisees found in Jesus Sirach and his sympathizers. We will say more about this in connection with Prov 19:18, where we read the warning about excessive corporal discipline. The issue here involves what we hear in the maxim "Spare the rod and spoil the child." An American professor of psychiatry humorously changed it to say, "Spare the Freud and save the child."[15]

---

15. Cited in McMillen, *None of These Diseases*, 124; the professor's name was Dr. Douglas Kelley, from the University of California.

Proverbs 14:1

> The wisest of women builds her house,
> but folly with her own hands tears it down.

"May the LORD make the woman, who is coming into your house, like Rachel and Leah, who together *built up* the house of Israel," said the people standing at the gate of Bethlehem when Boaz had taken Ruth in marriage (Ruth 4:11–12). They apparently understood the phrase "build a house" to refer to providing descendants. It is remarkable that Ps 127, which also talks about the blessing of children, begins with, "Unless the LORD *builds the house*" (cf. Exod 1:21 KJV). Should we not also think of that meaning in connection with this proverb? Does that not belong to "the wisdom of women," namely, that they should be prepared to bear children? But this proverb has more in view, of course, than "building a house" by having a family. A wife can make the house of her husband *flourish* in every respect, but she can also completely *ruin* his house. We find poignant illustrations of this with the queen mothers mentioned in the Bible. Some of them extended multigenerational blessing, but others were a curse for their husbands and children. Without exaggeration one can say that the spirit and tone of the royal houses in Israel, and thus of the history of Israel, were determined in large part by women.

Naamah, the Ammonite wife of Solomon, the mother of Rehoboam, must have exerted a detrimental influence on her son, and, through him, on all of Judah (1 Kgs 14:21–24). Jezebel, the daughter of a Baal priest-king, destroyed the house of her husband. Her daughter Athaliah married into the house of David, and almost exterminated it completely, so intense was her hatred of Yahweh (2 Kgs 11:1). By contrast, we learn of Abi(jah), the wife of the wicked King Ahaz! She built the house of her husband through her trust in God. She was a daughter of the high priest Zechariah, who throughout his life exercised such a great influence on the governing of King Uzziah (2 Chr 26:5; 29:1). King Hezekiah was a son of this godly, priestly daughter. Did not Judah owe the blessing that Hezekiah spread, humanly speaking, in part to his godly mother? Just as David the psalm writer had been a student of the prophet Samuel, who in turn had been instructed by . . . his own mother Hannah. The influence of mothers, especially on young children, reached very deeply and had lifelong effect. No subsequent influence could match it.

Therefore, it is really so very important for our young men that they know what kind of girls they should be pursuing. A girl can make or break a boy. She can either *build up* or *break down* his own nurture, his training, his income, his position in church and society, the nurture of his future children—in short, his entire "house." Therefore, we advise our young readers to become well acquainted with the portrait that Scripture provides in Prov 31 of the ideal woman. There you see what kind of girl you should pursue in order to build your "house." Such a woman needs to possess diligence, skill, friendliness, communication skills, frugality, dignity, good taste, and, last but not least, a talent for organization. For order and regularity constitute the natural basis for what is most important in a family: steadfast concourse with God and his Word.

This is the wisdom of women by which they build the "house" of their husbands. Blessed is the man who obtains such a woman, for that is a gift from God (we will say more about this in connection with Prov 18:22). Her entire life can be summarized in one sentence: "She does him good, and not harm, all the days of her life" (Prov 31:12).

Proverbs 14:4

> Where there are no oxen, the manger is clean,
>   but abundant crops come by the strength of the ox.

If a farmer sells his cows, he no longer needs to clean any dirty stall. No cows means no manure, no mess from hay and feed—but also no milk! For you cannot keep cows and keep your barn clean at the same time. Therefore, a farmer puts up with all the hassle and mess of his livestock, because he owes his income to those animals. This applies not just to agricultural work but to all labor, no matter what it consists of. You cannot rear children without experiencing any inconvenience from them, and you cannot fix a car without getting dirty hands. No work gets done without some mess and some dirtiness.

Of course, Solomon is not making a plea here for sloppiness, but he does advise us to put up with a certain amount of inconvenience in our work. One can exaggerate a love for order—no matter how praiseworthy and indispensable order may be—but then neatness can acquire a sterile character. "Where blade and saw are used, you'll get wood chips," says an old proverb. "Whoever wants never to make a mistake had better sleep day and night," says another proverb. If you need to live from milk production, then you need to deal with cows getting the barn dirty. That is unavoidable.

All work involves inconvenience, but let us not lose sight of the advantage that work provides us, despite all its inconvenience. It is being fussy, even foolish, to be more concerned about the manger that must remain spotless, than about the income acquired from an ox that ploughs the field.

Let mothers of young children draw comfort from this, for in such families the "manger" is not always "clean." Let all workers keep in view especially the *fruits* of their work. That helps us to put up with the inconvenience and may even lead to experiencing what was once vexing as no longer burdensome, because the harvest from the ox is more valuable than a clean manger.

Proverbs 14:12 (= 16:25)

> There is a way that seems right to a man,
>   but its end is the way to death.

Some things appear at first glance to be very promising, but they end up being a big disappointment. For that reason, the Preacher said, "Better is the end of a thing than its beginning" (Eccl 7:8)—especially if you want to evaluate that thing. The outcome of a matter is what discloses its value. Especially the broad path, life apart from God and his Word, can look very appealing, but it leads to destruction (Matt 7:13–14). Therefore, the book of Proverbs devotes attention in its wisdom lessons to caution, which leads a person to consider the outcome of a matter ahead of time, and to look beforehand at the consequences of an action.

Proverbs supplies various illustrations of things whose initial appearance is deceptive. Consider the strange woman: "For the lips of a forbidden woman drip honey, . . . but in the end she is bitter as wormwood. . . . And at the end of your life you groan, when your flesh and body are consumed" (Prov 5:3–4, 11; cf. chapter 9). So you see, "the end of joy may be grief" (14:13). That happens in more situations. "An inheritance gained hastily in the beginning will not be blessed in the end" (20:21). "Do not look at wine when it is red, . . . and goes down smoothly. In the end it bites like a serpent and stings like an adder" (23:31–32). "Do not hastily bring into court, for what will you do in the end, when your neighbor puts you to shame?" (25:8). "Whoever pampers his servant from childhood will in the end find him his heir" (29:21).

So Proverbs teaches us: Look before you leap.

Proverbs 14:15

> The simple believes everything,
>   but the prudent gives thought to his steps.

We recognize the simple person from our study of Prov 1:4, where we read that this kind of person appears especially among the youth, and the book of Proverbs offers a helping hand especially to these gullible persons. Characteristic of them is that their heart is susceptible to both good and bad influences. Everything that the spirit of the age wants to breathe into them can enter easily. Such a person is far too trusting, and fails to look out for himself. He acts impetuously and is easily misled.

What exactly causes this? Not an intellectual deficiency. In our day, someone who is "stupid" can easily have earned a couple of advanced degrees. But when you see how naive such a person can be after some ten years of schooling, you might readily identify him as a simpleton. Along with all his bookish facts, he displays a serious lack of self-understanding and a healthy critical capacity. We saw in Prov 7 how gullibly such a person was drawn in by a bad woman. And you should hear how childishly and naively such a person can talk about improving the world, as though Satan or demonic lies or terrorism did not exist.

Can we perhaps ascribe this gullibility to his lack of life experience? In part, yes, indeed, but, remarkably, many older people display the same lack of ability to discern. How many adult simpletons don't blindly believe what "people" say and eat whatever the media dish up as though it were candy? The Dutch cultural anthropologist Johan Huizinga noted already before World War II a "universal decline of the critical spirit." In his book *In the Shadow of Tomorrow* he foresaw a far-reaching naivete, when he observed that knowledge not integrated with life impedes judgment and obstructs wisdom. Employing in the original Dutch a pun that is impossible to translate into English (*Onderwijs maakt onder-wijs*, something like "Education makes one less wise"), Huizinga acknowledged that this hideous wordplay regrettably contains a profound truth.[16]

But if the problem is not a lack of education or experience, whence comes that naivete and gullibility on the part of so many people? It comes from losing the only suitable *standard* of good and evil: the Word of God! That is what young people must encounter at home. For with the Word of God you develop the capacity to distinguish between truth and falsehood, timely and untimely speech, valid and invalid conclusions. Holy Scripture is the only reliable norm for a healthy critical outlook. One who has been instructed in Scripture no longer believes "everything people say," for in God's Word all of life passes in review. One who knows biblical history knows about the power of the lie in the church and the world. He has learned from

---

16. Huizinga, *Shadow of Tomorrow*, 78; this sentence, which is omitted in the English translation, is found in the original Dutch essay. Huizinga, "In de schaduwen van morgen," 347.

the Lord Jesus what can come forth from the depths of the human heart (Mark 7:2–23), and as a result has obtained from him a better perspective than many unbelieving psychologists have.

Such students of Scripture are called in our proverb "the prudent." Such a prudent person "gives thought to his steps," because he lives with and from Scripture. Using that standard, he pierces through the slogans and placards giving voice to popular opinion, and he listens critically to the idols of the masses. He doesn't believe "what everybody says," not when people suggest that everyone must have an opinion about everything. He considers the flood of superficial information about "everything" as far too unreliable. Scripture has also cured him of his childish naivete and immunized him against an unrealistic idealism that tries to foist into his hand the master key of insight into everything in the world.

This healthy critical outlook fostered by Scripture protects him from much calamity, for "The prudent sees danger and hides himself, but the simple go on and suffer for it" (Prov 22:3; see our comments on this verse). Or as the apostle wrote, "So that we may no longer be children, tossed to and fro by the waves and carried about by every wind of doctrine, by human cunning, by craftiness in deceitful schemes. Rather, speaking the truth in love, we are to grow up in every way into him who is the head, into Christ" (Eph 4:14–15; cf. Matt 10:16).

Proverbs 14:19

> The evil bow down before the good,
>   the wicked at the gates of the righteous.

This will eventually be the outcome of world history. "Or do you not know that the Lord's people will judge the world?" (1 Cor 6:2–3; cf. Dan 7:18, 27; 2 Tim 2:12; Rev 20:4–6). At that time, every crooked relationship will be straightened, and "the rich man" will desire to receive a favor from "the poor Lazarus" (Luke 16:19–31). But before this definitive end, history will have shown the truth of this proverb many times over.

What Joseph's brothers could never have imagined nonetheless happened: they knelt down before him! And Simeon, who had cursed his king so viciously, threw himself down before David (2 Sam 19:18). Indeed, an entire church can have this experience. "I know that you have little strength, yet you have kept my word and have not denied my name," Jesus Christ wrote to the little church of Philadelphia. And he promised, "I will make those who are of the synagogue of Satan, who claim to be Jews though they are not, but are liars—I will make them come and fall down at your feet and acknowledge that I have loved you" (Rev 3:8–9).

Already in this dispensation God can in this way make the righteousness of his children "shine like the dawn" (Ps 37:6 NIV). But then they must follow the advice of Ps 37, and wait for his time: "Be still before the LORD and wait patiently for him. . . . Wait for the LORD and keep his way, and he will exalt you to inherit the land; you will look on when the wicked are cut off" (Ps 37:7, 34).

Proverbs 14:23

> In all toil there is profit,
> but mere talk tends only to poverty.

We have already discussed the benefit of diligent work (see our comments on Prov 10:2, 4; 11:18; 12:24; 13:4, 11). The second line of this proverb is a warning against wasting time. In addition to damaging your work, it is also unhealthy. As one physician has put it, unprofitable conversation is a waste of energy, something that leads to the exhaustion of your nervous system and the creation of stress. Just one more proof that it is surely true about the wisdom of the fear of the LORD: "It will be healing to your flesh and refreshment to your bones" (Prov 3:7–8; cf. our comments on Prov 10:2).

Proverbs 14:26–27

> In the fear of the LORD one has strong confidence,
> and his children will have a refuge.
> The fear of the LORD is a fountain of life,
> that one may turn away from the snares of death.

Solomon has already brought this to the attention of his readers very concretely in his Instruction Manual (Prov 1–9). The fear of the LORD is the ABC of wisdom (1:7). It supplies you in this life with the least chance for misery because in large measure it functions preventively. There is no better life insurance than the fear of the LORD, and the wisdom that blossoms from it. It offers "confidence," constitutes "a refuge" (for our children as well, when we nurture them in it), and leads us to escape "the snares of death."

In Prov 3 you can find examples galore of this life-protecting function of the fear of the LORD. For example, wisdom can protect you from poverty, indignity, various forms of disharmony, dangers to your health, and impediments to your nightly rest. It can also eliminate many a cause of premature death.

On the other hand, the fear of the LORD is a fountain of life or happiness in various arenas of life. Examples of this, too, Solomon supplies in his Instruction Manual. This happiness extends far beyond the arena of "spiritual life." You can savor it in your family life, your marital life, your business life, your civic life, your health, your nightly rest, and your income.

But, actually, throughout the entire book of Proverbs you can find examples connected with these *mashals*. For just like Prov 13:14 (see our comments of this verse), they constitute a brief summary of everything this Bible book is seeking to teach us: the fear of the LORD offers you powerful protection and is a fountain of happiness (see our comments on Prov 3:18).

Proverbs 14:30

> A tranquil heart gives life to the flesh,
>   but envy makes the bones rot.

The term *envy* can also be rendered as jealousy, resentment, anger, peevishness, indignation, in short, various feelings of hatred. This refers, then, to genuine infections that not only consume you from within through various kinds of stress but also severely undermine your physical health.

For a long time, medical science had a blind spot, as it were, regarding the connection between these phenomena. It failed to see that hatred, jealousy, discontent, and lack of love can drive a person not only to the psychiatrist's couch but also to the surgeon's operating table. During recent decades, however, health care professionals have become increasingly aware that there is a close connection between various organic (i.e., physical) symptoms of disease and what is going on within a patient's heart. Dr. S. I. McMillen (*None of These Diseases*) has enumerated about fifty diseases that can be *partially* caused by our mood. Various forms of hatred can have a disastrous effect on our thyroid, esophagus, skin, heart, lungs, liver, gall bladder, stomach, kidneys, and large intestine.

"Just wait, I'll get him!" But this is how a person "gets" a stomach ulcer. An outburst of rage flowing from pent-up hatred can give a person a heart attack or a stroke. "I could kill him!" Meanwhile, a person kills his own health and nerves through his "resentment-itis." Smoldering hatred and envy can give you eczema, boils, or gallstones. Intestinal infections are often closely related to antipathy or resentment that a person is harboring. Bitter comments and thought patterns saturated with chronic hatred cause and worsen many cases of high blood pressure. A dose of bicarbonate soda cannot develop in our stomach the amount of destructive acids that feelings of hatred and envy can produce there. And what about the negative influence of unconfessed sins, and of a spirit dominated by deception? David could speak about that: "For when I kept silent [about my sins], my bones wasted away, . . . my strength was dried up" (Ps 32:3–4).

But a tranquil heart gives life to the flesh!

Literally, the wise man is talking about a heart of equanimity (or meekness). A person is not born with this, although our temperament does have something to do with it. Meekness is a fruit of God's Spirit. For that, we must follow the Lord Jesus, who said, "Learn from me, for I am gentle and lowly in heart, and you will find rest for your souls [entire persons]" (Matt 11:29). "But I say, walk by the Spirit, and you will not gratify the desires of the flesh. . . . And those who belong to Christ Jesus have crucified the flesh with its passions [like hatred, quarreling, envy, jealousy, Gal 5:20] and desires" (Gal 5:16, 24). Then meekness will grow in our heart as a fruit of the Spirit, and from there it will benefit our body and spirit as well.

What is the secret to this wholesome effect? Why does God's Spirit accomplish through a meek heart what psychiatrists cannot accomplish after hours of conversation? Because such a meek heart *reacts spiritually* to various impulses of hatred and envy. After all, it is not the evil actions of others that endanger our health first of all, but our own wicked *reactions* to them. We deal daily with various things that could make us envious (stress factors) and could evoke hateful reactions from us. But whether they succeed in doing so depends primarily on *our attitude*. And for that, the fear of the LORD is "healing to your flesh and refreshment to your bones"(Prov 3:7–8). A meek heart fights against *the cause* of various psychosomatic ailments by remembering, "Do not be overcome by evil, but overcome evil with good" (Rom 12:21; Heb 12:14–15).

The meek person loves his neighbor, even if that neighbor is an enemy. Love is the only sufficient antidote against all those ailments that our flesh (i.e., our evil nature, Gal 5:16–17), and especially our hateful moods, can give us. For "love is patient and kind; love does not envy or boast; it is not arrogant or rude. It does not insist on its own way; it is not irritable or resentful. . . . Love bears all things, believes all things, hopes all things, endures all things" (1 Cor 13:4–5, 7). For immunizing us against the evil effect in our body of various stresses, there is no better means than this: "Love your neighbor as yourself."

The Christian who deals with his neighbor in the spirit of love and meekness spares the thyroid, gall bladder, heart, stomach, and intestines of both himself and his neighbor. He must daily process disappointments, but thanks to his meekness he does not succumb to frustrations. Rather, he accepts them with humility and dependence as divine lessons. He may well have to deal every day with spiteful people, but neighbor love and meekness protect him from gallstones and stomach ulcers, as well as from self-pity, which in the long run can be just as crippling to our health.

A meek heart is at the same time the best tranquilizer that you could take (Phil 4:6–7). It teaches you to listen to the encouragement of the apostle "and be thankful" (Col 3:15; cf. 1 Thess 5:18). Thereby such a heart can safeguard you from high blood pressure resulting from annoyance and envy. It grants you confidence to take to heart the advice of the Lord: "Come away by yourselves to a desolate place and rest a while" (Mark 6:31; cf. Eccl 4:6). A meek heart teaches us to see the limited scope of our task and responsibility, and thereby can free our body and nervous system from a lot of stress. Psalm 37 can point out and clarify for you the way forward in these matters. Additionally, Scripture provides this promise with a view to living on this earth: "Blessed are the meek" (Matt 5:5; for the connection between sin and sickness, see our comments on Prov 3:7–8, where additional proverbs are mentioned and discussed that deal with this connection).

Proverbs 14:32

> The wicked is overthrown through his evildoing,
>   but the righteous finds refuge in his death.

How did people ever come up with the idea that in the Old Testament believers did not yet see beyond death and the grave? "I know that he will rise again in the resurrection on the last day," said Martha to Jesus about her deceased brother Lazarus (John 11:24). She was verbalizing the confession of the church of God down through all the centuries. At any rate, she could also have read it in the proverb cited above, couldn't she?[17]

Proverbs 14:35

> A servant who deals wisely has the king's favor,
>   but his wrath falls on one who acts shamefully.

---

17. Cf. van Deursen, *Psalms I*, 237–43.

The first line you can see illustrated by Joseph and Daniel, each of whom by their prudent conduct obtained the favor of unbelieving world rulers. By contrast, the enemies of Daniel themselves ended up in the lions' den after their shameful murderous plot (Dan 6:25). Just like the vicious Haman, who forfeited his high-ranking position in the Persian palace because of his plan to exterminate the entire Jewish nation throughout the entire world on the same day.

Such opportunities are reserved not only for high-ranking nobility like Prince William of Orange, of whom Emperor Charles V was especially fond. The ordinary person can also find favor with people in high places: "Do you see a man skillful in his work? He will stand before kings; he will not stand before obscure men" (Prov 22:29). Of course, both Scripture and history show us exceptions to these rules, like that poor wise man who could have delivered the city but was despised (Eccl 9:13–16). Or the fool who occupied a high position, while princes walked on foot like slaves (Eccl 10:6). But what surpasses everything and will one day make everything good is this: the good pleasure of Jesus Christ, the King of kings and the Lord of lords, will be distributed to each of his servants who kept his Word and observed his commandments (Luke 19:11–27).

Proverbs 15:1

> A soft answer turns away wrath,
> but a harsh word stirs up anger.

With Yahweh's help, Gideon had given the marauding Midianites a severe defeat. Once they had taken to flight, he involved the tribe of Ephraim in the pursuit, who proceeded to kill both Midianite princes, Oreb and Zeeb (Judg 7). This offended the honor of Israel's greatest tribe, however, and the men of Ephraim accused Gideon, "What is this that you have done to us, not to call us when you went to fight against Midian?" (Judg 8:1).

Had Gideon been irascible, he could have, with a harsh response, heaped fuel on this fire and thereby unleashed an ill-fated fraternal quarrel that would have torn apart the concord of the tribes for a long time to come. For as the proverb says, "The beginning of strife is like letting out water, so quit before the quarrel breaks out" (Prov 17:14). That is what Gideon did: he mastered himself and his opponents by answering, "What have *I* done now in comparison with you? Is not the gleaning of the grapes of Ephraim better than the grape harvest of Abiezer? God has given into your hands the princes of Midian, Oreb and Zeeb. What have I been able to do in comparison with you?" (Judg 8:1–3).

But a hurtful word incites wrath. That is what King Rehoboam experienced. When asked to lighten the heavy yoke that had been put on the people, he responded harshly, "My father made your yoke heavy, but I will add to your yoke. My father disciplined you with whips, but I will discipline you with scorpions" (1 Kgs 12:14). With this answer the young prince needlessly incited the wrath of his people, so that ten of the twelve tribes declined to render obedience any longer to the house of David (1 Kgs 12).

Proverbs 15:18 gives approximately the same advice: "A hot-tempered man stirs up strife, but he who is slow to anger quiets contention." "A gentle tongue is a tree of life" (15:4).

Proverbs 15:8

> The sacrifice of the wicked is an abomination to the LORD,
>   but the prayer of the upright is acceptable to him.

Scripture is here pointing to such wicked people, not in the pagan world but in the midst of God's people.[18]

"Hear the word of the LORD, you rulers of Sodom! . . . you people of Gomorrah!" said Isaiah to the *church* of Judah and its leaders. "'What to me is the multitude of your sacrifices?' says the LORD; 'I have had enough of burnt offerings of rams and the fat of well-fed beasts; I do not delight in the blood of bulls, or of lambs, or of goats. When you come to appear before me, who has required of you this trampling of my courts? Bring no more vain offerings. . . . I cannot endure iniquity and solemn assembly. Your new moons and your appointed feasts my soul hates; they have become a burden to me; I am weary of bearing them. When you spread out your hands, I will hide my eyes from you; even though you make many prayers, I will not listen; your hands are full of blood'" (Isa 1:10–15).

This kind of religiosity, also in its Christianized form, God finds to be "an abomination," which is to say, equivalent to paganism. But God's ears are tuned day and night to the cry of the upright for help: "The eyes of the LORD are toward the righteous and his ears toward their cry. . . . When the righteous cry for help, the LORD hears and delivers them out of all their troubles"(Ps 34:15–22).[19]

---

18. See van Deursen, *Psalms I*, chap. 4.
19. See van Deursen, *Psalms II*, 102–14.

Proverbs 15:9

> The way of the wicked is an abomination to the Lord,
>   but he loves him who pursues righteousness.

Psalm 1 gives a wonderful explanation of this proverb.[20] "Blessed are those who hunger and thirst for righteousness, for they shall be satisfied" (Matt 5:6; cf. 6:33).

Proverbs 15:11

> Sheol and Abaddon lie open before the Lord;
>   how much more the hearts of the children of man!

"The heart is deceitful above all things, and desperately sick; who can understand it? I the Lord search the heart and test the mind" (Jer 17:9–10). Blessed are those who heartily fear the Lord and with David can pray, "O Lord, you have searched me and known me! . . . Even before a word is on my tongue, behold, O Lord, you know it altogether. . . . If I ascend to heaven, you are there! If I make my bed in Sheol, you are there!" (Ps 139). These Scripture verses are full of comfort for the upright.[21] But this is a frightening prospect for the outwardly pious wicked ones among God's people![22]

Proverbs 15:13

> A glad heart makes a cheerful face,
>   but by sorrow of heart the spirit is crushed.

One would be surprised how a crushed spirit can undermine someone's physical health. The heart's sorrow not only can rob someone of his appetite, industry, and nightly rest, but can also negatively affect his blood pressure and blood vessels. As one physician has put it, "It's not what you're eating, but what's eating you" (cf. our comments on Prov 14:30). But "a crushed spirit who can bear?" (Prov 18:14). Is there a prescription for overcoming sorrow?

Mothers in Western societies teach their sons from childhood not to cry when they are sad. But in Israel a man or a boy was allowed to let his

---

20. See van Deursen, *Psalms I*, chap. 5.
21. See van Deursen, *Psalms I*, 262.
22. See van Deursen, *Psalms I*, 86–90; Matt 10:26.

tears flow freely. "And he lifted up his voice and wept," we read about many an Israelite man. From this we see not only the nature of a group of people but also genuine wisdom. A certain amount of yielding to grief and a good cry are divine means for decreasing the stress and pressure that have built up in our spirit. Relaxing physical work is also a good means against depression. Muscle movement employs a different part of the brain than the one affected by suffering psychological pain. Thereby stress is shifted to a different part of the body (and brain), and that provides relief.

The best medicines for the Christian, however, are faith and hope. Count your blessings (and for a moment ignore your problems) and name them one by one. Take a paper and pencil, and write this: "I am thankful that I can hold this pencil and . . ." Proceed to write down, black on white, what God has allowed you to keep. And be persuaded that, at this moment, God's eye is upon you, for "This is the one to whom I [the Lord] will look: he who is humble and contrite in spirit and trembles at my word" (Isa 66:2). Read Pss 23, 27, 34, 37, and 56. Innumerable Christians who have suffered deep sorrow have experienced that these psalms provide medicine for heartache. "Why are you cast down, O my soul? Hope in God!" (cf. Ps 42).[23] "For I consider that the sufferings of this present time are not worth comparing with the glory that is to be revealed to us. . . . And we know that for those who love God all things work together for good, for those who are called according to his purpose" (Rom 8:18, 28).

This is one more example of the healing effect on one's body and spirit that can proceed from the fear of the Lord. Solomon had identified this earlier in his Instruction Manual (see our comments on Prov 3:7–8, and accompanying references).

Proverbs 15:15

> All the days of the afflicted are evil,
>   but the cheerful of heart has a continual feast.

In reply to Pharaoh's question about his age, Jacob answered, "The days of the years of my sojourning are 130 years. Few and evil have been the days of the years of my life, and they have not attained to the days of the years of the life of my fathers in the days of their sojourning" (Gen 47:9). Given the integrity of Jacob's confession of his faith (Heb 11:9–10, 13–16), and how pain-filled his life had been, did that term "evil" really describe all "the years of my life"? After all, he had just been given the chance to see his supposedly

---

23. Cf. van Deursen, *Psalms I*, chap. 13.

dead son as governor of Egypt, and would live another seventeen years to see how God was beginning to fulfill his promise to make Israel into a great nation (Gen 47:27–28). But in the eyes of dejected Jacob, at that moment, all his days had been evil.

By contrast, near the end of his life, Paul wrote differently, from his prison cell, "For I am already being poured out as a drink offering, and the time of my departure has come. I have fought the good fight, I have finished the race, I have kept the faith" (2 Tim 4:6–7).

Of course, our character plays a significant role in this connection, and we do not change that very easily (but where does Holy Scripture adduce that as an excuse?). But this is also a question of attitude, and you can change that. For a person could be feeling miserable as a result of his own resentment and discontent. Pessimism can be caused by little faith, and cheerfulness can be the fruit of great faith.

This is something Paul demonstrated in his challenging ministry. If anyone could talk of suffering "evil days," then this apostle knew many of them "by great endurance, in afflictions, hardships, calamities, beatings, imprisonments, riots, labors, sleepless nights, hunger; . . . through honor and dishonor, through slander and praise" (2 Cor 6:4–8). At that point, the apostle saw more than his persecution, and he confessed, "As dying, and behold, we live; as punished, and yet not killed; as sorrowful, yet always rejoicing; as poor, yet making many rich; as having nothing, yet possessing everything" (2 Cor 9:9–10). One cannot explain this satisfactorily from Paul's character. The apostle himself was putting into practice what he encouraged others to do: "Rejoice in the Lord always" (Phil 4:4).

By the power of faith, Christians can fight their depression and cultivate a certain degree of cheerfulness. What must one do to accomplish this? "Commit your way to the Lord; trust in him, and he will act" (Ps 37:5). Learn by heart such encouraging Scripture passages, and repeat them to yourself. At least once every day sing a Christian song, preferably a psalm. How often does not Scripture encourage us to sing? The word *hallelujah* literally means "Praise Yahweh!" Paul and Silas sang God's praise in prison in the middle of the night after their backs had been beaten (Acts 16:25). A physician has assured us that just as going to church and reading the Bible yields wholesome results for one's health and reduces stress, so too does singing psalms.

You can also follow the advice that the Preacher repeats, and enjoy with greater awareness the little pleasures of life, like eating and drinking (Eccl 2:24; 3:12; 5:17–18; 8:15; 9:9). That is how you cultivate cheerfulness. Are you perhaps working too hard? Are you perhaps overestimating your task and suffering depression because of that? Take some time off and relax

(Eccl 4:6; Mark 6:31). Are you suffering disappointments? Beware of self-pity, and follow the example of the apostle: "Forgetting what lies behind and straining forward to what lies ahead, I press on toward the goal for the prize of the upward call of God in Christ Jesus" (Phil 3:13–14). In this way, life will become for you—as it states literally in our proverb—"a continual feast," which you and yours will surely enjoy.

Proverbs 15:16

> Better is a little with the fear of the LORD
>   than great treasure and trouble with it.

A great treasure is often a source of deep trouble! Read the book of Ecclesiastes about that, especially Eccl 5:7—6:12, where we read this:

> He who loves money will not be satisfied with money, nor he who loves wealth with his income; this also is vanity. When goods increase, they increase who eat them, and what advantage has their owner but to see them with his eyes? Sweet is the sleep of a laborer, whether he eats little or much, but the full stomach of the rich will not let him sleep. There is a grievous evil that I have seen under the sun: riches were kept by their owner to his hurt, and those riches were lost in a bad venture. And he is father of a son, but he has nothing in his hand. As he came from his mother's womb he shall go again, naked as he came, and shall take nothing for his toil that he may carry away in his hand. This also is a grievous evil: just as he came, so shall he go, and what gain is there to him who toils for the wind? Moreover, all his days he eats in darkness in much vexation and sickness and anger. Behold, what I have seen to be good and fitting is to eat and drink and find enjoyment in all the toil with which one toils under the sun the few days of his life that God has given him, for this is his lot. (Eccl 5:10–18)

Proverbs 15:17

> Better is a dinner of herbs where love is
>   than a fattened ox and hatred with it.

In Israel, only the rich ate meat regularly (1 Kgs 4:22–23). The ordinary person ate meat only in connection with a sacrifice or when entertaining guests. Amos denounced eating veal as a luxury of the pampered (Amos 6:4). A fattened ox was, then, altogether the picture of great wealth and prosperity. Nevertheless, our happiness does not depend on that, for one who lives with only a little in a context of love is richer than one who bathes in luxury with hatred in his heart.

In this connection we need not think exclusively of hatred among those eating together. Hatred can take hold of our spirit in such a way that we see those whom we hate all around us. The object of our hatred sits as an unseen guest at our table, and lends to the most delicious meal a bitter aftertaste. He can even come into our bedroom and rob us of the blessing of an undisturbed nightly rest (see our comments on Prov 3:24). Hatred puts a damper on our enjoyment of the greatest luxury and can spoil the finest pleasures. To say nothing of the additional damaging consequences for our body and our spirit (see our comments about this in connection with Prov 11:17; 14:30; and 15:13). But fearing Yahweh and loving our neighbor are medicine for our body and refreshment to our bones (see our comments on Prov 3:7–8).

"Better is a dry morsel with quiet than a house full of feasting with strife," says a similar proverb (17:1). Human life is brief and difficult. Blessed are those who seek and find their happiness in a God-fearing family, where people love one another (Ps 133; see our comments on Prov 15:16). You will hardly find richer sources of earthly happiness.

Proverbs 15:27

> Whoever is greedy for unjust gain troubles his own household,
>   but he who hates bribes will live.

Even if one imposes tribute on a defeated foe, one must avoid unjust gain. God's commandments for economic life cannot be transgressed with impunity. After World War I, the victors demanded ruthlessly high reparations from the defeated and exhausted Germany. Afterward people saw how this led to the stock market crisis in 1929, when the international financial structure collapsed, followed by the infamous economic depression of the 1930s. The victors had destroyed their own house.

After World War II, the United States acted more wisely, as we observed in connection with Prov 11:18. Rather than demanding *reparations*, they provided *recovery* (the famous Marshall Plan). This led to a surprisingly fast global economic recovery. Although the proverb cited above would have in view first of all the payment of bribes, the United States experienced that a nation fares well economically if it shuns exacting war tribute from those who have been defeated.

Proverbs 15:30

> The light of the eyes rejoices the heart,
>   and good news refreshes the bones.

When Jacob's sons told him, "'Joseph is still alive, and he is ruler over all the land of Egypt,'" the old man could not believe it. But then they communicated Joseph's message, "and when he saw the wagons that Joseph had sent to carry him, the spirit of their father Jacob revived" (Gen 45:26–27; cf. Isa 52:7–8).

Proverbs 15:33

> The fear of the Lord is instruction in wisdom,
>   and humility comes before honor.

We discussed the first line of this proverb in chapter 4. The second line was fulfilled most beautifully in our Lord Jesus Christ, "who, though he was in the form of God, did not count equality with God a thing to be grasped, but emptied himself, by taking the form of a servant.... He humbled himself by becoming obedient to the point of death, even death on a cross. Therefore [!] God has highly exalted him and bestowed on him the name that is above every name" (Phil 2:6–9; see our comments on Prov 3:16).

Proverbs 16:3

> Commit your work to the Lord,
>   and your plans will be established.

"It is in vain that you rise up early and go late to rest, eating the bread of anxious toil; for he gives to his beloved sleep," says Ps 127:2 (also written by Solomon!). For that reason, the proverb cited above advises us literally, "*Roll* thy works *unto* the Lord" (KJV, alternate reading), for "the blessing of the Lord makes rich, and toils adds nothing to it" (Prov 10:22 ESV, alternate reading; cf. Ps 90:17; see our comments on Prov 3:24–25).

Proverbs 16:7

> When a man's ways please the LORD,
> he makes even his enemies to be at peace with him.

This is what Isaac experienced after Abimelech, the king of the Philistines, had sent him out of his land. After some time had passed, the king himself took up the matter again: "Isaac said to them, 'Why have you come to me, seeing that you hate me and have sent me away from you?' They said, 'We see plainly that the LORD has been with you. So we said, let there be a sworn pact between us.' . . . In the morning they rose early and exchanged oaths. And Isaac sent them on their way, and they departed from him in peace" (Gen 26:26–31).

This was also how God defended Jacob, when Laban angrily chased him and almost caught him. "But God came to Laban the Aramean in a dream by night and said to him, 'Be careful not to say anything to Jacob, either good or bad'" (Gen 31:24). And when, thereafter, Jacob's brother Esau met him with four hundred men, God made Esau's heart peaceable: "But Esau ran to meet him and embraced him and fell on his neck and kissed him, and they wept" (Gen 33:4). That was the same man who once had said, "'The days of mourning for my father are approaching; then I will kill my brother Jacob" (Gen 27:41).

David, too, had experienced the truth of this proverb in his life. God himself had turned the pro-Absalom sentiment, after his death, into a pro-David sentiment. "And all the people were arguing throughout all the tribes of Israel, saying, 'The king delivered us from the hand of our enemies and saved us from the hand of the Philistines, and now he has fled out of the land from Absalom. But Absalom, whom we anointed over us, is dead in battle. Now therefore why do you say nothing about bringing the king back?'" At that point, David's enemy, Shimei, who had cursed him, came to make peace with David and fell down before him (2 Sam 19:10–24). David's "ways" during the rebellion would have been very pleasing to Yahweh (2 Sam 15:25, 31; 16:1–12).

When the Babylonians captured Jerusalem, King Nebuchadnezzar gave Nebuzaradan, the captain of the guard, the following command: "Take him [Jeremiah], look after him well, and do him no harm, but deal with him as he tells you" (Jer 39:11–12). And that is exactly what happened, amid the confusion of battle (Jer 40:1–6).

These four examples—Isaac, Jacob, David, and Jeremiah—can encourage us to obey God rather than people. For this is what a related proverb states: "The fear of man lays a snare, but whoever trusts in the Lord is safe" (Prov 29:25).

Proverbs 16:12

> It is an abomination to kings to do evil,
>   for the throne is established by righteousness.

An Israelite king did not possess unlimited authority. He was, in fact, the vicegerent of Yahweh, Israel's great King, and, together with every other Israelite, he was under the Torah, or Law, of Yahweh (cf. Rom 13:1, 4). At his coronation, every king had to have a copy of the law made for himself, and he was to read from it throughout his entire life, so that he could know Yahweh, his God, and would keep all his statutes (Deut 17:18–19). If he did that, Yahweh promised him a long reign for both himself and his sons (Deut 17:20).

What did Yahweh see as the special task and place of the king in Israel? He gave several foundational indications of that in advance in what people term, all to broadly, "the law of the king" (Deut 17:14–20). An Israelite king was not to seek his honor with the use of the ancient Eastern status symbols that rulers of that time enjoyed: many wives, many horses, and much gold and silver. He needed no formidable military force, for he did not need to protect *the land*—Yahweh would take care of that (Exod 34:24)—but he had to protect *justice*, referring to God's judicial claim upon Israel. Therefore, the king would need to perform a domestic task: exercise the shepherding care of Yahweh's flock (1 Chr 17:6). With the shield of the Torah,[24] he was to protect the poor and the distressed against bullies and oppressors (Ps 72). In this way, the throne of the representative was to rest upon the same foundation as that of Israel's Supreme King, namely, on justice and righteousness (Ps 89:14; 97:2). People should be able to recognize the Supreme King in his representative.

Regrettably, many kings of Judah and Israel rejected the Torah, that order of life for Israel and for Christianity. This began with Saul, and it continued with Jeroboam, the son of Nebat, who made Israel to sin. This was followed by many others, kings like Ahab, Manasseh, and Ahaz, who acquired a sad notoriety in this regard. They were genuinely wicked—men who often with the appearance of religion violated Yahweh's royal claims upon Israel, who by their practices as rulers in fact dethroned Yahweh.

---

24. See van Deursen, *Psalms I*, 57–59.

King Jehoiakim can serve as a model of the kind of king who practiced wickedness. "Woe to him who builds his house by unrighteousness, and his upper rooms by injustice," Jeremiah the prophet scolded him,

> who makes his neighbor serve him for nothing and does not give him his wages, who says, "I will build myself a great house with spacious upper rooms," who cuts out windows for it, paneling it with cedar and painting it with vermilion. Do you think you are a king because you compete in cedar? Did not your father eat and drink and do justice and righteousness? Then it was well with him. He judged the cause of the poor and needy; then it was well. Is not this to know me? declares the Lord. But you have eyes and heart only for your dishonest gain, for shedding innocent blood, and for practicing oppression and violence. (Jer 22:13–17)

Many a ruler in the history of Christianity practiced the same wickedness, even though he could have known from God's Word what righteousness meant for a king.

The wise man declares very sharp disapproval of such a wicked ruler. He entitles such a king's mode of rule as an "abomination." In the Torah, this term was forged to describe something that is absolutely incompatible with serving Yahweh. Canaanite idolatry and immorality, using women as merchandise, child sacrifice, training Israelites boys to serve in idol temples—in the Torah, each of these practices was called an "abomination." Scripture places the wickedness of a ruler on the same line. Violate Yahweh's sacred claim on Israel? A *vicegerent* turning his back on his *Supreme King*? That is *to'abah*, an abomination! That is the Canaanite way! That kind of ruler is leading his people back into paganism.

In this way, Scripture shows us what subsequent history illustrates as well, that unbelief and revolution often begin in the higher echelons of society. European history knows of revolutionary *rulers* as well. Such rulers generally did not have a long-lasting dynasty, as we see from the history of the ten tribes of Israel, with its different royal houses. Our own House of Orange, by contrast, provides an attractive portrait of the second line of our proverb. For four centuries, the Netherlands received many blessings under the rule of the officials and kings belonging to this royal house. For the most part, they showed respect for the rights granted to them by their subjects, and thereby they practiced righteousness and justice.

By means of this wisdom concerning wicked rulers, the book of Proverbs also nourished Israel's messianic expectations. For in this way, it taught people to look forward to the coming of the Righteous King, whom we know as our Lord Jesus Christ. Of him, Gabriel said, "Of his kingdom there will be no end" (Luke 1:33). "Of the increase of his government and of peace there will be no end, on the throne of David and over his kingdom, to establish it and to uphold it with justice and with righteousness from this time forth and forevermore" (Isa 9:7; cf. 11:1–10; see our comments on Prov 25:5).

Proverbs 16:18

> Pride goes before destruction,
>   and a haughty spirit before a fall.

"The invincible fleet" is what people called the Spanish Armada, which in 1588 England and the Netherlands had to bring to its knees. Pride came before the fall. The British and the Dutch had the fleet on the run. At that point, an even more powerful opponent completed its destruction. Near Scotland, severe storms raged, which destroyed the arrogant Spanish invasion fleet. The provincial government of Zeeland minted a memorial coin with the inscription "God's breath has scattered them."

Proverbs 16:19

> It is better to be of a lowly spirit with the poor
>   than to divide the spoil with the proud.

This is true, of course, because all of Scripture teaches, "What is exalted among men is an abomination in the sight of God" (Luke 16:15). But "to the humble he gives favor" (Prov 3:34; Jas 4:6; 1 Pet 5:5). Therefore, the Lord Jesus taught, "Blessed are the poor in spirit, for theirs is the kingdom of heaven" (Matt 5:3).

Moreover, the lowly poor live more healthily than the rich who chase after plunder. Pride can sweep us to heights that lie beyond our capacities. To reach them, we strain our nervous system and exhaust our reserves of strength. We go to great lengths to prove that our ideas are the best, our church is the purest, our business is the leader, our political party can rescue the country, and so on. This is how many people run every day in the race to be the first; but colliding race cars cannot do greater damage than harm done to each other's health by people competing in their arrogance. The Preacher makes the same point: "Then I saw that all toil and all skill in work come from a man's envy of his neighbor. This also is vanity and a striving after wind" (Eccl 4:4).

The Lord Jesus warned about arrogant aspirations of leadership, "Whoever exalts himself will be humbled, and whoever humbles himself will be exalted" (Matt 23:10–12). David was indeed "humble in spirit with the poor" with whom he sat in the cave.[25] He sang, "O Lord, my heart is not lifted up; my eyes are not raised too high; I do not occupy myself with things too great and too marvelous for me" (Ps 131:1; cf. Rom 12:3).

One who fears the Lord by doing nothing "from selfish ambition or conceit" (Phil 2:3) will observe that this too is "healing to your flesh" (see our comments on Prov 3:7–8). Good for one's heart and circulatory system, good for your nerves and nightly sleep. The frustrations that belong to this world will not frustrate you, but you will accept them as daily exercises in humility. For such reasons, as well, it is "better to be of a lowly spirit with the poor than to divide the spoil with the rich" who do not fear God.[26]

Proverbs 16:24

> Gracious words are like a honeycomb,
>   sweetness to the soul and health to the body.

Naomi and Ruth experienced this! Distressed and destitute, both widows entered Bethlehem (Ruth 1:21–22). In hope of blessing, Ruth stepped out of her house to practice the breadwinning technique of the poor: gleaning behind the reapers. How would they treat her as a foreigner? But that evening she returned home elated. Her distressed heart had been refreshed by the graciousness of Boaz.

If you would like to hear someone speaking with gracious words, then you must listen to Boaz. Everything we learn from him in this Bible book is thoroughly gracious. After all, to Boaz Ruth was little more than an unknown gleaner from Moab, but Boaz spoke graciously to her. "Now, listen, my daughter, do not go to glean in another field or leave this one, but keep close to my young women. Let your eyes be on the field that they are reaping, and go after them. Have I not charged the young men not to touch you? And when you are thirsty, go to the vessels and drink what the young men have drawn" (Ruth 2:8–9).

These are words that must have tasted like honey to the lovely Ruth—and honey was a beloved delicacy in Palestine! "Sweetness to her soul," that is, to her entire person. She fell to the ground before Boaz and asked, "Why have I found favor in your eyes, that you should take notice of me, since I

---

25. See van Deursen, *Psalms II*, 66–80.
26. See van Deursen, *Psalms I*, 106–13.

am a foreigner?" (v. 10). In response, Boaz continued in the same gracious tone, "All that you have done for your mother-in-law since the death of your husband has been fully told to me, and how you left your father and mother and your native land and came to a people that you did not know before. The LORD repay you for what you have done, and a full reward be given you by the LORD, the God of Israel, under whose wings you have come to take refuge!" (vv. 11–12). When mealtime approached, Boaz invited her with graciousness, "Come here and eat some bread and dip your morsel in the wine." Then he passed to her roasted grain (v. 14).

"There is one whose rash words are like sword thrusts, but the tongue of the wise brings healing" (Prov 12:18). The latter is what the gracious words of Boaz accomplished. With these words, he must have made the heavy hearts of Naomi and Ruth leap, and he must have poured drops of balsam oil on the wounds of their hearts! Such words penetrate so deeply and in this way can benefit a person physically as well. Talk about tools that are useful for strengthening someone!

Gracious words are among the *least expensive medicines*. Someone who fears the LORD can spare, indeed can even promote the health of his neighbor by means of the free medicine of a few gracious words. In addition, one thereby spares his own health as well, for Boaz's graciousness naturally benefited not only his reapers' nerves but also his own. "A man who is kind benefits himself" (Prov 11:17; see our comments on this proverb). An environment in which a person constantly growls and snarls confirms by means of various smaller and larger ailments the truth of the proverb "Envy makes the bones rot" (Prov 14:30; see our comments on this proverb). But where a person fears the LORD also with his words, he creates not only a pleasant but also a wholesome climate for working and living (see our comments on Prov 12:25), one that is healthy for the heart and the stomach, healthy for gall bladder and nerves. In other words, here we have a tonic for our entire system. (For the connection between the fear of the LORD and our health, see our comments on Prov 3:7–8; there we mentioned other proverbs as well that are related to this topic and that we discuss; see our comments on Prov 3:17 as well.)

Proverbs 16:25

> There is a way that seems right to a man,
>   but its end is the way to death.

See our comments on Prov 14:12.

Proverbs 16:31

> Gray hair is a crown of glory;
> it is gained in a righteous life.

Of course, as faithful to reality as it is, Scripture does not gloss over the fact that old age involves limitations. In their old age, Isaac, Jacob, and the prophet Ahijah had poor eyesight. David's body warmth decreased with age (1 Kgs 1:1). King Asa had diseased feet (1 Kgs 15:23). Zest for living diminished, as with the aged Barzillai (2 Sam 19:35–36). Nevertheless, Scripture tells us about Abraham, Gideon, and David, "He died in a good old age" (Gen 15:15; 25:8; Judg 8:32; 1 Chr 29:28). The proverb cited above talks about gray hair as "a crown of glory," that is found "in the way of righteousness" (KJV; see our comments on Prov 20:29).

For rather often those who perpetrate unrighteousness die before their time. But, in many respects, the fear of the LORD can extend a person's life, so that he comes to wear the ornate crown of gray hair (see our comments on Prov 3:1–2).

Proverbs 17:8

> A bribe is like a magic stone in the eyes of the one who gives it;
> wherever he turns he prospers.

Although this verse speaks of a "bribe" (see our comments about this in connection with Prov 17:23), that is not necessary (cf. Prov 17:8 KJV, NKJV, which use "gift" and "present" respectively). Throughout history, people have given gifts as proof of affection or as a show of honor. Saul and Jehoshaphat received gifts when they became king (1 Sam 10:27; 2 Chr 17:5). Jesse gave David ten cheeses for his brothers' army commander (1 Sam 17:18). Solomon himself received gifts from the queen of Sheba (1 Kgs 10:2; cf. 2 Chr 9:24; Ps 72:10). Elisha received gifts from Benhadad (2 Kgs 8:7–8). Daniel was loaded down with gifts from Nebuchadnezzar (Dan 2:48). The wise men from the East honored the newborn king of the Jews with gold, frankincense, and myrrh (Matt 2:11). Even today, business relationships function with gifts of various kinds.

Indeed, from the perspective of the giver, as Solomon says, it is "like a magic stone" (as the Hebrew puts it, "a stone of favor," a lucky stone?). As we observed, we need not immediately think that this involves bad practices. Small gifts keep a friendship warm, says one proverb; later, one can experience pleasure from such a good relationship. Solomon mentioned this more often, as we learn from this proverb: "A man's gift makes room for him and brings him before the great" (Prov 18:16). Doors are opened that otherwise would remain closed. Do not missionaries take this into consideration? They acquire affection by means of their schools and hospitals, don't they? Why should not a businessman bait a hook to catch a big fish?

Gifts can also help to mend *broken relationships*: "A gift in secret averts anger, and a concealed bribe, strong wrath" (Prov 21:14). Why should we need to think immediately of bribes in this context? When Jacob had to meet his brother Esau, he wrestled with God throughout the night to receive the promised blessing. But he did not neglect to send ahead a large present for his brother Esau. "For he thought, 'I may appease him with the present that goes ahead of me, and afterward I shall see his face. Perhaps he will accept me'" (Gen 32:20). Was that not wise on Jacob's part? And was it not wise of Abigail as well to first send a gift to the enraged David before pleading her case to him (1 Sam 25:18–19)? Perhaps these were not examples of "a *secret* gift," but they do illustrate the power of gifts to "avert anger," as Solomon teaches in Prov 21:14. A small gift can quiet an angry heart, indeed can make it turn like a leaf on the tree. As one flower merchant wrote above his sidewalk flower stand, "Do you need to make something right today?"

No, you never lose out through generosity, but instead you receive more. We saw this earlier in connection with Prov 11:24. You gain, for example, *hearts*. Later you can do a lot with that advantage. Did not our Lord Jesus Christ give us the same advice: "I tell you, make friends for yourselves by means of unrighteous wealth, so that when it fails they may receive you into the eternal dwellings" (Luke 16:9)? He praised the unrighteous steward, who, just before he was fired from his job, had cultivated much goodwill by means of gifts.

Proverbs 17:9

> Whoever covers an offense seeks love,
> but he who repeats a matter separates close friends.

A good memory is a wonderful gift, but with it a person can also remember a thousand and one little issues that we people can have with each other. And then, if we are not walking in love, we easily come to the point of repeatedly bringing up the "transgression" that a friend has committed against us. We can do this by explicitly rubbing his nose in it, or by indirect insult, or by outright mistrust. In this way you can eventually alienate your best friend, since he will get the impression that this issue from long ago continues to live between both of you, even though he thought it had been resolved. This is something that damages a friendship.

Does not God himself give us a better example? He declares that he is ready to *cover* our sins (Ps 32:1), to remember them no more (Isa 43:25), and to cast all our sins into the depths of the sea (Mic 7:19). That is different from bringing them up repeatedly. One who is aware of having to live daily from this forgiving love of God does not drag up bygones or rake up old issues.

There are more proverbs with which Solomon binds it upon our hearts to be careful toward our friends and brothers. "A dishonest man spreads strife, and a whisperer separates close friends" (Prov 16:28). "Hatred stirs up strife, but love covers all offenses" (Prov 10:12; cf. 1 Cor 13:7). Surely we should forget about that "debt" of a few pennies (Matt 18:28)! Far better to help others to forget such slights as well. A Chinese proverb says, "A friend is someone who says good things about you behind your back." Our friends will reward us with mutual trust for having such an attitude.

Proverbs 17:22

> A joyful heart is good medicine,
>   but a crushed spirit dries up the bones.

A person can shiver from fear, be paralyzed by shock, tremble with rage, and feel his heart race with joy. Mood swings can have so many effects on a body's health (see our comments on Prov 14:30 and 15:13). When emotions return repeatedly or persist, however, they can impact our internal organs negatively. Dr. G. A. Lindeboom has pleaded for a psychosomatic approach to health care: "For example, it happens frequently that a serious disease turns someone who merely has gallstones into someone who suffers from gallstones. And it is no accident when severe illness-related events, like a stroke, a stomach ulcer, a heart attack, sometimes in recurring form, occur in cases of intense emotion or in times of intense inner tension."[27] In his practice, this physician has observed the effects of emotions "in connection with illnesses of the heart and lungs, stomach and liver, skin and kidneys."[28]

Undoubtedly many more physicians could confirm the truth of the proverb cited above in connection with many of their patients. "The manner in which the patient relates to his sickness is often of decisive significance for the outcome of the therapeutic involvement of the doctor. A negative

---

27. Lindeboom, *De ziel der geneeskunde*, 9.
28. Lindeboom, *De ziel der geneeskunde*, 15.

attitude toward life can occasionally make the best medical treatment ineffective."[29]

Of course, a person's own temperamental nature plays a role here, but Christian joy is rooted not in the Christian but in Christ (Phil 3:1; 4:4, 10). Each temperament may need this encouragement: "The joy of Yahweh is your strength" (Neh 8:10). With that encouragement, Paul and Silas sang during the night as they were in prison following a severe beating (Acts 16:25). That singing was simultaneously medicine for their wounds. (For the connection between the fear of the Lord and our health, see our comments on Prov 3:7–8, where other proverbs relating to this matter are mentioned. Cf. Sir 30:20–24.)

Proverbs 17:23

> The wicked accepts a bribe in secret
> to pervert the ways of justice.

Israel, "you shall not pervert justice. You shall not show partiality, and you shall not accept a bribe, for a bribe blinds the eyes of the wise and subverts the cause of the righteous" (Deut 16:19; cf. Exod 23:8; 18:21). "For the Lord your God is God of gods and Lord of lords, the great, the mighty, and the awesome God, who is not partial and takes no bribe" (Deut 10:17). He had Israel herself swear, "'Cursed be anyone who takes a bribe to shed innocent blood.' And all the people shall say, 'Amen'" (Deut 27:25).

Nevertheless, later Israel abominably violated God's covenant in this regard, so that Yahweh angrily said, "Your princes are rebels and companions of thieves. Everyone loves a bribe and runs after gifts. They do not bring justice to the fatherless, and the widow's cause does not come to them" (Isa 1:23; cf. 5:23; Ezek 22:12; Mic 3:11; Zeph 3:3). Although Samuel himself declared that he had never turned aside for a bribe, his sons did twist justice to do exactly that (1 Sam 8:3; 12:3; Ps 15:5; 26:10).

Solomon plainly calls this bribery *wicked*. Gifts strip the judge of his freedom. Even members of ecclesiastical gatherings must not accept favors from those whose judicial cases they are called to adjudicate. Perhaps the addition of the words "a bribe *from the bosom*" (ESV, marginal reading), referring to the excess material of a shirt or vest that could be used as a pocket, is pointing to the sneaky character of this business. Apparently the judge was impartial, but the guilty party had secretly taken something from under his garment that the judge had furtively hidden among his possessions. This

---

29. Lindeboom, *De ziel der geneeskunde*, 15.

calls to mind poor countries and poor people where the sigh goes up with regard to the government and judicial system, "With money you can buy any verdict."

Here are two related proverbs: "He who justifies the wicked and he who condemns the righteous are both alike an abomination to the LORD" (17:15). "It is not good to be partial to the wicked or to deprive the righteous of justice" (18:5).

Proverbs 17:28

> Even a fool who keeps silent is considered wise;
> when he closes his lips, he is deemed intelligent.

A Latin proverb says something similar: "If you had kept silent, people would have considered you a philosopher" (*Si tacuisses, philosophus mansisses*). (See our comments on Prov 10:19 as well.)

Proverbs 18:1

> Whoever isolates himself seeks his own desire;
> he breaks out against all sound judgment.

You could also translate the opening phrase somewhat more literally, "Whoever remains aloof." What drives a solitary person to his self-induced isolation? He breaks out against all sound judgment. That validates the assumption that folly has played a role. Is he harboring resentment, and for that reason remains aloof from friend and foe? Does he feel misunderstood, and for that reason separates himself from people and from the church? The verse doesn't say, and so there could be any number of reasons. In any case, he is no philanthropist. He prefers to be alone and enjoys being around others like he enjoys a toothache.

This attitude makes him aggressive. Perhaps he appears to be content, but he is ready to blow up toward everyone. If someone approaches him with reasonable advice ("don't focus so much on yourself"), he responds viciously. In that way he alienates himself from everybody. This serves to drive him even more deeply into his egocentricity. Filled with egotistical self-defensiveness, he goes his own way, devoting attention only to himself and being consumed with his own interests. The polemicizing of such people is fanatical and bitter.

What may well be the deepest source of such a distorted relationship toward the community? The poet does not tell us. One could therefore think of social disorders resulting from certain psychological illnesses. But we should exclude this entirely when we consider other instances of forsaking the second table of the law: "You shall love your neighbor as yourself" (Matt 22:39–40). For then this impulse to isolation belongs—leaving aside the unhealthy social disorders—together with its envy, its outbursts of anger, and its self-centeredness, to what Paul calls "the works of the flesh" (Gal 5:19). The loner fails in neighbor love.

What is characteristic of all forms of lovelessness is true of self-imposed isolation as well, namely, that a person cannot always pursue this without causing injury to himself. Psychiatrists observe this as well when giving counsel: "Someone who does not show interest in his neighbor has the greatest difficulty in his life and commits the greatest injustice against others," according to the world-renowned psychiatrist Alfred Adler.[30] You must live with *an outward focus*, be focused on others, and not be so consumed with yourself. This is remarkable advice. But what supplies a person with the required driving force to do that? Only faith in Christ and the power of his Word and Spirit can help a person to struggle effectively against his isolation. Christian neighbor love is the only effective medicine against this. For we know that "love is patient and kind; love does not envy or boast; it is not arrogant or rude. *It does not insist on its own way*; it is not irritable or resentful" (1 Cor 13:4–5). Love is what a person desperately needs to *receive* during childhood, but also what a person learns during childhood to *give*.

Proverbs 18:7

> A fool's mouth is his ruin,
> and his lips are a snare to his soul.

O that tongue! The smallest of our members, yet it boasts of great things! "With it we bless our Lord and Father, and with it we curse people who are made in the likeness of God" (Jas 3:9). The book of Proverbs talks often about this evil, too often for us to enumerate. With a large number of examples it shows how we, with a foolish or sinful use of our tongue, can wound and hurt our neighbor.

Here is a selection of those proverbs: "The mouth of the righteous is a fountain of life, but the mouth of the wicked conceals violence" (Prov 10:11).

---

30. Adler, *What Life Should Mean*, 258, cited in McMillen, *None of These Diseases*, 78.

"The wise lay up knowledge, but the mouth of a fool brings ruin near" (10:14). "The lips of the righteous know what is acceptable, but the mouth of the wicked, what is perverse" (10:32). "With his mouth the godless man would destroy his neighbor, but by knowledge the righteous are delivered" (11:9). "By the blessing of the upright a city is exalted, but by the mouth of the wicked it is overthrown" (11:11). "The words of the wicked lie in wait for blood, but the mouth of the upright delivers them" (12:6). "There is one whose rash words are like sword thrusts, but the tongue of the wise brings healing" (12:18). "The heart of him who has understanding seeks knowledge, but the mouths of fools feed on folly" (15:14). "It is an honor for a man to keep aloof from strife, but every fool will be quarreling" (20:3). Each of these illustrates what James said about the sins of the tongue: "It is a restless evil, full of deadly poison" (Jas 3:8). This is true, first of all, for the neighbor.

But also for *the sinner himself*! That is what Solomon is referring to in the proverb cited above. A fool with his wicked words injures *himself* (literally: his soul). He gets ensnared by his own words. We read the same thing in Prov 12:13a: "An evil man is ensnared by the transgression of his lips." This goes for the speaker himself! "The righteous hates falsehood, but the wicked brings shame and disgrace" (13:5; cf. 11:6).

In this context we might think of rash promises, empty claims, false accusations, unjust assumptions about things, unnecessary disclosures, but also of false *teaching* and false *prophecy* along with speaking prematurely (cf. 18:13). These are deadly snares! They lay in wait in every area of life: social, political, ecclesiastical, marital, physical, and spiritual. The result is that we can observe in every area of life the "ruin" of which Solomon speaks in the proverb cited. "If only I had not said that! If only we had not promised that!" Life is full of this (unexpressed) complaint.

An Amalekite claimed that he had killed Saul, and this lie cost him his life (2 Sam 1:13-16). Daniel's false accusers talked themselves into the lions' den (Dan 6). And Jerusalem is an altogether frightening example: "His blood be on us and on our children!" the people shouted (Matt 27:25). Similarly, America and Europe have adopted the foolish slogan "Liberty, Equality, and Fraternity." What a snare that slogan has turned out to be, and what destruction has resulted from it (see our comments on Prov 11:11). For the unbreakable law applies also to our words and slogans: "Whatever one sows, that will he also reap" (Gal 6:7). Whoever sows the wind with his mouth will reap the whirlwind. In every area of life.

How can we escape this ruin? "Whoever keeps his mouth and his tongue keeps himself out of trouble" (Prov 21:23). This is true now already, in this life. But later it will be completely true, for our Lord said, "I tell you, on the day of judgment people will give account for every careless word they speak" (Matt 12:36). At that time, blessed is the one who is justified through the blood of the Lamb, for that believer will experience fully: "An evil man is ensnared by the transgression of his lips, but the righteous escapes from trouble" (Prov 12:13; see our comments on Prov 3:17 and 10:11 as well).

Proverbs 18:10

> The name of the LORD is a strong tower;
> the righteous man runs into it and is safe.

The name of Yahweh is not merely a sound for recognition, but it is in fact a complete book of biblical history summarized in four Hebrew consonants: YHWH. It is the microfilm version of that miraculous age from the ten plagues to the death of Joshua. Yahweh means: He is with us. And that is what he has shown! Whoever names the name of Yahweh is calling to mind a series of *mighty deeds*. The plagues upon Egypt, the drying of the Red Sea, Israel's food supply in the desert, the quaking at Sinai, the victory over Amalek, the drying of the Jordan, the shock Israel experienced among the Canaanites, the collapse of the walls of Jericho, the sun standing still at Gibeon, and other events in the starry heavens. Holy Scripture summarizes all these miracles with the simple phrase: the name of Yahweh. All those facts display his faithfulness, his almighty power, and his lovingkindness.

Our proverb calls that name a strong tower or fortress. Thus, given that Scripture equates God's *name* with his *accomplishments*, Solomon is teaching us here that the deeds of Yahweh, the narrative of his powerful miraculous deeds, the fame of his liberating power, Yahweh himself, as we know him from his powerful deeds, is a strong tower. To this fortress, the righteous run quickly in faith and prayer, and they dwell in safety. What a beautiful description of what it means to pray and to believe: to take refuge in the name of Yahweh!

Yet, we know him now in terms of his still more beautiful name: the God and Father of our Lord Jesus Christ. This name, too, is a history book in a nutshell. In this name you must hear the entire powerful narrative of God's redemptive work through Jesus Christ. A narrative that began with his conception by the Holy Spirit, and included his resurrection from the dead and being exalted to the right hand of God. In that name, "our Father," we hear God's complete redemptive power, rescuing us from the power of Satan and death, through Jesus Christ. The name of God now refers to everything that his Word and other works reveal to us about him. This includes God's deeds in Gen 1:1 all the way to the fulfillment of Rev 22. Read the proverb in that way once: "The *accomplishments* of our heavenly Father are a strong tower, the righteous man runs into it and is safe." Indeed, more safe than in a nuclear shelter. And surely better protected than the rich, who imagine that their fortune is a fortress, as we learn from the next proverb.

Proverbs 18:11

> A rich man's wealth is his strong city,
> and like a high wall in his imagination.

That is how the rich fool was thinking in the *mashal* of our Lord (Luke 12:16–21). But his *life* was not safe in the fortress of his money, for God said: "'Fool! This night your soul is required of you, and the things you have prepared, whose will they be?' So is the one who lays up treasure for himself and is not rich toward God" (Luke 12:20–21). One could better find safety in the name of Yahweh! (See our comments on Prov 10:15, and compare 1 Tim 6:17–19.)

Proverbs 18:12

> Before destruction a man's heart is haughty,
> but humility comes before honor.

"Is not this great Babylon, which I have built by my mighty power as a royal residence and for the glory of my majesty?" said Nebuchadnezzar when he was looking around while walking on the roof of his palace. He had not yet finished speaking when he lost his mind and was humiliated by being reduced to a crazy, grass-eating man (Dan 4). But the humble captive, Daniel, ascended from being a prisoner of war to the second in command within this Babylonian kingdom.

Our Lord Jesus, who knows his Father better than anyone (John 1:18), once said, "What is exalted among men is an abomination in the sight of God" (Luke 16:15). That is a lesson that permeates the entire Scripture. Therefore, he repeatedly taught this using the same words: "Whoever exalts himself will be humbled, and whoever humbles himself will be exalted" (Matt 23:12; cf. Luke 14:11; 18:14; 1 Pet 5:5).

Proverbs 18:22

> He who finds a wife finds a good thing
> and obtains favor from the LORD.

When Jesus walked on earth, some laughingly asked a man who was married, "Will it be *matza* or *motze*?" They were doing a wordplay on the proverb cited above: "He who finds [*matza*] a wife finds a good thing." They were simultaneously alluding to this saying of the Preacher: "I found [*motze*] more bitter than death the woman who is a trap, whose heart is snares and nets, whose hands are fetters" (Eccl 7:26 NRSV).

Solomon was referring, of course, to a good wife, one who builds her house and does not destroy it through folly (see our comments on Prov 14:1). You can see her portrait in Prov 31:10–31. You cannot inherit such a wife; not even your father and mother can provide you with such a wife. She is indeed a gift from God, whom he gives you as a proof of his favor. "House and wealth are inherited from fathers, but a prudent wife is from the LORD" (Prov 19:14). When Eliezer had to seek this kind of wife for the son of his master, he prayed that God would point her out to him, as a proof of his favor (Gen 24:12–14, 27).

Why should young men not follow that example today?

Proverbs 19:3

> When a man's folly brings his way to ruin,
> his heart rages against the LORD.

Folly is another word for sin, rebellion against God, despising his Word and counsel, going one's own way.[31] That is what Adam did in the beginning. And in his excuse, do we not hear an undertone of accusation? "The woman whom you gave to be with me, she gave me fruit of the tree, and I ate" (Gen 3:12). Do we not hear the claim that he actually could not help it? Since then, every person is by nature inclined to charge not himself but God with the consequences of his folly.

This happens among God's people as well. Why were the people of Judah sitting in captivity so far from home? Because they were so foolish as to break God's covenant, though they blamed their distress on God: "Yet your people say, 'The way of the Lord is not just,' when it is their own way that is not just" (Ezek 33:17, 20; cf. 18:25, 29). Isaiah was familiar with that

---

31. See van Deursen, *Psalms I*, 93–96.

mentality as well. First throw God's Word and warnings to the wind, and then they "will be enraged and will speak contemptuously against their king and their God" (Isa 8:21).

How many young and old from Christian homes do we not hear making the same accusation? Against better knowledge, they despised the good path of God's commandments, they stubbornly refused to listen to their parents and leaders, and they wanted to determine their own path. Ultimately, they had to pluck the fruit of their own folly, and came to realize that they themselves had messed up their lives. But all of a sudden, it was God's fault, or the church's fault. Even though they might not say it in words, they think it in their hearts, says Solomon. First despise God's order, and then accuse him of the resulting disorder. Numerous life stories can confirm this.

Especially when people in effect tear the first page out of the Bible, they easily arrive at such hateful ideas about God. At that point they are suppressing in unrighteousness the fundamental truth that God created everything good, and, for that reason alone, we cannot blame God for all the misery that exists in the world. Acting as though Gen 1 and 2 are not in the Bible, people rudely quarrel with their Maker, asking questions like, "If he exists, how could a loving God allow . . . ?" The Preacher would say, "See, this alone I found, that God made man upright, but they have sought out many schemes" (Eccl 7:29).

Evolutionism, which denies the fall, displays its bad fruit at this point as well. For, with this perspective, people are tempted no longer to acknowledge their sin or folly as *a culpable debt*, but as *fate*, a disruption of the evolutionary process, for which "higher powers" are responsible. In this way, belief in evolutionism can lead a person into the sin that Solomon is identifying here: First shatter your life happiness, and then become angry at God!

At this point we recognize that the author of Lamentations was speaking the truth. After the fall of Jerusalem, he told his brothers, "Why should a living man complain, a man, about the punishment of his sins?" (Lam 3:39). If anyone has a right to make an accusation, then it is not we against God, but God against us! What have we human beings done with life upon his good earth? What have we as his people done with his good commandments? That is what he has complained about and questioned: "And now, O inhabitants of Jerusalem and men of Judah [add: Christians], judge between me and my vineyard. What more was there to do for my vineyard, that I have not done in it? When I looked for it to yield grapes, why did it yield wild grapes?" (Isa 5:3–4).

Proverbs 19:11

> Good sense makes one slow to anger,
> and it is his glory to overlook an offense.

We might translate this more literally, "The discretion of a man *deferreth* his anger" (KJV). Our heavenly Father does the same thing: "For my name's sake I defer my anger, for the sake of my praise I restrain it for you, that I may not cut you off" (Isa 48:9). God takes his time before he unleashes his wrath.[32] "Who is a God like you, pardoning iniquity and passing over transgression for the remnant of his inheritance?" (Mic 7:18). With the phrase "passing over," Scripture is clearly referring to a *forgiving* passing over. From this we infer that in the proverb cited above, Solomon is encouraging us to be imitators of God, such that we ourselves forgive our neighbor's trespasses against us, and pass over them with a forgetful spirit. We must do so to the extent that God's honor and the edification of others require that.[33]

A person's *understanding* can lead him to that goal. This is so, of course, if he is being led by faith and love, for "hatred stirs up strife, but love covers all offenses" (Prov 10:12; cf. 1 Cor 13:7). Love opens our eyes to see various mitigating circumstances, which in turn disposes us to be mild and prepares us to leave the judgment in God's hands. Faith teaches us to see God's hand in everything, a mighty hand that can employ so much evil for good.

A moving illustration of this proverb is the magnanimous and forgiving attitude that Joseph displayed toward his brothers. They had committed unspeakable evil against him. But he looked above them to see God's hand, and at that point Joseph's believing understanding restrained his anger to such an extent that it never came to expression against his brothers. On the contrary, when he identified himself to them, he comforted them magnanimously: "And now do not be distressed or angry with yourselves because you sold me here, for God sent me before you to preserve life . . . and to keep alive for you many survivors. So it was not you who sent me here, but God" (Gen 45:5–8).

This patience adorned David as well. You know what Saul did to him. In spite of that, David spared the life of his deadly enemy twice (1 Sam 24, 26). When news of Saul's death reached David's ears, David composed a moving obituary, in which he lovingly passed over all the injustice that Saul had perpetrated against him, and testified to nothing but the praiseworthy deeds of the king who had been killed (2 Sam 1:17–27).

---

32. See van Deursen, *Psalms II*, 197–98.
33. Haak, *Dutch Annotations*, ad loc.

If someone displays "slowness to anger," then Scripture describes this as "his splendor." This radiated most beautifully in the life of our Savior himself, who has fulfilled this proverb by "mak[ing] intercession for the transgressors" (Isa 53:12; Luke 23:34). When Peter asked him, "Lord, how often will my brother sin against me, and I forgive him? As many as seven times?" Jesus answered him, "I do not say to you seven times, but seventy-seven times" (Matt 18:21–35; cf. Prov 25:21; Rom 12:17–21).

By recommending that we be slow to anger, Scripture is giving us healthy counsel! Think about it. Do not overlook the transgressions of your neighbor! Comment on every little thing and raise a fuss about the least little injury, continually focus on what others have done against you, and then you will run a great risk that you will pay for this continual anger with your own health, for "a tranquil heart gives life to the flesh, but envy makes the bones rot" (Prov 14:30; see our discussion of this proverb). Being long-suffering instead benefits your heart and blood vessels, your stomach and intestines, and spares you from insomnia (you can find more about the connection between the fear of the LORD and our health in our comments on Prov 3:7).

Here are a number of related proverbs: "A man of quick temper acts foolishly, and a man of evil devices is hated" (14:17). "Whoever is slow to anger has great understanding, but he who has a hasty temper exalts folly" (14:29). "A hot-tempered man stirs up strife, but he who is slow to anger quiets contention" (15:18).

Proverbs 19:18

> Discipline your son, for there is hope;
> do not set your heart on putting him to death.

Solomon thinks differently than modern pedagogues about the use of corporal punishment in connection with nurture. He taught, "Whoever spares the rod hates his son, but he who loves him is diligent to discipline him" (Prov 13:24; see our discussion of this proverb). The Torah prescribed corporal punishment in connection with judicial verdicts as well, but limited the judge to the maximum of forty blows (Deut 25:2–3; cf. 2 Cor 11:24). So there was chastisement, but it was obviously able to be modified and not excessive.

In the proverb cited above, Solomon also warns against excessive punishment of children. In that regard, the instruction of Israel's wisest king differs in principle from that of the later author Jesus Sirach in the apocryphal book bearing his name.

There you will find several pedagogical recommendations that breathe the harsh spirit of the later Pharisees, which also show us their intensification of the "Law."

> He who loves his son will whip him often,
> > so that he may rejoice at the way he turns out.
> Pamper a child, and he will terrorize you;
> > play with him, and he will grieve you.
> Do not laugh with him, or you will have sorrow with him,
> > and in the end you will gnash your teeth.
> Give him no freedom in his youth,
> > and do not ignore his errors.
> Bow down his neck in his youth,
> > and beat his sides while he is young. (Sir 30:1, 9–12a)

The Spirit of Jesus Christ gives us more mild counsel in Holy Scripture. The wise men did not shun the rod, but neither did they view it as a miracle tool. For them, discipline is, first of all, kind leading by instruction (see our comments on Prov 1:2–3). Listen to how tenderly David spoke to his son Solomon when the latter was a child (Prov 4, especially vv. 3–4 and 11). Listen as well to how kindly the mother of King Lemuel taught her son: she called him "son of my womb" and "son of my vows" (Prov 31:2). That is the basic tone of the discipline taught by the wise men, who also devoted such sensitive words to parental love and parental pain (see our comments on Prov 10:2; cf. 15:20; 17:6; 23:24–25; 31:1–9).

Genuine parental love does not shun physical chastisement in connection with child-rearing, if needed (see our comments on Prov 13:24). It recognizes the wholesome effect of the rod, which can drive out foolishness (see our comments on Prov 22:15), which in turn can deliver a person from death (see our comments on Prov 23:13–14), can supply wisdom (see our comments on Prov 29:15), and provide the one giving instruction with joy and rest (Prov 29:17). But then one should use it in a *timely* manner, "while there is still hope," as Solomon says in our proverb. This means that we must do this early on, for a child who is toddler and just beginning school can still be improved, and at that age surely there is still hope (see our comments on Prov 13:24).

But although the wise men warn against excessive sensitivity about this—"he will not die" (see our comments on 23:13)—those giving instruction should be watchful for excessive chastisement and for coldheartedness in administering discipline. The strict predecessor of the Pharisees Jesus Sirach diverged from Solomon in this regard, as we observed above. But the converted Pharisee Saul of Tarsus agreed entirely with Solomon in giving his admonitions, "Fathers, do not provoke your children to anger, but bring them up in the discipline and instruction of the Lord" (Eph 6:4). "Fathers, do not provoke your children, lest they become discouraged" (Col 3:21).

The wise men also knew the heart of mothers and fathers, as we see from their warning "Do not set your heart on putting him to death."

This proverb, then, can teach us two things.

First, it teaches that *love* for Christ's will is the chief value undergirding Christian discipline. If this is the case, we will not reach quickly and immediately for the rod, and then we will not punish incessantly or unfairly or irregularly. We will not act out of vindictiveness and will be averse to giving beatings à la Jesus Sirach. Christian nurture is therefore far softer toward the sinner than that of the Pharisee. It takes account of the limits of ability of sinful people. That gives the appearance of not being all that concerned about sin. In essence, however, it is far more concerned. For the "righteousness" of Christians surpasses that of the Pharisees. Christian love practices tough patience in order to instruct our weak, young brother and sisters in the Lord, to lead the stout, and to let the unruly feel discipline with a few taps.

This requires the prudent discernment of time, place, and child. "Luther ascribed the regrettable outworking of the strict nurture that he had received to the fact that his parents, who nonetheless did mean well, did not know how to distinguish between children's characters: the very sensitive boy, who could certainly have been guided with a soft word, instead learned through the frequent use of the rod to view his father as a judge, and to see in the heavenly Father only the avenger of evil. For others, however, strict discipline is desperately needed, if they are not to stray entirely from the right path."[34]

Second, this proverb can encourage us to reflect on *the limits of children's abilities* with regard to good and evil. Christian discipline in the spirit of love requires of the one administering it that he or she treat the child according to the child's nature, and guard against fanaticism when it comes to nurture. Fanatics lack patience to wait for the new earth, which will arrive when Jesus returns—no, they want that world to dawn here and now. The tools of fanaticism par excellence are "power and force." This can lead a pedagogue to reach with excessive haste for the rod. But this needed respect for the limits of children's abilities we have discussed more extensively in connection with the proverb "Train up a child in the way he should go; even when he is old he will not depart from it" (Prov 22:6).

---

34. Wielemaker, *Lichtstralen uit het Woord*, 79.

Proverbs 20:3

> It is an honor for a man to keep aloof from strife,
> but every fool will be quarreling.

When our Savior was on earth, someone approached him with the request, "Teacher, tell my brother to divide the inheritance with me." However, even though the Lord knew that as the Son of God he was the Cocreator and future Judge of the whole earth, he replied, "Man, who appointed me a judge or an arbiter between you?" (Luke 12:13–14 NIV). In so doing, the Master acted according to the wisdom of the proverb cited above, and he stayed far away from the family quarrel in which the man wanted to entangle him (cf. Matt 12:19).

In humility our Savior knew his place! He had received no divine mandate to function already then as judge, and for that reason, he remained obedient as the humiliated mediator within the confines of his calling. Surely he also knew the proverb "Whoever meddles in a quarrel *not his own* is like one who takes a passing dog by the ears" (Prov 26:17). This explains his question, "Who *appointed* me a judge or arbiter over you?" This insight into the limits of his task restrained him from getting entangled in an inheritance dispute that did not concern him. The question, "Am I indeed *called* to do this?" can help us stay far away from many quarrels, and prevent us from suffering as a meddler (1 Pet 4:15).

Here again we see the wisdom of God in contrast to that of this world, where often people with big talk are put on a pedestal. But Scripture calls this meddlesome outburst characteristic of a fool. By contrast, it praises the disciples of the Lord Jesus who are at peace with all men, insofar as it depends on them (Matt 5:9; Rom 12:18; cf. Mark 9:50). "The Lord's servant must not be quarrelsome but kind to everyone" (2 Tim 2:24).

Here are some related proverbs: "A dishonest man spreads strife, and a whisperer separates close friends" (16:28). "The beginning of strife is like letting out water, so quit before the quarrel breaks out" (17:14; see our comments on Prov 3:30).

Proverbs 20:9

> Who can say, "I have made my heart pure;
> I am clean from my sin"?

No one can say this! "For there is no one who does not sin!" That too is a saying of Solomon, from his prayer in connection with the dedication of the temple (1 Kgs 8:46). This is confirmed throughout all of Scripture. Solomon's father David confessed, "Behold, I was brought forth in iniquity, and in sin did my mother conceive me" (Ps 51:5). "Enter not into judgment with your servant, for no one living is righteous before you" (Ps 143:2). "Surely there is not a righteous man on earth who does good and never sins" (Eccl 7:20). "If we say we have no sin, we deceive ourselves, and the truth is not in us" (1 John 1:8; cf. Gen 8:21; Job 4:17b; 14:4; Ps 130:3; John 8:7).

To this rule there is but one exception: our Lord Jesus Christ. He could ask, "Which one of you convicts me of sin?" (John 8:46). We can both complain and boast, "For all have sinned and fall short of the glory of God, and are justified by his grace as a gift, through the redemption that is in Christ Jesus" (Rom 3:23–24).

Proverbs 20:12

> The hearing ear and the seeing eye,
>   the Lord has made them both.

Do you have ears with which you can hear, and eyes with which you can see? Then you have God to thank directly for those invaluable gifts. The eye clinics and institutions for the blind and the deaf remind us that our hearing and our sight are not automatic capacities, and that we may praise God often, "I praise you that I can *see*! I thank you that I can *hear*!"

But then as the Creator, God has the right to ask us to account for our use of our eyes and ears. For naturally he has given us ears in the first place to listen to his voice, and eyes to observe his great deeds. Even if you had but one ear, then with it you must listen well to God's Word (Rev 2 and 3).

For that matter, in Hebrew, just as in Dutch, *hear* is a term for *obey*, and *see* is a term for *understand* (cf. our maxim: If he will not listen to advice, he needs to feel the consequences). Samuel used the same Hebrew word that we find in the proverb cited above when he said to Saul, "Behold, to obey is better than sacrifice, and to listen than the fat of rams" (1 Sam 15:22). According to Isa 6, with respect to God's Word, someone can be deaf though hearing, and blind though seeing—meaning that such a person does not obey and does not understand.

In our proverb we also hear this lesson: If you have ears that truly hear God's voice through his Word, and eyes that truly see his deeds in Scripture and in history, then do not boast about that, for that is a gift of God (Matt

13:11; Eph 2:8). The disciples of the Lord Jesus saw and heard in him the promised King, and at that point he congratulated them, "Blessed are your eyes, for they see, and your ears, for they hear" (Matt 13:16).

Proverbs 20:22

> Do not say, "I will repay evil";
> wait for the LORD, and he will deliver you.

As a young man, Solomon's own father did this in such an exemplary way that he thereby became "the man after God's heart." David obeyed the Torah: "You shall not take vengeance or bear a grudge against the sons of your own people, but you shall love your neighbor as yourself: I am the LORD" (Lev 19:18). For that reason, during his persecution by Saul, he followed the code "*Al tashkheth!*" ("Do not destroy!"; cf. the superscription of Pss 57, 58, 59, and 75). Do not destroy your hostile brothers, but love them and hand over your just cause to God.[35] Even when one thrust of the spear could have put an end to David's distress, he did not take revenge against Saul for his evil (1 Sam 24, 26).

In many a psalm, David confessed this humble faith and stirred his listeners in similar instances to wait for God's intervention.[36] Psalm 37 especially strongly urges us to leave to God the defense of our righteousness. With this reliance upon God, David was not put to shame at all. Without David himself killing one of his enemies in Israel, Yahweh saw to it that people came to offer to David the kingship over Judah and Israel.

No one has practiced this wisdom as perfectly, however, as David's great Son, our Lord Jesus Christ. He could have brought down fire from heaven upon his enemies and called upon legions of angels for help against them (Luke 9:54; Matt 26:53), but he did neither. "When he was reviled, he did not revile in return; when he suffered, he did not threaten, but continued entrusting himself to him who judges justly" (1 Pet 2:23). Indeed, even when he was on the cross, Jesus prayed for his enemies, "Father, forgive them, for they know not what they do" (Luke 23:34). He showed in a perfect way what "waiting on God" can mean, and, in his time, "God has highly exalted him and bestowed on him the name that is above every name" (Phil 2:9).

Nevertheless, let no one infer from this that it cost David and our Lord no hardship to have to wait years for God's deliverance. Because people

---

35. See van Deursen, *Psalms II*, 14–17.
36. See van Deursen, *Psalms II*, 85–86, 103–5.

often think that a Christian must always "do" something, you can interpret this waiting on God as merely being "passive." As though such waiting did not go directly against our fleshly desires that so easily take refuge in unbelieving impetuosity. As though being able to "do" nothing cannot bring our faith under severe stress. Waiting on God constitutes perhaps one of the most weighty assignments that our faith can receive. No, Solomon is not giving us easy advice, but certainly good advice, as many children of God have discovered. They put this proverb into practice, and in God's time received his help.

One who rejects Solomon's counsel, however, and repays evil with evil, generally unleashes a chain reaction of continuously fresh evil. In addition, he is using the same sinful weapons that his opponent is using. But what he especially loses from view is that vengeance is a right that belongs to God alone, and to his servant, the government and its judges. Those functionaries must indeed repay evil. But in this proverb, Solomon does not have in view judges but *individuals*, and for the latter the rule applies: "Beloved, never avenge yourselves, but leave it to the wrath of God, for it is written, 'Vengeance is mine, I will repay, says the Lord'" (Rom 12:19; Deut 32:35; 1 Thess 5:15; regarding seeking justice in the private and public sectors, see our comments on Prov 24:29).

Here, for the umpteenth time, we learn that the fear of the LORD is medicine for our body and refreshment to our bones (see our comments on Prov 3:7–8). For whoever pursues vengeance is pouring salt into his own wounds. Whoever says to himself, "I'm going to get him!" often does great damage to his spiritual and physical health (see our comments on Prov 14:30). Here is one more related proverb: "If your enemy is hungry, give him bread to eat, and if he is thirsty, give him water to drink, for you will heap burning coals on his head, and the LORD will reward you" (Prov 25:21–22; cf. Rom 12:20).

Proverbs 20:25

> It is a snare to say rashly, "It is holy,"
> and to reflect only after making vows.

"Help, beloved holy Anna! I want to become a monk!" cried the deathly scared student, Martin Luther, when on July 2, 1505, as he was traveling from his parental home in Mansfeld to the university in Erfurt, he was caught in a severe thunderstorm.[37] God used this vow to create a great tran-

---

37. Berkhof, *Geschiedenis der Kerk*, 151.

sition in church history, but that is not to deny that this was nevertheless not the proper manner for making a vow.

When someone in Israel pledged something to Yahweh, he apparently cried out, whether or not in reference to the gift, "Holy!" (This is holy from now on.) That is to say, this is separated from the world and intended for the service of God. One could also assign to Yahweh a particular votive sacrifice: "If you grant me this or that benefit, then I will give you this or that." Such votive sacrifices belonged to the peace offerings. Once you had made such a vow, you were bound to fulfill it: "If you make a vow to the LORD your God, you shall not delay fulfilling it, for the LORD your God will surely require it of you, and you will be guilty of sin. But if you refrain from vowing, you will not be guilty of sin. You shall be careful to do what has passed your lips, for you have voluntarily vowed to the LORD your God what you have promised with your mouth" (Deut 23:21–23; Ps 50:14).

Although now we no longer bring bloody peace offerings as Israel did, we may nonetheless still make vows. This is certainly not limited to the Old Testament. The mother of King Lemuel talked about her "son of my vows" (Prov 31:2). In this way she had apparently entreated for him, just as Hannah did (1 Sam 1:11). During a particular vow Paul let his hair grow (Acts 18:18). Why would we not be allowed to promise God so many (hundreds of) dollars if he fulfills this or that beloved wish of ours?

But we must not make such vows impulsively, as Luther did, under the sudden force of a number of sharp thunderclaps You must do this kind of thing prayerfully, after serious reflection, before the face of God. Otherwise, we could be promising more than we can deliver. Imagine that someone makes this impulsive vow: "If you provide my son with a God-fearing wife, then I will give ten thousand dollars for your kingdom." If he would be unable to pay anything close to that amount, he would be putting himself in great difficulty because of his vow, and his family as well. Regarding such a rash vow, our proverb would say, "It is a *snare* to say [in this case, financially] rashly, 'It is holy,' and to reflect only after making vows."

If we reflect on a vow for the first time after we have made it, then we can simultaneously fall into the temptation to break it, something that Scripture explicitly forbids (see above, regarding Deut 23:21–23). Scripture did provide for Israel the possibility of paying a dispensation for an unfulfilled vow, but of course that is different than breaking the vow (see Lev 27:1–8). With his sudden vow, Luther brought much sorrow to his father, for he didn't have much use for monks. For that reason, let us take to heart the advice of the Preacher that corresponds to our proverb: "Be not rash with your mouth, nor let your heart be hasty to utter a word before God. . . .

It is better that you should not vow than that you should vow and not pay" (Eccl 5:1–7; cf. Deut 23:22; Sir 18:23).

Proverbs 20:29

> The glory of young men is their strength,
> but the splendor of old men is their gray hair.

As a young man, you are at the pinnacle of your physical strength. If you fear the LORD, perhaps at the end of your life-education he will give you gray hair as the adorning crown of wisdom.

In the world, the differences between young and old often constitute a source of quarreling, and in that connection people often talk about a generation *gap*. People cannot tolerate each other, they are jealous about each other's gifts and position, and make the most serious accusations against each other. But according to God's order, a grandpa and his grandson are not opponents but supporters in the struggles of life. One has more life-*strength*, the other more life-*wisdom*. Together they supplement each other nicely. With the Preacher, we may say, "He has made everything beautiful in its time. . . . For there is a time and a way for everything" (Eccl 3:11; 8:6).

What sweet peace proverbs like the one above (and Prov 16:31 as well) can establish. They encourage us to take grateful and conscious pleasure in the joys afforded us at every age in life. At the same time, they can lift God's people over the unwholesome generation gap that often so unwholesomely separates the children of this world from each other.

Proverbs 21:1

> The king's heart is a stream of water in the hand of the LORD;
> he turns it wherever he will.

You could take the entire book of Esther as an illustration of this proverb. Yahweh mightily took in his hand the heart of that world ruler Ahasuerus, and thereby all his actions! For all of one's actions proceed from his heart, "from it flow the springs of life" (Prov 4:23). Yahweh inclined that royal heart toward his divine plans just as easily as an Israelite farmer dug a water channel in his vegetable garden—with no effort at all. You know what Haman had in mind: to destroy all the Jews in the Persian Empire on the same day, including the Jews who had returned to Jerusalem. But Yahweh wanted to keep this people alive, for he would cause the Savior of the world to come from this people.

Therefore, God took the heart of that mighty Ahasuerus in his hand at that point. Everyone thought that Ahasuerus was doing what he wanted, but, in reality, he was doing only what God wanted. Yahweh inclined the heart of the ruler first to choose, from numerous beauty queens, the Jewish Esther as successor to the repudiated Queen Vashti. Next Yahweh filled the heart of Ahasuerus with sympathy for Esther, who could thereby implement Haman's fall and Israel's deliverance.

This is how Yahweh has, throughout history, inclined the hearts of the greatest people on earth toward his plans. *He* incited Pharaoh's heart, for he wished to glorify himself through Pharaoh (Exod 4:21; 14:4). *He* placed a lying spirit within Ahab's prophets, for he wanted to entice him to undertake what would be a fatal military campaign (2 Chr 18:18–22). *He* used the mighty Assyrian Tiglath Pileser because *he* needed a rod with which to discipline Judah (Isa 10:5). One hundred years later, *he* employed Nebuchadnezzar in his service, because *he* wanted to lead Judah into captivity. But seventy years later, *he* moved the spirit of Cyrus, because *he* wanted to redeem Judah from captivity (Ezra 1; Isa 41:2–4). *He* had emperor Augustus order a census, for *he* wanted to fulfill the prophecy that the Messiah would be born in Bethlehem (Mic 5:1; Matt 2:6; Luke 2). All these mighty ones were of the firm opinion that they themselves were implementing their own plans. But, in fact, they were serving in submission to *God's* plans. To that end he guided their royal heart just as easily as a farmer digs an irrigation channel measuring less than half a foot wide. He is the King of kings.

Even today, all those who are mighty and powerful, from the highest to the lowest, are so completely in God's power that they are unable either to maneuver or to move (Ps 33). He inclined the hearts of Napoleon and Hitler to undertake a Russian campaign, which resulted in their defeat and our liberation. Whether they acknowledge it or not, all the mighty people throughout the earth rule by the grace of God, and must serve his plans, and they do so not one minute longer than he needs them.

Proverbs 21:9

> It is better to live in a corner of the housetop
>   than in a house shared with a quarrelsome wife.

No, Solomon is not making a joke here. You can easily sympathize with a man who has married such a woman. The backgrounds of such perpetual quarreling certainly do not provide material suitable for humor. We see here how deeply sin can corrupt the shared life of a husband and wife. For God has not intended marital life to go this way, of course, so that husband and wife eventually would prefer to flee from each other.

"I will make him a helper fit for him," said God the LORD when he proceeded to create a wife for Adam. When Adam saw her, he cried out, "This at last is bone of my bones and flesh of my flesh; she shall be called Woman, because she was taken out of Man" (Gen 2:18–25). That is the opposite of *walking away* from her in discouragement, like the Israelite who got tired of the nagging and went to sit down on the flat roof of his house, perhaps in a small room constructed on the roof (2 Kgs 4:10). There he sat by himself, perhaps even in the rain, but there he could at least enjoy some peace and quiet.

But how did it happen that a wife lived with her husband with such a quarrelsome attitude? You cannot dismiss this with a reference to irritable character, though that does play a role, of course. The deepest roots lie, however, in the sin that such a wife did not want to view her husband as her *head*. Already in paradise, the LORD had predicted that reluctance. One of the results of sin would be that the husband would no longer exercise his leadership with love and pleasure, but that he would have to fight his wife for that.

How many husbands saw their marital life corrupted by this rebellion, if they appeared to have married a wife who resisted God's ordained design for marital life? What then comes to expression is perpetual strife, unceasing criticisms, tantrums and pouting, self-pity, abuse, and bluster. We can easily imagine what else flows from these in a marriage. A husband must indeed govern his wife (1 Tim 2:12–15; cf. Gen 3:16; 1 Tim 3:2–5). But how can he do so *in love* in such a situation—if he is even able to govern? For as another proverb puts it, "A continual dripping on a rainy day and a quarrelsome wife are alike; to restrain her is to restrain the wind or to grasp oil in one's right hand" (27:15–16). Many a husband, too wise to return insults, and tired of useless arguing, has therefore eventually fled out of the house in order to find some peace and quiet in "a corner of the rooftop."

According to Solomon, that is "better" than living with a "quarrelsome wife," but in saying this, of course, he is not arguing that such fleeing is ideal. Such withdrawal is and remains a disruption of God's order, and lifelong sorrow for such a husband. He misses a cozy home and a friendly glance, which for other husbands are sources of pleasure and encouragement. In addition, the proverb tacitly assumes that a marriage may not be dissolved for *these* reasons (Matt 5:32). He may well think, "A soft answer turns away wrath" (see our comments on Prov 15:1). And, "It is an honor for a man to keep aloof from strife, but every fool will be quarreling" (see our comments on Prov 20:3). But it remains a burdensome assignment. A related proverb states, "It is better to live in a desert land than with a quarrelsome and fretful woman" (21:19). Naturally, a wife can be married to a quarrelsome and irritable husband who makes her sigh and weep her entire life. But in this proverb Solomon is limiting himself to the quarrelsome wife.

Blessed is the husband who receives from God a wife who submits to the divine command "Wives, submit to your own husbands, as to the Lord. For the husband is the head of the wife even as Christ is the head of the church, his body, and is himself its Savior. Now as the church submits to Christ, so also wives should submit in everything to their husbands" (Eph 5:22–24). That makes it much easier for her husband to fulfill God's mandate for him, which is in fact more challenging than her mandate: "Husbands, love your wives, as [!] Christ loved the church and gave himself up for her. . . . In the same way [!] husbands should love their wives as their own bodies" (Eph 5:25–28).

Let no one render the Word of God powerless regarding this point, by feminist claims or by declaring on one's own authority that this is "time bound." For no better safeguards exist for our marital happiness and that of our young men and women than God's marriage ordinances, concerning which he has also said, "The person who does them will live by them" (i.e., find happiness).

Proverbs 21:13

> Whoever closes his ear to the cry of the poor
> will himself call out and not be answered.

"For judgment is without mercy to one who has shown no mercy" (Jas 2:13). That happens already now, but surely at the last judgment. The Lord Jesus has portrayed that in a *mashal*: "There was a rich man who was clothed in purple and fine linen and who feasted sumptuously every day. And at his gate was laid a poor man named Lazarus, covered with sores, who desired to be fed with what fell from the rich man's table. Moreover, even the dogs came and licked his sores" (Luke 16:19–21). But the rich man appeared never to have noticed the human misery at his gate. Until he opened his eyes in pain, and was pointed by father Abraham to "an unbridgeable gap" between him and Lazarus.

Remember that Solomon spoke this proverb and the Lord Jesus told this parable to *Israelite* ears. Such things happened and happen within the force field of God's Word that from beginning to end proclaims mercy to us and demands mercy from us. Therefore, we must not think in the first place of what pagans did but of what Christians did to their poor in connection with what the Lord tells us in Matt 25 about the last judgment.

When, at that time, he takes his seat in full majesty upon his throne, and has separated all of humanity into two groups, he will say to the unmerciful on his left, "Depart from me, you cursed, into the eternal fire prepared for the devil and his angels. For I was hungry and you gave me no food, I was thirsty and you gave me no drink, I was a stranger and you did not welcome me, naked and you did not clothe me, sick and in prison and you did not visit me."

And when they fail to understand anything he is saying, he will answer, "'Truly, I say to you, as you did not do it to one of the least of these [my *brothers*, v. 40], you did not do it to me.' And these will go away into eternal punishment, but the righteous into eternal life" (Matt 25:31-46; see our comments on Prov 3:27-28, 34; 11:26; cf. Matt 5:7; 18:32-35; Prov 14:21; Sir 4:1-6).

Proverbs 21:24

> "Scoffer" is the name of the arrogant, haughty man
>   who acts with arrogant pride.

The name "scoffer" is one of the nicknames of the wicked. Perhaps we think that it refers more to rough fellows who make shameless jokes about God and his service. As we have argued more extensively elsewhere,[38] in Scripture the scoffer refers more to a figure *inside* the church rather than *outside* the church. They often wrap themselves in a cloak of religiosity or even of theological erudition. The apostles pointed them out *within* the Christian churches.

In the proverb cited above, Solomon is pointing out what makes the apostate person a scoffer: his unbridled arrogance, his egomania and pride. He is the reckless person who does not know his limit with respect to God, and in that connection measures incorrectly. He is the counterpart to the poor and meek, and the opposite of the wise, for "a wise son hears his father's instruction, but a scoffer does not listen to rebuke" (13:1).

By means of his autonomous attitude, he barricades himself from the discipline of God's Word and renders himself almost irremediable: "A scoffer does not like to be reproved; he will not go to the wise" (15:12). Or

---

38. See van Deursen, *Psalms I*, 96-100.

else someone needs to punish him sternly; that might help, because that is the only language he understands (21:11).

In this way, he acts every day with the immeasurably arrogant notion that he knows everything better than God, and that he need not take the slightest notice of the order disclosed in God's commandments and works. Perhaps he feels in this connection that he is too humane or too civilized to scoff outright at the Bible, but his *arrogant attitude* nonetheless characterizes him as a genuine scoffer. (See our comments on Prov 3:34.)

Proverbs 22:3 (= 27:12)

> The prudent sees danger and hides himself,
> but the simple go on and suffer for it.

The "simple" is the gullible person, the inexperienced and naive young person, and the much too unsuspecting older person. We have already met this person in connection with Prov 1:4 and 14:15 (see our comments on these verses). A characteristic example of such a simple person who went his own way and had to pay the price is the young man of Prov 7 who let himself be seduced by the bad woman. "All at once he follows her, as an ox goes to the slaughter, . . . till an arrow pierces its liver" (Prov 7:22; cf. chapter 9: adultery and prostitution are the crown of folly). On that point, Joseph showed himself in similar circumstances to be genuinely more "clever": he saw the disaster that sexual relations with the wife of Potiphar would occasion and attempted to flee.

Proverbs 22:6

> Train up a child in the way he should go;
> even when he is old he will not depart from it.

What does Solomon mean by "the way he should go"? Is he referring to nurturing with a view to the child's *later* life? Or taking into account the child's life *as a child*? With a view to his *calling* or according to the measure of his *ability*? In our view, the one does not exclude the other, and both pieces of wisdom are included in this *mashal*.

"He who loves him is diligent to discipline him" (Prov 13:24). As we saw with the discussion of this proverb, children are most sensitive to admonition and most susceptible to improvement in early childhood. The proverb cited above points to the same thing. Wise nurture begins immediately at birth.

Solomon's proverb allows room for thinking of babies as well, for the Hebrew word he uses here for "child" is *na'ar*, which in Exod 2:6 refers to the infant Moses in his basket of rushes. Not that one should spank a young child, for the wise men thought that discipline refers first of all not to corporal punishment, but to love-filled parental guidance through instruction, warning, and prohibition. If necessary, parents can let a disobedient child feel the pain of this authority received from God. Whoever allows the early years of a child's life to pass by without such nurture is neglecting the best opportunity for this, and will perhaps regret this later with tears (Prov 29:15).

Of course, we think the phrase "the way he should go" refers to the capacity for every good word and work to which God will call the child in his or her life. In the life-walk with God, the educator must *initiate* the child, as the Hebrew states literally. The Dutch States Translation (SV) puts it this way: "Teach the child *the first principles*," to be understood as referring to the right that God has to our entire life, by virtue of his covenant. Thus, it refers to nurture arising from deep respect for God's ordinances in Scripture and creation (cf. chapter 4, dealing with Prov 1:7).

As early as possible, children should receive basic instruction about sin and grace, as well as about their cleansing through the blood and Spirit of Jesus Christ. Accustom them early to serving the Lord according to the will of God by teaching them daily from the Word. Timothy knew the Scriptures *from his childhood* (2 Tim 3:15). The exceptions that are ignored in this proverb confirm that in the kingdom of God, as well, the rule applies: What you learn while young you do when you're old!

In addition to receiving an encouragement to begin nurture as early as possible, one can hear in this proverb also a warning to take into consideration *the nature and age* of the child. That too is "the way he should go." God created everything according to its kind, including the child. His ordinances for childhood are different than those for adulthood. The young child is still living in his own sphere. A child does not yet know his life calling, and lacks the zeal and sense of obligation that characterizes a grown man. Children are absorbed with playing. Already in this respect God has established limits to the ability of children, which we must respect.

In addition, our children are conceived and born in sin. Just as in our own lives, this accounts for various deficiencies and shortcomings in their childhood as well. They can no more attain the ideal than we can. Harsh pedagogues like Jesus Sirach attempt to force this sad reality by beating his sides (see our comments on Prov 19:18). But disciples of Solomon show respect in connection with the nurture of their children for the limits of their ability with regard to good and evil. That, too, is "according to the way he should go" (cf. Ps 103:8–14).

This is not to say that we have complete peace with the sins and deficiencies of our children, or that we should passively acquiesce to them. Far from it! But let our zeal be for the improvement of the sinful nature of our children, a zeal that proceeds from a meek and humble heart, one that recognizes its own sin and misery. Let us remember that, also in connection with the nurture of sinful children of human parents, everything cannot be made straight at once, but we must first sow and weed the crop patiently before we can begin to harvest.

Proverbs 22:14

> The mouth of forbidden women is a deep pit;
> he with whom the LORD is angry will fall into it.

In Prov 5–7, with the use of practical examples, Solomon has shown extensively how such a woman can whine with her mouth and how one falls into such a pit (cf. chapter 9, about adultery and prostitution, the crown of folly).

Proverbs 22:15

> Folly is bound up in the heart of a child,
> but the rod of discipline drives it far from him.

In Scripture, folly is not something innocent, like childish stupidity, but another word for sin.[39] Folly identifies evil as a manifestation of stupidity. Regrettably, it has become attached to (bound up in) the hearts of our youngest children, as the proverb writer had to confirm as well. No one needs to teach his children disobedience to God's commandments. "The intention of man's heart is evil from his youth" (Gen 8:21; Ps 51:5; Job 14:4), unless we are regenerated by the Holy Spirit.

Holy Scripture teaches us here that folly is not always removed from a child's heart without pain, but one may harbor good expectations that such may be achieved with the use of the rod. Folly can be removed from a child's heart with a few taps on the fingers, or, if necessary, with a firm slap. Be especially alert to the problem of waiting too long. "He that loveth [his son] chasteneth him betimes" (Prov 13:24 KJV). From this we deduce that the best time for physical discipline occurs before the child enters school, because experience teaches that usually during the earliest years of life a child

---

39. See van Deursen, *Psalms I*, 93–96.

responds best to physical discipline. Children who have become familiar with the rod of discipline before starting school will generally hardly need that rod once they are in school. They will have learned already at home to toe the line. (On the use of the rod of discipline in connection with nurture, see our discussion of Prov 13:24; 19:18; 22:6; 23:13–14; and 29:15.)

2. SOME SAYINGS OF OTHER SAGES

Proverbs 22:17 begins the third of seven collections that make up the book of Proverbs (or if one wishes to view Prov 24:23–34 separately, the third and fourth of eight collections). Until we come to Prov 24:34, we are not reading proverbs of Solomon but of other sages, as we learned at the beginning: "Incline your ear, and hear *the words of the wise*" (22:17; cf. 24:23).

In comparison with the subjects treated in the preceding collections (1–9 and 10–22), the subjects in this collection are not new. The form of the *mashals* resembles that in Prov 1–9; they display more of a connection and contain more than two lines. They are also addressed somewhat more directly to the hearers and readers than in Prov 10–22.

Proverbs 22:17–19

> Incline your ear, and hear the words of the wise,
>   and apply your heart to my knowledge,
> for it will be pleasant if you keep them within you,
>   if all of them are ready on your lips.
> That your trust may be in the LORD,
>   I have made them known to you today, even to you.

God gave us the book of Proverbs not to page through it once in awhile, but to put it *in our hearts*. For that reason, I have advised you several times already to underline the proverbs in the Bible that catch your attention, and then to reread these a number of times, until you know them by heart. What fills the heart crosses the lips. The wise men call it *pleasant* when we season our conversations with their proverbs. In this way our confidence will also grow, confidence in God and in the order for living that he has made known in his Word and other works (on this, see chapter 4).

Proverbs 23:13-14

> Do not withhold discipline from a child;
>   if you strike him with a rod, he will not die.
> If you strike him with the rod,
>   you will save his soul from Sheol.

Parents who have to spank their children often feel the most pain. For that reason alone, this warning against all too much softheartedness is not superfluous. But in our time this warning is especially relevant, because Christian people who are falling away from God and his Word are surrendering to increasingly greater insubordination. The spirit of the age has proclaimed for many years the mantra of "a free-spirited upbringing" or an upbringing "without constraints," and has nothing good to say about corporal punishment, to say nothing of the rod, from which the proverb writers expected so much good.

To the extent that it is necessary for us to defend their counsel over against the revolutionary spirit of our time (Isa 40:8; 2 Cor 13:8), we declare emphatically that the following statement applies also to those proverbs about the rod of discipline: "All Scripture is breathed out by God" (2 Tim 3:16). The Spirit of wisdom is speaking also through the admonition of the proverb writer that we have cited above. In this way, all the proverbs about corporal punishment are elevated for us beyond all criticism.

Now, although God's Spirit gave us this wisdom through the ministry of men, these were nonetheless not calloused moral tyrants. Their tender form of address, "My son," already betrays the warmhearted sensitivity of these teachers, who viewed their pupils as their children. In connection with Prov 19:18 we called attention to the warm affection of the wise men for their pupils. Consider carefully Prov 23:15-16, immediately after our proverb, and more or less the result of that proverb: "My son, if your heart is wise, my heart too will be glad. My inmost being will exult when your lips speak what is right." Does such language come from an insensitive soul?

Moreover, for these wise men discipline is not equivalent to a spanking, and surely not to an unwise use of the rod (see our comments on Prov 19:18). In Proverbs, discipline is first of all the friendly, fatherly guidance by means of instruction and admonition, which can be supplemented for young children if needed with a couple of taps.

Please do not label this as "Old Testament," for Heb 12—we pointed this out earlier—cites Prov 3:11-12 with approval and asks, "For what son is there whom his father does not discipline?" It does so in order to observe soberly that this discipline naturally provides the child "for the moment no joy but pain." But what is the ultimate fruit? "The peaceful fruit of righteousness" (Heb 12:11). The writers of our proverb here are also pointing that out.

You probably know the objections that people raise against physical discipline. It is supposedly inhumane and too harsh. Would the wise men also have heard this latter accusation in ancient Israel? They reply soberly, "He will not die!" Isn't that true? You do see the issue in its proper proportions, don't you? Then follows the crowning argument, "If you strike him with the rod, you will save his soul from Sheol!" With this observation, have they not swept most of people's objections off the table? The child will not only survive but will survive *by this means*! Discipline can save lives!

By contrast, just look at children who were raised without discipline. Children who are three years old, whose grabby hands should have been disciplined to keep to themselves, and sometimes die from pulling a pan of scalding water on themselves or ingesting poison. Of course, the best discipline cannot prevent an accident, but in many cases proper discipline could have saved a child from death. Who can count the number of those who ended up in the electric chair or on the scaffold, or who in another manner experienced a premature death, because discipline was withheld from them when they were young?

Being without discipline leads to a premature death (see our comments on Prov 3:1–2). That is a rule. The exceptions do not invalidate the rule. By virtue of the fact that with parental authority all authority lies in one hand, as it were, the neglect of parental discipline has consequences in every area of life. Parents who leave the "rod" unused could sometimes occasion God reaching for his rod. At that point, nations and churches, marriages and schools, associations and enterprises find out that the folly of being undisciplined leads to destruction. For undisciplined children grow up to be undisciplined citizens, unfaithful church members, unfaithful spouses, and unreliable coworkers. That is what the "rod"—used in a timely manner, that is, in early youth—could have prevented! (For more on physical punishment, see our comments on Prov 13:24; 19:18; 22:6; and 22:15.)

Proverbs 23:17–18

> Let not your heart envy sinners,
>   but continue in the fear of the LORD all the day.
> Surely there is a future,
>   and your hope will not be cut off.

Who are those sinners, actually? Christians are known to say, "We are all sinners." No doubt they have good intentions, but they are not really expressing themselves correctly. In Scripture, the term *sinner* is, like the terms *scoffer, arrogant, evildoer*, and *fool*, one of the words the Bible uses to identify *the wicked*.[40] In Scripture, the wicked or the sinner is the counterpart to the righteous.

But what characterizes a person as a sinner? Because we often view sin and evil exclusively in an ethical sense, we think the term *sinner* refers only to those who perpetrate various moral offenses, like social injustices, murder, robbery, sexual sins, and other violations of the second table of the law. But the righteous can also fall into those sins (which is different than living in such sins); but Scripture does not on that basis call them sinners. People are called sinners in Scripture far more with a view to the ground motive of their life-attitude. In connection with sinners, that consists of their imagined right to self-determination.[41]

For that reason, the term *sinner* should make us think not only of bank robbers, adulterers, and murderers, but also of many who, to all outward appearances, live a very decent life. For, according to the measure of Scripture, they too belong among the sinners, even though a patina of humanistic self-righteousness, or even a tinge of religiosity, covers their lives. In spite of this, they are guilty of the *greatest evil* that a person can commit: proudly ignoring the God and Father of our Lord Jesus Christ, his Son, his Spirit, his Word, and his covenant, and demanding for themselves complete autonomy. That is the primeval sin, which cannot be committed so insolently as by apostate Christians who were born under the canopy of God's covenant.

The life motto of the sinner is "*Ni Dieu, ni maître*"–no God, no master. That motto determines all of his actions: his view of duty, obedience, authority, justice, nurture, recreation. In all these areas he insolently misunderstands *God's* right to and claim on our life, and has no shortage of rhetoric about *his* "right" to this and that (social security, free time, sexual gratification, etc.).

Keep in mind that Proverbs is intended especially for young people (see chapter 3). At that point in life, they are still expecting a lot from life: a happy marriage, a harmonious family, social progress. Their lack of life experience, however, exposes them to the danger of falling under the influence of the lifestyle of sinners, and they themselves being envious of them. Just as the godly Asaph was embittered by the prosperity of the wicked (his Ps 73 constitutes, together with Ps 37, a wonderful commentary on this

---

40. See our extensive discussion in van Deursen, *Psalms I*, 99–106.
41. Cf. van Deursen, *Psalms I*, 106–9, with regard to the proud.

proverb). But the wise men here warn their young readers not to be jealous of the self-assured sinners, because a person can harbor well-founded expectations for the future only if "throughout the whole day" he pursues the fear of the LORD.

For no more effective means exists for healing this broken human life, and for discovering the path of least distress through this crooked world, than the fear of the LORD. This refers to believing reverence for the life-order that God has revealed in his Word and in his other works (cf. chapter 4). In that connection the book of Proverbs constitutes an excellent guide, focused entirely and completely on the practices of daily living. If you follow the guidance of that book, you have obtained the best possible life insurance. Then you need not find a lawyer to guide you through a divorce process, or visit you in prison as a criminal. "Surely there is a future, and your hope will not be cut off," says our proverb.

Our Bible book contains even more *mashals* with the same emphasis: "The hope of the righteous brings joy, but the expectation of the wicked will perish" (10:28). "When the wicked dies, his hope will perish, and the expectation of wealth perishes too" (11:7). "Be not envious of evil men, nor desire to be with them, for their hearts devise violence, and their lips talk of trouble" (24:1–2). "Fret not yourself because of evildoers, and be not envious of the wicked, for the evil man has no future; the lamp of the wicked will be put out" (24:19–20; cf. 24:14).

The apostle John would write later, "Do not love the world or the things in the world. If anyone loves the world, the love of the Father is not in him. For all that is in the world—the desires of the flesh and the desires of the eyes and pride of life—is not from the Father but is from the world. And the world is passing away along with its desires, but whoever does the will of God abides forever" (1 John 1:15–17).

Proverbs 23:29–35

> Who has woe? Who has sorrow?
>   Who has strife? Who has complaining?
> Who has wounds without cause?
>   Who has redness of eyes?
> Those who tarry long over wine;
>   those who go to try mixed wine.
> Do not look at wine when it is red,
>   when it sparkles in the cup
>   and goes down smoothly.

> In the end it bites like a serpent
> and stings like an adder.
> Your eyes will see strange things,
> and your heart utter perverse things.
> You will be like one who lies down in the midst of the sea,
> like one who lies on the top of a mast.
> "They struck me," you will say, "but I was not hurt;
> they beat me, but I did not feel it.
> When shall I awake?
> I must have another drink."

Here you have a frank description of an alcoholic, or any other kind of addict, for that matter. For Proverbs may well be talking here about wine, but of course we may readily apply this lesson to any alcoholic beverage, to drug use, and to other forms of addiction. You watch a drunkard, staggering down the street, his eyes blurred, his clothes disheveled, his face bloodied from a drunken brawl. Tomorrow he will wake up with a hangover and look with surprise at his bruises when he looks in the mirror. Who would have beaten him up last night? No matter; later he will reach once again for the bottle, for king alcohol still keeps its slaves, and he gets no day off.

In connection with Scripture passages like this one, people like to point out that the Bible does speak positively about wine. Indeed, the Preacher says, for example, "Go, eat your bread with joy, and drink your wine with a merry heart, for God has already approved what you do" (Eccl 9:7). Thus, you can hardly maintain that Scripture simply forbids *all* enjoyment of wine (cf. Gen 27:28; Ps 104:15; Isa 55:1; John 2:1–11; 1 Tim 4:4–5; 5:23). But then please do not cite these Scripture passages to enervate and to ignore the *many warnings* in the very same Bible against alcohol abuse.

For prophets, sages, and apostles univocally warn against drunkenness. Isaiah threatened, "Woe to those who are heroes at drinking wine, and valiant men in mixing strong drink" (Isa 5:22; cf. 28:1). Are such warnings communicated often enough nowadays in sermons? In Israel that was not always the case, since those who were supposed to communicate the warnings were themselves often drunk: "The priest and the prophet reel with strong drink, they are swallowed by wine" (Isa 28:7). Stated in today's language: elders, ministers, and professors in theology are overindulging in drinking. But they are not at all concerned about "the ruin of Joseph" (Amos 6:6), the ruin of the Christian life. You can see at once that alcohol abuse occurs in every age and among all classes. Even children can become addicted.

Let us be careful not to view alcohol addiction as horrible *disease*, as often happens, but as an offensive *sin*, whereby a person can lose his salvation! "Do not be deceived: neither the sexually immoral, nor idolaters,

... nor *drunkards* ... will inherit the kingdom of God" (1 Cor 6:9–10). Drunkenness belongs among "the works of the flesh," concerning which Paul warned that "those who do such things will not inherit the kingdom of God" (Gal 5:19–21; cf. Rom 13:13; Eph 5:18). Now we know that God denies no one entrance into the kingdom because he is *sick*, but because he will not repent and turn from his *sin*. Therefore, drunkards need first of all not to be *healed*, but to *repent and turn* from their sin.

From the *mashals* cited above, we can learn how easily, and therefore how insidiously, we can be lured into this evil. Did not the writers of these proverbs point this out with such artistry by the very location of this warning in this collection? It comes right after a warning about the unchaste woman! People often talk about "wine, women, and song" as though the trio is inseparable. The Germans have a similar saying: "Where Bacchus rules, Venus is not far away" (*Wo bacchus regiert, ist venus nicht weit*). We were also acquainted with the prophet Hosea, who said, "Harlotry, wine, and new wine enslave the heart" (Hos 4:11 NKJV; cf. Hab 2:15). The apocryphal book Jesus Sirach said, "Wine and women lead intelligent men astray" (19:2; cf. 31:25–31).

For that reason, the wise men began with a warning against the *sphere* within which this evil is most often perpetrated: late evening or nighttime ("tarry long over wine," Prov 23:30), conversations about its appearance ("look at wine when it is red, when it sparkles in the cup"), and the quality of the drinks ("those who go to try mixed wine," v. 31). The prophets and apostles point out as well that alcohol abuse occurs especially in the evening and during the night. Isaiah also knew of those "who tarry late into the evening as wine inflames them!" (Isa 5:11). "Those who get drunk, are drunk at night," Paul writes (1 Thess 5:7). With respect to this matter, anyone who thinks that he stands, take care that he not fall. Many an alcoholic began to abuse alcohol in the social sphere of nighttime festivity and conviviality.

But there is where the venomous snake came crawling insidiously into one's life! The wise men have sketched it in a lively manner. "[Wine] goes down smoothly. In the end it bites like a serpent and stings like an adder" (Prov 23:31–32). That is the invoice that everyone must pay for excessive use of alcohol. It lifts you out of your cares and helps the tensions slide off you, but woe to you if you surrender to it! Then you will find out that venomous snakes are hiding in those seductive wine glasses, serpents that will bite you, all of a sudden, and inject their poison into your body. Take that last observation literally.

Alcohol poisons your understanding, it undermines your strength of will, and it robs you of the normal use of your senses. Verses 33–35 show us the tragic outworking of this serpent's bite. "Your eyes will see strange things, and your heart utter perverse things" (v. 33). The drunkard has lost his view of reality, just like the one addicted to drugs. An alcoholic can even suffer from permanent delusions, such as, for example, that his wife is being unfaithful. Perhaps Proverbs is alluding here to the hallucinations suffered by one who is severely addicted, who suffers from delirium tremens. Because the drunkard achieves very little, he often surrenders to childish fantasies and bragging.

A person who loses control of his senses in this way, who has also lost every sense of direction and can hardly walk, exposes himself to various *deadly hazards*. Verse 34 points this out with biting irony: "You will be like one who lies down in the midst of the sea, like one who lies on the top of a mast." We think in our own day of the thousands upon thousands of victims that alcohol produces around the world in connection with traffic accidents. This is part of our daily news reports. Our modern health care has sufficiently eliminated formerly terrifying plagues and cholera epidemics. But in 1898 the Dutchman O. G. Heldring wrote a book about alcohol abuse with the title *Gin Is Worse Than Cholera* (*De jenever erger dan de cholera*). According to American studies, an alcoholic is seven times more likely to suffer a fatal accident than a non-alcoholic.

In a time when the world loves to talk about freedom, alcohol and drugs have not yet surrendered their enslaving power, but continue to hold in their chains millions of their victims. Verse 35 describes the tragedy of these slaves: "'They struck me,' you will say, 'but I was not hurt; they beat me, but I did not feel it. When shall I awake? I must have another drink.'" If alcohol merely robbed its victim of various pleasures as long as he "was under the influence," that would be bad enough. But even when he is sober, alcohol deprives him of the most valuable things in life. As a rule, the alcoholic forfeits the respect and love of his wife and children. He never gets around to enjoying good music, edifying conversations, a wonderful hobby, or other forms of recreation. According to verse 35, the drinker asks, "When shall I awake? Then I will look for another drink [another 'high']." Someone who had been addicted to alcohol for years confirmed this: "In fact, I missed out on the entire childhood of my children."

Real alcoholics become less suited or even completely unsuitable for society. They lose their (occasionally excellent) jobs and are declared unemployable. And to think that, according to respectable studies in the United States, around 4 percent of all adults are alcoholics! In France this percentage must be around 10 percent. Proverbs 23:29–35 is talking about a reality that is extremely relevant, extends throughout the whole world, and is therefore indescribable.

But wisdom can protect you! The fear of the LORD can preserve you from untold suffering! That was the pervasive lesson of Solomon's Instruction Manual for Proverbs (Prov 1–9). In that connection, alcoholism provides a striking illustration! Or have you ever observed that an alcoholic lives more happily than one who totally abstains from alcohol? Or that someone lost his job because he did not drink? Or of a physician who said, "You need to drink"? Or of an employer who prefers to appoint people to executive positions who are addicted to drinking? Or of a wife who complained, "If only my husband drank more, then we would live more happily and keep more of our income for our household needs and enjoyments"?

No more powerful motivation exists for handling alcohol with care than the wisdom that one receives through the fear of the LORD. Through such wisdom, one can protect one's life from all the suffering that results from alcohol abuse! For then you need not smash into a tree with your car and terminate your life prematurely. You need not destroy your marriage, forfeit the respect of your children, drown your money and possessions, end up in financial ruin, forfeit your health through liver disease or mental illness, lose your job and your social standing, and have to go to court because of driving while intoxicated and because of manslaughter. If only you take to heart the Scripture passage cited above!

Proverbs is a book for young people. If they would like to live long and happily and enjoy the good things of this world, then they must know and put into practice Prov 23:29–35. For that is the gospel and "is the power of God for salvation to everyone who believes" (Rom 1:16).

Here are several other proverbs that warn against abusing alcohol: "Wine is a mocker, strong drink a brawler, and whoever is led astray by it is not wise" (Prov 20:1). "Whoever loves pleasure will be a poor man; he who loves wine and oil will not be rich" (21:17). And finally this:

> It is not for kings, O Lemuel,
>   it is not for kings to drink wine,
>   or for rulers to take strong drink,
> lest they drink and forget what has been decreed
>   and pervert the rights of all the afflicted.
> Give strong drink to the one who is perishing,
>   and wine to those in bitter distress;
> let them drink and forget their poverty
>   and remember their misery no more.
> Open your mouth for the mute,
>   for the rights of all who are destitute.
> Open your mouth, judge righteously,
>   defend the rights of the poor and needy. (31:4–9)

Proverbs 24:11–12

> Rescue those who are being taken away to death;
>   hold back those who are stumbling to the slaughter.
> If you say, "Behold, we did not know this,"
>   does not he who weighs the heart perceive it?
> Does not he who keeps watch over your soul know it,
>   and will he not repay man according to his work?

What is involved here, of course, is condemning to death someone who is *innocent*. In this connection we can think of abominable mass murder through abortion. In this manner, millions of unborn people are being murdered nowadays in the womb of their mother. Within totalitarian states, God provides little or no power of appeal by raising one's voice against this evil, but in our Western democracies we still possess the requisite civic liberties to register our appeal. Are we using those means in order to warn of God's wrath upon this form of mass murder? In light of this proverb, he is not satisfied with excuses like "We knew nothing about it" or "That was none of my business." He sees through such excuses and could one day come to repay apostate Christianity in terms of such passivity. Perhaps in the form of mass slaughter of those whom they did not prevent from being born?

We do not want to withhold from our readers the comments of the German commentator Helmut Lamparter in connection with this proverb. "You cannot read these words," he writes, "without recalling the deepest shame at how evangelical Christianity in Germany failed when they dragged the sons of Israel to slaughter. (The courageous protests on the part of a few individuals may not be forgotten, but they were so infrequent that as the exceptions they were, they merely served to confirm the rule.) The widespread excuse, 'We knew nothing about it!' is here torn from our hands. Unfamiliarity with the Old Testament was in this instance avenged so bitterly. Was there in all of Germany one pulpit in which this Bible text was preached during those years?"[42]

It is as though the writer of these verses had a premonition of the indescribable suffering that would one day come upon his people. These verses can be read as a somber prophecy of the march of millions of deported sons of Israel who were led to slaughter. And "nobody knew about it."

---

42. Lamparter, *Das Buch der Weisheit*, 251–52.

Proverbs 24:21–22

> My son, fear the LORD and the king,
>   and do not join with those who do otherwise,
> for disaster will arise suddenly from them,
>   and who knows the ruin that will come from them both?

How faithfully David did this! Recall that he had been anointed by Samuel to be king, and he had at his disposal an armed force, and still he never rebelled against Saul! Even though the latter had treated him very unjustly, and had even wanted to kill him. David nonetheless continued to acknowledge him as "the anointed of Yahweh," whom he refused to (have) kill(ed) (1 Sam 24, 26). When he had cut off the hem of Saul's robe, his heart pounded (1 Sam 24:6), in fear that he may have angered God, because he had committed this insult against Saul.[43] "This feeling of reverence, and even of piety, we owe to the utmost to all our rulers, be their characters what they may."[44]

Daniel also performed faithfully what we read above: "My son, fear Yahweh and the king." With loyalty he served King Nebuchadnezzar in a high-ranking position, even though this king had destroyed Jerusalem and had led Judah away into captivity. But Daniel feared Yahweh and therefore he acknowledged that Nebuchadnezzar had received his authority over the world of that day from God (Dan 2:21, 37; 5:18). Therefore, Daniel sought the peace of Babylon, and he surely would have prayed to God for that, as the prophet Jeremiah had commanded (Jer 29:7).

But the most striking example of obedience to God and the king was provided by our Lord Jesus Christ during his life on earth. "Therefore render to Caesar the things that are Caesar's, and to God the things that are God's," he taught (Matt 22:21). This is what he did perfectly when the governments (of Rome and the Jews) perpetrated the most abominable injustice against him that was ever committed on this earth. What else was his imprisonment, his judicial hearing, his sentence, and his condemnation, than the grossest injustice in all of world history? Nevertheless, he did not resist the governments that perpetrated this against him, even though he was the Son of God! Nor did he resist the government servants who arrested and crucified him. When, in that context, Peter reached for his sword, Jesus forbade him emphatically, "Put your sword back into its place. For all who take the sword will perish by the sword" (Matt 26:52). Jesus honored the governor of the Roman emperor, who was occupying Israel's inheritance, in his government office with the words, "You would have no authority over me at all

---

43. Haak, *Dutch Annotations*, ad loc.
44. Calvin, *Institutes*, 4.20.29.

unless it had been given you from above. Therefore he who delivered me over to you has the greater sin" (John 19:11; cf. 18:36).

His apostles instructed the church in the same spirit. Peter wrote, "Be subject for the Lord's sake to every human institution, whether it be to the emperor as supreme, or to governors as sent by him" (1 Pet 2:13–14). The proverb under consideration here is echoed in Peter's command "Fear God. Honor the emperor" (1 Pet 2:17).

When the churches in the cosmopolitan city of Rome were persecuted during Nero's reign of terror, Paul did not incite them to commit violent resistance against this government, but he wrote carefully to these terrorized churches, "Let every person be subject to the governing authorities. For there is no authority except from God, and those that exist have been instituted by God. Therefore whoever resists the authorities resists what God has appointed, and those who resist will incur judgment" (Rom 13:1–2; cf. vv. 3–7). Once more, keep in mind that these words were referring, first of all, to Nero (cf. also Acts 23:5; 1 Tim 2:2)!

History also knows, however, of "godly" rioters, who despised governments with an appeal to Holy Scripture, but thereafter experienced firsthand the "disaster" and "ruin" spoken of in Prov 24:22. The bloody drama of the Anabaptist Christians in the Netherlands during the first half of the sixteenth century serves as a striking illustration of this. Blinded by fanatic notions of the kingdom of God, they sang their imprecatory psalms against the authorities and even took up the sword against them in the name of Christ—only, thereafter, to fulfill Christ's word to Peter, when they "perished" by the sword.

In his *Institutes*, Calvin fervently warned against these "pious" insurrectionists (4.20.17–32), and wrote to Admiral De Coligny, "If a single drop of blood were spilled, floods of it would deluge Europe."[45] These prophetic words were fulfilled in a terrifying manner in the Huguenot Wars of 1562–1598 (with the so-called blood wedding on St. Bartholomew's night).

"A good soldier of Christ Jesus" (2 Tim 2:3) is the absolute opposite of a revolutionary and a guerrilla fighter. For this reason, Reformed believers in the sixteenth century were repeatedly pressed to prove that they were not rebellious Anabaptists. The Belgic Confession was also pressed into service at this point. Strictly speaking, the main intention of article 36 is to speak about an office or task not of the *government* but of the *church*, and of all Christians toward the government. "Behold," the church is declaring in that article, "I am so loyal to authority, not despite God's Word, but because of

---

45. Calvin, *Letters*, 176.

God's Word. For the preaching of this Word does not incite confusion, and thus it deserves not your oppression but your protection, O government!"[46]

Read the humble letter that Guido de Bres, the author of the Belgic Confession, wrote to King Philip II: "We assure you, Sire, that in your Netherlands there are more than one hundred thousand people who advocate and follow the religion whose confession we present you, and that among none of them has there been any sign of revolt."[47] De Bres wrote that to a government that was persecuting faithful Christians with fire and sword and would one day come after him! But even when he was standing at the top of the steps leading to the gallows where he would be hanged, he used the closing moments of his life to call the spectators to obey the authorities!

Just as Calvin did, so too de Bres judged that, for a Christian, God's Word does not allow one to throw off "the cross of Christ" through rebellion against the government. It is our political calling of the first order as followers of Jesus Christ to obey all those who have been appointed to be over us ("conservative" and "liberal," mild and harsh governments), and to stay far removed from the world's revolutionary agitation. Of course, it is also written, "We must obey God rather than men" (Acts 5:29; cf. 4:19). But how quickly we forget as we use this Scripture verse that it states that we must *obey* people (who have been appointed over us), and, even beyond and *above* those people, we must obey God himself.

In our Western world, revolution (for our understanding of this word, see our comments on Prov 3:5–6) causes an awful crisis of obedience, and its life endangering ideas poison many Christians as well. God's Word warns us in one and the same breath to fear God and the king, but the French Revolution cried, "No God, no master!" God's Word teaches that the government is the servant of God, but millions believe today that it is the servant of the people. By virtue of the revolution principle of popular sovereignty they think that the people possess the authority to appoint governments or to dismiss them.

In his important book *Unbelief and Revolution*, Groen van Prinsterer identified the source of our national and international calamities. Nowadays we see on a global scale what Scripture pointed out on a small scale in the history of the ten tribes of Israel. One palace revolution came after another military mutiny, and those must have opened up streams of blood throughout poor Israel. But what a river of European blood would have flowed after the French Revolution?

---

46. Vonk, *De Nederlandse Geloofsbelijdenis*, 661; cf. 631, 648.
47. Vonk, *De Nederlandse Geloofsbelijdenis*, 580–81; cf. 579–81.

Proverbs is a book for young people, and often young people can be so impetuous when it comes to political events. Let especially our Christian young people, then, keep in mind the wise counsel of Prov 24:21-22 and not become involved with revolutionary agitators. Not even if they conduct their campaigns in the name of Christ, allegedly on behalf of the kingdom of God. So walk away, young people, when the police starting advancing with their batons or when armored vehicles are coming down the street. At least if you value your life! It happens often that a stray bullet has killed a naive spectator or left him with a severe handicap. "For disaster will arise suddenly from them," warns God's Word, "and who knows the ruin that will come from them both?" (Prov 24:22; cf. the premature death of Absalom; see our comments on Prov 3:1-2 as well).

To prevent misunderstanding, we would also point out that Proverbs certainly does not praise every ruler. In many *mashals*, the book mentions requirements that a *good* ruler must meet—he must give a good example (Prov 29:12); live moderately and modestly (31:3-5); defend the poor and oppressed (29:14; 31:6-9); establish his throne through righteousness (16:12; 25:5; 29:14); choose good counselors (11:14; 15:22; 24:6); and rule with gentleness and compassion (20:28). But we may not turn these into norms according to which we as subjects or citizens evaluate a sovereign, or decide whether we will obey a harsh or less competent government.[48]

Proverbs 24:23b

> Partiality in judging is not good.

For Yahweh does not do that, either. How often do we read that in Scripture (cf. 1 Sam 16:7; 2 Chr 19:7; Acts 10:34; Rom 2:11; Gal 2:6; Eph 6:9; Col 3:25; 1 Pet 1:17)? Therefore, as righteous Judge, he does not tolerate that those who substitute for him on earth would judge with partiality. "Justice, and only justice, you shall follow!" he commanded in the Torah. This was to be done also by providing *impartial* judges (Deut 16:18-20; Lev 19:15). Proverbs—which is seeking to teach justice and righteousness as well (1:4)—warns literally in the proverb cited above, "Paying attention to *the face* is not good." Implementing justice in such a way is even to act in a pagan manner.

---

48. For further study of this topic, we refer anyone who reads Dutch to the discussion of Belgic Confession, art. 36, in Vonk, *De Nederlandse Geloofsbelijdenis*, 549-663; there you can see how Calvin and de Bres communicated the teaching of Scripture about the task and calling of both government and citizens.

The well-known ancient Near Eastern Code of Hammurabi contained separate laws for the higher classes, separate laws for the middle class, and separate laws for the slaves. Yahweh detested that, and it was in part because Israel perpetrated injustice that he punished her with the Babylonian captivity. So let us for that reason be very fearful, if we are called to administer justice, that we are not unrighteously giving preferential treatment to members of our own group, our own party, or our own family. Not only in those circumstances but also in our ordinary interaction as brothers and sisters within the church. "My brothers, show no partiality as you hold the faith in our Lord Jesus Christ, the Lord of glory" by not giving preferential treatment to someone "wearing a gold ring and fine clothing" above a poor brother. The apostle James warns explicitly against this evil (Jas 2:1–13).

Let us give thanks to God if we may live in a country where jurisprudence indeed still proceeds from the fundamental principle that each citizen is equal before the law. In that blessing we may see a precious fruit of the Word of God in our society. Many nations are jealous of that. For where the judicial order is attacked, there the order of life is attacked, and there people curse their government and forfeit the blessing of prosperity (cf. Prov 24:24–25).

Proverbs 24:27

> Prepare your work outside;
>   get everything ready for yourself in the field,
>   and after that build your house.

Young people, don't be too eager to get married! First build the nest and then capture the bird. Or, first be able to earn a living and only then start a family (i.e., build a house; see our comments on Prov 14:1). Also in the arena of love, you should not pick the fruit before it has ripened. With such refinement, the Song of Solomon points that out to young ladies in its refrain, "I adjure you, O daughters of Jerusalem, by the gazelles or the does of the field, that you not stir up or awaken love until it pleases" (Song 2:7; 3:5; 8:4).

Proverbs 24:29

> Do not say, "I will do to him as he has done to me;
>   I will pay the man back for what he has done."

Solomon had offered similar advice back in Prov 20:22: "Do not say, 'I will repay evil'; wait for the LORD, and he will deliver you." With this good advice these proverbs are not speaking about *judges*, for it is precisely they who must pay back the guilty party for what he has done. No, this proverb involves enduring injustice in our personal life. We need to distinguish those two aspects very carefully in connection with such Bible words: *public justice*, which involves justice provided by the *judge*, and enduring injustice in one's *private life*.

When Jonathan defended his friend David, Saul hurled at him this insult: "You son of a perverse, rebellious woman, do I not know that you have chosen the son of Jesse to your own shame, and to the shame of your mother's nakedness?" (1 Sam 20:30). Jonathan swallowed that insult and that injustice, but he defended the matter of public justice involving his friend: "*Why* should he be put to death? What has he done?" (v. 32).

In this way he was distinguishing very carefully between obtaining public justice for his friend and enduring injustice in his personal life. Is that refined distinction not lacking far too often nowadays? When someone brings his complaint to the judge, people occasionally think that such action conflicts with Christian love. After all, Jesus did say, "If anyone slaps you on the right cheek, turn to him the other also" (Matt 5:39). But why did God provide us with courts and a judicial system? And why did God himself instruct the Israelite judges, "An eye for an eye and a tooth for a tooth" (the punishment must correspond to the crime)?

People turn the entire matter upside down! Where *justice* must be pronounced, people rave about forgiveness and love. And where love must be practiced, people point to the need for justice to be done. From the *judge* who by virtue of his office is supposed to avenge wrong, people demand "love," and in the private sector where love is supposed to cover everything, people cannot endure a shred of injustice, and people take revenge against each other for minutiae.

The proverb cited above applies precisely to that personal arena: "Do not say, 'I will do to him as he has done to me; I will pay the man back for what he has done.'" In the private sector, Jesus' saying applies: "If anyone slaps you on the right cheek, turn to him the other also" (Matt 5:39). "And if anyone would sue you and take your tunic, let him have your cloak as well" (Matt 5:40). In this way Jesus was teaching us to resolve issues among ourselves with amiability and accommodation. But when he was standing before the Sanhedrin and people slapped his face, he asked as he was standing *before the judge's bench*, "Why do you strike me?" (John 18:23). In our personal lives, our restrained anger and our quiet endurance of injustice must be so intense that after a slap on the right cheek we are prepared possibly to receive another on our left.

As a private individual, Jonathan put up with the insults of his father. In that arena we may not say, "Now I'm sick and tired of it. I've reached the end of my rope. I will pay him back!" But in the arena of public justice Jonathan defended as long as possible the just cause of his friend: "Why must David die? What has he done?" Even as Jesus asked in a *public trial*, "If what I said is wrong, bear witness about the wrong; but if what I said is right, why do you strike me?" (John 18:23).

However, when the public administration of justice on the part of both Saul and the Sanhedrin failed, Jonathan and Jesus could not expect justice any longer from another person. Then they had to expect justice only from the Supreme Judge, who would one day administer justice, and who promised, "Commit your way to the LORD; trust in him, and he will act. He will bring forth your righteousness as the light, and your justice as the noonday. Be still before the LORD and wait patiently for him" (Ps 37:5–7a).

3. SOME MORE PROVERBS OF SOLOMON (PROV 25–29)

"These also are proverbs of Solomon which the men of Hezekiah king of Judah copied" (Prov 25:1). That is the superscription above the third collection of the Proverbs of Solomon in this Bible book. Back in chapter 2, we discussed his share in the composition of this Bible book. The collection from which we have selected a few more *mashals* for discussion was gathered by the committee appointed by Hezekiah.

Proverbs 25:2

> It is the glory of God to conceal things,
>   but the glory of kings is to search things out.

"For my thoughts are not your thoughts, neither are your ways my ways, declares the LORD. For as the heavens are higher than the earth, so are my ways higher than your ways and my thoughts than your thoughts" (Isa 55:8–9). That is the glory of God's majesty. "He knows what is in the darkness, and the light dwells with him" (Dan 2:22; cf. Job 28:27–28; 1 Kgs 8:12). That led the apostle to exclaim, "Oh, the depth of the riches and wisdom and knowledge of God! How unsearchable are his judgments and how inscrutable his ways!" (Rom 11:33). His sovereign will is responsible for *whether* and *what* and *when* he will reveal to us something of those ways.

But with the glory of kings the matter is just the opposite. In Israel, they were the supreme judges, and, as such, the cases set before them they were supposed to not conceal but *investigate* thoroughly. They were supposed to investigate the testimony of witnesses and examine suspects. Two women stood before Solomon claiming, "No, O king, the child is mine!" It was Solomon's glory that he got to the bottom of this matter.

Let us be grateful if God allows us to live in a society whose administration of justice includes processes of careful scrutiny, untangling the statements of witnesses, investigating traces of blood, and checking fingerprints. What blessing can be enjoyed through the work of astute judges and lawyers, forensic laboratories and detectives. Let us pray that we may continue to be preserved from a government that does not investigate legal matters, but conceals them.

Proverbs 25:4–5

> Take away the dross from the silver,
>   and the smith has material for a vessel;
> take away the wicked from the presence of the king,
>   and his throne will be established in righteousness.

Naturally, you may well be thinking in this context primarily of the influence of bad counselors. King Rehoboam lost the largest part of his kingdom because of them (1 Kgs 12). But don't ignore the influence of *false prophecy*! According to Scripture, the wicked can sometimes pose as prophets, but they are shown to be genuine liars,[49] who steer not only the people but also the government in the wrong direction. Many a ruler has lost, through false prophecy, the correct insight into the situation, and was thereby led astray, which in turn cost him his throne and his crown.

It was the wicked prophets around the throne of Ahab who spurred him on to the fatal campaign against Ramoth in Gilead (1 Kgs 22). It was false prophets who blinded the last king of Judah to the real situation in the world. God was giving Nebuchadnezzar authority over the entire world of his day (Jer 27:6; Dan 2:37–38). The faithful prophet Jeremiah was calling him to humble himself under God's chastisement (Jer 27). But kings Jehoiakim, Jeconiah, and Zedekiah gave more credence to the apparently principled yet unfounded "peace preaching" of false prophets like Pashur (Jer 20) and Hananiah (Jer 28; cf. Jer 23:9–32).

---

49. See van Deursen, *Psalms I*, 115–18.

The French Revolution, that ongoing fire-spewing volcano, was also a fruit of wickedness *in the palaces*! In his analysis of the origin and source of the French Revolution, Groen van Prinsterer argued that it came from the top down, when the king (Louis XVI) followed the lead of philosophers and philanthropists (Turgot, Malesherbes, Necker).[50] We are afraid that, today in the West, this history is being repeated on a large scale, in part because God is withholding from us the historic vocation of "removing the wicked people surrounding the king."

In this regard, Solomon acted more wisely. Immediately at his coronation, he removed harmful figures and in this way established his kingship (2 Kgs 2, especially vv. 45–46). Rulers like Jehoshaphat and Joash surrounded themselves with godly officials and established their governments through righteousness (see 2 Chr 17–20; "Joash did what was right in the eyes of the LORD all the days of Jehoiada the priest," 24:2; cf. David's portrait of a ruler in Ps 101:4–7).

Here are several related proverbs: "It is an abomination to kings to do evil, for the throne is established by righteousness" (Prov 16:12; see our comments on this verse). "A wise king winnows the wicked and drives the wheel over them" (20:26). "Steadfast love and faithfulness preserve the king, and by steadfast love his throne is upheld" (20:28). "If a king faithfully judges the poor, his throne will be established forever" (29:14).

Proverbs 25:16

> If you have found honey, eat only enough for you,
>   lest you have your fill of it and vomit it.

The ancient Greek physician Hippocrates (ca. 400 BC) is said to have advised that to remain healthy, one needs to take two precautions: eat less than you can, and work. With his deep insight into the life benefits of (self-)discipline, Solomon had given this advice long before in the proverb cited above.

Israel lived in a land "flowing with milk and honey" (Exod 3:8). Samson, Jonathan, and John the Baptist found wild honey (Judg 14:8–9; 1 Sam 14:25–30; Matt 3:4). For the Israelite, honey was a proverbial delicacy (Deut 8:8; Ps 19:11; 119:103). Moreover, it was healthy and nutritious, so that the wise men also said, "My son, eat honey, for it is good, and the drippings of the honeycomb are sweet to your taste" (Prov 14:13). Nevertheless, they also realized that "it is not good to eat much honey" (Prov 25:27a). This explains

---

50. For a thorough and penetrating analysis of the differences between revolution and reformation, see van Prinsterer, *Unbelief and Revolution*.

why Solomon provided the warning we have cited above, which we might also translate this way: "If you find honey, eat only enough; for too much can make you vomit."

Naturally, you can understand this metaphorically, and hear in this proverb a warning against excess in various areas. It remains striking, however, that the proverb writer intentionally chose honey as his example. In Israel, where sugar was not yet known, honey was not first of all a nutrient but a stimulant. So we would be faithful to the text if we hear first of all a warning against excessive use of *stimulants*. Among us, this includes things like sugar and various fats, the excessive use of which can cause diseases of the heart and circulatory system.

In addition, the proverb is also shaking a finger of warning against extravagant eating in general. Surely this warning is not out of place for Christians living in the opulent West, where many people dig their graves with their own teeth. How many people are fatally oblivious to the difference between a healthy appetite and unhealthy gluttony? "You are what you eat."

In point of fact, however, the truth that excess is harmful can be said of all good things. Living a disciplined life in every area is one of the most important conditions for physical and psychological health.[51] One English-language commentator wrote this heading above our proverb "Knowing when to stop"![52]

This applies to every area of life, including the enjoyments of friendship. And O how the wise men knew the value of friendship (Prov 28:24; 27:9; etc.)! Remarkably, immediately after the warning against excessive eating of honey they placed a warning against excessive visiting of a friend: "Let your foot be seldom in your neighbor's house, lest he have his fill of you and hate you" (Prov 25:17). This too is a poignant illustration of the life lesson that, even in the best things, one must practice moderation. Some people are intellectual gluttons, who sacrifice their sleep for their reading addiction. In the same way, alcoholics are generally people who lack moderation in many areas of life. Often you will see heavy drinking combined with immoderate smoking, snacking, etc.

In the apocryphal book, the Wisdom of Jesus Sirach, we read a similar piece of advice.

> My child, test yourself while you live;
>   see what is bad for you and do not give in to it.
> For not everything is good for everyone,
>   and no one enjoys everything.

---

51. Tournier, *Healing of Persons*, chap. 9.
52. Kidner, *Proverbs*, 159.

Do not be greedy for every delicacy,
> and do not eat without restraint;
for overeating brings sickness,
> and gluttony leads to nausea.
Many have died of gluttony,
> but the one who guards against it prolongs his life. (Sir 37:27–31)

Was Sirach inspired by Prov 25:16 to write these words?

In any case, in this seemingly irreligious proverb, we hear the echo of all biblical wisdom: "The fear of the Lord is the beginning of knowledge" (Prov 1:7). After all, it opens our eyes to the *limits* that God has established in every area for our well-being (see our comments on Prov 1:7). At the same time, this is yet one more proverb that teaches us that the fear of the Lord is also healthy (for the other proverbs, see our comments on Prov 3:7).

Proverbs 25:24 (= Prov 21:9)[53]

> It is better to live in a corner of the housetop
> > than in a house shared with a quarrelsome wife.

Proverbs 26:2

> Like a sparrow in its flitting, like a swallow in its flying,
> > a curse that is causeless does not alight.

The classic illustration of this is Balaam, who had to acknowledge, "How can I curse whom God has not cursed? How can I denounce those whom the Lord has not denounced?" (Num 23:8). With the metaphor of the birds flying away aimlessly, the proverb is rejecting the superstition that a curse is a kind of magical arrow that flies unjustifiably to its target.

Proverbs 27:3

> A stone is heavy, and sand is weighty,
> > but a fool's provocation is heavier than both.

---

53. See our comments there.

Abigail, the wife of Nabal, and his employees could talk about this (1 Sam 25). For months David and his destitute companions had stood like a wall surrounding Nabal's flocks, and had never stolen from his thousands of sheep and goats. But when David was appealing to nomadic justice, when at the shepherd's feast he asked if, by their faithful guarding of the livestock, they had not "earned" something, Nabal snapped at them and showed himself to be a genuine fool. Although his own wife saw that Yahweh was in the process of exalting David as ruler over Israel (v. 30), Nabal asked mockingly, "Who is this David?" (v. 10 NIV). Evidently Nabal had no clue about the entire revival movement of return to Yahweh, and his Word that had begun with Samuel and that Abigail now saw being advanced by David.

In the proverb cited above, Solomon is speaking about "a fool's provocation." You can certainly believe that people in Nabal's immediate surroundings knew that perfectly well. "He is such a worthless man," complained one of his servants, "that one cannot speak to him" (1 Sam 25:17). The heavy farm labor of lifting stones would not have been as oppressive to this farmhand as the daily irritation with his foolish master Nabal.

For the term *provocation*, one could substitute a term like *pain, sorrow*, or *hurt*. In Abigail's situation, would not those terms be better suited? How much sorrow this wise woman must have suffered at the hands of the fool to whom she was married. "For as his name is, so is he," she told David. "Nabal is his name, and folly [Heb., *nabal*] is with him" (v. 25). Remember in this connection that Scripture does not call someone a fool because he does stupid things—the naive person does that too (see our comments on Prov 14:15)—but especially because he does wicked things (Isa 32:6). A fool is someone who does not seriously consider Yahweh (Ps 14:1; 53:1).[54] Because of this, Nabal did not know his *historical time* (a period of wrestling for a return to Yahweh), his *moral duty* (to feed the hungry), and his *personal limit* (he was heavily intoxicated). Abigail lived with this kind of husband. While she herself was watching David fight the battles of Yahweh (1 Sam 25:28), on account of which he had brought upon himself the demonic hatred of Saul, she heard her husband railing in mockery, "There are many servants these days who are breaking away from their masters!" (v. 10). Such folly can weigh heavily on a wise heart!

In this context, we might also think of the irritation caused by fools occupying high positions (Eccl 10:6). Or of the foolish prophets whom one encounters in every period of covenant abandonment. While God's judgments descended upon his people, they continued calmly declaring "Peace, peace!"—homilies and antics designed to close the eyes of God's people

---

54. See van Deursen, *Psalms I*, 93–96.

to Yahweh's chastising hand (Ps 28:5).[55] Brothers like Micaiah, the son of Imlah (2 Chr 18), and Jeremiah must have felt severe irritation, indeed intense pain, in connection with this foolish activity of these blind leaders (Jer 20:7-18; 23:9-32). Especially in times when the great majority of God's people go astray (Jer 5:21), the godly remnant experiences the truth of our proverb in a painful way.

Indeed, carrying stones and moving sand is heavy work. But not as heavy as enduring the pain and offense on account of the power of fools in the church and the world. The Preacher knew this as well. Learning to distinguish between wisdom and folly brings with it much sorrow. One who increases his knowledge in this respect, increases his sorrow as well (Eccl 1:17-18).

Proverbs 28:2

> When a land transgresses, it has many rulers,
>   but with a man of understanding and knowledge,
>   its stability will long continue.

You could also render this proverb as follows: "When a land commits *covenant breaking*," for the Hebrew Bible uses the same word (*pesa*) for *sin*, *evil*, *rebellion*, and *covenant breaking*. The indebtedness leading to the bankruptcy of justice and righteousness is often paid for with societal chaos and political instability. You can see this clearly in Ephraim, another name for the ten tribes of Israel.

That nation lived continually in rebellion against God. As a result of that, in the span of two hundred years the nation had no fewer than *nine* royal dynasties, each succeeding its predecessor by means of rebellion and regicide (cf. Hos 7:7; 8:4; 13:11). God's promise to David (2 Sam 7) protected the nation of Judah, which often was just as sinful, for that nation lived for three-and-a-half centuries under the single royal house of David.

Does not the revolutionary era in European history after 1789 in many countries offer a striking illustration in connection with the proverb cited above? The more that our continent despises (commits *pesa* against) God's covenant and his Word, the more it can expect domestic chaos and foreign threats. (See our comments on Prov 11:11 and 29:18.)

---

55. See van Deursen, *Psalms II*, 141-42.

Proverbs 28:4

> Those who forsake the law praise the wicked,
> but those who keep the law strive against them.

As so often, here too the Hebrew term *law* (*torah*) means the teaching of *God's Word*. In that day, it was the teaching of Moses, the prophets, and the wise men; nowadays it is also that of Christ and his apostles. The more that our once Christianized continent abandons that Word, the deeper it sinks back into paganism from which God once delivered it. And the more striking will be its resemblance to the ancient pagan world that Paul describes in the second half of Rom 1. Are we not able to say about our nation, "They exchanged the truth about God for a lie and worshiped and served the creature rather than the Creator, who is blessed forever!" (Rom 1:25)? For that reason, God has surrendered "us" to every form of malice and wickedness that Paul summarizes in Rom 1:18–31.

His conclusion, therefore, constitutes a remarkable commentary on the first line of our proverb. "Though they know God's righteous decree that those who practice such things deserve to die, they not only do them but give approval to those who practice them" (Rom 1:32). Do you not recognize in those words the public opinion of our modern world and the spirit of our own age? Many righteous people have the same experience today as Lot had in Sodom, "(for as that righteous man lived among them day after day, he was tormenting his righteous soul over their lawless deeds that he saw and heard)" (2 Pet 2:8). Let them reach for the psalter, then, which is full of the laments of the godly, who formerly suffered under the dominion of the wicked among God's people.[56]

"Hot indignation seizes me because of the wicked, who forsake your law," complains the poet in Ps 119:53. The man was suffering under their wickedness: "My eyes shed streams of tears, because people do not keep your law" (v. 136; see also our comments on Prov 28:28).[57] But be comforted: the Judge is standing at the door! Isaiah, who endured the same suffering, prophesied, "Woe to those who call evil good and good evil, who put darkness for light and light for darkness, who put bitter for sweet and sweet for bitter!" (Isa 5:20).

---

56. See van Deursen, *Psalms I*, chap. 4.
57. See van Deursen, *Psalms II*, 319–20.

Proverbs 28:5

> Evil men do not understand justice,
> but those who seek the LORD understand it completely.

In this context you should not think exclusively of our thick lawbooks that only lawyers and judges know how to navigate. With the term *justice*, Solomon is referring simply to God's justice, his sovereign divine right over everything and everyone. This comes down, in fact, to the knowledge of God's will for daily living, as he had revealed in the Torah. Put another way: it refers to the practical applications of the first commandment: no other gods beside Yahweh. Wicked people understand nothing of that.

Solomon is speaking literally about "people of *badness*." He wants to conjure up the image not only of what people in our society understand by "bad people," like murderers and robbers. Solomon had in view, first of all, Israel, or God's people. Among them he saw autonomous people who were following their own "counsel" or principles, apart from God's Word (Ps 1:1).[58] These may very well be the kind of folk who live respectable public lives, who perhaps pepper their speech with Bible verses.[59] But they do not acknowledge God's covenantal sovereignty over everything, his sovereign Creator rights to enlist everything and everyone into his service. Therefore, neither do they acknowledge in the practices of daily living "what is the good and acceptable and perfect will of God" (Rom 12:2 ASV). Stated more strongly still, ultimately they are not permitted by God himself to know that will (Rom 1:28). Therefore it is something to be feared, that with the disappearance of God's Word from public society, the sense of justice will diminish.

But those who seek Yahweh "understand all things" (Prov 28:5 ASV). They are engaged with God's Word day and night, and that makes them wise (Ps 1:2).[60] That also makes them increasingly more congenial and adaptive toward the order of life that God reveals in his Word and other works (cf. chapter 4). That simultaneously supplies their judgment with a standard and thereby imparts to it the requisite power.

In contrast to those who reject God's Word, they discover keys that fit the doors of crooked reality in this fallen world. Paul prayed for this gift on behalf of the Philippians, "That your love may abound more and more, with knowledge and all discernment" (Phil 1:9; cf. Ps 119:66;[61] 119:100; 1 Cor 2:14–15; 1 John 2:20).

58. See van Deursen, *Psalms I*, chap, 4, and 129–32.
59. See van Deursen, *Psalms I*, 86–90.
60. See van Deursen, *Psalms I*, 133–34.
61. See van Deursen, *Psalms II*, 327–29.

Proverbs 28:26

> Whoever trusts in his own mind is a fool,
> but he who walks in wisdom will be delivered.

This applies to religion as well. What is decisive is not what we judge about ourselves in *our own heart*, but what *God* declares about us in Jesus Christ and in his Word, both for our benefit and for our judgment. Walking in this wisdom can spare you much anxiety and distress, which have darkened many lives along the path of various kinds of subjectivistic religiosity.

After all, the source of true wisdom lies not within us but outside of us. Not in our sick and straying heart but in the fixed order that God has revealed to us in his Word and his other works. Wisdom is then practically another word for piety (on this, see chapter 4).

In that respect, it squarely opposes every form of subjectivism, including religious subjectivism (see our comments on Prov 3:5–6).

In Prov 1–9, Solomon has shown how wholesome this wisdom is for our entire life, and how it can function preventively in combatting all sorts of evil. There is no better life insurance than this wisdom insurance!

Proverbs 28:28

> When the wicked rise to power, people go into hiding;
> but when the wicked perish, the righteous thrive. (NIV)

This is no surprise, since the wicked reject God's Word and thereby overturn the foundations of society. In such a situation, Ps 11:3 asks, "If the foundations are destroyed, what can the righteous do?" For it is a misunderstanding to think that they must always *do* something. If God has withdrawn from the godly their power to make an appeal in the public square, they can better retreat and stay in the background. "Therefore he who is prudent will keep silent in such a time, for it is an evil time" (Amos 5:13). Humble David understood that, and therefore fled from wicked Saul to hide in caves and deserts. Perhaps it was in such circumstances that he prayed Ps 12, "Save, O Lord, for the godly one is gone; for the faithful have vanished from among the children of man" (v. 1).

Our own history shows striking examples of this. In 1560, when our land was groaning under the tyranny of King Philip II, three hundred and fifty men fled across the ice to Emden, which received the nickname "the inn for God's oppressed people." Others fled from our country, through

Germany and Poland to England, where in London the Dutch refugee church Austin Friars can still be found.

One hundred years later, the Huguenots fled to our country, and in that example you can see immediately how the righteous increase when the power of the wicked is snapped. For two centuries the free Republic of the Seven United Netherlands could serve as a refuge destination for those in Europe who were being persecuted for their faith. The Lord Jesus had promised that to them (Mark 10:29-30).

Here are some related proverbs. "When it goes well with the righteous, the city rejoices, and when the wicked perish there are shouts of gladness" (11:10). "When the righteous triumph, there is great glory, but when the wicked rise, people hide themselves" (28:12). "When the righteous increase, the people rejoice, but when the wicked rule, the people groan" (29:2).

Proverbs 29:15

> The rod and reproof give wisdom,
> but a child left to himself brings shame to his mother.

"The intention of man's heart is evil from his youth" (Gen 8:21; cf. Job 14:4; Ps 51:5-6). For that reason, parents must curb the evil in the hearts of their children very early by means of the wall of discipline. The Israelite sages were not thinking, in connection with discipline, first of all of a spanking, but of the guidance that you give through friendly instruction in the fear of the LORD (see our comments on Prov 4). Blessed are the parents who can persevere in this! Blessed are the fathers and mothers who can lead their growing children with a single word. Such obedience, however, generally rests upon the foundation that parents have laid already during the early years in the hearts of their children.

In that period, parents discover the truth of the proverb "Folly is bound up in the heart of a child." During that stage of life, they do not eliminate that folly with words alone! Understanding parents will also act according to the rest of this proverb: "But the rod of discipline drives it far from him" (Prov 22:15; see our comments on this verse). With these words Solomon is not referring only to the rod—perhaps we would identify it as the paddle—but has in view all corporal punishment, from a tweak of the ear to a tap on the fingers to a chore. Modern educators and child psychologists dismiss corporal punishment, but Holy Scripture points often to the blessed function of the rod (see our comments on Prov 13:24; 22:15; 23:13-14; cf. Prov 10:13; 26:3).

Of course, the one administering discipline must know the proper "time and manner" (Eccl 8:5). When raising their child, righteous parents will take into consideration the child's nature and disposition, as well as the limits of the child's ability with regard to good and evil. We discussed this in connection with Prov 22:6. In this context, it seems to us significant that the proverb cited above mentions rod and correction together. In those words we hear the encouragement to let *physical* discipline always be accompanied with rational and serious *verbal* correction (cf. Eph 6:4). In this way, under God's blessing, the pain of the rod and the lesson of punishment can together teach the child wisdom.

The earlier you start with this, the better. We saw that truth in connection with the proverb "Whoever spares the rod hates his son, but he who loves him is diligent to discipline him" (Prov 13:24). Because the nurture of the young child falls especially to the mother, she has the calling to lay the foundations of obedience in the child's heart. Here is one of her greatest and principal tasks. Apparently Solomon saw in his day, as well, that mothers were neglecting this duty. Out of a mistaken love or personal laziness they were leaving their children to themselves. Our proverb is speaking literally about a young person who was "sent away."

From undisciplined children, however, all kinds of things can emerge: undisciplined citizens, unfaithful church members, unfaithful spouses, unreliable coworkers, and so forth. The damage that goes along with this descends on the head of their mothers, however. She is the one, after all, who failed to erect at the appropriate time the restraining wall of life-discipline around her child. She forsook her calling by leaving her young child to him- or herself. In this way mother's little darling became mother's overwhelming shame. The spankings she spared then come down upon her own heart.

Clearly, Scripture is speaking here about a different mother than we hear weeping in Prov 17:25, of whom it is said, "A foolish son is a grief to his father and bitterness to her who bore him." She had indeed disciplined him—at the appropriate times—but he refused to listen. Her final but very powerful means of remedy are God's covenant, and the pleading intercessions that she raises on the basis of that covenant.

Nurture with the rod and with discipline during early youth not only brings about *wisdom* but also promotes spiritual and physical *health*. Children who have grown up unbridled often appear as adults to be a bad match for the inevitable counterpunches that come in life. Discipline teaches a child early to adapt to resistance and to handle disappointments. Mothers who withhold restraining discipline from their children are also eliminating the opportunity to develop a healthy resilience.

According to one American professor of psychiatry, the fear of restraining children has changed modern child-rearing into a desert. And this is the result: We now have a generation of children who have not learned the discipline needed to make it in the world. Out of fear for psychological damage we have all too enthusiastically refused to teach them self-discipline. That deficiency can later give them far more psychological and physical suffering than the rod of discipline in their early youth could ever have caused! The professor concludes with this witticism: "Spare the Freud and save the child!"[62] (See our comments on Prov 13:24 and 22:15.)

Once again we see with this proverb that the fear of the LORD is also medicine for the flesh. You can read more about the connection between godliness and our health in connection with Prov 3:7–8, where we mention other proverbs that deal with this matter.

Proverbs 29:18

> Where there is no prophetic vision the people cast off restraint,
>   but blessed is he who keeps the law.

Whether in this context Solomon had in mind only the Torah of Moses (Genesis–Deuteronomy), or also the *torah* (i.e., instruction) of the sages and prophets, makes little difference. All of this secondary teaching about God and his service rested upon the foundation of the Torah of Moses. That was the source of wisdom and the starting point of prophecy. The echo of Moses resonates throughout the Prophets and the Psalms, into the Apostolic writings.

We have seen more frequently that God through Moses instructed his people not only about religious matters but also about *comprehensive living in his covenant*.[63] So it was that the Torah contained not only prescriptions for sacrifices but also laws pertaining to property, business, marriage, and regulations protecting widows, orphans, sojourners, the poor, even animals. All of these ordinances were supposed to serve to provide God's covenant partner Israel with a righteous society, without class conflict and landlordism. This was to be a society in which wholesome laws were supposed to prevent social extremes and contrasts. After all, if there is one who knows what is good for human living, that is Yahweh, the God of life. Regarding his

---

62. Cited in McMillen, *None of These Diseases*, 124; the professor's name was Dr. Douglas Kelley, from the University of California.

63. See van Deursen, *Psalms I*, 33–34.

statutes he gave this assurance: "The man who [believingly] obeys them will live [happily] by them. I am the LORD" (Lev 18:5 NIV).[64]

This divine covenantal instruction, or *torah*, constituted the foundation of Israel's society.[65] For that reason, Yahweh threatened disasters if Israel forsook that Torah, not only because Israel had to fear God's covenant curse upon all of life (Lev 26; Deut 28) but also because the train of Israel's society would jump the tracks of God's good ordinances, with all of the disastrous consequences of such a derailment. But then Yahweh sent prophets to call Israel back to his Word and covenant. "Back to the Torah! Back to obeying God's covenant!" That was the motto of the prophets, and Yahweh was attempting through their preaching to preserve Israel from punishments that were even more severe.

But it happened that Yahweh was so deeply offended that he silenced the warning voice of prophecy. Or he no longer sent any prophets, or he refused to let Israel understand their preaching. The first occurred in Samuel's youth. At that time, "the word of the LORD was rare" (1 Sam 3:1). The second happened in the days of Amos and Isaiah. At that time, God made it so that his Word could not be found (Amos 8:11–12). At that time, Isaiah with his prophecy made Judah deaf while hearing, and blind while seeing (Isa 6:10–11; cf. 2 Chr 15:3; Ps 74:9).[66]

About such times, Solomon says briefly and concisely, "Where there is no prophetic vision the people cast off restraint." They "run wild." For a nation stands or falls with the proclamation and observance of God's ordinances (Prov 14:34). That had appeared in the time of the judges, which in Solomon's time was relatively fresh in Israel's memory. At that time, Israel "ran wild," all the way to tyranny and sodomy (Judg 19–21). Later, Isaiah saw the society of his day descend into licentiousness. "And the people will oppress one another, every one his fellow and every one his neighbor; the youth will be insolent to the elder, and the despised to the honorable" (Isa 5:15). This is a revolution at its best!

Does not the cause of modern secularism, in fact, of today's global instability, lie precisely here? Europe, once exalted to heavenly heights, has rejected the prophetic word and thereby surrendered to "running wild." If God does not preserve Europe, we are heading with giant strides toward our demise. Does not our society constitute a striking illustration of Solomon's proverb? Is not everything "running wild"? Marriages, families,

---

64. See van Deursen, *Psalms I*, 205.
65. See van Deursen, *Psalms I*, 21–22.
66. See van Deursen, *Psalms II*, 148–49.

morals, fashions, amusement, authority, sense of duty, business, art, and jurisprudence?

But God's Word had predicted this to us: "But understand this, that in the last days there will come times of difficulty. For people will be lovers of self, lovers of money, proud, arrogant, abusive, disobedient to their parents, ungrateful, unholy, heartless, unappeasable, slanderous, without self-control, brutal, not loving good, treacherous, reckless, swollen with conceit, lovers of pleasure rather than lovers of God, having the appearance of godliness, but denying its power" (2 Tim 3:1–5a).

Has not Europe sown the weeds of its unbelief everywhere in the world? If it had stayed more closely to the Torah, the world would look very different. Then we would not be seeing the racial strife that has arisen from our slave trading. But now the entire problematic of rich and poor countries, foreign aid, doing "justice," the authority crisis, the lethal struggle between socialism and capitalism—all of these seem to be unsolvable because people refuse to listen to the prophetic Word of God. And without prophecy, a nation descends into anarchy.

"But blessed is he who keeps the law [Heb., *torah*]," says the second line of Prov 29:18. We could interpret it this way: "Blessed is the *nation* that keeps the Law." That is a scriptural truth (Ps 33:12; see our comments on Prov 11:11). Our country and our continent owe our inestimable blessings to the wholesome power of the Word of God. A comparison with countries that have not had the benefits of Christianity can still open our eyes to the many fruits of the influence of the Word that is coming to an end in our society.

But Solomon does not mention the word *nation* in the second line, so we could perhaps better go with what he says literally, "*He* who keeps the law, blessed is he!" In that connection we can think of the remnant,[67] that in times of general covenant abandonment may nonetheless still understand and keep the Word of God. The poet of Ps 119 lived in such a time,[68] and he too assured us, "Blessed are those whose way is blameless, who walk in the law of the LORD!" (Ps 119:1). That can occur even when, as a general condition, there "is no prophecy."

Indisputably, the righteous must often suffer along with the wicked in such times. Therefore we cannot turn Solomon's *mashals* into ironclad rules that are supposed to be valid always and everywhere. Nevertheless, God desires to extend to his godly remnant a variety of blessings. God's laws are unto life, and those who keep them should discover blessing in doing so.

---

67. See van Deursen, *Psalms I*, 74–81.
68. See van Deursen, *Psalms II*, 314–20.

Reviewing everything once more, we have every reason to pray the ancient church prayer, "O Lord, do not withdraw from us your word and Spirit!" That is the best means for healing and binding together every life relationship. If that does not help, then nothing else will help. Not even in churches that are "running wild." May our prayers ascend on behalf of the coming generation, for what will become of our children if there is no more prophecy? Will there be religion, but no summoning back to the Word of God's covenant? Then far better to live as a church in the catacombs with prophecy than in a cathedral without prophecy!

Proverbs 29:20

> Do you see a man who is hasty in his words?
> There is more hope for a fool than for him.

Later Jewish wisdom emphasizes the same point: "All my days have I grown up among the wise and I have not found anything better for a person than silence," said Rabbi Simeon (AD 150). Rabbi Akiva (AD 125) taught, "There are seven things that characterize a boor, and seven that characterize a wise man. A wise man does not speak before one who is greater than him in wisdom or age. He does not interrupt his fellow's words. He does not hasten to answer. His questions are on the subject and his answers to the point. He responds to first things first and to latter things later. Concerning what he did not hear, he says, 'I did not hear.' He concedes to the truth. With the boor, the reverse of all these is the case."[69]

Proverbs 29:25

> The fear of man lays a snare,
> but whoever trusts in the LORD is safe.

The first line actually says, "*Shivering* before people." The notion is one of *quaking, trembling* before others. Who has never experienced this? Even the greatest in the kingdom of God have.

Yahweh had ceremoniously promised that Sarah would be the mother of a great nation. In spite of this, Abraham was ensnared by the fear that Pharaoh could take his pretty wife Sarah from him and put him to death. For that reason he surrendered to the fear of man: "Say that you are my

---

69. Gemser, *De Spreuken van Salamo*, 146.

sister" (Gen 12:10-20). Later he trembled for the same reason before King Abimelech (Gen 20).

Peter certainly was no meek soul, for fearful people in those days did not dare to disclose that they were disciples of Jesus (John 7:13; 19:38). Nevertheless, this tough fisherman quaked before a servant girl. And that fear of another person struck him a very fatal blow. For he insisted, with verbal intensity, concerning his Master whom he so intimately loved, "Girl, I do not know that man!"

Later, he once again stepped into a dangerous snare on account of fearing other people. The apostle was lodging with the church in Antioch, when on a given day brothers from Jerusalem visited him. On this occasion, Peter once again was burdened with the fear of man. What would those Jerusalem believers say about the fact that as a Jew he was sitting at the same table with Gentile believers to eat unclean food? Out of fear of those Jewish brothers, he began to eat kosher again. But that fear of man struck him another dangerous blow, for now he was giving the impression—even as an apostle!—that there were in fact two kinds of believers: first class Christians who lived as Jews, and second class Christians from among the Gentiles who ate unclean food. Because of this undermining of the gospel and of Christian freedom, Paul had to give him a public reprimand (Gal 2).

But who would criticize Abraham and Peter harshly for these failures? "Dare to be a Daniel, dare to stand alone!" But that isn't easy. It is not easy toward the unbelieving world, and toward the religious world it is even less so. Fear of other people can whisper to us so seductively, "Is that really necessary? Think about your status. What will others say?" At that point, we are fearing other people more than we fear the Lord.

"But whoever trusts in the Lord is safe." You see this magnificently with David. As a tender lad, he faced Goliath, a fellow standing more than nine feet tall, with a helmet on his head, a shield of one hundred seventy-five pounds, and a spear that weighed more than a weaver's beam. David had only a slingshot and some stones. But he confessed his trust in God, "You come to me with sword and spear and javelin; but I come to you in the name of the Lord of hosts, the God of the armies of Israel, whom you have defied" (1 Sam 17:45). You know the rest of the story.

Whom else could we put forward as an example? Moses before Pharaoh? Samuel before Saul? Hezekiah before Sennacherib? Jeremiah and Baruch before the rulers? Daniel before Nebuchadnezzar and Darius? Let us look to the one who was perfect in his trusting in God, and completely free from fear of people: our Lord Jesus Christ.

He was constantly surrounded by Pharisees and Sadducees. Filled with religious hatred—and no hatred is more intense—they lay in wait against him to find a pretext for a death sentence. Nevertheless, he never compromised the truth. He attacked Pharisaical self-righteousness and Sadducean leniency without fear or respect of persons. The result was that when he hung on the cross, even his enemies had to admit in their scorn, "He trusts in God; let God deliver him now, if he desires him" (Matt 27:43).

A disciple is not above his master. Therefore the Lord warned, "I tell you, my friends, do not fear those who kill the body, and after that have nothing more that they can do. But I will warn you whom to fear: fear him who, after he has killed, has authority to cast into hell. Yes, I tell you, fear him!" (Luke 12:4–5; cf. Isa 51:12–16; 2 Tim 1:7).

4. SOME PROVERBS OF AGUR, THE SON OF JAKEH (PROV 30)

We don't know who this Agur was, but he must have been a humble man, someone who thought very highly of God and very little of himself (see Prov 30:1–4). He sensed deeply that we know God only because he has *revealed* himself to us in his Word. Agur talked about that very respectfully. That too belongs to our wisdom for daily living: living constantly under the realization of the purity, the reliability, the wisdom, and the perfection of God's Word.

That is what Agur teaches us in the following proverb.

Proverbs 30:5–6

> Every word of God proves true;
>   he is a shield to those who take refuge in him.
> Do not add to his words,
>   lest he rebuke you and you be found a liar.

The psalmists also praise God's Word this way: "The words of the LORD are pure words, like silver refined in a furnace on the ground, purified seven times" (Ps 12:6). The poet sang in Ps 119, "Your promises have been thoroughly tested, and your servant loves them" (v. 140 NIV).[70] In fact, his psalm is one chain of praises of the Word of God (cf. Ps 18:30; 19:7–8; 33:4; 56:4, 10; 2 Tim 3:16; 2 Pet 1:20).

But God, the Speaker of this Word, "never lies" (Titus 1:2; Heb 6:18). Therefore Agur says that "*every* word of God" is pure, unmixed with lies

---

70. For an overview, see van Deursen, *Psalms II*, 321.

(which is why the Bible simply has nothing to "demythologize"). This "word of our God will stand forever" (Isa 40:8; cf. Matt 24:35). It is our only certainty as we live on earth. Because the eternal God has spoken it, and because he is the true one, therefore he is a faithful shield for those who take refuge in him (Prov 30:5).

Agur appears to have known very well that God's Word, from beginning to end, is a *covenant book*. It is the document of God's covenants with his people. First, the old covenant with Israel, but, since Pentecost, the new covenant as well, with believers from the Gentiles, like us. Every word of Holy Scripture is covenantally determined and colored. Take, for example, the term *shield*. Naturally you can think of the familiar defensive weapon used in antiquity, but in the language of ancient Near Eastern covenants, it is a fixed term for the Suzerain. "I am your Shield," God said to Abraham (Gen 15:1), and Abraham surely heard the language of covenant in that term, for that is how vassals addressed the great king with whom they had made a treaty: "You are my shield" (cf. the Ten Words). The Jews called the book of Deuteronomy—which is a covenant document through and through, filled with covenant stipulations—"These are the *words*"!

In the world of that day, people considered alterations in the text of a treaty document to be scandalous. After the ratification of such a document, people obviously did not add to or subtract from it. Tinkering with a *covenant text* was viewed as *covenant breaking*. This applied even more strongly, of course, to God's covenant. Therefore Israel understood very well that Moses was speaking covenant language when, in Deut 4:2, he spoke as Yahweh's agent, "You shall not add to the word that I command you, nor take from it, that you may keep the commandments of the LORD your God that I command you" (cf. Deut 12:32).

Agur sounds the same warning, also in covenantally tinted wording. "Do not add to *his words*" means "Do not add to *his covenant stipulations*." Agur is in fact warning against introducing high-handed alterations in the stipulations of the blessings and curses of God's covenant. For violating covenant documents, as we said, comes down to violating the covenant itself!

This respect applies to us today even more with regard to the completed Holy Scripture. If we read it as it presents itself to us—as the document of the old and new covenant of God—then we will hear a covenantal echo in the threat with which it ends: "I warn everyone who hears the words of the prophecy of this book: if anyone adds to them, God will add to him the plagues described in this book, and if anyone takes away from the words of the book of this prophecy, God will take away his share in the tree of life and in the holy city, which are described in this book" (Rev 22:18–19).

Nevertheless God's people have often committed this wickedness.

Jeroboam, the son of Nebat, added his own religious inventions to God's covenant stipulations (1 Kgs 12:25–32). He was reproved on account of this (1 Kgs 13–14), and was shown to be "a liar," someone who led God's people astray.[71] But that happened also during Jesus' life on earth. "In vain do they worship me, teaching as doctrines the commandments of men" (Matt 15:9). "So for the sake of your tradition you have made void the word of God," Jesus accused the Pharisees and scribes (Matt 15:6).

Autonomous human knowledge always "puffs up," and, if in addition it is mixed with knowledge of Scripture, this often constitutes a source of argument and divisions among God's people. It is striking that, after discussing the splits with the church in Corinth, Paul recalls what at the time was perhaps a well-known maxim: "Do not go beyond what is written" (1 Cor 4:6 NIV). For it is precisely additions to God's Word that in many cases eventually injure the faith of the church.

That is what medieval church history shows in a gripping manner. At that time, people were adding the philosophy of Aristotle to the knowledge of Holy Scripture, and that mixture robbed the churches of the key of knowledge. Until in his mercy, in the sixteenth century, God had compassion on his people and taught them to live once again by Scripture alone. At that time, the Reformed church confessed in Belgic Confession, article 7,

> For since it is forbidden to "add unto or take away anything from the Word of God," it does thereby evidently appear that the doctrine thereof is most perfect and complete in all respects.
>
> Neither may we consider any writings of men, however holy these men may have been, of equal value with those divine Scriptures, nor ought we to consider custom, or the great multitude, or antiquity, or succession of time and persons, or councils, decree or statutes, as of equal value with the truth of God, since the truth is above all: "for all men are of themselves liars, and more vain than vanity itself."[72]

The publisher of the Dutch States Translation (SV) placed Prov 30:6, among other passages, immediately after the preface of their Bible translation! It did this in order to warn every Bible reader in advance against any tinkering, whether clothed with piety or not, with the covenant document that the Holy Scripture in fact is.

For the danger of making high-handed additions to God's Word is a continuing threat, in various ways. Luther himself had many dealings with sectarians who came with their "revelations" that supposedly proceeded

---

71. See van Deursen, *Psalms I*, 114.
72. Dennison, *Reformed Confessions*, 2.427.

from "the Spirit" apart from God's Word, and the same phenomenon occurs everywhere today. But we can still learn from Agur that we do not have the right to add Rev 23 and 24 to Holy Scripture. Recall Rev 22:18–19. Scripture is complete. And recall Agur: Add nothing to it!

For this reason, we must be on guard for the theologians. Calvin warned emphatically against *speculations* with regard to the knowledge of God.[73] Scientific-theological handling of Holy Scripture, and systematizing its content, conceal no small dangers. How easily the theologian manages in his thinking to go *further* than God permits, given the limits to our knowledge of him that God has established in Scripture. At that point, the danger of forbidden additions raises its head! Or the systematizing scientific thinking distorts the practical-prophetic language of Scripture in such a way that it shortchanges the richness of Scripture. Unintentionally or not, it seeks to make the purpose of the gospel more "acceptable" to an arrogant humanity. At that point, the danger of forbidden reductions raises its head!

The apostle Paul warned Timothy about the dangers of so-called Gnosticism or knowledge (1 Tim 6:20). In that connection he identified the recurring consequence of any gnostic-theological handling of the Word of God: "irreverent babble" (1 Tim 6:20; 2 Tim 2:16). Of what use is that to a modern person?

Therefore we are on the safest ground when we listen to Peter: "Whoever speaks, [let him speak] as one who speaks *oracles of God*" (1 Pet 4:11). Return to the language of Holy Scripture! The closer we remain to it, the more perfectly we will speak.

Proverbs 30:7–9

> Two things I ask of you;
>   deny them not to me before I die:
> Remove far from me falsehood and lying;
>   give me neither poverty nor riches;
>   feed me with the food that is needful for me,
>   lest I be full and deny you
>   and say, "Who is the LORD?"
>   or lest I be poor and steal
>   and profane the name of my God.

---

73. Calvin, *Institutes*, 1.4.1, contains but one of many such warnings.

Precisely because Agur acknowledged God's Word as the only perfect truth, he feared two dangers: (1) falsehood and lying, and (2) poverty and riches. For that reason, he prayed that God would preserve him from these.

With falsehood and a lying tongue, Scripture has more in view than only ordinary lies, whereby a person presents twisted facts. It is, in fact, referring to all words, deeds, things, and people upon which eventually you cannot rely and in which you cannot place your trust. So Agur was praying not only, "Preserve me from lies like false accusations, perjury, and deceptive business practices," but also, "Do not let me put faith in false notions about God and his Word" (cf. v. 6).[74]

His second petition consists of three parts: Give me (1) no poverty, (2) no riches, and (3) simply my daily bread. Agur had the same humble spirit that David had, who prayed, "O LORD, my heart is not lifted up; my eyes are not raised too high; I do not occupy myself with things too great and too marvelous for me" (Ps 131:1). "Keep back your servant also from presumptuous sins; let them not have dominion over me!" (Ps 19:13). Because he feared these things, he sought to be continually preserved from poverty as well as riches.

For poverty is nothing but catastrophe (see our comments on Prov 10:15). One has no money to be able to buy life's basic necessities! Agur was afraid that he would then assault God's name (i.e., God's Word, the narrative of God's great deeds), and perhaps fall into stealing. Only God knows how many of today's atheists have descended from great-grandparents who in the 1800s were driven by their poverty into unbelief. "How can God tolerate having one person living in a palace and another subsisting in a shack?"

Regrettably, many of them did not hear in the church that God has never wanted those great extremes to exist among his people, but has attempted to prevent them! He had the land (the means of production) of Canaan divided honestly. He stipulated that in the fiftieth year a Jubilee was to be held, for the purpose of balancing the imbalanced social relationships A Torah full of wholesome ordinances he had lifted up as a protective shield over the poor (cf. our comments on Prov 3:27–28 about the poor person's God-given *right* to assistance).[75] But when Christians break that shield, what then?

At that point, contrary to what the adage claims, our emergency needs do not always teach us to pray, but at times to curse. Especially when preachers and pastors walk around in slums with placards saying, "The Lord sends it, the Lord knows it, and the Lord will turn it." At that point, the

---

74. See van Deursen, *Psalms I*, 113–18.
75. See van Deursen, *Psalms I*, 57.

seed of socialists and communists does not fall in stony soil. How great a temptation arises at that point to bid farewell to God and his service. When you together with your young children work your fingers to the bone from early morning until late at night, and you still suffer bitter poverty! For that reason, Agur was so wise in praying that God would preserve him from that. He added, "Before I die"—in other words, for his entire life.

Let us be sensitive to the fact that God could plunge our prosperous world into such bitter poverty in no time at all. Well-heeled Dutchmen could not foresee in 1925 that within twenty years they would be walking more than ninety miles for a sack of wheat or to obtain green peas, as happened in 1944. At that time, Lam 4:4 was fulfilled: "The children beg for food, but no one gives to them." Would *we* at that point keep God's name holy and not end up stealing? Asaph acknowledged that, when he saw the prosperity of the wicked and his own distress, "my feet had almost stumbled, my steps had nearly slipped" (Ps 73:2–15; cf. Deut 8:11–17; Job 21:7–15; Isa 8:21).

But Agur was just as afraid of *riches*, for great temptations come with that as well! (See our comments on Prov 10:15; cf. 14:20; 18:16; 18:23; 19:4; 19:6.) Unnoticed, the roles are reversed, and the owner comes to be possessed by his own wealth. Agur feared that he would then not remain humbly dependent on God, but would feel "satiated" and deny him. It is not easy, when you can buy everything that your heart desires, to feel *dependent* on God! "But those who desire to be rich fall into temptation, into a snare, into many senseless and harmful desires that plunge people into ruin and destruction" (1 Tim 6:9). At that point we are called to believe that God has given us all of this "to do good, to be rich in good works, to be generous and ready to share" (1 Tim 6:17–19). With a view to the many people who are possessed by their possessions, our Lord said, "How difficult it will be for those who have wealth to enter the kingdom of God!" (Mark 10:23).

Nehemiah confessed that Israel had fallen away from God *in part* through material prosperity (Neh 9:25–26). How many within Christianity today have turned away from God and his Word, because they were "satiated"? For that reason, Agur prayed for "the food that is needful for me." Later, our Lord Jesus Christ would talk about "our daily bread." This is the middle way between riches and poverty. What this means concretely depends, of course, on the time and place in which we are living. In 2016 the middle way is different than in 1916, and in our country it is different than in the Third World. Agur would have been praying for suitable life sustenance according to the standards of the time and place when and where God has put us.

In view of his godliness and wisdom, Agur was apparently free of greed and covetousness. Perhaps because he knew very well that our happiness does not depend on riches. His petition for "the food that is needful for me" shows that he knew contentment. Agur knew that God determines the standard of our prosperity, and that often this is connected to the measure of our *gifts* and *capacities*, which are also determined by God. Blessed is the one who submits to that divine ordination, even as the apostle Paul wrote, "I have learned in whatever situation I am to be content. I know how to be brought low, and I know how to abound" (Phil 4:11–12; cf. Heb 13:5). "But if we have food and clothing, with these we will be content" (1 Tim 6:8).

13

Proverbs 31:10–31
Hymn to a Proficient Wife[1]

DON'T YOU THINK THAT is remarkable? The only occupation about which the Bible sings a hymn is that of homemaker! More than a thousand pages are filled with the work of prophets, priests, and kings, but one of them contains a hymn to what she accomplishes every day. Apparently the LORD God thought it was necessary and not beneath the dignity of Holy Scripture that someone would write—and do so down to the smallest details—about what the God-fearing Israelite wife had to accomplish every day.

Once again we see that the Bible is not the kind of religious book in which only religious matters are discussed, like the forgiveness of sins, prayer, and singing spiritual songs. For Scripture praises that wife not because she is occupied from morning until evening with religious activities, like a monk or a nun, but because she maintains an orderly home so proficiently, and, in addition, does her best to earn some income besides. And what is the most wonderful of all? When you do that year after year as a believing wife, then Scripture calls you "a woman who fears the LORD"!

What are the activities of such a woman? You can see this in the portrait of her that an unknown sage has drawn. In twenty-two verses you get the most beautiful and complete description of a good, believing wife who, through her wisdom and proficiency, is a blessing to her family, a credit to her church, and a pillar of society.

---

1. Translator's Note: This chapter, authored by Frans van Deursen, did not appear in the Dutch original, and has been added to this translated volume.

The poet sketches a portrait of a wise Israelite woman as she would have lived three thousand years ago. His painting naturally shows ancient Near Eastern colors and hues. Since that time, irreversible social and cultural developments have occurred. But when we take these into account, this poem continues to be a relevant didactic poem despite differences in time and culture.

This is surely important now in a time when the evil one is directing such severe attacks against Christian marriage and family life, and he often sows confusion among Christians about the relationship between husband, wife, and children. In so doing, the foundations of society are being dislodged. In this situation, this didactic poem can open our eyes to God's wholesome order for marriage and family.

Our young men should study this portrait in Prov 31 attentively. It can teach them what kind of young ladies they should look for when they go in search of a godly, wise wife. After all, some young men can be rather blind! They pass up proficient young ladies who fear God and with whom they can be happy in prosperity and adversity, and they stare themselves blind at "beauty and charm." But woe to them when their eyes are opened later. And our young ladies should take as their example not movie stars but this wise woman of Prov 31.

> An excellent wife who can find?
> She is far more precious than jewels. (Prov 31:10)

The point is not that such a woman is virtually nonexistent, for many of them function competently (cf. v. 29). But you have to search for them, for they are extraordinarily rare. You can find such a woman only among those who fear the LORD (v. 30). This kind of woman is as valuable as wisdom itself, which is more valuable than jewels (3:15; 8:11). Whoever finds such a woman "obtains favor from the LORD" (see our comments on 18:22). She is a gift of God and "the crown of her husband" (12:4), for whom he may thank God often. Young men who would like to find this kind of wife must pray earnestly to God for that. Similarly, godly parents act wisely when in due time they, too, ask the LORD to provide such a wife for their sons.

> The heart of her husband trusts in her,
> and he will have no lack of gain. (Prov 31:11)

The Hebrew says literally, "the heart of her *ba'al* [lord, owner]." The point is not that she is his spineless slave, who must be kept in submission with a whip. The following verses show something quite different. There is no indication here that she would feel inferior to her husband and try to wrestle free from his authority. Nor do we see anything to do with inhibitions or frustrations due to restrictive stipulations. On the contrary, for this woman being a wife is obviously a delight.

In the term *baʿal* we do hear an echo of God's order in which the husband is appointed as the head of his wife. A man should not underestimate the serious responsibility that God thereby places upon the husband! As her head, he is called to provide for her and to protect her *as his own body*! As head of the family he also bears the ultimate responsibility toward God. She in turn exercises authority on his behalf over the children and domestic personnel.

This is not "typically Old Testament" or ancient Near Eastern, for the New Testament teaches the same divine order: "But I want you to understand that the head of every man is Christ, the head of a wife is her husband, and the head of Christ is God" (1 Cor 11:3; cf. Eph 5:22-24). Husbands must love their wives "as Christ loved the church," (Eph 5:25; Col 3:19). When they do this, they cannot possibly become domestic tyrants, just as the husband of this proficient wife is not.

On the contrary, she has his heart and is his comrade, his confidant, one with whom he can completely be himself and with whom he can talk about everything (cf. v. 26). Whenever he works outside his home, he can safely leave domestic matters in her hand, without fear that she will perpetrate follies. He allows her to be fully independent and gives her his full trust. She does not embarrass such confidence. What follows in this poem shows the manifold kinds of benefit that she provides through her activities, and how highly he values her because of that.

> She does him good, and not harm,
> all the days of her life. (Prov 31:12)

As his helper, created by God and suited to him (Gen 2:18), she brings him only happiness and no unhappiness. That is how she began her marriage as a young woman, and that is how she continues as the mother of adult sons (Prov 31:28). And if she outlives him, she continues to do well by him as she provides for his children, stewards his wealth, and honors his good name. In her marriage, she is not self-centered, focused on her own personal welfare, but she is primarily oriented toward *giving* and not toward getting. In the next verses we read how she devotes all her gifts on behalf of her husband and his interests.

She is undoubtedly stimulated by the trust and esteem (v. 29) that he gives her. The word *love* is not mentioned in this poem. But in every line it displays the ripened fruits of the love with which husband and wife inspire one another back and forth in surprising harmony.

> She seeks wool and flax,
> and works with willing hands. (Prov 31:13)

The Israelite wife could not buy any ready-made clothes. She had to make all the family's clothes by hand and without a sewing machine, from wool and flax. Before she could spin these into yarn, she had to do a lot by way of preparation. Especially linen over- and undergarments were of high quality. Sturdy ropes and lampshades were made out of flax. This wife did all of this handily and cheerfully, literally, "to the satisfaction of her hands" (cf. Col 3:23).

> She is like the ships of the merchant;
> she brings her food from afar. (Prov 31:14)

In addition to her domestic qualities she has something of the entrepreneurial spirit of a businessman, who sends his ships on distant voyages to obtain expensive cargo. No difficulty is too great for her when it involves supplying the life necessities of her family. If necessary, she obtains these necessities from distant places, if conditions there are better than nearby. Some young men and grown men have too narrow a perspective: "Housekeeping? Cooking meals? Doing the laundry? There is nothing to those chores!" They harbor such an illusion despite the reality that those tasks demand a great deal more organizational talent, economic insight, self-discipline, industriousness, handiness, physical strength, good taste, and creativity than many an outside job!

> She rises while it is yet night
> and provides food for her household
> and portions for her maidens. (Prov 31:15)

She is definitely not lazy, for the night is hardly finished and she has already risen from her bed to provide her family and domestic servants with food. For in an Israelite home, baking was a daily activity. Exhausting work, for the barley or wheat needed first to be ground into meal with a hand grinder or a stone. Only then could she proceed to bake her cakes.

This order and regularity itself, on which her entire family life depended, already testifies to her expertise. She also taught her children from their youth to become accustomed to this. In this, too, her fear of the Lord was manifest, for obviously he too observes fixed times for this and that. You need look only at his work in nature and the regularity of the seasons, and recall that he too loves cleanliness (Deut 23:13).

> She considers a field and buys it;
> with the fruit of her hands she plants a vineyard. (Prov 31:16)

Apparently an Israelite woman could function quite independently, though she would not have done so entirely apart from her husband. Excavations have brought to light that this was the case also among the Sumerians, the Babylonians, and the Assyrians. This Israelite wife looked beyond the walls of her house, and had her own financial means at her disposal. Or did she manage her husband's finances? After all, a sizeable investment of activity was needed for planting a vineyard (Isa 5:1-2).

> She dresses herself with strength
> and makes her arms strong. (Prov 31:17)

She digs into her work with gusto and rolls up her sleeves (cf. v. 25). She is not afraid of heavy work.

> She perceives that her merchandise is profitable.
> Her lamp does not go out at night. (Prov 31:18)

Under her capable leadership, everything runs smoothly. A telltale sign of this order and prosperity is the small oil lamp. Usually this was a saucer in which the potter with his thumb and forefinger had pinched a lip on which rested the pit. Most often it contained olive oil. It had to burn night and day, serving also as an igniter fire for cooking, since matches had not yet been invented. If through neglect the oil was not supplied and the lamp's fire had gone out, one had to find an elaborate way to reignite the flame. But under her management, the lamp was always burning.

> She puts her hands to the distaff,
> and her hands hold the spindle. (Prov 31:19)

The distaff was a long stick around which the thread was wound. The spool was a round staff or iron. Originally spindles were nothing more than a pair of sticks, between which threads were woven horizontally. The interwoven threads were inserted by hand, after which one would compress them with a piece of wood. Weaving was typically women's work.

They produced mainly woolen items. For a coarser weave, they also used goat and camel hair. With these they made tents, bags, mourning garments, and thick coats for shepherds (cf. Matt 3:4). This God-fearing Israelite woman would never weave wool and linen together, however. For the LORD had forbidden that, as a symbolic reminder of Israel's separation from the pagans, and as an inducement to keep far away from their abominable lifestyle (Deut 22:11; cf. Lev 19:19).

> She opens her hand to the poor
> and reaches out her hands to the needy. (Prov 31:20)

She is not only industrious but also compassionate and generous. For she acts according to God's command regarding the poor: "You shall give to him freely. . . . You shall open wide your hand to your brother, to the needy and to the poor, in your land" (Deut 15:10–11). Although she is a spick-and-span homemaker, her interests extend beyond the limited world of her family, and the poverty and misery outside her home do not escape her observant glance.

> She is not afraid of snow for her household,
> for all her household are clothed in scarlet. (Prov 31:21)

Careless wives can be surprised by the sudden arrival of cold temperatures, but this proficient wife does not need to fear the arrival of snow. With time to spare she has supplied her entire household with warm and beautiful clothes. Everyone is wearing scarlet, a light red dyed, fine wool fabric, whereby one recognized affluent people (cf. 2 Sam 1:24; Jer 4:30).

> She makes bed coverings for herself;
> her clothing is fine linen and purple. (Prov 31:22)

In the heart of even the poorest women God has placed the need and creativity for keeping her house clean and for creating a unique atmosphere there. In that regard, the ancient Near Eastern wife was no different than a modern apartment dweller. Even today, Eastern women make tapestries that Western women use for decorating their homes. For that purpose this lady also made colorful "blankets," which could have included quilts and handwoven tapestries.

Her good taste was evident from the beautiful clothing that she herself wore. She was dressed in fine linen and purple. In ancient Israel, people were also familiar with "harlot's attire" (Prov 7:10), but the outward appearance of this godly Israelite woman radiated feminine dignity. In that regard, she is the counterpart of many modern women, who dress lasciviously and shamelessly.

But with her, beauty and morality, taste and fashion, go hand in hand (cf. 1 Pet 3:3–4). That, too, shows that she fears the LORD. A Christian young lady who follows her example can be engaged preservatively by means of her mode of dress wherever God places her. It depends on her whether the good morals in our country will continue to be preserved, or disappear altogether. "You are the salt of the earth" (Matt 5:13).

> Her husband is known in the gates
> when he sits among the elders of the land. (Prov 31:23)

In the cool spaces of the city gate, the heart of society's life is beating (see our comments on 1:20–21 and 8:2–3). There the Israelite conducted business, talked with his friends, made agreements, sought companionship, and there the elders exercised jurisprudence and looked after the interests of the city. In this civic government her husband is a well-known and respected figure (cf. Job 29:7–11). But this honored position he owed in part to her. Thanks to her care of his private interests, he can devote himself to matters of public interest (cf. Prov 31:11). His honor is part of her honor.

> She makes linen garments and sells them;
> she delivers sashes to the merchant. (Prov 31:24)

She also has an instinct for business. She not only sees to it that her family is wearing good and beautiful clothes (vv. 13, 21) but wearing her own self-made garments, she conducts business. She makes luxurious items like linen garments (presumably fine undergarments, Isa 3:23) and leather or woven belts that she has decorated. Itinerant merchants want to offer her a good price for her goods, to sell them in the world market in Tyre. The profit that she earns she invests in real estate: a field or a vineyard (Prov 31:16).

To do this, her husband generously provides her the necessary opportunity (cf. vv. 14, 16, 18a). Not that she is resisting him in an unspiritual manner, for she has no need to compete with him or overshadow him. She is and remains his wife in the fullest sense. Societies that withhold from women these opportunities for development are thereby doing great damage to themselves.

> Strength and dignity are her clothing,
> and she laughs at the time to come. (Prov 31:25)

Although she does provide them for herself, it is not her outward appearance and clothing that make the greatest impression. Whether she is smart we are not told. She makes an impression through the inner strength and beauty that radiate from her entire appearance, or through "the hidden person of the heart" (cf. 1 Pet 3:4). You recognize that strength in the carefree laugh with which she talks about tomorrow. She has already made the necessary preparations with time to spare, so that she fears no unpleasant surprises in her work.

> She opens her mouth with wisdom,
> and the teaching of kindness is on her tongue. (Prov 31:26)

Thoughtful speech belongs, according to Proverbs, to the highest wisdom. That is how you maintain good relationships This woman practices this everyday. What she says and how she says it both testify to her wisdom. When necessary, she instructs, rebukes, and warns her children and domestic servants in a gentle and tactful manner. For that reason, the wise men often said, "My son, do not forget your mother's teaching" (cf. Prov 1:8; 6:20). Long after she closed her eyes for good, her life lessons can continue to spread blessing: "Mother used to say . . ." Such a wife is "the crown of her husband" (12:4). He likes to ask her opinion and to listen to her wise counsel. We considered the portrait of her counterpart, a quarrelsome, moody wife, in connection with Prov 21:9.

> She looks well to the ways of her household
> and does not eat the bread of idleness. (Prov 31:27)

Although she conducts business on a limited scale (vv. 16, 24), she does not on that account neglect her primary calling. While she collaborates industriously with her servants, she pays close attention to the course of events in her home. Someone has properly coined the modern title for every competent homemaker: household engineer! Not many occupations are as variegated as this one. In a single person she combines something of a pedagogue, economist, nutritionist, interior designer, counselor, catechist, nurse, seamstress, and social worker.

> Her children rise up and call her blessed;
> her husband also, and he praises her:
> "Many women have done excellently,
> but you surpass them all." (Prov 31:28–29)

Her grown sons and daughters do not consider it something automatic that their mother has everything under control at home. Now and then, as at a family commemoration, they spontaneously stand up to praise her. What gifts of head, heart, and hands she has received! They give audible expression of their gratitude for her faithful care, her wise counsel, her example, and her love. She is a mother to be proud of! They are well aware "parents are the pride of their children" (Prov 17:6b NIV).

Regrettably, some husbands appear to be blind to the accomplishments of their wives. With gross injustice they wound her by criticizing or denigrating her work. They never come to the point of openly esteeming her work, and thereby cause her much hidden sorrow.

But this husband does not carelessly ignore the accomplishments of his wife. On the contrary, he is very aware of the fact that she represents his interests splendidly. He sees that what he enjoys in his home is not the case everywhere. His wise wife builds her house (Prov 14:1). He recognizes and acknowledges her talents and the zeal with which she employs them. He hold her is high esteem, both in his heart and with his lips Now and then he says aloud, "There are many good wives, but you are the best of them all!" Such words never annoy her, and always warm her heart! (For the power of gentle words, see our comments on Prov 12:25 and 16:24.)

This praise also testifies to his wisdom. As we have said, the word *love* does not appear in this poem, but high esteem is an essential component of love, and this is what he generously gives to her! From this we see that he loves her very much. He realizes that a marriage does not survive automatically, but that spouses must work at it for their entire lives. Before the apostles had written it, the spirit of Christ has already taught him, "Husbands, love your wives, and do not be harsh with them" (Col 3:19); "Show honor to her" (cf. 1 Pet 3:7; cf. Eph 5:25–33). God's order for marriage (see our comments on v. 11) keeps him from exercising tyranny, and for her this order is no burden, but a longing.

> Charm is deceitful, and beauty is vain,
> > but a woman who fears the LORD is to be praised. (Prov 31:30)

Now the poet himself takes the floor in order to identify her most important quality. He doesn't tell us if he has in view a smart woman. Scripture does not despise feminine beauty. It tells us that Sarah, Rebekah, Rachel, Abigail, Bathsheba, and Esther were beautiful in appearance. But the wise men did warn their young readers never to desire a woman on account of her outward beauty, because that can seriously deceive you as a man.

Good looks and godliness do not always go together. An attractive appearance can bring to mind a gold ring in a pig's snout (see our comments on Prov 11:22). Many a man who was blind to that has brought great damage to himself. "Do not desire her beauty in your heart" (6:25). "Turn away your eyes from a shapely woman, and do not gaze at beauty belonging to another; many have been seduced by a woman's beauty, and by it passion is kindled like a fire" (Sir 9:8; cf. chapter 9 above, section 3.3). Moreover, physical beauty is as transitory and fleeting as a mist, and like the most beautiful flower, it too is doomed to fade.

So the person who must be praised is not the beauty queen on TV, but the woman who fears the LORD and submits to his order for being a woman. What does this mean for a married woman? That in her day and culture, she must follow the example of the wife in Prov 31. All the activity of this wife is rooted in her fear of the LORD. Her respect for her husband, the support and comradeship that she offers him, her care for their children, her warm heart for those in distress, her industry and wisdom, her use of time and money, are all motivated by her respect for the Creator of the family and for the fundamental principles that he has established for being a wife. To the eye of a believing husband, these supply a charm that is not a threat, and an unfading grace that blossoms all the way into her old age.

> Give her of the fruit of her hands,
> and let her works praise her in the gates. (Prov 31:31)

Such a wife deserves a sizeable portion of the wealth that the family has acquired through her care and industry. The satisfaction that she experiences from making her garments and clothing (v. 22) returns to her. If you meet such a woman, do not withhold from her your acknowledgement and esteem. Her husband and sons praise her (vv. 28–29), but in the city gate as well, where everyone meets everybody (see our comments on v. 23), the entire city lifts up a song of praise about her. When you see the ornate shirt that she has woven for her husband, then her work praises its maker.

Were this husband and wife perfect? No, since in all of world history there has been only one *perfect* marriage: that of Adam and Eve before the fall. At that point, she had a perfect husband, and he had a perfect wife, but since then no one else has had such a spouse. Between imperfect people, no perfect marriage is possible any longer.

But the example of the competent wife and her husband that we find in Prov 31 can teach us that through the fear of the LORD, *Christian* marriages can exist in this broken world. Driven by the spirit of Christ, an imperfect husband and an imperfect wife can compete in such a marriage to *serve* each other, each is their own place and each according to their own abilities and calling.

Submitting to God's order for marriage in this way, they may experience repeatedly what the book of Proverbs proclaims from beginning to end: "The fear of the LORD is a fountain of life, so that one may avoid the snares of death" (Prov 14:27).

Bibliography

Adler, Alfred. *What Life Should Mean to You*. Boston: Little, Brown, 1931.
Albright, W. F. *From the Stone Age to Christianity: Monotheism and the Historical Process*. 2nd ed. Garden City, NY: Doubleday Anchor, 1957.
Andel, J. van. *Vademecum Pastorale*. Kampen: Kok, 1920.
Berkhof, H. *Geschiedenis der Kerk*. Nijkerk, Netherlands: Callenbach, 1947.
Calvin, John. *Institutes of the Christian Religion*. 2 vols. Translated by Ford Lewis Battles. Library of Christian Classics. Louisville: Westminster John Knox, 1960.
———. *Letters of John Calvin*. Vol. 4. Edited by Jules Bonnet. Translated by Marcus Robert Gilchrist. Philadelphia: Presbyterian Board of Publication, 1858.
Dennison, James T., Jr. *Reformed Confessions of the 16th and 17th Centuries in English Translation*. 4 vols. Grand Rapids: Reformation Heritage, 2008–14.
Deursen, Frans van. *Psalms I*. Edited by Jordan J. Ballor and Stephen J. Grabill. Translated by Nelson D. Kloosterman. Opening the Scripture. Grand Rapids: Christian's Library, 2015.
———. *Psalms II*. Edited by Jordan J. Ballor and Stephen J. Grabill. Translated by Nelson D. Kloosterman. Opening the Scripture. Grand Rapids: Christian's Library, 2015.
Gemser, B. *De Spreuken van Salamo*. Vol. 1. Groningen: Wolters, 1929.
Haak, Theodore. *The Dutch Annotations upon the Whole Bible*. London: Rothwell, Kirton, and Tomlins, 1657.
Huizinga, Johan. "In de schaduwen van morgen. Een diagnose van het geestelijk lijden van onzen tijd." In *Geschiedwetenschap: Hedendaagsche cultuur*. Verzameld werken 7, 313–428. Haarlem: Tjeenk Willink en Zoon, 1950. https://www.dbnl.org/tekst/huiz003gesc03_01/huiz003gesc03_01_0021.php.
———. *In the Shadow of Tomorrow*. Translated by J. H. Huizinga. New York: Norton, 1936.
Kidner, Derek. *Proverbs: An Introduction and Commentary*. Tyndale Old Testament Commentaries 17. Nottingham, England: Tyndale, 1964.
Lamparter, Helmut. *Das Buch der Weisheit*. Stuttgart: Calwer Verlag, 1955.
Lindeboom, G. A. *De ziel der geneeskunde*. Inaugurele rede Vrije Universiteit. Haarlem: Bohn, 1950.
McMillen, S. I. *None of These Diseases*. London: Marshall Morgan and Scott, 1966.
Poel, D. C. van der. *Hoofdlijnen der Economischen en Sociale Geschiedenis*. Vol. 2. Utrecht: De Haan, 1953.
Prinsterer, Guillame Groen van. *Unbelief and Revolution*. Edited and translated by Harry Van Dyke. Lexham Classics. Bellingham, WA: Lexham, 2018.

Ridderbos, Herman. *Paul and Jesus: Origin and General Character of Paul's Preaching of Christ*. Translated by David H. Freeman. Grand Rapids: Baker, 1958.

Schuringa, H. David. *The Dordrecht Bible Commentary*. Vol. 3, *The Wisdom Literature*. Translated by Theodore Haak. N.p.: North Star Ministry, 2019.

Sikkel, J. C. *Het Beginsel der Wetenschap—naar aanleiding van Spreuken 1:7a*. Amsterdam: Wormser, 1889.

Tournier, Paul. *The Healing of Persons*. Translated by Edwin Hudson. New York: Harper and Row, 1965.

Vondel, Joost van den. *Lucifer: Adam in ballingschap, of Aller treurspelen treurspel; Noah, of Ondergang der eerste wereld*. Edited by M. A. Schenkeveld-van der Dussen. Amsterdam: Bert Bakker, 2004. Originally published 1654. https://www.dbnl.org/tekst/vond001luci11_01/vond001luci11_01_0006.php.

Vonk, C. *De Nederlandse Geloofsbelijdenis: Art. 22–24 en 27–37*. De Voorzeide Leer IIIb. Barendrecht, Netherlands: Drukkerij "Barendrecht," 1956.

———. *Exodus*. Edited by Jordan J. Ballor and Stephen J. Grabill. Translated by Theodore Plantinga and Nelson D. Kloosterman. Opening the Scriptures. Grand Rapids: Christian's Library, 2013.

———. *Genesis*. Edited by Jordan J. Ballor and Stephen J. Grabill. Translated by Theodore Plantinga and Nelson D. Kloosterman. Opening the Scriptures. Grand Rapids: Christian's Library, 2013.

Wielemaker, K. *Lichtstralen uit het Woord*. Goes, Netherlands: Oosterbaan en Le Cointre, 1927.

Subject Index

Abigail, wife of Nabal, 256, 304
Abi(jah), wife of King Ahaz, 232
Abimelech, king of the Philistines, 249
Abiram, ground split open and
    swallowed, 118
Abner, killed by Joab, 122
abomination
    devious person as, 124–25
    exalted among men as, 128, 252,
        259, 263
    false balance as, 49
    kings doing evil as, 250–52, 301
    religiosity as, 242
    way of the wicked as, 243
    wickedness as, 165, 259
abortion, 292
Abraham, 48, 255, 314, 315
Absalom, 89, 90, 118, 122, 150
abstractions, 70
abundance, plans of the diligent leading
    to, 203
accomplishments, of our heavenly
    Father, 263
Achan, hid stolen gold and silver, 78
activism, Jesus' parables applying to, 12
Adam, 264, 277
addiction, 288
Adler, Alfred, 260
administration of justice, 300
admonition, 104, 280
Prince Adonijah, premature death of, 89
adulterer, suffering and shame of, 119
adulteress
    costs of, 143, 144–52
    smooth words of, 140

staying away from, 154
unfaithfulness of, 82
adultery
    arming yourself against, 152–60
    beginning of, 138–42
    bringing indelible shame, 36
    capital punishment for, 82, 149
    consequences of, 81–82
    as deadly, 151
    as folly, 137–60
    mashals on, 150
    outcome of, 155–56
    progression of, 142–52
advisors, importance of good, 215
affection, gifts as proof of, 255
the afflicted, God not forgetting, 220
age, wisdom going hand in hand with,
    169
Agur, the son of Jakeh, 23
    on "every word of God" as pure,
        316–17
    free of greed and covetousness,
        321–22
    prayed for protection from poverty,
        206
    selected Proverbs of, 316–22
    words of, 27
Ahab, 118, 213, 276, 300
Ahasuerus, 275–76
Ahithophel, treachery of, 122
Albright, William, 183
alcohol abuse, 288, 289–90
alcoholics, lacking moderation, 302
alienation, 259
all knowing, 61

an Amalekite, claimed that he had killed Saul, 261
Prince Amnon, violated his half-sister, Tamar, 90, 150
Amos, 220, 247
Amsterdam, exalting of, 213
Anabaptist Christians, "perished" by the sword, 294
"Anakim," "the people of the necklaces," 92
anarchy, nations descending into, 313
anger, 241–42, 266–67
angry heart, small gift quieting, 256
animal welfare, wisdom in, 221
animal world, under the curse upon the earth, 222
anti-revolutionary movement, in church and world history, 94
anxiety, weighing down in a man's heart, 226–27
apocryphal books, 176–78
apostate Christianity, youth living in the atmosphere of, 67
apostles, 53, 189, 227. *See also* disciples of Jesus
apostolic fathers, 178
Arian struggle, 179–80
Arius, 161–62, 179
arrogance, people competing in, 252
arrogant pride, of the scoffer, 279–80
King Asa, had diseased feet, 255
Asaph, 124, 125, 225, 286, 321
associative sayings, proverbs as, 34
Assyrian empire, led the ten tribes into captivity, 25
Assyrian-Aramean proverbs of Achiqar, educating youngsters from the ruling class, 40
Athaliah, married into the house of David, 232
atheists, 320
attitude of life, of pride or humility, 128
audacity, of scoffers, 127
Augustus, ordering a census, 276
author(s)
    of proverbs, 28
    of *Wisdom of Solomon*, 177

authoritative guidance of God, as discipline, 104
authority, 60, 170, 171
autonomous human knowledge, 318
autonomous people, 127, 307
autonomy, declaring toward God, 60

Babylon, captivity of the Jews in, 2
bad company, ruining good morals, 229
bad women, using their eyes as a snare, 155
badness, people of, 307
baking, in an Israelite home, 326
Balaam, 222, 303
balance, false, as an abomination to the LORD, 49
Barnabas, 219
Barzillai, as "very old" at eighty, 87
Beatitudes, 7
beautiful woman, without discretion, 218
beauty, not desiring in your heart, 331
bed coverings, wife making, 328
Belgic Confession, 294, 295, 318
believers, God always preserved a remnant of, 94
believing attitude, as best chance for happiness, 175
benefits, gaining from wisdom, 135
the benevolent, God will reward, 121
Bezaleel, construction insight of, 44–45
Bible translations, use of the word "wisdom," 34
"birth," of mountains and sea, 172–73
black death, 98–99
blessed
    fathers and mothers as, 309
    the meek as, 240
    nations keeping the Law, 313
blessing(s)
    bringing as enriching, 219–20
    bringing life to full bloom, 126
    counting, 244
    making rich, 248
    proceeding from the fear of the LORD, 84–85
blunt formulations
    mashals containing, 85

SUBJECT INDEX

in Proverbs and Ecclesiastes, 13–18
Boaz, 72, 207, 232, 253–54
bones, crushed spirit drying up, 257–58
book of Proverbs. *See* Proverbs (book of)
book of Wisdom, exercised some influence, 179
booklets of proverbs, 26, 27
books of proverbs, biblical and extrabiblical, 21
the boor, as the reverse of the wise man, 314
borrower, as the slave of the lender, 206
bribes, 143, 247–48, 258
bridegroom, whispering pure love, 155
broad path, apart from God leading to destruction, 234
broken relationships, gifts help to mend, 256
broken world, living in, 98
"build a house," meaning of, 232
business
  as not a form of charity, 220
  relationships, 255
  wife having an instinct for, 329
  wisdom of Tyre, 35
  Yahweh involved with, 48–49
"by me kings reign," 183–84
bygones, not dragging up, 257

Caesar, rendering to, 293
Calvin, warned against speculations, 319
Calvinists, understanding of revolution, 94–95
Canaanite literature, hymns in praise of wisdom, 183
Canaanite paganism, 165
Canaanites, Baal festivals, 145
Canaanitism, adultery as the purest form of, 149
canonical place, of Prov 8, 181
capacities
  determined by God, 322
  discerning between good and evil, 20–21
  for speech as "a fountain of life," 110
capital punishment, 90–91, 149

carelessness, 152, 328
caution, 168, 234
cave of Machpelah, cost of, 48
Emperor Charles V, 241
chastisement
  of children, 267, 268
  by God, 104, 105–6
cheated spouse, blind rage of, 150
cheerful of heart, having a continual feast, 244–46
cheerfulness, as the fruit of great faith, 245
children
  able to get along without corporal discipline, 231
  bringing shame to mothers, 309–11
  calling their mother blessed, 330
  disciplining early on, 268
  folly in the hearts of, 282–83
  inconvenience of rearing, 233
  learning God-fearing customs and attitudes, 65
  not withholding discipline from, 284–85
  training up, 280–82
  treating according to their nature, 269
  walking in the truth as great joy, 201
children and domestic servants, gentle and tactful instruction of, 330
children of men, as the crown of God's creational work, 173–74
chokma (wisdom), possessing a wider meaning than our word wisdom, 34
Christ. *See* Jesus Christ
Christians, 94, 98, 284
church members, terrifying future for wicked, 125
circumcision, oath of, 82
citizens, each equal before the law, 297
city, exalted by the blessing of the upright, 212–14
city gate, activities at, 329
the clap, contracting through sexual intercourse, 145
Cleanthes, 208
clothing, 142, 328, 329

SUBJECT INDEX

collaborator, wisdom as in God's works, 178
collective term, *mashal* as, 2
commentators, organizing the book of Proverbs, 26
comparison, proverb lines containing, 7
compassion, 220, 222, 223
competence, 36, 47
comprehensive living, of ordinances, 311
concealing *mashals*, of Jesus, 10–13
condemning to death, an innocent person, 292
confidence, 85, 237–38
consequences, of actions, 29
consistency, truth showing, 223
contemporary society, permissiveness of, 138
contention, quieting, 242
"a continual feast," life becoming, 246
contradictions, between Proverbs and Ecclesiastes, 14–15
cooperation, wisdom exercised at creation, 176–77
Corinth, easy access to brothels, 158
"a corner of the rooftop," husband finding peace and quiet in, 277
corporal punishment, 229, 267, 309
correction, in the "discipline of Yahweh," 104
corruption, reaping from the flesh, 192
counsel
    influence of bad, 300
    of Lady Wisdom, 162–64, 167
    needing good, 168
    safety in an abundance of, 215
"the counsel of the wicked," Proverbs opposed to, 1
courtroom, Yahweh's concern with, 51
covenant, living in, 1
covenant abandonment, times of, 313
covenant breakers, "pious," 213
covenant breaking, land committing, 305
covenant demand, of benevolence, 120
covenant documents, violating, 317
covenant promises, of the upright, 212
covenant wisdom, Proverbs containing, 16

covenant words, love and faithfulness of, 92
covenantal language, of circumcision, 82
craftsmanship skills, wisdom from, 34, 56–57
creation, 54, 55, 71, 113
critical capacity, lack of, 235
critical outlook, fostered by Scripture protecting from calamity, 236
crops, abundant from the strength of the ox, 233–34
"the crown of her husband," wife as, 324, 330
cruel man, hurting himself, 215
cruelty, teaching children to avoid, 222
crushed spirit, drying up the bones, 257–58
cunning men, craftsmen as, 34–35
Cupid's disease. *See* syphilis (the curse of Venus)
current order, in the book of Proverbs, 25–26
curse
    causeless not alighting, 303
    of God, 16, 126, 213
    from taking a bribe to shed innocent blood, 258
cursing, of people made in the likeness of God, 260
Cyrus, Yahweh moved to redeem Judah, 276

daily living, 55, 163, 187
dangers, of wealth, 108
Daniel, 241, 263, 293
dark figures, encountering in Proverbs, 81
Dathan, ground split open and swallowed, 118
David
    taught Solomon, 268
    accepted divine chastisement, 107
    on afflictions of the righteous, 13, 225
    appealing to nomadic justice from Nabal, 304
    betrayed by a friend, 125
    composed wisdom psalms, 131
    connected with the Psalms, 204

SUBJECT INDEX

died in a good old age, 255
encouraging us to obey God, 249
faced Goliath, 315
fled from wicked Saul, 308
God promised to protect the nation of Judah, 305
as "humble in spirit with the poor," 253
on keeping silent about sins, 117, 239
killed a lion and a bear, 222
lay down and slept, 116–17
lost four sons and observed adultery of three of them, 106
never rebelled against Saul, 293
obeyed the Torah in not taking vengeance, 272
shamed by his son Absalom and his counselor Ahithophel, 122
Simeon threw himself down before, 236
in sin his mother did conceive him, 271
spared the life of Saul, 266
strengthening us by means of his psalms, 227
student of the prophet Samuel, 232
succumbed to the charm of a woman, 139
taught Solomon, 131–36
day and night, divine separation between, 55
day laborer, paying in a timely manner, 49
day of death, as God's decision, 88
day of judgment, accounting for every careless word, 261–62
day of wrath, 210–12
days of the afflicted, as evil, 244–46
de Bres, Guido, author of the Belgic Confession, 295
dead-end path, of the counsels of the wicked, 2
death
 adultery leading to, 151
 as dissolution of human life, 196
 escaping a premature, 88–89
 righteousness delivering from, 201–3, 210–12

turning away the snares of, 81, 228–29
as the wages of sin, 195
deceit, 224
deceitful people, 136
deception, 165
deceptive initial appearance, illustrations of, 234
delusions, alcoholics suffering from permanent, 290
desire, fulfilled as a tree of life, 228
destruction, sudden during peace and security, 118
Deuteronomy, as a covenant document, 317
devious person, as an abomination, 124–25
"devourers," God sending, 101
dew, as heavy evening mist in Palestine, 112
the diligent, hand of, 203–4, 225–26
diligent work, benefit of, 237
disbursements, God transforming into income, 219
discernment, 39–40, 164
disciples of Jesus. *See also* apostles
 asking for further explanation, 11
 asking "Why do you speak to them in *mashals*? 3
 opened their hearts, 190
 at peace with men, 270
 promoting life-happiness of their neighbor, 205
 saw and heard the promised King, 272
disciples of Solomon, 281
discipline
 bowing under God's, 103–7
 as first friendly instruction, 229–30, 309
 fools despising, 59–60
 as God's guidance, 38, 39
 knowing the proper "time and manner," 310
 lack of, 159
 as love-filled parental guidance, 281
 not withholding from a child, 284–85

discipline (*cont.*)
    promoting the good, 37
    Proverbs understanding of, 132
    strict not needed for Luther, 269
    teaching a child early, 310
    of Yahweh, 103–5, 230
disciplined life, living, 302
discourses, in the book of Proverbs, 2
discretion, 81, 218, 266
disease, not viewing alcohol addiction as, 288
disgrace, pride bringing, 209–10
dishonest man, spreading strife, 270
disobedience, restraining, 37
dissolute people, looking down, 136
dissoluteness, putting in chains, 37
distaff, 327
distresses, of the righteous, 127
divine attributes, of wisdom, 178
divine being, wisdom as, 177
divine covenantal instruction, or *torah*, 312
divine order, 36, 325. *See also* God's order
divine wisdom, 134, 171
doing good, not growing weary of, 219
doing to others what you would have them do to you, 216
Dorcas, 93
drunkenness, 90, 288, 289
Dutch Bible, on every slave ship, 217
Dutch population, three-fifths died of black death, 99
Dutch Republic. *See* Republic of the Seven United Netherlands
Dutch States Translation (SV), 36, 318
dwelling secure, after listening to Lady Wisdom, 80
dying, before your time, 87–89

ears, for hearing, 271
earthly pope, calling for a heavenly pope, 183
earthly possessions, God blessing people with, 107
Eastern status symbols, of kings, 250
eating, excessive, 55–56, 302
Ecclesiastes, 15, 178, 225
Ecclesiasticus, also called by its author "The Wisdom of Jesus [the son of] Sirach," 176
economic righteousness, followed with restoration of the global economy, 217
efficiency, Wisdom loving, 173
Egyptian books of proverbs, as textbooks for young officials, 35
Egyptian wisdom books, 40, 208
Egyptian wisdom teachers, 66
Egyptians, associating literature with the name of a renowned king, 21
election campaigns, not mentioning the word wisdom, 168
Eliezer, seeking a good wife for Isaac, 264
Elijah, survived famine, 119
Eliphaz, on Job speaking far too rashly, 169
Elisha, 13, 213–14
emergency needs, not always teaching us to pray, 320–22
emotions, impacting internal organs negatively, 257
empathy, with someone's sorrowful heart, 226
end of a thing, as better than its beginning, 234
enemies, 249–50, 272, 273
enigmatic writing style, of Proverbs and Ecclesiastes, 10
enjoyment, finding in toil, 246
Enlightenment, ideas of, 214
enslaving power, of alcohol and drugs, 290
entrepreneurial spirit, 204
envy, 238–40, 252, 254, 267
Ephraim (tribe or nation of), 241, 305
Ephron, the Hittite, 48
Esau, God made his heart peaceable to Jacob, 249
Esther, successor to Queen Vashti, 276
eternal decree, some Christians believing in, 88
eternal life, reaping from the Spirit, 192
eternal salvation, "perhaps" not applying to, 211
eternity, Israelite meaning of, 171

Europe
    surrendered to "running wild," 312
    weeds of unbelief everywhere, 313
European history, effects of revolution in, 75
European ladies, sat in Japanese camps, 210
Eve, as a mother, 201
evil
    afflicting the evildoer, 75, 119
    all rebellion against God as, 61
    bowing down before the good, 236–37
    devising, 224
    greatest that a person can commit, 286
    as a manifestation of stupidity, 282
    not repaying, 272–73, 298
    overcoming with good, 239
    shunning as understanding, 175
"evil days," Paul knew many of them, 245
evil devices, hated, 267
evil man, 261, 262, 287, 307
evil practices, 81, 100
evolutionary paradigm, playing a role, 20
evolutionism, denying the fall, 265
exaggeration, making a point more clearly, 14
exalted among men, as an abomination in the sight of God, 128, 252, 263
excavations, poetic works found resembling Proverbs, 22
exceptions, not invalidating the rule, 91, 109
expensive well, lawful spouse and her charms compared to, 156–57
experience, 42–43, 73
extramarital love relationships, 90
eyes
    of the adulteress, 141, 142
    for seeing, 271
eyesight, of Isaac, Jacob, and the prophet Ahijah, 255
Ezekiel, on throwing silver into the streets, 210

fabricator, wisdom as, 178
faith, 244, 260, 266
faith confession, on lifespan, 88
"faith healers," 97
faith-expectation, wafting throughout Proverbs, 118
faithfulness, 70, 223
fallen grapes, leaving for the poor and the sojourner, 50
false accusers, of Daniel, 261
false guides, with corrupt judgment, 208
false prophecy, 214, 300
false witness, bearing, 51
falsehood and lying, feared by Agur, 320
family, supporting church, state, and society, 201
family life, depending on the wife's order and regularity, 326
family quarrel, staying far away from, 270
famine, righteous suffering along with everyone else, 13
fanaticism, "power and force" as tools of, 269
farmer, 56, 221, 222
father
    authority through friendly instruction, 38
    with a wise or foolish son, 201
father and mother
    consequences of cursing, 91
    guiding children with a firm hand, 38
    honoring, 153
    listening carefully to godly, 64
father and teacher of young children, Proverbs speaking often to, 42
fattened ox, as the picture of great wealth and prosperity, 247
favor, on a servant dealing wisely, 240–41
fear, of man, 250, 314–15
fear of the LORD
    as the beginning of knowledge, 29, 44–63, 303
    as the beginning of wisdom, 45–47, 191, 223
    as the best life insurance program, 76
    better than great treasure, 246

fear of the LORD (*cont.*)
    continuing in, 285–87
    doing nothing "from selfish ambition or conceit," 253
    entailing a rich reward, 101
    extending a person's life, 255
    as a fountain of happiness, 238
    as a fountain of life, 332
    as hatred of evil, 166
    healing effect proceeding from, 244
    as healing to your flesh and refreshment to your bones, 100
    as healthy, 147
    imparting wisdom not to pick a quarrel, 123
    as instruction in wisdom, 248
    leading a person to knowledge, 53
    leading to accepting chastisement humbly, 107
    leading to life, 117
    learning at home, 65
    life-protecting function of, 237–38
    lifting humanity out of the morass, 208
    as medicine for our body, 273, 311
    not mentioning the name of the LORD, 57–59
    nurturing children in, 201
    placing a stamp on one's conduct, 109
    practical consequences of, 86
    preserving from untold suffering, 291
    pursuing "throughout the whole day," 287
    remembering the teaching in, 153–54
    reward for as riches and honor and life, 108
    as the root of all knowledge, 59
    showing respect for God's regulations, 114–15
    Solomon on living in, 129–30
    when spending money, 101
    as wisdom, 55, 175
feminine beauty, Scripture not despising, 331
fictional person, seeing wisdom as a, 180
financial damage, of adultery, 143

financial wisdom, of giving to Yahweh, 101–2
the first principles, teaching the child, 281
fisheries, followed by cargo trade, 203
fixed order, of the light of the sun, moon, and stars and the waves of the sea, 54
folly (*nabal*)
    adultery and prostitution as, 137–60
    of being undisciplined leading to destruction, 285
    bound up in the heart of a child, 282–83, 309
    bringing to ruin, 264–65
    calling someone a fool, 304
    despising wisdom and discipline, 59
    discounting reality, 37
    as disorder, 60
    dividing generations, 133
    by nature our heart loves, 79
    not viewed as a real person, 182
    pride as, 210
    robbed many of their old age, 91
    set in many high places, 129
    synonyms Proverbs using for, 193
food, withholding from people, 220
fool(s)
    accusing among God's people, 76
    as another term for the wicked, 193
    companion of suffering harm, 229
    complacency of, 75
    despising wisdom and discipline, 59–60, 128–29
    expressions describing, 5
    imagines he has attained wisdom, 43
    injuring himself with wicked words, 261
    keeping silent considered wise, 208, 259
    laughing at the order of God, 73–74
    meddlesome outburst characteristic of, 270
    mouth of bringing ruin, 205
    occupying a high position, 129, 168, 241
    provocation of as heavier than stone or sand, 303–5

refusing to adapt to Yahweh's
    statutes, 60
refusing to suffer under the iron fist
    of reality, 37
self-exaltation and despising of
    God's Word, 72
trusting in his own mind, 308
foolish son, 201, 310
foolishness, 115, 193
"a fool's provocation," Solomon speaking
    about, 304
forbidden women, mouth of as a deep
    pit, 282
forgiveness, that you may be feared, 160
forgiving passing over, imitating God,
    266
foundation of heaven and earth, wisdom
    lying at, 112–13
fountain of life
    drinking from, 112
    fear of the LORD as, 237–38
    mouth of the righteous as, 205
    teaching of the wise as, 81, 114
"a free-spirited upbringing," mantra of,
    284
French Revolution, 295, 301
friends, 257, 270, 302
fruit, picking from a tree of life, 111
fruits, of work, 234
frustrations, 240, 253

Gabriel, 252
gangsters, 68, 69
the gate, Lady Wisdom standing at, 163
gate area, as the only open areas, 72
gathering little by little, increasing
    wealth, 228
general rule, emphasis placed on in
    Proverbs, 14
generation gap, people often talk about,
    275
generations, wisdom binding to one
    another, 133
generosity and charity, resting on
    righteousness, 120
gentle words, power of, 331
Gideon, 213, 241, 255

gift(s)
    determined by God, 322
    keeping a friendship warm, 255–56
gift of God
    good wife as, 264, 324
    wisdom as, 44–45, 191
Gilead, known for its criminality, 68
girl, making or breaking a boy, 232–33
giver, obligated, 120
giving freely, growing all the richer,
    218–19
glad heart, making a cheerful face,
    243–44
gleanings, leaving for the poor and the
    sojourner, 50
global economic recovery, after World
    War II, 247
glory of God and kings, 299–300
gluttony, evils of, 303
gnostic heretics, 158
Gnosticism, 176, 179, 183, 319
God. *See also* "our Father"; Yahweh
    allowing the good to suffer, 211
    asking us to account for use of eyes
        and ears, 271
    bestowing or withholding wealth,
        101
    came with his judgments upon his
        arrogant church of Judah, 209
    chastising his children individually,
        106
    created everything wisely, 113, 173
    creating a wife for Adam, 147, 277
    discipline of, 103–5
    established the rule for using wine,
        58
    esteemed marriage to be holy and
        righteous, 149
    extending to his godly remnant a
        variety of blessings, 313
    as Father interested in our bodily
        well-being, 99
    feeding a remnant among his people
        dwelling in caves, 16
    gave the day for working and the
        night for sleeping, 115
    inseparable from Wisdom, 170

SUBJECT INDEX

God (cont.)
    Moses instructed his people about comprehensive living, 311
    never needed to ask anyone for advice, 44
    never wanted great extremes to exist among his people, 320
    not demanding that we walk through walls to spread the truth, 190
    not needing to punish adulterers at all, 159
    plunging our prosperous world into bitter poverty, 321
    providing courts and a judicial system, 298
    putting into practice our love toward, 80
    ready to cover our sins and remember them no more, 257
    "removing the wicked people surrounding the king," 301
    scoffer knowing everything better than, 280
    seeing you everywhere, 158–59
    seeking too late, 74
    the Speaker of this Word, "never lies," 316
    speaking intimately with us in Proverbs, 125
    specifying the boundaries of our power, 167
    superintending Proverbs, 25
    supplying wisdom in an indirect way, 169
    taking his time before unleashing his wrath, 266
    took the heart of Ahasuerus in his hand, 276
    transforming our subtraction into multiplication, 219
    use of wisdom in creating heaven and earth, 112
    wanting to interact with his upright children, 125
God the Son, preexistence of, 175
God-fearing woman, in Prov 31, 110
godless man, destroying his neighbor, 261
godliness, 119, 136, 223
the godly
    not always having it good, 15
    wise in living, 36
"godly" rioters, who despised governments, 294
God's chastisement, not all suffering as, 105–6
God's commandments, rich reward for keeping, 84–130
God's justice, Solomon referring to, 307
God's name, equating with his accomplishments, 262
God's order. *See also* divine order
    despising, 265
    for marriage, 325, 331
God's people, 12, 75, 213
God's Word
    Agur appears to have known very well, 317
    danger of making additions to, 318
    despising the discipline of, 208
    disappearance of from public society, 307
    eating, 188
    on the last days as times of difficulty, 313
    life-advancing working of, 85
    as pure words, 316
    teaching learning and knowing reality, 61
    warning us to fear God and the king, 295
    the wicked rejecting, 308
    wisdom drawing from, 47–53
God's work, drawing wisdom from, 54–59
God's wrath, burden of, 179
gold digger, quarrying for wisdom, 78–79
goldsmith, wisdom of, 35
Goliath, David faced, 315
gonorrhea, 144, 145, 146
good and evil, children's abilities regarding, 269, 310
good health, sleep as essential for, 114
good name, value of, 109

good news, refreshing the bones, 248
good sense, 109, 116
good soldier of Christ Jesus, 294
good word, making a man glad, 226–27
governments, 183, 184, 293
governor, wisdom as, 178
gracious words, 253, 254
grain, not withholding in the face of famine, 121, 220
grandchildren, as "the crown of the aged," 87
grandpa and his grandson, as mutual supporters, 275
graphic language, of many *mashals*, 8
grasp of reality, wise person characterized by, 46–47
gratitude, of a good wife's children for her faithful care, 330
gray hair, 13, 255, 275
great gain, Godliness with contentment as, 85
Greek morals and customs, author of *Wisdom of Solomon* influenced by, 177
Greek philosophers, never made their ideas common property, 40
Greek philosophical training, among the early Christians, 178–79
Greek philosophy, opponent of fell under its spell, 177
Greek thought, Proverbs 8 not influenced by, 182–83
grief, yielding to, 244
groaning, when flesh and body are consumed, 144–45
grown sons and daughters, praising their mother, 330
guests, of Lady Folly in the depths of Sheol, 195
guidance
  as first of all friendly, fatherly, 284
  obtaining, 43
gullible persons, 42, 235, 280. *See also* the simple

hallelujah, literally meaning "Praise Yahweh!" 245
Haman, 241, 275
Hananiah, 189, 300
hand of the diligent, will rule, 226
Hannah, instructed Samuel, 232
happiness, 111, 157, 325
harsh word, stirring up anger, 241–42
harvest time, as one of God's ordinances, 58
hateful thought, costing many hours of sleep, 116
hatred
  effects on health, 238
  of evil, fear of the Lord as, 166
  forms of, 116
  stirring up strife, 257
  taking hold of our spirit, 247
haughtiness of man, shall be humbled, 210
haughty eyes, the Lord abhorring, 209
haughty spirit, going before a fall, 252
head of a wife, as her husband, 325
health
  adulteress costing you, 144–47
  wisdom promoting, 97–100
heaping burning coals, on your enemy's bread, 116
hearing ear, made by the Lord, 271–72
heart(s)
  of the children of man open to the LORD, 243
  everything proceeding from, 135
  gaining through generosity, 256
  haughty before destruction, 263
  humble toward God, 191
  of the king as a stream of water, 275–76
  the Lord abhorring proud, 209
  making pure, 270–71
  not desiring beauty of the adulteress, 155
  opening fully for wisdom, 175
  putting proverbs in, 283
  raging against the LORD, 264–65
  ruled by love, 93
  trusting in one's own, 60
  weighing a person down, 226
  where wisdom is stored, 45
  of the wicked as of little worth, 205
heartbreak, adulteress costing you, 152

heartfelt trust, characterizing the father-son relationship, 67
heavenly Father
    nurturing Israel, 229
    as "the only wise God," 44
heavy work, wife not afraid of, 327
Hebrew language, having no word for "square" or "plaza," 72
heir of the world, Jesus Christ as, 184
Heldring, O. G., 290
hell, Lady Folly's guests in the depths of, 196
herbs, dinner of a better where love is, 246–47
Herod, Jesus made no answer to, 189
"hero's death," not required needlessly, 227
Hezekiah, 24–25, 88, 213, 232, 299
hidden treasure, the ground still preserving, 78
high blood pressure, 239, 240
high esteem, as an essential component of love, 331
Hippocrates, 301
hired worker, not oppressing, 121
historical narrative, Solomon seeing through his window, 137–38
historical time, Nabal not knowing, 304
Holy Scripture. *See also* Scripture
    containing ordinances for authority over children, 231
    on folly as not always removed from a child's heart without pain, 282
    as the infallible textbook, 47
    as the norm for a healthy critical outlook, 235
    as not a book of science, 99
    proceeding from a certain kind of inequality, 66
    recognizing no autonomous human knowledge, 61
    returning to the language of, 319
home
    path to wisdom beginning at, 29
    where all discipline begins, 38
"home catechism," providing by the time a child is about ten, 231
homemaker. *See* wife

honesty, of Lady Wisdom, 167
honey
    as a beloved delicacy in Palestine, 253
    eating just enough, 55–56, 301–3
    gracious words are like, 227
honor
    gracious woman getting, 215
    humility coming before, 248, 263
    for a man to keep aloof from strife, 270
    wisdom lending, 108–9
    wisdom making one inherit, 128–29
hope, 228
Hosea, 68, 289
hot-tempered man, stirring up strife, 242
house, of the adulteress as a danger, 141
House of Orange, righteousness and justice of, 251
house of the wicked, reality of God's curse on, 126
house with seven columns, Lady Wisdom living in, 186
household, providing food for, 326
household engineer, as the modern title for homemaker, 330
Huguenot Wars, 294
Huguenots, fled, 309
Huizinga, Johan, 235
human beings, possessing no wisdom in themselves, 191
humanitarianism, 92
humble person, as the counterpart to the scoffer, 128
humble spirit, of Agur and David, 320
humility
    as the beginning of wisdom, 191–92
    coming before honor, 109, 248, 263
    of Jesus Christ, 270
    reward for, 108
    wisdom as, 167
    wisdom beginning with, 46
hunger, idle person suffering, 204
hurtful word, inciting wrath, 242
husband(s)
    bearing ultimate responsibility toward God, 325
    governing his wife in love, 277

SUBJECT INDEX

as the head of the wife, 278
   loving their wives, 278, 325, 330–31
   providing necessary opportunity, 329
hymn, to a proficient wife, 323–32
hypostasis, 180, 181

ideal woman, 27, 218, 233
idle person, suffering hunger, 204
idleness, not eating the bread of, 330
"I'll do as I please" attitude, of some Christians, 94
illnesses, continuing to bring people to the grave, 98
illness-related events, severe, 257
image gallery, of *mashals*, 8
"immortality," wisdom providing a person with, 178
impartial judges, providing to follow justice, 296
imperfect people, no perfect marriage is possible, 332
imperious church, Roman Catholic notions of, 184
impulse to isolation, leading to "the works of the flesh," 260
In the Shadow of Tomorrow (Huizinga), 235
indebtedness, 305
the "inexperienced," struggle between Wisdom and Folly involving, 194
inheritance, gained hastily as not blessed in the end, 234
injustice, food swept away through, 17
insight
   discovering for living, 79–80
   gaining from good precepts, 135
   not leaning on your own, 96
   possessing, 168
   respect for the Holy One as, 192
   teaching why one thing is good and another evil, 39
insomnia, sin and, 115–16
instruction, 104, 132, 207–8
Instruction Manual for Proverbs (Prov 1–9), 27–30, 64, 161, 170, 185–96. *See also* Proverbs (book of)
instruction unto wisdom, fear of Yahweh as, 46

intermediaries, *logos* as, 177
intestinal infections, from antipathy or resentment, 238
irritation, caused by fools in high positions, 304
Isaac, 249
Isaiah
   on calling evil good and good evil, 81, 306
   compared Israel to a vineyard, 8
   on drunkenness, 288
   on pride of the men of Judah, 209
   saw licentiousness, 312
   on throwing God's Word and warnings to the wind, 264–65
   watched wanton eyes walking the streets of Jerusalem, 155
Israel
   all the laws as covenant stipulations, 120
   experiencing covenant curse, 213
   forsaking God's covenant, 214
   lived in a land "flowing with milk and honey," 301
   repeatedly abandoned God and his Torah, 52
   sought to avoid any pain when disciplined, 106
Israelite(s), 180–81, 186, 274
issues
   raking up old, 257
   resolving among ourselves, 298
it's not your time, as fatalistic, 88

Jacob, 244–45, 248, 249, 256
James, on not giving preferential treatment, 297
jealousy, making a man furious, 90, 149–50
Jehoiada the priest, on Joash doing what was right, 301
king Jehoiakim, as a model of wickedness, 251
Jehoshaphat, godly officials of, 301
Jeremiah
   calling Nebuchadnezzar to humble himself, 300
   cast unceremoniously into a pit, 16

Jeremiah (*cont.*)
   as an example encouraging us to obey God, 249
   feeling pain in connection with blind leaders, 305
   on God's hand keeping him outside "the sod of revelers," 125
   lived in a time of covenant forsaking, 147–48
   men of Anathoth plotted evil against, 122
   not entering into endless discussions with the false prophet Hananiah, 189
   saw few promises fulfilled, 16
   scolded king Jehoiakim, 251
   whole land striving and contending with, 224

Jeroboam, the (son of Nebat), 106, 127, 207, 250, 318

Jerusalem, trampled on by the Gentiles, 210

Jerusalem church, members sold houses and fields for the sake of the poor, 217

Jesus Christ
   accused the Pharisees and scribes of making void the word of God, 318
   on being gentle and lowly in heart, 123
   betrayed by one of his disciples, 122
   called himself "the bread of life," 188
   as completely free from fear of people, 315–16
   condemning Jewish revolutionary and military messianic expectations, 12
   deity of, Proverbs 8 and, 181–82
   on dividing inheritance, 270
   expected justice only from the Supreme Judge, 299
   followed closely the didactic style of those who wrote proverbs, 17
   gave way to evildoers at times, 227
   "Give, and it will be given to you," 219
   on giving account for every careless word, 209
   on giving to the one who begs from you, 121
   giving us mild counsel in Holy Scripture, 268
   good pleasure of, 241
   having the words of eternal life, 205
   on the heart of man, 135
   his name enduring forever, 204
   honored the governor of the Roman emperor, 293–94
   "I have not came to bring peace, but a sword," 224
   increased in wisdom and in stature and in favor with God and man, 93
   learning wisdom from, 52–53
   making intercession for transgressors, 267
   on the man born blind, 97
   not condemning the woman caught in adultery, 160
   not counting equality with God as a thing to be grasped, 248
   not reviling in return, 272
   not throwing pearls before pigs, 189
   not yet the sovereign of all the kings on earth, 184
   obedience to God and the king, 293
   as the one greater than Solomon, 5, 23, 169
   on "our daily bread" as the middle way, 321
   parables of, 3
   parallelism in the preaching of, 7
   on Pharisees and scribes as blind guides, 207
   on the poor in spirit, 252
   promised "If anyone serves me, the Father will honor him," 129
   provided help on the Sabbath, 122
   as scorned king, 12
   as sinless, 271
   sleeping in a boat during a storm at sea, 117
   speaking as one who personified wisdom, 116

speaking style of, 8–9
standing before the judge's bench, 298–99
subject to his parents, 66
taught with *mashals* that obscured his teaching, 10
warned about arrogant aspirations of leadership, 253
Jesus Sirach (Wisdom book)
  pedagogical recommendations of the harsh spirit of later Pharisees, 268, 281
  reaching back beyond Ecclesiastes and Job once again to Proverbs, 15
  on seeing what is bad for you, 302–3
  on wine and women leading men astray, 289
  on wisdom as from eternity, 176–77
jewels, wisdom as more valuable than, 107–8
Jewish wisdom, suppressing in the face of Greek wisdom, 177
Jews
  rejected Jesus, 11, 190
  speculated about a fictious "Wisdom," 178
Jezebel, 118–19, 232
Joab
  killed Abner, 122
  pierced Absalom dead, 118
Joash, surrounded himself with godly officials, 301
Job, 3, 15, 97, 106, 121, 225
John (apostle), on not loving the world, 287
Jonathan, 211, 226–27, 298, 299
Joseph
  brothers of knelt down before him, 236
  flight from Potiphar's wife, 228, 280
  flight from Potiphar's wife as a hero's escape, 93, 141
  forgiving attitude toward his brothers, 266
  opened all the storehouses and sold to the Egyptians, 220
  as the opposite of a naive person, 42
  sent wagons to carry his father to Egypt, 248
Joshua, 196
joyful heart, as good medicine, 257–58
Jubilee, balancing imbalanced social relationships, 320
Judas, betrayed the Son of Man with a kiss, 122
judges, supposed to avenge wrong, 298
judging, partiality in, 296–97
judicial basis, of caring for the poor, 119
judicial knowledge, LORD as the beginning of all, 51
just balance and scales, as the LORD's, 49
justice, 123, 167–68, 250, 258–59, 298, 300, 307
juvenile criminality, warning against, 68

kind man, benefiting himself, 215
kindness, 330
king(s)
  abomination to do evil, 250–52, 301
  honored in ancient Egypt by a collection of proverbs, 20
  in Israel as the supreme judges, 300
  of Judah, lifespans of, 87
  wise winnowing the wicked, 301
king of Babylon, 3, 9
the kingdom, painted by Jesus, 8
kingdom of Christ, coming through his Word and Spirit, 183
kingdom of God, 168, 218
kingdom of heaven, not coming through fleshly activism, 12
knowing the right thing to do and failing to do it, as sin, 122
knowledge
  applying your heart to, 283
  discovering well-considered, 166
  of God, the wicked hating, 74
  God's wisdom excluding autonomous, 60–61
  as a matter of our heart, 45
  proceeding from respect, 46
  the wise laying up, 205
"the knowledge of the Son of God," attaining, 191

Korah, ground split open and
    swallowed, 118

Laban, 213, 249
Lady Folly, 182, 185, 193–96
Lady Sin. *See* Lady Folly
Lady Wickedness. *See* Lady Folly
Lady Wisdom
    addressing city inhabitants at gate
        areas, 72
    being intimate with, 154
    as the best counselor, 162–67, 174
    displaying her advanced age, 170, 172
    guests eating life-food, 186–88
    invitation and admonition of, 73
    issuing an appeal to everyone, 164
    listening to, 64, 69–77
    as not a divine being, 176–84
    offering a real feast, 186, 195
    offering the food of life, 185
    as the personification of wisdom, 77
    as a prophetess for young and old,
        71–72
    providing life, 174–75
    quest of, 166
    refusing to cast her pearls before
        swine, 188–92
    showing her nobility credentials,
        169–74
    speaking noble things, 165
    speaking to us, 28
    as a street evangelist, 71–76
    summoning you to listen to her, 175
    supplying her friends with power
        and profit, 167–69
lamp, burning under management of
    the wife, 327
Lamparter, Helmut, 292
the land, protected by Yahweh, 250
landmark, not moving a neighbor's, 50
laughter, as destruction, 73–74
the Law, 47, 268, 306, 311
"law of jealousy," placing under Yahweh's
    curse, 149
lawlessness, 70
Lazarus (poor man), desired to be fed at
    the rich man's table, 278

leadership, oldest men in the
    community exercising, 67
Leah and Rachel, built up the house of
    Israel, 232
learning, never too old for, 43
legal appeal, of the poor for help, 120
King Lemuel, 23, 27, 268
"length of days," meaning of, 86–87
Lenin, 223
"Liberty, Equality, and Fraternity," as a
    foolish slogan, 261
lies, 224, 320
life
    adulteress costing you, 148–52
    as another word for happiness, 111,
        136, 151
    as brief and difficult, 247
    Lady Wisdom providing, 174–75
    righteousness preventing the
        dissolution of, 211
    undisciplined bringing injury to
        health, 100
    wisdom extending, 86–92
life and death, age-old choice between,
    196
life experience, 133, 169, 187
life insurance, fear of the LORD as, 237
life lessons, 5, 9, 133, 154, 330
life motto, of the sinner as "*Ni Dieu, ni
    maître*"- no God, no master, 286
life to the flesh, tranquil heart giving,
    239–40
life-food, at the table of Lady Wisdom,
    188
lifespans, before and after the flood,
    86–87
life-strength, versus life-wisdom, 275
life-walk, with God, 281
life-wisdom, 33–43, 103, 171, 199
life-wisdom-through-fearing-the-
    LORD, 133
lifted up, shall be brought low, 209
light of the eyes, rejoicing the heart, 248
Lindeboom, G. A., 257
linen garments, wife making and selling,
    329
lines of proverbs
    clarifying each other, 5, 6

composing with balanced, 7
lips
    of a fool as a snare to his soul, 260–62
    of a forbidden woman drip honey, 140
    restraining as prudent, 208–9
listening
    to God-fearing parents, 65, 153
    to Lady Wisdom on fearing Yahweh, 76
    making one wise, 29, 64–77
    to wisdom, 132–34
little children, enjoying Bible stories, 231
livestock, farmer putting up with, 233
living
    discovering insight for, 79–80
    earning before starting a family, 297
    peaceably with all, 93
living person, description of wisdom as, 161
Logos, identified, 178–79
long and happy life, as a wonderful ideal, 86
longevity, Lady Wisdom mentioning adding to, 192
long-suffering, wisdom making a person, 110
LORD of hosts, against all that is proud and lofty, 209
Lord's people, will judge the world, 236
Louis XVI, 301
love
    characteristics of, 239
    for Christ's will, 269
    not tolerating evil within a child's heart, 230
    opening our eyes, 266
    as patient and kind, 260
    providing the outer limit for punishment, 230
    seeking by covering an offense, 256–57
    of your neighbor as yourself, 121
love and faithfulness, 92, 93
love song [of Yahweh], concerning his vineyard Israel, 3
lovelessness, of self-imposed isolation, 260
loveliness, wisdom bestowing, 110
lowly in spirit, will obtain honor, 109
lowly poor, living more healthily than the rich, 252
loyalty, required toward Yahweh and the neighbor, 120
Lues Venerea (the curse of Venus). *See* syphilis (the curse of Venus)
Luther, Martin, 273–74, 318–19
luxury, bathing in with hatred in his heart, 247
lying tongue, as but for a moment, 223–24

Malachi, 102
man and his wife, becoming one flesh, 147
man born blind, experience of, 97
man or a boy, in Israel allowed to let tears flow freely, 243–44
managerial wisdom, of Joseph, 35
man's heart, intention of as evil from his youth, 282, 309
man's ways, before the eyes of the LORD, 159
manual. *See* Instruction Manual for Proverbs (Prov 1–9)
marital fidelity, giving life to the flesh, 147
marital happiness, 138, 152–59
"the marketplace of life," Lady Wisdom lifting up her voice, 163
marriage
    Christian can exist in this broken world, 332
    evil one now directing severe attacks against, 324
    God's order for, 331
    not being too eager for, 297
    not dissolving for a quarrelsome wife, 277–78
    only one perfect of Adam and Eve, 332
    watchword for a happy, 157–58
Marshall Plan, 217, 247
Martha (sister of Lazarus), 240

SUBJECT INDEX

Mary (mother of Jesus), on God's regard for the lowly, 128
mashal(s)
    categorized under more than one of the Ten Commandments, 26
    as characteristic of the speaking style of the Lord God, 8–9
    collected in Proverbs written over the course of many years, 19
    as a collective term, 2–3
    containing a blunt formulation, 13–18
    designed to grab and hold the hearer, 9, 15
    displaying Hebrew parallelism, 4–7
    eye-catching features of, 3–18
    Jesus taught in the form of, 97–98
    as lessons from real life, 199
    on listening to mother and father, 153
    manner of speaking unique to, 85
    "neutral" grouped together, 57–58
    not always applying to everyone, 117
    not mentioning exceptions, 91, 93
    not speaking impiously or "humanistically," 59
    as proverbs of wise men who discovered rules, 17
    speaking enigmatically, 9–13
    speaking graphically and containing a comparison, 8
    teach the correct way of living, 37
Mashals of Solomon, translation as *Proverbs of Solomon*, 3
the measure you use, will be measured to you, 216
meat, only the rich ate regularly in Israel, 246–47
the meek, will inherit the earth, 125
meek heart, 239, 240
memory, 7, 204
men
    all are of themselves liars, 318
    consequences of gonorrhea, 145
    "the men of Hezekiah," collection of proverb compilations by, 26
mercy, judgment without, 278
Messiah, 11, 128

Micaiah, the son of Imlah, 305
mighty deeds, of Yahweh, 262
mighty people, ruling by the grace of God, 276
Miriam (Moses sister), became a leper, 106
misery, 94–96, 113, 121, 124, 146–47
misle, plural form of *masal* (transliteration *mashal*), 2
mist, aiding fertility and causing crops to grow, 176
misunderstanding, preventing, 97–98
mockers, 72, 73–74, 75, 188–89, 192. *See also* scoffer
moderation, 55–56, 302
modern life, artificial light of, 115
money, 107, 206, 207, 217, 246
mood, diseases partially caused by, 238
mood swings, effects on a body's health, 257
moral duty, Nabal not knowing, 304
Moses, 106, 126, 196, 213
mothers, 201, 232, 310, 330
mouth
    of the adulteress, 142
    of a fool bringing ruin, 205, 261
    setting a guard over, 209
    of wicked people, 214

Naamah, Ammonite wife of Solomon and mother of Rehoboam, 232
na'ar
    as child or infant, 281
    as youth, 41
Nabal, 118, 207, 304
naïve ones, defenseless against temptations, 164
name of the LORD, as a strong tower, 262–63
Naomi, 253
Napoleon, God used for chastisement, 214
Nathan, 3
national health, of Israel, 98
nations, 17, 202, 312
natural laws, not existing autonomously, 54
nature, 162, 164

nature and age of a child, 281
navigation, of life, 43
Near Eastern Code of Hammurabi, 297
neatness, acquiring a sterile character, 233
Nebuchadnezzar, 249, 263, 276, 293, 300
negative attitude
    toward God and his Word, 75
    toward life, 257–58
Nehemiah, 321
neighbor
    focusing on, 216
    helping as soon as possible, 121
    love of, 219, 260
    mutual solidarity toward one's, 119
    not desiring the wife of, 155
nephesh, of an ox and donkey, 222
Netherlands
    economic prosperity in the seventeenth century, 203
    German occupation, 209–10
    hunger winter of 1944–1945, 13
    Reformed people could have known that God hates oppression, 217
neurotic phenomena, resulting from sinning, 146–47
new covenant, with believers from the Gentiles, 317
new earth, believers will inherit, 83
new morality, 144
night, God giving for resting, 114–17
Nineveh, many animals in, 221
nobility credentials, of Lady Wisdom, 169–74
Northern Kingdom, plagued with revolutions, 89
nurture
    of children, 201, 280–81, 310
    Luther described the outcome of strict, 269

obedience, 67–68, 98–99, 173, 309
observation, gift of, 57
occupation, 57
occupational know-how, applying to daily living, 35
offense, glory to overlook an, 266–67
Oholiab, construction insight of, 44–45

oil lamp, as a sign of order and prosperity, 327
old age, 88, 91, 235, 255
old and new covenants, Proverbs belonging to the canonical books of, 16
old covenant, with Israel, 317
Old Testament, 182, 292
olive oil, burning night and day, 327
opening eyes and ears, while living with father and mother, 134
oppressors, God abominates, 125
order
    in Proverbs, 19
    Wisdom loving, 173
order of life, attacked, 297
ordinances
    for childhood, 281
    for the conduct of God's people, 46
    of God, 99, 100, 278
    of heaven and earth, 54–57
    for teaching activity, 66
Oreb and Zeeb (princes of Midian), 241, 242
orphans, Yahweh prohibited the oppression of, 50
"our Father." *See also* God; Yahweh
    rescuing us from the power of Satan and death, 262
outcome, of a matter disclosing its value, 234
outward adornment, not seeking strength in, 92
outward beauty of a woman, deceiving a man, 331

pagan fantasies, role in the book of Wisdom, 177
pagan nature in us, 37
pagan world, wisdom of, 62–63
paganism, 88, 179
parable, also called a *mashal*, 3
parables, of Jesus, 10, 190–91
parallelism, mashals displaying, 4–7
parental discipline, 68, 285
parental home, 131, 153–54
parental instruction, for young people, 68
parental love, 268

parents
　　asking the LORD to provide good wives for their sons, 324
　　authority over young persons, 66
　　considering a child's nature and disposition, 310
　　curbing evil in the hearts of children very early, 309
　　listening well to, 65–68
　　obtaining "guidance" from Proverbs, 43
　　as the pride of children, 330
partiality, in judging as not good, 51
Pashur, 300
passing away, before the "time to die," 89–92
path(s)
　　of life, 112
　　making straight, 96
　　of the righteous and of the wicked, 62
　　to wisdom, 28, 29, 45
　　of wisdom and folly, 62–63
patience, 266, 269
Paul
　　on everything created by God as good, 107
　　fought the good fight and kept the faith, 245
　　gave Peter a public reprimand, 315
　　on Gnosticism, 319
　　on not going beyond what is written, 318
　　not inciting violent resistance against Nero, 294
　　on not provoking children to anger, 268–69
　　not viewing Jesus Christ as the preexistent Wisdom of Proverbs 8, 181
　　putting into practice what he encouraged others to do, 245
　　as a servant of Christ Jesus, 183
　　on sin, 70
　　on wisdom regarding sexual immorality, 158
Paul and Barnabas, fled a dangerous situation, 227
Paul and Silas, 245, 258

peace, 11, 17, 110, 224
peace offerings, 140, 274
"peace preaching," of false prophets, 300
peacemakers, as blessed, 124, 224
pedagogues, harsh like Jesus Sirach, 268, 281
Pekah, as victim to the sword after regicide, 89
penicillin, discovery of, 216
a people falls, where there is no guidance, 215
permissiveness, 156
personal life, enduring injustice in, 298
personal limit, Nabal not knowing, 304
personal metaphors, Israelites loved speaking in, 180–81
personal representations
　　Israelites loved, 162
　　Lady Folly as, 193
　　Lady Wisdom as, 162
personification
　　versus hypostasis for Wisdom, 180–84
　　Israelites fond of, 70–71
pessimism, can be caused by little faith, 245
pestilence, Yahweh promised and threatened, 98
Peter, 117, 190, 205, 267, 293, 315
Pharaoh, Yahweh glorifying himself through, 276
Pharisaical self-righteousness, Jesus attacked, 316
Pharisees, 207, 231
King Philip II, tyranny of, 308
Philo, 177, 179
philosophers, spoke of a logos, 177
philosophy, wisdom not the same as, 35
physical beauty, as transitory, 331
physical benefit, of a life of faith, 97
physical discipline, 105, 282–83, 285, 310
physical health, crushed spirit undermining, 243
physical strength, pinnacle of as a young man, 275
physical work, as a good means against depression, 244
piety, 92, 308

Pilate, Jesus silent before, 189
pithy manner, of speech, 13, 14
planning peace, bringing joy, 224
playing, children absorbed with, 281
playing child, wisdom presented as, 182
poetry, reading strong *mashals* as, 14
politicians, calling themselves progressive, 208
the poor. *See also* the weak
  better to be than to divide spoil with the proud, 252–53
  closing ears to the cry of, 278–79
  generosity to, 50
  king faithfully judging, 301
  king protecting, 250
  receiving as the right of, 218
  referring to the godly in Scripture, 206
  shield of protection around, 49–50
  Solomon's powerful assurance to, 124–25
  standing up for, 119
  tracing misery to lack of money, 206
  wife opening her hand to, 328
poor wise man, could have delivered the city but was despised, 241
pope, ruling authority of, 183
pornography, new morality and, 144
possessions
  as not improper, 206
  wisdom increasing, 101–3
Potiphar, blessed for the sake of Joseph, 213
poverty
  burdens and dangers of, 119
  as catastrophe, 320
  mere talk tending only to, 237
  of the poor as ruin, 206
  slack hand causing, 203–4
poverty and riches, feared by Agur, 320
power, with which God created everything, 113
powers of the heavens, will be shaken, 118
practical knowledge, 62
praise songs, 170
prayers, 242, 314
precepts, giving good, 38

predatory killers, in ancient Israel, 68
preexistent wisdom figure, Apostles not identifying Christ with, 181
preferential treatment, in administration of justice, 297
premature death, 92, 192, 285
prescientific knowledge. *See* practical knowledge
prevention, as the best cure, 152
pride, 209–10, 252
primeval sin, committed by apostate Christians, 286
private life, enduring injustice in, 298
profiteers, cursed by desperate fathers and mothers, 220
proper time and procedure, for all things, 59, 231
prophecy
  false, 214, 261, 300
  taking away from the words of Revelation (book of), 317
  voice of wisdom and, 74
  Yahweh silencing, 312
prophetess, wisdom as, 71
prophets, 52, 164, 312
  wicked, 300
prosopopoeia, stylistic device personification, 69
prosperity, God determining, 322
prosperous nations, God making, 203
prostitution, 137–60, 193
protection
  wisdom providing, 79
  for your life, 80–83
proverb compilations, eight in the book of Proverbs, 26–27
proverbial wisdom, delivering from the way of evil, 81
proverbs
  arranging according to topics, 26
  defined, 169
  duplicated in Proverbs (book of), 25–26
  Israelites passed them on orally, 24
  many not mentioning God's name, 57–59
  needing to be read more than once, 10

proverbs (*cont.*)
   not praising every ruler, 296
   one supplementing the other, 14
   opening the "actual" book of, 199
   other composers of, 23–24
   pagan collections of directed to a select public, 40
   people composing for hundreds of years, 22
   resting on facts, 4
   warning against abusing alcohol, 291
   writers of, 39, 40
Proverbs (book of). *See also* Instruction Manual for Proverbs (Prov 1–9)
   ascribing to Solomon alone, 21
   beginning with a preface, 33
   belonging to the books of the old and new covenants, 1
   consisting of selections from various collections, 200
   containing only about eight hundred proverbs, 23
   design and arrangement of, 25–27
   designed "for attaining wisdom and discipline," 104
   fostering abilities of discernment, 39–40
   as a guide focused on daily living, 287
   introducing wisdom in many different ways, 180
   nourished Israel's messianic expectations, 251
   as "optimistic," 225
   origin of, 19–30
   on pain and injustice in the life of the righteous, 15
   proceeding from God's redemption through his Son, 182
   as profitable for teaching, 67
   reading and rereading, 79
   reading as one of the books of the old and new covenants, 15–18
   selection from, 199–322
   serving "to know wisdom and instruction [discipline]," 132
   Solomon's name mentioned in, 22–23
   as a special book for the youth, 40–43
   on staying close to God and his Word, 124
   teaching discipline, 37–39
   teaching wisdom, 34–37
   as a title that does not entirely fit the contents, 2–3
proverbs of Solomon, 20–24
   belonging to the family or the category of the parables of our Savior, 3
   as an oracle for life's questions, 1
   which the men of Hezekiah copied, 25, 26
provocative clothes, as a warning, 140
prudence, 40–41, 58, 59
the prudent, 37, 42, 234–36, 280, 308
prudent conduct, of Joseph and Daniel, 241
psalmists, on "lying lips," 164–65
psalms, providing medicine for heartache, 244
psychiatry, modern on Christian neighborly love, 216
Ptah-Hotep, Egyptian proverbs of, 22
public justice, involving justice provided by a judge, 298
pupils, called "my son" and "my daughter," 66–67
Pythagoras, on learning to listen and to be silent, 208

quarreling, 36, 123, 270
queen of Sheba, 212
quick temper, acting foolishly, 267

Rachel and Leah, built up the house of Israel, 232
racial strife, arisen from slave trading, 313
rage, giving a heart attack or stroke, 238
rain clouds, efficiency of, 173
rationalism, 60
reactions, to the evil actions of others, 239

Rebekah, complained to Isaac about Esau, 201
rebellion, marital life corrupted by, 277
rebellion against God, 75, 95, 96, 167
Reformation, rescued Europe from superstition, 95
Reformed church, 214, 318
Rehoboam, 169, 215, 242, 300
rejection of their King, Israel's unbelief as, 11–12
reliability, truth as another word for, 223
religion, unchastity under the guise of, 140
religiosity, as "an abomination," 242
religious life of the seventeenth century, blessing of God's covenant in, 213
religious people, wicked helped destroy the Dutch state, 214
remorse, 152
reproof, rejecting, 207–8
Republic of the Seven United Netherlands, 214, 217, 226, 309
reputation, adulteress costing you, 147–48
respect, 46, 128, 231
revelation, 54, 73, 162
revenge, 116
revolution, 75, 89, 94, 95, 96
revolutionary agitation, 89, 295, 296
revolutionary rulers, 251
rewards, for keeping God's commandments, 13, 84–130
the rich, 218, 246
rich fool, 210, 263
rich man, 206, 278, 321
"the rich man," desiring to receive a favor from "the poor Lazarus," 236
Cardinal Richelieu, on the Dutch of his day, 225
riches, 210–12, 215, 321
riddles, Israelites fond of, 9
right(s)
    of the poor, 120
    of Yahweh, 102, 103
the righteous
    avoiding all sorts of adversity through piety, 225
    crying for help will be heard by the LORD, 242
    distresses of, 127
    escaping from trouble, 262
    falling into sins, 286
    finding refuge in death, 240
    getting a sure reward, 217
    going into eternal life, 279
    as a guide to neighbors, 227–28
    hating falsehood, 261
    having regard for the life of his beast, 221–23
    hiding in the inner room, 17
    life-wisdom of, 37
    as a minority in Israel and in Christianity, 124
    mouth of as a fountain of life, 205, 260
    possessing honor before God, 129
    promises given to, 82
    standing as a lasting foundation, 126
    suffering of, 16, 122, 313
    thriving when the wicked perish, 308–9
    trusting in rescue from death, 211–12
    wages of leading to life, 207
righteous and the wicked, 63, 118, 190
Righteous King, Jesus Christ as, 251–52
righteous man, 43, 211, 306
righteousness
    defending, 167–68
    delivering from death, 201–3, 210–12
    establishing a throne, 250–52
    Jesus called alms a matter of, 120
    of Lady Wisdom, 165
    leaving to God the defense of, 272
    one who sows getting a sure reward, 217
    as the only means of rescue, 210–11
    pursuit of loved by the LORD, 243
    rescuing economic life, 203
    shining like the dawn, 237
    suffering for the sake of, 105
    supplying rest, 117
    throne established by, 301
"ripe age," as someone approaching seventy, 87

rivers of living water, flowing out of the heart, 135–36
robbers and killers, spreading their own snare, 69
Robespierre, 223
Rockefeller, John D., Sr., 215, 216
Rockefeller Foundation, 216
rod of discipline
   driving folly away, 282–83, 309
   proverbs about, 284
   and reproof giving wisdom, 38
   sparing hating his son, 229–31
   wholesome effect of, 268
Rousseau, establishing the utopia of, 223
ruin, entering the life of the adulterer, 74
ruler
   requirements of a good, 296
   revolutionary, 251
   unwise, 168
rules of thumb, to avoid adultery, 141–42, 159–60
ruling, only wisdom equipping a person for, 168
Ruth, 253

Sabbaths, God gave Israel as sources of rest, 114
sacrifice, of the wicked, 242
sacrificing, of first fruits, 102
Sadducean leniency, Jesus attacked, 316
safety, in the name of Yahweh, 263
sages, 14, 15, 24, 283–99
Samaritan woman, Jesus teaching to, 121–22
Samson, 139
Samuel, 93, 258, 271
sand, as weighty, 303–5
Sanhedrin, "pious" wicked members of, 223
Sarah, 314
Satan, 94, 95–96
Saul, 122, 272, 293, 298
Savior. *See* Jesus Christ
saying
   mashal as a, 2
   we have no sin as deceiving ourselves, 271
scale, accuracy of, 48

scandal, continuing to use the word, 148
scarcity, determining value, 220
"school of discipline," 38
school of wisdom, never graduating from, 43
science
   as an early Dutch word for knowledge, 62
   elevating above the wisdom of Solomon, 17
   Scripture transcending, 99
scientific knowledge, 62, 96, 194
scientific thinking, distorting the language of Scripture, 319
scoffer, 127, 279–80. *See also* mockers
Scripture. *See also* Holy Scripture
   as complete, 319
   destructive activity of criticism, 22
   golden rule of interpretation, 181
   knowing from childhood, 281
   in the language of ordinary experience, 172
   learning passages by heart, 245
   portraying the teacher-student relationship, 133
   praising the wife, 323
   speaking with living words, 88
   teaching that God alone possesses immortality, 178
seamanship, 34, 35
season of harvest, resting upon divine ordinances, 54
secularism, causing today's global instability, 312
seductive speech, of the adulteress, 139
seeing eye, made by the Lord, 271–72
self-determination, imagined right to, 286
self-discipline, learning, 39
self-esteem, poverty injuring, 206
self-pity, being aware of, 246
self-understanding, lack of, 235
sensitivity, not preventing cruelty, 223
Sermon on the Mount, 7, 9
sex, without love, 157–58
sex tourism, new morality and, 144
sexual diseases, 144, 145, 147
sexual enjoyment, not restricting, 152

sexual immorality, 137, 154
sexual pleasure, "to eat" and "to drink water" referring to, 195
sexual sins, results of, 90
shalom. *See* peace
shame, 129
shameless words, as a warning, 140
sharing, 101, 219
Sheba, premature death of, 89
Sheol and Abaddon, lie open before the LORD, 243
shield
    as a fixed term for the Suzerain, 317
    wisdom functioning like, 114
Shimei, came to make peace with David, 249
Shimel, premature death of, 89
"shivering before people," laying a snare, 314–16
Shrewdness, as the daughter of Lady Wisdom, 166
shrewdness, gaining, 42
signet ring, 67
Sikkel, J. C., 193–94
silence, 208, 314
silver, taking away the dross from, 300–301
"silver fleets," of Spain, 201–2, 204
Simeon, threw himself down before David, 236
the simple. *See also* gullible persons
    believing everything, 42, 234–36
    going on and suffering for it, 280
    killed by their turning away, 75
    Proverbs understanding of, 41
sin(s)
    all suffering on earth as a result of, 105
    as an attack upon one's own life, 192
    becoming clean from, 270–71
    children conceived and born in, 281
    connection with sickness, 99
    corrupting the shared life of marriage, 277
    as fate instead of a culpable debt, 265
    folly as another word for, 282
    insomnia and, 115–17
    leading perpetrators to fall into adversity, 225
    negative influence of unconfessed, 239
    parent misperceiving the power of in children, 230
    as so pretty and seductive to our evil nature, 195
    tied to words, 208
"sincere brotherly love," taught by the apostles, 123
sinners, 64, 68–69, 285–87
sixth commandment, shall not murder, 68
slack hand, causing poverty, 203–4
slave trade, profiting from, 217
sleep, wisdom benefiting your, 114–17
the slothful, putting to forced labor, 225–26
slothfulness, 109, 204
"slowness to anger," displaying, 267
snares
    of death, 228–29, 237
    fear of man laying, 314–16
    to say rashly, "It is holy," 273–75
    of sin, 119
snow, wife not afraid of, 328
social disorders, from psychological illnesses, 260
social knowledge, beginning with the fear of the LORD, 49
social reformers, calling themselves progressive, 208
soft answer, turning away wrath, 241–42
sojourners, shield of protection around, 49–50
solitary person, 259
Solomon
    acknowledging his own lack of wisdom, 191
    advising us to put up with inconvenience, 233
    asked God for wisdom at his coronation, 168
    composed three thousand proverbs, 23
    concluding in a couple of wonderful metaphors, 185

Solomon (*cont.*)
    on excessive punishment of children, 267
    governed with advisors, 215
    instruction about blessing and cursing, 126
    learned as a child from his father David, 131–36
    memory of remaining a blessed one, 204
    mentioned three times in Proverbs, 22–23
    no one who does not sin, 271
    omitted mention of tragic situations, 98
    Proverbs of, 20–24, 200–283, 299–316
    provided the largest amount of material, 19
    received gifts from the queen of Sheba, 255
    removed harmful figures immediately at his coronation, 301
    saw a reward connected to the fear of the LORD, 96
    treated his mother with great respect, 65
    two women claiming the same child and, 300
    warned about the eyes of the strange woman, 155
    wisdom of, 1
    youthful gangsters speaking some words, 68–69
Son of God, Lord Jesus Christ as, 176
sons, 231, 243
Sophia (wisdom), myth of, 179
soul
    having regard for a beast's, 222
    saving from Sheol, 285
sound judgment, having, 218
sovereign right of supremacy, of God over the entire creation, 46
sovereign will, of God, 299
"space of heart," given to Solomon, 21
Spain, 201, 202

Spanish Armada, as "the invincible fleet," 252
speaking, with much coming much sinning, 208
speech, thoughtful belonging to wisdom, 330
spirit
    crushed by sorrow of heart, 243–44
    governing many young people, 67
Spirit of God, 38, 75, 184, 239
Spirit of wisdom, driving all of the authors, 24
"spiritual life," happiness extending far beyond, 238
spouses, working at it, 331
springs of life, flowing from the heart, 135
stability, of a man of understanding and knowledge, 305
"statutes and ordinances," God has established, 54
steadfast love, 70
stimulants, warning against excessive use of, 302
stolen money, of Spain, 202
stomach ulcer, person getting, 238
stone, as heavy, 303–5
strange women, 140, 144, 155–56, 234, 267
street evangelist, Lady Wisdom as, 71–76
strength, 143, 168, 275, 329
strife, 241, 267, 270
strong tower or fortress, Yahweh as, 262
subjectivism, 308
suffering, not all as God's chastisement, 105–6
superscriptions, on Proverbs, 26
sweet sleep, of a laborer, 246
sympathetic listeners, obeying, 28
synagogue of Satan, falling down before the church of Philadelphia, 236–37
synonyms, Proverbs teeming with, 5–6
syphilis (the curse of Venus), as more horrible than gonorrhea, 146
systematic knowledge, excluding from the force of God's Word, 62

table, of Lady Wisdom, 186–87
table fellowship, as life fellowship for an Israelite, 188
table of contents, of the book of Proverbs, 33
"taking up one's cross," as a kind of suffering, 105
talent for organization, 233
talk, tending only to poverty, 203
Tamar, 90, 150, 160, 193
taste, determining what is good, 218
taunts, *mashals* as, 2–3, 9
teachers, 66–67, 284
teaching
    directing to those who want to listen, 189
    false, 261
    fundamental ordinances for all, 66
    as a substitute for "discipline," 132
    those who are straying, 38
    of the wise as a fountain of life, 228–29
temple, built by the wise men, 34–35
temptation, 154, 274, 321
Ten Commandments, organizing proverbs by, 26
testing
    faith, 102
    what "people" are claiming, 42
theologians, going further than God permits, 319
things in daily life, source of wisdom for, 55–57
thinking, authority of, 60–61
those who keep the law, striving against the wicked, 306
those who seek the LORD, understanding justice, 307
Tiglath Pileser, 276
tithe, involving the best portion, 102
to dust you shall return, illnesses as causes of death, 98
toil, profiting in all, 237
tongue
    as a fountain of loveliness, 110
    of the righteous as choice silver, 205
    sins of, 261
    of the "strange woman" or the wife of another man, 140
    of the wise bringing healing, 254
    wounding or hurting a neighbor, 260
Torah
    on God's compassion extending to the animal world, 221
    learning wisdom from, 48–51
    many kings of Judah and Israel rejected, 250
    prescribed capital punishment for adultery, 149
    as a protective shield over the poor, 320
    teaching about God and his service, 311
Tournier, Paul, 115
traffic accidents, alcohol in connection with, 290
tranquil heart, giving life to the flesh, 238–40, 267
"transgressions," repeatedly bringing up, 256
treasure hunter, looking for wisdom, 78–83
treasures
    gained by wickedness as not profit, 201–3
    as often sources of deep trouble, 246
tree of life, wisdom letting you eat from, 110–12
trespasses and sins, being dead in, 196
trouble, wicked filled with, 13
trust, 96, 122–23, 315
truth, 165, 223, 236, 314
truth and falsehood, distinguishing between, 235
"turning away," death, 88–89
two swords, Roman Catholic doctrine of, 183
two ways, as the way of the righteous and the way of the wicked, 196

"Unbelief and Revolution," sowing the seed of, 94
Unbelief and Revolution (Groen van Prinsterer), 75, 295

uncertainty of life, 117
unchastity, destroying one's taste for God's will, 82
unconfessed sins, keeping us awake, 117
understanding
 departing from evil as, 55
 human standing above Holy Scripture, 214
 leading a person to good, 266
 slow to anger having, 267
 subject to the Word of God, 60
 wisdom leading to, 79
United States, acted wisely after World War II, 217, 247
universal genius, Solomon as, 21
unjust gain, 247–48
unknown composers, of proverbs, 23–24
unmerciful, at the last judgment, 279
unprofitable conversation, as a waste of energy, 237
unrighteous wealth, 256
unrighteousness, 117, 255, 265
unspiritual people, viewing wisdom as foolishness, 166
"unto life" or "unto sin," as the great distinction, 207
unwise rulers, implementing "iniquitous decrees," 168
upbringing, "without constraints," 284
upright people, 136, 212
Uriah, 106, 122, 211

value
 of life, 111
 of wisdom, 28–29, 64–65
van Andel, J., 53
van Prinsterer, Groen, 75, 94, 95, 96, 99, 295, 301
vanity, 126
venereal diseases, coming back with intensity, 144
vengeance, leaving to the wrath of God, 273
vineyard, activity needed for planting, 327
violence, 124, 205, 215
voice of wisdom, resemblance to prophecy, 74

vows, reflecting on only after making, 273–75

wages of sin, as death, 195
waiting on God, as merely being "passive," 273
walking with God, nightly rest and, 116–17
walking with the wise, becoming wise, 169
warning, against excess in various areas, 302
wasting time, warning against, 237
"the way he should go," meaning of, 280–82
way of the wicked, as an abomination to the LORD, 243
way seeming right to man, as the way to death, 234, 254
ways, of God as higher than your ways, 299
the weak. *See also* the poor
 blessed is he who has regard for, 227
weakness, God's power perfected in our, 105
wealth
 dangers of, 108
 describing a person having "a full stomach," 109
 gained hastily will dwindle, 228
 honoring the LORD with your, 101
 of a rich man as his strong city, 206, 263
 wife deserving a sizeable portion of, 332
 wisdom lending, 108–9
wealthy Jews, gold of in AD 70, 210
weaving, as typically women's work, 327
weights
 honesty of, 48
 specified, 49
wellbeing, Word of God directed to our, 95
"what everybody says," not believing, 236
whisperer, separating close friends, 270
whoever trusts in the LORD, as safe, 250, 314–16

SUBJECT INDEX

the wicked
    accepting a bribe in secret to pervert the ways of justice, 258–59
    arrogance of, 207
    being cut off (circumcised) from the land, 82
    bringing shame and disgrace, 261
    condemning the righteous as an abomination, 259
    distress of in perplexity, 118
    earning deceptive wages, 217
    exposed to various terrors, 119
    filled with trouble, 225
    gain of leading to sin, 207
    at the gates of the righteous, 236–37
    living according to autonomous principles or counsels, 73
    mercy of as cruel, 221–23
    in the midst of God's people, 242
    mouth of, 205, 212–14, 260
    name of will rot, 204
    as nothing but worthless chaff, 124
    overthrown through evildoing, 240
    quick and unexpected demise for, 118
    refusing to fear God in humility, 189
    reproving, 189
    riddle of prosperity and long lifespans of, 91
    rising to power causing people to go into hiding, 308–9
    sinners as one word identifying, 286
    sorrows of, 192
    taking away from the presence of the king, 300–301
    those who forsake the law praise, 306
    way of leading them astray, 227–28
    as wealthy, 124
wicked woman, life-destroying seduction of, 28
wickedness, 165, 251
wife
    doing good all the days of her life, 325
    effects on the house of her husband, 232
    enjoying the love of your own, 156–58
    as a good thing, 264
    house shared with a quarrelsome, 276–78, 303
    hymn to a proficient, 323–32
    looking beyond the walls of her house and financial means at her disposal, 327
    not overshadowing her husband, 329
    proficient not fearing the arrival of snow, 328
    proficient not quarrelsome, 330
    supplying life necessities of her family, 326
Prince William of Orange, 241
willing hands, wife working with, 326
wine
    Bible speaking positively about, 288
    biting like a serpent and stinging like an adder, 234
    going down smoothly but biting like a serpent, 289
    of a mocker, 58
    not drinking a lot of, 56
wisdom
    all coming from God, 24
    beginning with respect for God's revelation, 167
    beginning with the fear of the LORD, 4, 45–47
    beholding its dwelling blessed by God, 126–27
    benefiting sleep, 114–17
    as better than jewels, 166
    book of Proverbs teaching, 34–37
    canticle celebrating, 161–84
    catastrophic lack of, 168
    co-creating the world, 176
    of the craftsman, 37
    delivery of he who walks in, 308
    despising to own injury, 74
    as a divine person, 177–78
    encompassing and blessing life, 129–30
    exalting a person, 186
    extending life, 64–77, 86–92
    fools despising, 59–60

wisdom (cont.)
- in the form of a wise woman, 69
- as the foundation of everything, 172, 175
- functioning preventively, 76
- as a gift of God, 44–45, 191
- of God, 60–62, 180, 270
- from God's word, 47–53
- from God's work, 54–59
- health and, 99–100
- with the humble, 209–10
- identified, 178–79
- increasing possessions, 101–3
- as indispensable for creation, 170
- initiated into the knowledge of God, 178
- intoxicated with joy in God's work, 174
- of Israel, 177
- keeping us on the path toward eternal life, 83
- leading into intimate interaction with God, 124–25
- leading to life, 188
- leading to the least amount of misery, 94–96
- leading us to recognize wisdom, 166
- lending wealth and honor, 108–9
- letting you eat from a tree of life, 110–12
- leveling the path for the blessing of Yahweh, 108
- listening to, 29, 45, 132–34
- lying at the foundation of heaven and earth, 112–13
- making a person helpful and benevolent, 119–22
- making a person more humble, 128
- making alive, 134–36
- making alive, adorning you, and protecting you, 113–14
- making one inherit honor, 128–29
- making one peace-loving, 123–24
- making you sympathetic to God and others, 92–94
- as more valuable than jewels, 107–8
- need for, 1
- not abusing trust, 122–23
- obtained from God, 24
- obtaining God's good pleasure, 127–28
- obtaining treasures of, 71
- offering protection, 81
- as older than the world, 184
- path to, 28, 29
- as a personification and not as a (semi-)divine being, 170
- placing on the stage as though it were speaking person, 161
- placing you under the favor of the LORD, 192
- of a poor man as despised, 129
- presented as a playing child, 182
- preserving you while the wicked are perishing, 118–19
- as priceless but obtainable for everyone, 166
- promoting health, 97–100
- promoting nightly rest, 116, 117
- protecting against unspeakable evil, 113
- providing with tangible wealth and honor, 169
- putting us on familiar terms with God, 125
- quarrying for like a gold digger, 78–79
- required for making the world, 171
- rod and reproof giving, 309–11
- role of in connection with the creation, 174
- seeking as richly rewarded, 78
- Solomon possessed unprecedented, 20–21
- source of lying outside of us, 308
- taking to heart, 131, 162
- teaching one to bow under God's discipline, 103–7
- teaching to render speedy benevolence, 121
- value of, 28–29, 64–65, 112
- wife opening her mouth with, 330
- of women, 232, 233
- Yahweh prohibited the oppression of, 50

Wisdom (God's Son), as God's first creation according to Arius, 179
wisdom and folly, choice between, 196, 305
wisdom literature, Solomon wrote genuine, 21–22
Wisdom of Solomon, 182, 183
Wisdom of Solomon, apocryphal wisdom book, 177–78
wisdom psalms, of David, 131
Wisdom-hypostasis, Judaism pulled back from speculations about, 180
the wise
- expressions describing, 5
- famous, 22
- hearing the words of, 283
- inheriting honor, 109, 128, 129
- laying up knowledge, 205
- as a minority in Israel and in Christianity, 124
- needing to be corrected, 190
- not always experiencing things in the same way, 17
- not always sitting in the seats of government, 168
- not always striking it rich, 109
- as not perfect, 190
- paying attention to gifts and callings, 36
- preserving their knowledge for the right moment, 205
- walking with as becoming wise, 229

wise heart, 58, 108, 231
"wise in their own eyes," fools as, 59
wise man, 43, 314
wise or foolish, becoming as a process, 190
wise son, making a glad father, 201
wise woman, wisdom as, 162
wisest of women, building her house, 232–33
withdrawal of a husband, as a disruption of God's order, 277
withholding what should be given, suffering want, 218–19
witness, truthful saving lives, 51
woman
- caught in adultery brought to Jesus, 160
- consequences of gonorrhea, 145
- ideal, 27, 218, 233
- must be able to discern, 218
- as not always the one guilty, 159–60
- portrait of a wise, 324
- ruthless, 143
- as a trap, 264
- turning away your eyes from a shapely, 155, 331
- who fears the LORD, 323, 331
- young man hooked by, 138

women and maidens, Yahweh raising up a shield over, 160
Wonderful Counselor, Jesus Christ as, 23
wool and flax, family's clothes made from, 326
woolen items, produced by the wife, 327
Word, was with God, and the Word was God, 176
Word of God
- childlike respect for, 153
- coming to us with things, 8
- daily reading and discussion of, 230
- of God constituting an inexhaustible fountain of wisdom, 45
- as the only suitable standard of good and evil, 235
- as the preeminent source of wisdom, 53

words
- as the best tool of discipline, 230
- man hasty in, 314
- not lacking transgression, 208–9
- of the wise, 26, 283

work
- all involving inconvenience, 233
- committing to the LORD, 117, 248
- of God, 54–59
- manner of can be crippling for our rest, 117
- requiring some mess and some dirtiness, 233

work space, knowing, 36
workers, zealous succeeded by lazy grandchildren, 204

"works of darkness," 158
"the works of the flesh," 289
the world, accepting as it is, 37
worldly supremacy, papal claims to, 183
worthless pursuits, bringing poverty, 203
wrath
    day of, 210–12
    of God, 179, 266, 273
    of the king, 240–42
writers, of proverbs as godly artists, 4–5

Yahweh. *See also* God; "our Father"
    ate meat as a guest of Abraham, 222
    blessing all types of life, 212
    Daniel feared, 293
    did not spare even his own Son to redeem human life, 48
    fearing and loving our neighbor as medicine, 247
    as God and Father of our Lord Jesus Christ, 262
    honoring continuing instruction, 46
    as Israel's God and Deliverer, 102
    not letting the righteous go hungry, 13
    possessing wisdom, 170
    promised that Sarah would be the mother of a great nation, 314
    protected the existence of marriages among his people, 150
    protecting the godly in times of judgment, 119
    revulsion to those who commit violence, 125
    silencing the warning voice of prophecy, 312
    on the special place of the king in Israel, 250
    wanted to keep this people alive, 275–76
"You are my shield," 317
"You shall not steal," 203
young men, seduction of, 141, 280, 324
young people (youth)
    ages of, 41–42
    impetuous about political events, 296
    Lady Folly calling, 194
    life-wisdom for, 33–43
    listening well to the priest and Levite, 65
    obedience adorning, 67–68
    Proverbs (book of) for, 40–43, 187, 286, 291
    sages wanted to nurture, 14
    struggle between Wisdom and Folly involving, 187, 194
    teaching about a potential wife, 218

Zechariah, 232
Zephaniah, 210, 211
Zimri, 89

Scripture Index

OLD TESTAMENT

Genesis

1	265
1:1	176, 262
1:4	115
1:14–18	55
1:16	55
1:21	221
1:25	221
1:29	55
2	265
2:7	100
2:18	325
2:18–25	277
2:24	147, 158
3:5–6	195
3:12	264
3:16	277
3:16–19	105
3:22	110
4:1	201
8:21	271, 282, 309
8:22	54, 115
11:10–32	86
12:10–20	315
15:1	317
15:15	255
16	205
16:2–4	142
17:14	82
18:1	117
18:7–8	222
18:17	125
19:1	138
20	315
20:6	142
21:22	41
23:16	48
24	172
24:12–14	264
24:27	264
25:8	255
26:26–31	249
27:28	288
27:41	249
27:46	201
28:8	201
28:18	92
30:3	142
30:27	213
31:24	249
32:20	256
33:4	249
37:2	41
38:14	193
38:18	67
39:5	213
39:7–10	141
39:8–10	93
39:21–23	93
41:39	35, 44
41:46–57	213
41:56–57	220
45:5–8	266
45:26–27	248
47:9	244
47:25	213, 220
47:27–28	245

Exodus

1:21 KJV	232
2:6	41, 281
2:16–20	172
3:8	301
4:6	142
4:21	276
4:23	229
12:15	82
12:19	82
13:9	153
14:4	276
15:26	98
18:21	258
20:9–10	221
20:14	82
20:17	155
21:16	217
21–22	90
22:1–4	148–49
22:8	123
22:22–24	50
22:25	49
23:1–2	51
23:3	51
23:8	258
23:9	49
23:11	49
23:12	49
28:3	45
28:3 KJV	34
31:2–3	45
31:3–11 KJV	34
34:24	250
35:10 KJV	34
35:26 KJV	34
35:31 KJV	34
35:35 KJV	34
36:1 KJV	34
36:4 KJV	34

Leviticus

3	140
7:11–21	140
18:5	99
18:5 NIV	312
19:9–10	50
19:13	49, 51, 121
19:15	51, 296
19:18	121, 272
19:19	328
19:35–36	49
20	90
20:10	148, 149, 150
24	90
25:23	102
25:35–55	217
25:39–40	49
26	16, 126, 312
26:1–13	212
26:3–13	101
26:14–26	105
26:25	98
27:1–8	87, 274

Numbers

4:3	87
5:11–31	149
8:23–26	87
8:25	87
12	106
15	90
16	118
20	106
23:8	303
25	90
35	90

Deuteronomy

	26, 317
1:17	51
4:1	99
4:6	46, 47
4:26	82
5:13–14	221
5:33	99
6:6–8	48
6:6–9	153
6:7	133, 153
8:1	99
8:8	301
8:11–17	321
10:17	258

11:17	82	28:60	98
11:18	48	30:15	111
11:19	153	30:15–20	111
12:32	317	30:16	99
15:11	121	30:18	82
16:18–20	296	30:19	99, 111
16:19	51, 258	30:19–20	111, 196
16:20	40, 99, 211	30:20 NASB	85
17:14–20	250	32:4	51
17:18–19	250	32:35	273
17:20	250	33:10	153
19	90–91		
19:14	50	**Joshua**	
22	90–91		105
22:1–4	121	7:21	78
22:6–7	221	24:15	196
22:11	328	25:6–7	186
22:13–21	160		
22:13–30	160	**Judges**	
22:22	149, 150	4:4	71
22:22–24	148	7	241
22:25–27	160	8:1	241
22:28–29	160	8:1–3	242
23:2–3	229	8:32	255
23:13	326	14	9
23:21–23	274	14:8–9	301
23:22	275	19:11–21	138
23–24	217	19–21	312
24	90–91		
24:14	51	**Ruth**	
24:14–15	121	1:21–22	253
24:17	50	2:8–9	253
25:2–3	267	2:10	254
25:4	221	2:11–12	254
25:13–16	49	2:14	254
26:1–11	102	4	72
26:5	102	4:11–12	232
26:9–10	102		
27:17	50	**1 Samuel**	
27:25	258	1:11	274
28	16, 111, 126, 312	1:24	41
28:1–12	101	2:1–10	128
28:1–14	212	2:3	191
28:15	105	2:26	93
28:20–21	98	2:30	129
28:27	98		
28:35	98		
28:37	3		

1 Samuel (cont.)

3:1	312
8:3	258
9:11	172
10:12	2
10:27	255
12:3	258
14:25–30	301
15:22	271
16:7	296
17:18	255
17:34–35	222
17:45	315
18:14	118
18:21–25	122
19:9	122
20:30	298
20:32	298
23:16–17a	227
24	266, 272, 293
24:6	293
24:12	66
24:14	2
25	304
25:3	218
25:10	304
25:10 NIV	304
25:17	304
25:18–19	256
25:25	304
25:28	304
25:30	304
25:38	118
26	266, 272, 293

2 Samuel

1:13–16	261
1:17–27	266
1:24	328
3:27	122
4:5	117
7	305
11:8–13	122
12	8, 106
12:5–6	9
13	90, 150
14	23

14:2	162
14:27	41
15	122
15–19	89
15:25	249
15:31	249
16:1–12	249
17:33	41
17:42	41
18:5	41
18:12	41
18:32	41
19:10–24	249
19:18	236
19:32	87
19:35–36	255
20	89
20:16–17	162
20:16–22	23, 71

1 Kings

	22
1:1	255
2	89
2:9	13
2:19	65
3:4–15	21
3:7	41
3:7–9	191
3:9	39, 134, 168
3:12	24, 44
3:14	36
3:28	71
4:20	212
4:22–23	246
4:29	21, 24
4:30	22
4:30–33	62
4:31	22
4:32	22, 23
4:33	21
4:34	22, 71
5	23
5:12	44
7:2–7	186
7:14 KJV	35
8	212

8:12	299
8:46	271
9:7	3
10:1–10	22, 24
10:2	255
11:29–39	207
12	242, 300
12:6	215
12:14	242
12:25–32	318
12:33—13:34	207
13	106, 127
13–14	318
14:13	91
14:21–24	232
15:23	255
16	89
17	119
18	16, 17
18:4	119
22	300
22:34–36	118
22:52	207

2 Kings

1	210
2	301
2:12	66
2:45–46	301
4:10	277
6:21	66
6:24–33	13
7:1	72
8:7–8	255
9:30–37	119
11:1	232
15	89
22:14	71

1 Chronicles

17:6	250
19:14	103
22:5	41
22:15 KJV	34
23:24	87
29:1	41
29:28	255
32:27–29	213

2 Chronicles

2:7 KJV	35
9:24	255
12:6	17
13:7	41
15:3	312
16:9	159
17:5	255
17:7–9	71
17–20	301
18	305
18:18–22	276
19:7	296
24:2	301
26:5	232
29:1	232
34:3	41

Ezra

1	276

Nehemiah

8	153
8:10	258
9:17	74
9:25–26	321

Esther

5:4	187
6:14	187

Job

	15, 225
1	106
1:1	97
1:9–12	105
2:7–8	97
3:21	78
4:17b	271
5:27	45
8:8	45
8:8–10	133

Job (cont.)

11:18–19	117
13:12	3
14:4	190, 271, 282, 309
15:7	170
15:7–10	169
15:10	133
15:18 NIV	169
19:19	125
21:7–15	321
24:15	158
27:1	3
28	44
28:8–9	172
28:14	70
28:15–19	108
28:25–28	55
28:27–28	175, 299
28:28	45, 46, 61, 178
29:1	3
29:4	125
29:7–10	72
29:7–11	329
29:21–22	72
31	106
31:16–22	121
33:16–33	107
34:22	159
38:33	54
39:1–3	221
42:16–17	87

Psalms

	7, 16, 33, 51, 59, 62, 85, 196, 204
1	62, 124, 196, 243
1:1	1, 73
1:2	307
1:4	124
1:4–6	82
1:6	2
2:3	95
2:6	171
2:9	184
3:5	116, 167
4:8	117
6:1	106, 107
9:2	172
9:12	220
9:18	220
10	220
10:2	237
10:4	237
10:11	205
10:22 ESV	248
11	123
11:3	52, 308
11:18	237
11:19	211
12	123
12:1	308
12:1–2	165
12:6	316
12:24	237
13:4	237
13:11	237
13–14	124
14:1	59, 304
14:23	237
15:5	258
16:11	110
18:27	128
18:30	316
19	71, 85
19:2	115
19:4–5	71
19:7	47
19:7–8	316
19:7–11	167
19:9	85
19:11	85, 301
19:13	167, 320
21:9	276
23	244
23:1	227
23:4	227
24:1	103, 207
25:3	105
25:14	125
26	107
26:10	258
27	244
27:4	110
28:5	305
28:28	306

31:15	87, 88	57	272
32:1	257	58	272
32:3	117	59	272
32:3–4	239	66:10–12	105
32:10	192	72	212, 250
33	276	72:10	255
33:4	316	72:17	204
33:12	313	73	91, 124, 225, 286
34	131, 244	73:2–12	124
34:12	111	73:2–15	321
34:15–22	242	73:17	125
34:19	13, 225	73:28	125
35:7	105	74:9	312
36:6	221	74:16	115
36:9	205	75	272
37	82, 91, 125, 220, 225, 237, 240, 244, 272, 286	78:2	3
		78:3–4	153
		81:11–13	74
37:5	245	84:12	129
37:5–7a	299	85	70, 71
37:6 NIV	237	85:10–11	70
37:7	237	89:14	250
37:10	125	89:41	206
37:11	125	90:17	110, 248
37:13	125	96:11–12	70
37:29	125	97:2	250
37:34	237	101:4–7	301
41:1 NIV	227	103:8–14	281
41:1–2	220	104:15	288
41:9	122	104:20	115
42	244	104:21	221
44	106	104:23	115
44:22	105	104:24	54, 112, 172
45:10	66	104:27	221
46	16	104:35	82
49	210	107:27	34, 35
49:4	3	111:2	59, 173
50:14	274	111:10b	46
51:5	271, 282	112:9	120, 219
51:5–6	309	114:3–7	70
53:1	304	119	47, 313, 316
53:2	59	119:1	313
55:12–14	122	119:11	79
55:12–19	122	119:53	306
55:14	125	119:66	40, 218, 307
56	244	119:67	105
56:4	316	119:96 NIV	55
56:10	316	119:100	307

Psalms (cont.)

119:103	301
119:105	192
119:136	306
119:140 NIV	316
120:7	224
127	232
127:2	248
128:5–6	87
130	160
130:3	271
131:1	47, 253, 320
133	247
138:6	128
139	243
139:1–12	159
139:16	87
141:3	209
141:5	190
143:2	271
145:15–16	221
148	54

Proverbs

1	28, 34, 64, 75, 78
1:1	19, 20, 22, 27, 34
1:1 NIV	104
1:1–6	33–43
1:1–7	27, 64
1:1—9:18	26
1:2	36, 38, 39, 132
1:2–3	128, 230, 268
1:2–5	43
1:2–6	34
1:2b–3	39
1:3	40, 120, 123
1–3	134, 135
1:4	40, 41, 42, 67, 139, 156, 187, 235, 280
1:5	43
1:6	10, 225
1:7	4, 16, 29, 36, 37, 44–63, 54, 57, 58, 64, 128, 167, 186, 191, 218, 237, 281, 303
1:7 SV	62
1:7a	45, 47
1:8	29, 38, 65, 71, 133n2, 153, 330
1–8	175, 185
1:8–9	27, 64
1:9	67, 109, 113, 186
1–9	3, 20, 22, 25, 27–30, 64, 75, 80, 104, 111, 129, 131, 134, 161, 181, 182, 199, 200, 211, 237, 283, 291, 308
1:10–19	64, 68–69
1:20	164, 180
1:20–21	72, 329
1:20–33	64, 69–77, 79, 119, 162, 182
1:22	72
1:23	73
1:24	73
1:24–25	73, 75
1:24–33	192
1:26–28	74
1:29	59
1:29–30	74
1:31–32	75
1:33	76, 80, 84
2	28, 34, 78–83
2:1	86, 114
2:1–4	78–79, 82
2:4	166
2:5	86, 167
2:5–10	79–80
2:6	24, 44
2:7	80
2:8	80
2:9	135
2:10	45
2:11	81, 84, 135
2:11–22	80–83
2:12	81
2:12–15	81
2:14	81
2:16	25, 140
2:16–19	81, 140, 151
2:17	140, 143
2:19	82
2:20–22	82

SCRIPTURE INDEX

2:21	82, 135
2:22	82
3	28, 84–130, 101, 108, 111, 130, 188, 237
3:1	111, 196
3:1–2	84, 86–92, 97, 108, 175, 192, 255, 285, 296
3:2	126, 135
3:3	48, 113
3:3–4	84, 92–94
3–4	92
3:4	111
3:5–6	84, 94–96, 135, 295, 308
3:5–7	60
3:6	111
3:7	59, 90, 267, 303
3:7–8	55, 84, 97–100, 135, 147, 216, 227, 228, 237, 239, 240, 247, 253, 254, 258, 273, 311
3:8	111, 124
3:9	111
3:9–10	84, 101–3, 108, 169, 204
3:10	102
3:11	104, 105
3:11–12	84, 103–7, 230, 284
3:13–15	84, 107–8, 169
3:14	166
3:15	25, 324
3:16	84, 86, 108–9, 111, 135, 204, 248
3:17	80, 84, 110, 111, 205, 254, 262
3:18	84, 110–12, 113, 135, 229, 238
3:19	84, 172, 178
3:19–20	112–13
3:21	135
3:21–23	85, 113–14, 229
3:21–26	135
3:23	111
3:24	85, 114–17, 124, 135, 247
3:24–25	248
3:25	135
3:25–26	85, 118–19
3:27	119, 120
3:27–28	119–22, 279, 320
3:28	120, 122
3:29	85, 122–23
3:30	85, 123–24, 270
3:31–32	85, 124–25
3:32	111
3:33	85, 111, 126–27, 135
3:33–35	169
3:34	85, 127–28, 210, 252, 279, 280
3:35	85, 109, 128–29
4	28, 38, 65, 86, 131–36, 175, 268, 309
4:1	133
4:1–2	38, 132, 135
4:2	133
4:3–4	268
4:3–4a	132
4:4	38, 111, 133, 135
4:5	133, 135
4:5–9	71
4:6	114, 133, 134, 135
4:6–7	81
4:6–9	162, 180, 182
4:7	134, 135
4:8	134
4:8–9	109, 135
4–9	130
4:10	86, 134, 135
4:10–13	66
4:11	38, 135, 268
4:12	114, 135
4:13	134, 135
4:14	135
4:16	135
4:17	188
4:18	135
4:19	135
4:20	134
4:21	134, 135

Proverbs (cont.)

4:22	100, 135, 227	6:35	150
4:23	93, 135, 275	7	42, 143, 146, 149, 235, 280
4:24–27	136	7:1–4	154
4:25	136	7:2	111, 154
4:26	136	7:3	48
5	138, 143, 156, 158	7:4	71, 162, 180, 182
5:1–23	3, 140	7:5	25
5:3	140	7:7	139, 156
5:3–4	156, 234	7:8	140
5:4	142	7:10	138, 328
5:5–6	151	7:12	138
5:6	112	7:14–23	139
5–7	28, 74, 82, 104, 119, 137–60, 282	7:15	140
		7:18	195
5:8	140, 154	7:20	149
5:8–10	143	7:21	141
5:11	100, 144–45, 146, 234	7:22	141, 280
		7:22—7:23a	146
5:12–13	152	7:26–27	151
5:13	138	7:27	195
5:14	148, 149	8	28, 71, 75, 133, 161–84, 170, 175, 176, 178, 179, 180, 181, 182, 183, 184, 185
5:15	188		
5:15–16	157		
5:15–20	156, 157, 195		
5:16	157		
5:17	157	8:1	163
5:18	157	8:1–3	161, 187
5:19	157	8:1–5	162–64, 166, 174, 175
5:21–23	159		
5:23	137, 159	8:1–6	167
6:14	123	8:1–36	3
6:18	123	8:2–3	163, 329
6:20	66, 330	8:3	163
6:20—7:27	3, 140	8:4–5	164
6:20–23	153	8:5	164, 166
6:20–35	48	8:6	165
6:22	162, 180, 182	8:6–13	161, 164–67, 174
6:23	112	8:7	165
6:25	141, 155, 331	8:7–13	167
6:26 NIV	143	8:8	165
6:27–29	142	8:8–31	174
6:30–35	150	8:9	165
6:31	149	8:10	166
6:32	143	8:10–11	166
6:33	36, 148	8:11	25, 324
6:34	90, 149, 150	8:12	166
		8:13	61, 166

SCRIPTURE INDEX

8:14–16	167, 168	9:12	28, 36, 84, 129, 192
8:14–21	161, 167–69, 174	9:13–14	193
8:15	165, 183, 184	9:13–18	193–96
8:15–16	183, 184	9:15–16	194
8:17	79, 164, 168, 229	9:17	195
8:18	109	9:18	195, 196
8:18–21	169	10:1	19, 20, 22, 25, 27, 68, 117, 199, 201
8:19	166		
8:22	162, 170, 171, 176, 179, 181	10:1—22:16	25, 26
8:22 KJV	178	10:2	201–3, 204, 237, 268
8:22–23	180, 181, 182		
8:22–30	113	10:3	13, 117
8:22–31	24, 161, 163, 169–74, 175, 176, 178, 180	10:4	6, 109, 203, 217, 226, 228
		10:5	58, 109
8:23	171	10:6	21
8:24 NIV	171	10:7	126, 204
8:25–27	172	10:11	110, 112, 260, 262
8:27	172	10:12	257, 266
8:27–31	178	10:13	38, 229, 309
8:28–31	173	10:14	79, 110, 205, 261
8:30	181, 182	10:15	119, 206, 263, 320, 321
8:30–31	182		
8:31b	173	10:16	207
8:32	171, 175	10:17	112, 207
8:32–36	161, 170, 174–75	10:19	208, 259
8:33	37	10:20	205
8:34	175	10:21	60, 110, 205
8:35–36	75	10:22	14
8:36	77, 111	10–22	200, 283
9	28, 71, 175, 180, 182, 183, 185–96, 234	10–22:16	20
		10:23	224
		10:25	126
9:1	162, 180, 182, 186	10:26	7
9:1–6	186–88	10:27	90, 126
9:2	186	10:28	126, 287
9:3	187	10:30	82, 126
9:4	187, 195	10–31	27, 28, 29, 30, 74, 75, 79, 83, 100, 104, 161, 170, 185, 186, 188, 192, 199, 200
9:5–6	187		
9:6	111		
9:7–8	73, 189		
9:7–12	188–92		
9:9	43, 190	10:32	261
9:10	4, 45, 186, 191, 192	11:1	49
		11:2	128, 129, 209
9:10b	46	11:4	210
9:11	21, 86, 192	11:6	261

Proverbs (*cont.*)

11:7	287
11:8	127, 204
11:9	261
11:10	126, 309
11:11	16, 212, 261, 305, 313
11:14	215, 296
11:14–16	57
11:16	108, 215
11:17	100, 207, 215, 216, 228, 247, 254
11:18	126, 207, 217, 219, 220, 247
11:19	75, 90
11:22	7, 9, 218, 331
11:24	121, 217, 218, 256
11:24–26	121
11:25	121, 217, 219
11:26	121, 220, 279
11:28	126
11:30	111, 112
11:31	126
12:4	324, 330
12:6	261
12:8	109
12:10	221
12:10b	223
12:13	262
12:13a	261
12:15	59, 66
12:18	110, 129, 254, 261
12:19	223
12:20	123, 224
12:21	13, 225
12:24	109, 225
12:25	100, 226, 228, 254, 331
12:26	227
12:27	109, 204
13	111
13:1	201, 279
13:5	129, 261
13:8	119
13:9	90
13:11	203, 204, 228
13:12	100, 111, 112, 228
13:14	81, 88, 112, 114, 228, 238
13:14a	205
13:15	109
13:20	169, 229
13:21	116
13:23	17
13:24	38, 42, 132, 201, 229, 267, 268, 280, 283, 285, 309, 310, 311
13:24 KJV	282
13:25	126
14:1	232, 264, 297, 331
14:4	233
14:7	6, 229
14:8a	37
14:8a ASV	36
14:11	127
14:12	26, 155, 234, 254
14:13	155, 234, 301
14:14	116
14:15	42, 139, 234, 280, 304
14:17	267
14:19	236
14:20	26, 108, 119, 206, 321
14:21	50, 121, 279
14:23	14, 109, 203
14:25	51
14:26	85, 114
14:26–27	81, 237
14:27	88, 108, 111, 112, 205, 332
14:29	267
14:30	100, 147, 228, 238, 243, 247, 254, 257, 267, 273
14:31	50
14:32	126, 240
14:34	312
14:35	240
15:1	205, 241, 277
15:4	110, 111, 112, 242
15:5	59, 126, 201
15:8	126, 242
15:9	243

15:10–11	328	17:21	68, 201
15:11	243	17:22	6, 100, 226, 228, 257
15:12	279		
15:13	100, 228, 243, 247, 257	17:23	255, 258
		17:23 ESV	258
15:14	261	17:24	60
15:15	100, 228, 244	17:25	201, 310
15:16	246, 247	17:27	6, 208
15:17	100, 228, 246	17:28	208, 259
15:18	242, 267	18:1	100, 259
15:20	25, 68, 201, 268	18:5	259
15:22	296	18:6	38, 229
15:23	205	18:7	205, 260
15:24	88, 91	18:8	60
15:25	50	18:9	204
15:27	217, 247	18:10	262
15:29	126	18:11	206, 263
15:30	248	18:12	109, 210, 263
15:33	46, 52, 109, 210, 248	18:13	261
		18:14	243
15:35	45	18:15	43
16:3	117	18:16	256, 321
16:7	249	18:17	110
16:11	49	18:20	116
16:12	250, 296, 301	18:22	233, 264
16:15	155	18:23	108, 206, 321
16:16	108, 166	19:3	75, 264
16:18	210, 252	19:4	26, 119, 321
16:19	252	19:5	51
16:22	75, 112, 205	19:6	321
16:24	100, 110, 205, 227, 228, 253, 331	19:7	206
		19:9	51
16:25	26, 234, 254	19:10	129
16:28	257, 270	19:11	100, 110, 116, 266
16:31	13, 91, 255, 275	19:11 KJV	266
17:1	247	19:13	201
17:2	226	19:14	264
17:6	87, 268	19:15	204
17:6b NIV	330	19:16	91
17:7	129	19:17	121
17:8	255	19:18	42, 201, 231, 267, 281, 283, 284, 285
17:8 KJV	255		
17:8 NKJV	255	19:19	6
17:9	256	19:20	37, 66, 155
17:14	8, 36, 123, 241, 270	19:22	94
		19:23	108, 117
17:15	51, 259	19:24	9
17:19	6	19:26	201

Proverbs (cont.)

19:29	38, 229
20:1	58, 291
20:2	89
20:3	110, 123, 261, 270, 278
20:4	109
20:9	270
20:10	49
20:11	201
20:12	271
20:13	109
20:13 NIV	109
20:19	275
20:20	91, 201
20:21	155, 234
20:22	272, 298
20:25	273
20:26	301
20:28	296, 301
20:29	255
20:30	38, 229
21:1	275
21:5	109, 203
21:9	303, 330
21:11	280
21:13	278
21:14	256
21:15	224
21:16	88, 91
21:17	291
21:19	278
21:23	261
21:24	127, 192, 279
22:1	109
22:3	236, 280
22:4	107, 108, 109, 210
22:6	42, 132, 269, 280, 283, 285, 310
22:7	119, 206
22:9	50, 121
22:11	94
22:14	282
22:15	38, 42, 132, 201, 229, 231, 268, 282, 285, 309, 311
22:16	201
22:17	20, 23, 283
22:17–19	283
22:17—24:22	26
22:19	86
22:29	241
23:4	108
23:10–11	50
23:13	132, 268
23:13–14	38, 42, 229, 268, 283, 284, 309
23:15–16	284
23:17–18	285
23:18	155
23:19	66
23:24–25	268
23:25	66
23:26	135
23:27–28	151
23:29–35	3, 56, 90, 287–88, 290, 291
23:30	289
23:31	289
23:31–32	234, 289
23:32	155
23:33	290
23:33–35	289
23:34	290
23:35	290
24:1–2	287
24:6	296
24:9	60
24:11–12	292
24:13	55
24:14	155, 287
24:19–20	287
24:20	155
24:21–22	89, 293, 296
24:22	294, 296
24:23	23, 51, 283
24:23–24	26, 283
24:23b	296
24:24–25	297
24:27	297
24:29	273, 297
24:34	283
25:1	19, 20, 22, 25, 299
25:1—29:27	26
25:2	299

25:4–5	300	29:17	268
25:5	252, 296	29:18	17, 52, 305, 311, 313
25:8	123, 155, 234		
25:16	56, 100, 228, 301, 303	29:20	314
		29:21	155, 234
25:17	302	29:23	109
25:18	51	29:25	250, 314
25:21	267	30	316
25:21–22	116, 273	30:1	20, 23
25:24	303	30:1–4	316
25:27	56	30:1–33	27
25:27a	301	30:5	317
25–29	20, 299	30:5–6	316
26:1	129	30:6	320
26:2	303	30:6 SV	318
26:3	38, 229, 309	30:7–9	108, 319
26:4	14	30:8	206
26:5	14	30:9	119
26:7–8	129	30:15–16	21
26:17	270	30:17	66
27:3	8, 303	30:18–20	21
27:4	149	30:20	195
27:9	302	30:24–31	21
27:11	68	31	28, 110, 157, 218, 233, 324, 332
27:12	280		
27:15–16	277	31:1	20, 23, 66
28:2	305	31:1–9	27, 168, 268
28:4	306	31:2	268, 274
28:5	307	31:3–5	296
28:5 ASV	307	31:4–9	291
28:7	68, 201	31:6–9	296
28:12	309	31:10	324
28:13	117	31:10–31	23, 27, 264, 323–32
28:16	59		
28:19	17, 109, 202, 203	31:11	324, 329, 331
28:19 NIV	109	31:12	233, 325
28:24	302	31:13	326, 329
28:26	60, 308	31:14	326, 329
28:27	50, 121, 220	31:15	326
28:28	17, 308	31:16	327, 329, 330
29:2	309	31:17	327
29:3	68, 201	31:18	327
29:7	120, 121	31:18a	329
29:12	296	31:19	327
29:14	296, 301	31:20	328
29:15	38, 66, 100, 132, 229, 230, 268, 281, 283, 309	31:21	328, 329
		31:22	328, 332
		31:23	329, 332

Proverbs (cont.)

31:24	329, 330
31:25	329
31:26	66, 325, 330
31:27	330
31:28	325
31:28–29	330, 332
31:29	324, 325
31:30	218, 324, 331
31:31	332
55:24	91
111:10	45

Ecclesiastes

	13, 15, 225
1:15	114
1:17–18	305
2:16	45
2:24	245
3:1–2	88
3:7	189, 205
3:11	205, 275
3:12	245
4:4	252
4:6	117, 240, 246
5:1–7	275
5:7—6:12	246
5:10–18	246
5:11	117
5:17–18	245
6:8	129
7:1	109
7:8	155, 234
7:12	81, 170, 206
7:15	124
7:17	87–88, 150
7:18	114, 146
7:20	271
7:26	147, 155
7:26 NRSV	264
7:29	265
8:5	310
8:5b NIV	58
8:5b–6 NIV	231
8:6	275
8:8	87, 88, 178
8:10	124
8:12–13	127
8:13–14	124
8:14	126
8:15	245
8:16	117
9:2	124
9:7	288
9:9	157, 178, 245
9:11	109
9:13–16	75, 129, 168, 241
9:15	24
10:6	129, 168, 241, 304
10:10	36, 117
10:12	93
10:16	168
10:16–17	215
12:11	10, 12, 24
12:13	45

Song of Solomon

2:7	297
3:5	297
4:9	155
4:9–10	154
4:12	157
4:13–15	195
5:1–2	154
8:4	297
8:6	70, 92

Isaiah

1:2	70
1:10–15	242
1:23	258
2–4	209
2:6	209
2:12	209
2:17	210
2:20–21	210
3:5	68
3:12	208
3:16	155
3:16–32	209
3:18	209
3:23	329
5	8

5:1-2	327	50:2	74
5:1-7	3	51:12-16	316
5:3-4	265	52:7-8	248
5:11	289	53:12	267
5:15	312	55:1	288
5:20	81, 306	55:6	74
5:22	288	55:8-9	299
5:23	258	58:10-11	216
6	271	59:14	70, 164
6:9-10	11, 189	65:2	74
6:10-11	312	65:12	74
7:14-15	17	66:2	244
7:21-25	17	66:4	74
8:16	189		
8:20	65		
8:21	265, 321		

Jeremiah

1:6	41
2:8	153
2:13	205
3:2	193
4:30	328
5:7-8	147
5:21	305
5:24	54, 58
6:15	147
7:13	74
8:5	76
8:9	74
11:11	74
11:19	122
11:21	122
13:10	74
15:10 NIV	224
15:16	188
15:17	125
16:5	17
17:5-8	196
17:9-10	243
17:13	205
20	300
20:7-18	305
22:13-17	251
23:9-32	300, 305
24:9	3
26:23	211
27	300
27:6	300
28	300

9:6	23
9:7	252
10:1	168
10:3	210
10:5	276
11:1-10	168, 252
11:2	23, 24, 52
14	9
14:4	3
14:4-21	2
19:12	22
21:4	138
26	17
26:3	227
28:1	288
28:7	288
28:23-29	56
28:26	45, 58
30:9	164
30:10	11
32:1-8	168
32:6	304
32:9-15	66
33:6	79
38:10	88
40:8	223, 284, 317
40:13-14	44
40:28	44, 113
41:2-4	276
43:25	257
45:3	78
48:9	266

Jeremiah (cont.)

28:11	189
29:7	293
29:21–23	140
31:20	230
31:26	117
31:29	2
31:36	54
33:25	54, 58
39:11–12	249
40:1–6	249
41:8	78
45	17
49:7	22
50:35	22
51:57	22

Lamentations

	265
3:22	214
3:29	211
3:39	265
4:4	321

Ezekiel

2:5	76
7:19 NIV	210
8:18	74
12:22–23	2
13:9	125
16:31	193
17:2	3
18:2	2
18:2–3	2
18:25	264
18:29	264
22:12	258
23:45–49	150
28:4–5	35
28:12	35
33:17	264
33:20	264

Daniel

	17
1:9	93
2:21	44, 293
2:22	299
2:37	293
2:37–38	300
2:48	255
3:30	93
4	263
4:27	120
5:18	293
6	261
6:25	241
7:18	236
7:27	236
12:2–3	129

Hosea

4:2	164
4:11 NKJV	289
6:8–9	68
7:7	305
8:4	305
11:1	229
13:11	305

Amos

3:6	106
5:13	17, 308
5:15 NIV	211
6:4	247
6:6	288
8:5–6	220
8:7	220
8:11–12	74, 312

Jonah

4:11	221

Micah

3:4	74
3:11	258
5:1	276
7:18	266
7:19	257

Habakkuk

2:15	289
3:2	119

Zephaniah

1:18	210
2:1–3 NIV	211
3:3	258

Zechariah

4:6	12
4:10	159
7:13	74

Malachi

	105
2:7	153
2:14	82
3:8–11	102
3:11	101

ANCIENT NEAR EAST TEXTS

Code of Hammurabi

	297

Ptah–Hotep, proverbs of (Maxims of Ptah–Hotep)

	22

DEUTEROCANONICAL BOOKS

Sirach (Jesus Sirach/Ecclesiasticus)

	15, 161, 176–77, 231, 267, 302
1:4 NRSV	176
1:9 NRSV	176
1:14 NRSV	176
4:1–6	279
9:1–9	154
9:3–9	155
9:8	155, 331
18:23	275
19:2	289
23:18–21	158
24:3 NRSV	176
26:9 NRSV	155
30:1	268
30:9–12a	268
30:20–24	258
31:25–31	289
37:27–31	303
47:14–12	22

Wisdom of Solomon

	177–78, 179, 182
1:5 NRSV	177
6:19 NRSV	178
7:12	182
7:12 NRSV	178
7:21 NRSV	178
7:22	177, 178, 182
7:23	178
7:23 NRSV	178
7:25 NRSV	177
7:27	178
8:1 NRSV	178
8:3	177
8:4	178, 182
8:13 NRSV	178
8:17 NRSV	178
9:4	177
9:9–10	177
9:11	178

ANCIENT JEWISH WRITERS

Philo	177, 179

NEW TESTAMENT

Matthew

2:6	276
2:11	255
3:4	301, 327
3:7	210
3:17	176
5:1–12	7
5:3	7, 252
5:4	7
5:5	83, 125, 240
5:6	243
5:7	216, 279
5:9	124, 224, 270
5:11–12	129
5:13	329
5:20	102
5:25	123
5:27–32	154
5:28	155
5:28–30	154
5:29–30	17
5:32	277
5:39	298
5:40	116, 298
5:40–42	123
5:42	7, 121
6:1–2	120
6:26	221
6:33	102, 243
7:6	189, 205
7:7	79
7:12 NIV	216
7:13–14	136, 196, 234
7:15	9
7:21	7
8:24	117
9:22	66
10:14	189
10:16	236
10:23	227
10:26	243n22
10:34	224
10:34–35	11
11:16	72
11:19	166
11:29	11, 123, 239
12:1–14	122
12:19	270
12:36	262
12:36–37	209
12:42	5, 23, 52, 169
13	8
13:3	10
13:9	18
13:10	3, 10
13:10–17	11
13:11	271–72
13:12	12, 43, 166, 190
13:13	11
13:14–15	11, 189
13:15	11
13:16	13, 272
13:18	3
13:18–23	11
13:24	3
13:31	3
13:33	10
13:33–34	3
13:36–52	11
13:43	129
13:44	78
13:45–46	108
15:6	318
15:9	318
15:14	207
16:16	176
16:24	105
18:15	123
18:16	123
18:17	123
18:21–35	267
18:28	257
18:32–35	279
19:5	158
19:12	18
19:23	108
19:28	186
20:3	72
21:27	189
21:31	11
22:4	187
22:21	186, 293
22:37–40	92

22:39–40	260	2:52	23, 93
23:10–12	253	4:16	153
23:12	128, 263	6:36	223
23:16	9	6:38	121, 216, 219
23:16–17	207	7:42–43	11
23:23	102	8:9	11
23:24	9	9:54	272
23:34	75	10:36	11
24:16	227	12:4–5	316
24:30	118	12:13–14 NIV	270
24:35	317	12:16–21	210, 263
25	279	12:20–21	263
25:18	78	12:47–48	229
25:31–46	216, 279	13:34	74
25:40	279	14:11	263
25:40–45	121	14:16–17	186
25:41–46	122	14:17	187
26:23	122	14:35	18
26:52	293	15:30	143
26:53	272	16:9	256
26:63–64	176	16:15	128, 252, 263
27:25	261	16:19–21	278
27:43	316	16:19–31	210, 236
		18:14	128, 263
		19:11–27	241
Mark		21:20–21	119, 211
4:10	11	21:23–24 NIV	210
4:11	11	21:25–26	118
4:12	11	21:28	118
6:31	117, 240, 246	22:16	186
7:2–23	236	22:20	186
7:21	137, 155	22:48	122
7:21–23	135	23:9	189
9:50	270	23:34	267, 272
10:7	147		
10:23	321	**John**	
10:29–30	309	1	178, 179
		1:1	178, 182
Luke		1:1–3	176
1	128	1:14	176
1:33	252	1:18	263
1:46–55	128	1:30	176
1:51–52	66	2:1–11	288
2	128, 276	3:16	48
2:14	128	4	122, 172
2:34–35	12	4:14	136
2:40	23	4:34	188
2:40–52	153		

John (cont.)

6:22–59	188
6:27a	18
6:56	188
6:68	205
7:13	315
7:38	135
7:38–39	205
8:3–11	160
8:5	148
8:7	271
8:46	271
8:58	176
8:59	227
9:3	97, 105
9:4	115
11:24	240
12:26	129
12:36	227
15:14–15	125
15:18	105
16:33	105
17:3	136
17:17	223
18:23	298, 299
18:36	294
19:11	294
19:38	315

Acts

2:45	219
2:46–47	219
2:47	93, 109, 128
4:19	295
4:32	219
4:33	219
4:34–37	217
5:29	295
9:36–39	93
10:34	296
12:6	117
13:51	189
14:5–6	227
16:25	258
17	177
18:18	274
23:5	294

Romans

1	306
1:4	176
1:16	46, 291
1:18–31	306
1:18–32	127, 194
1:20	46, 71
1:22	37, 194
1:24–32	154
1:28	307
1:32	81, 306
2:11	296
3:23–24	271
5:1	212
6:12	70
6:17–18	70
6:23	70, 195
7:21	137
8:11	99
8:17	105
8:18	244
8:22	222
8:23	99
8:28	225, 227, 244
8:32	176
9:5	176
11:33	299
11:33–36	44
12:2 ASV	307
12:3	253
12:9	123
12:17–21	267
12:18	93, 123, 270
12:19	273
12:20	273
12:21	239
13:1–2	294
13:1–6	184
13:1–7	89
13:3–7	294
13:6	183
13:8	122
13:12–13	158
13:13	289
15:16	183
16:19	53
16:27	44, 170

1 Corinthians

1:24	162, 181
1:30	162, 181
2:6	181
2:14–15	166, 307
3:13	224
4:6 NIV	318
5:1	148
6:2–3	236
6:4	123
6–7	154
6:9–10	289
6:12–20	148
6:18	154
7	158
7:2	158
7:3–6	158
7:5	142
8	181
11:3	325
11:30	106
13:4–5	239, 260
13:7	239, 257, 266
15:33	229
15:35–49	99
15:42	129
15:54	178
15:58	224

2 Corinthians

3:18	129
4	181
6:4–8	245
9:6	122, 219
9:6–11	219
9:9	120
9:9–10	245
10:5	191
11:24	267
12:9	105
13:8	224, 284

Ephesians

2:1	196
2:8	272
2:12	228
4:13–15	191
4:14–15	236
4:22	37
4:26	116, 123
4:28	202, 203, 207
5:11	158
5:18	289
5:22–24	278, 325
5:25	325
5:25–28	278
5:25–33	331
5:28	157
6:4	133, 153, 201, 269
6:9	296

Philippians

1:9	307
1:9–10	40, 218
1:9–11	191
2:3	253
2:6	176
2:6–9	248
2:9	184, 272
3:1	258
3:8	107
3:13–14	246
3:21	99, 129
4:4	245, 258
4:6–7	227, 240
4:10	258
4:11–12	322
4:13	227
4:19	227
16:3	248

Colossians

	181
1	182
1:15	162, 179, 181
2:3	23, 162, 181
2:8	194
3:15	240
3:18–19	154
3:19	157, 158, 325, 331
3:21	133, 269
3:23	326
3:25	296

1 Thessalonians

4:4	158
4:11	202, 203
4:13	228
5:2–3	118
5:4–7	158
5:7	115, 289
5:15	273
5:18	240

2 Thessalonians

2:5–6	94
2:12	81
3:6–12	203
6:6–12	202

Galatians

2	190, 315
2:6	296
5:16	239
5:16–17	239
5:19	154, 260
5:19–20	137
5:19–21	289
5:20	239
5:22	216
5:22–23	154
5:24	239
6:7	261
6:7–8	75
6:7–9	192
6:7–10	219
6:9–10	219
6:10	120

1 Timothy

1:5	123
1:17 KJV	170, 191
2:2	294
2:9–10	92
2:12–15	277
3:2–5	277
3:5	133
3:7	109, 128
4	158
4:4	107
4:4–5	288
4:8	83, 85
4:8–10	136
5:23	288
6:3	216
6:6	85
6:8	322
6:9	108, 321
6:9–10a	217
6:16	178
6:17–19	207, 263, 321
6:20	194, 319

2 Timothy

1:7	316
2:3	294
2:12	236
2:16	319
2:22	154
2:24	270
3:1–5a	313
3:12	93
3:15	53, 281
3:16	19, 24, 67, 158, 284, 316
4:6–7	245

Titus

1:2	316
1:6	229
1:10	229

Hebrews

1:1–2	182
1:3	184
1:13	184
3:16	120
5:14	40
6:18	316
10:13	184
11:9–10	244
11:13–16	244
12	284
12:4–11	105
12:5–11	231
12:10–11	107

12:11	106, 285
12:14–15	239
13:4	154
13:5	322

James

1:2–4	105
1:5	79, 169, 191
1:12–18	105
1:19	208
1:26	208
2:1–13	297
2:13	216, 278
2:15–16	122
3:2–12	208
3:8	110, 261
3:9	260
4:6	128, 252
4:17	122
5:4–6	207
5:7–11	105
5:16	117

1 Peter

1:6–9	105
1:17	296
1:22	123
2:9	103
2:13–14	294
2:17	294
2:23	123, 272
3	154
3:3–4	328
3:3–6	93
3:4	329
3:7	331
3:14	105
4:11	226, 319
4:15	270
4:15–16	105
5:5	67n1, 128, 252, 263
5:6	106
5:7	227

2 Peter

1:20	316
1:21	19, 24
2:8	306
2:14	154
3:3–4	72

1 John

1:8	271
1:15–17	287
2:20	307
2:23	176
3:14	216
3:19	166
4:1–6	166

3 John

4	201

Jude

18–19	72
25 KJV	170

Revelation

1:7	118
2	271
2:11	212
2:13	211
2:20–23	140
3	271
3:8–9	237
6:15–17	211
10:10	188
19:7	186
19:9	186
20:4–6	236
20:6	212
20:14	196
22	262
22:11	190
22:15	154
22:18–19	317, 319
23	319
24	319

www.ingramcontent.com/pod-product-compliance
Lightning Source LLC
Chambersburg PA
CBHW071437300426
44114CB00013B/1478